Praise for *Evolve You...* W9-AGE-058

"Dr. Joe Dispenza delves deep into the extraordinary potential of the mind. Read this book and be inspired to change your life forever."
—**Lynne McTaggart**, author of
The Field and *The Intention Experiment*

"A beautifully written book that provides a strong scientific basis for how the power of the human spirit can heal our bodies and our lives."
—**Howard Martin**, executive vice president of HeartMath and coauthor of *The HeartMath Solution*

"Joe Dispenza gives you the tools to make real changes in your life."
—**William Arntz**, producer/director of
What the Bleep Do We Know!?

"A groundbreaking work on what I call the 'yoga of the mind.' A perceptive and insightful look at how our mental and emotional bodies function and how we can create a more healthy and purposeful life."
—**Bikram Choudhury**, author of *Bikram Yoga*

"Through the integration of personal experience, Western science, and Eastern thought, Dr. Joe brings a lucid and inspiring story that will change your life."
—**Michael T. Lardon, M.D.**, consulting psychiatrist for the San Diego Olympic Training Center and the PGA Tour

"*Evolving Your Brain* isn't just a book; it is an opportunity for anyone who is serious about becoming more and having more to learn exactly how to do it from the inside out."
—**John Assaraf**, author of
The Street Kids Guide to Having It All
and founder of Onecoach

"Approachable, accessible, and empowering, Joe Dispenza helps make sense of this wacky world we call reality."
—**Betsy Chasse**, writer/director/producer of
What the Bleep Do We Know!?

EVOLVE Your BRAIN

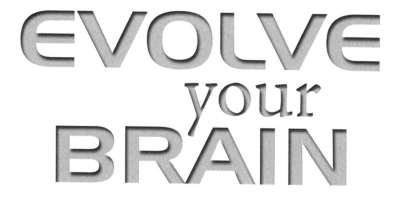

EVOLVE *your* BRAIN

The Science of Changing Your Mind

JOE DISPENZA, D.C.

Health Communications, Inc.
Deerfield Beach, Florida

www.hcibooks.com

The content of this book is published for educational and informational purposes only. The content of this book should not be used for the diagnosis or treatment of any condition or disease. The case histories presented are provided for illustrative purposes only. No express or implied guarantee of results is made. If you are currently being treated by a physician or other healthcare practitioner for any condition or disease, consult with that provider prior to changing or modifying any treatment program.

Library of Congress Cataloging-in-Publication Data
is available through the Library of Congress.

© 2007 Joe Dispenza, D.C.
ISBN-13: 978-0-7573-0765-2 (paperback)
ISBN-10: 0-7573-0765-5 (paperback)
ISBN-13: 978-0-7573-9779-0 (e-book)
ISBN-10: 0-7573-9779-4 (e-book)

Publisher: Health Communications, Inc.
            3201 S.W. 15th Street
            Deerfield Beach, FL 33442-8190

R-10-08

Cover design by Larissa Hise Henoch
Interior book design and formatting by Lawna Patterson Oldfield
Interior illustrations by Larissa Hise Henoch

FOR JACE, GIANNA,
AND SHENARA

CONTENTS

ACKNOWLEDGMENTS

Creation is such an interesting phenomenon. The process is riddled with a landscape of peaks and valleys with indeterminate views. There are moments when we feel truly inspired and uplifted, because we have made some progress in climbing to a new level to see a better view. In the next moment, when we see that there are bigger obstacles to overcome, we wonder if we even made a difference and if our efforts were really worth it. Like the birthing process, creation comes with labor pains, complications, nausea, fatigue, sleepless nights, and even woeful moments of thinking about the future. Questions lurk about our personal abilities, what we know, what we don't know, who our critics are, who we are doing this for anyway, and why. I have had such moments in writing this book.

And yet, it is almost natural that we fret with such encumbrances, because somewhere inside us, we know that the only terrain we are overcoming is our limited view of ourselves. It's a process, and most certainly, there are speed bumps along the way. I must say that this book has been a great and wonderful teacher for me. I am different today because I continued on in spite of the many reasons to stop. I understand better now why I wrote this book. My sole purpose and hopeful intentions were to contribute toward helping people change their lives. If this book makes a difference in even one person's life, then the whole process was worth it. *Evolve Your Brain* was not written primarily for the scientist, the researcher, or the academic, but for the average person who wants to understand that science supports our ability to change, and that we, as human beings, have great potential.

I certainly do not know everything there is to know about the brain. What I have come to learn, to experience, to research, and to personally conclude are only doorways to greater understandings. Some might say to me, why didn't you discuss this topic or that topic in the book? Simply, I have chosen to keep this body of work about the science of changing our mind and what implications this has for our health and our well-being. There are many more subjects I could have discussed about energy, mind, quantum physics, and our greater abilities that would make this book too broad to be useful. My epilogue suggests greater applications.

I do want to acknowledge several people who have supported, influenced, and inspired me to complete the book. First, I want to thank my publishers at HCI, Peter Vegso and Tom Sand, who believed in me. A special thank you to my editor, Michele Matrisciani. I also want to express my appreciation to Carol Rosenberg for being such a thorough managing editor and to Dawn Von Strolley Grove and Lawna Patterson Oldfield for their production expertise.

To Tere Stouffer, my copy editor, who helped me with perspective. Also, to Sara Steinberg, my content/copy editor, who taught me about the tortoise and the hare and who showed such caring and love . . . I am grateful. To Gary Brozek, your contribution to my work is truly appreciated. My graphic artist Larissa Hise Henoch showed her true talent in this book.

I also want to give my acknowledgments to my staff for keeping up with my pace. Thanks to Bill Harrell, D.C., Jackie Hobbs, Diane Baker, Patty Kerr, Charlie Davidson, and Brenda Surerus. Your sincerity is invaluable to me. Special gratitude is given to Gabrielle Sagona for her assistance, encouragement, and fabulous energy. Thank you for everything. To Joanne Twining, Ph.D., I am expanded by your skills, your knowledge, and your patience. To Will Arntz, James Capezio, and Rebecca Capezio for their important feedback with the manuscript. To Marjorie Layden, Henry Schimberg, Linda Evans, Anne Marie Bennstrom, Ken Weiss, Betsy Chasse, and Gordon J. Grobelny, D.C., for true encouragement and support. My immense appreciation goes to Paul Burns, J.D., D.C., who helped me in innumerable ways.

I also want to give thanks to JZ Knight for giving her life to help humanity.

To Ramtha, who inspired me to write this book and from whom I have learned enough to think about for a hundred lifetimes. To the students at RSE, who live their lives with a passion for adventure and a love of God. I am always inspired by their dedication to the great work.

My gratitude to Amit Goswami, Ph.D., for his brilliant intellectual mind, true compassion, and willingness to be an individual. You are a maverick. Thank you as well to Nick Pappas, M.D., Margie Pappas, R.N., M.S., and John Kucharczyk, Ph.D., who played an important role in informing me about the brain, mind, and body.

I want to personally thank John and Katina Dispenza and my mother, Fran Dispenza, for having strong shoulders to lean on. And finally, a profound thank you should be written across the sky to my lovely lady Roberta Brittingham, for naturally being and living everything that I have tried to explain in this book. I am always inspired by your humility and greatness.

FOREWORD

S ince you are holding this book in your hand, you may already be aware of the paradigm shift that is going on in science. In the old paradigm, your consciousness—you—is regarded as an epiphenomenon of your brain. In the new paradigm, your consciousness is the ground of being and your brain is the epiphenomenon. Feel better? Then you are ready to reap the benefit of this book.

If consciousness is the primary ground and brain is secondary, then it is natural to ask how to use the brain in an optimal fashion to fulfill the purpose of consciousness and its evolution. The new paradigm research has been going on for a while, but this is the first book that addresses this question and brilliantly guides you toward that end. Truly, Dr. Joe Dispenza has written a user's manual par excellence for the brain, from the new primacy-of-consciousness perspective.

Dr. Dispenza, not being a quantum physicist, does keep the primacy of consciousness implicit, not explicit, until the very end of the book. Because it requires quantum physics to see the primacy of consciousness explicitly, it may be useful for you, dear reader, to receive a little background information from a quantum physicist; hence, this foreword.

To go back to the beginning of the new paradigm revolution, quantum physics has a fundamental interpretational problem. It depicts objects not as determined "things," but as waves of possibility. How do these possibilities become actual "things" of our experience when we observe or "measure" them?

If you think that our brain—being the site of us, or our consciousness—has the capacity to change possibility into actuality, think again. According to quantum physics, the brain itself consists of quantum possibilities before we measure it, before we observe with it. If we, our consciousness, were a brain product, we would be possibilities as well, and our "coupling" with the object would change neither the object nor us (our brain) from possibility to actuality. Face it! Possibility coupled to possibility only makes a bigger possibility.

The paradox only thickens if you think of yourself dualistically—you as a nonmaterial dual entity, not bound by quantum laws and separate from your brain. But if you are nonmaterial, then how do you interact with your brain, with which you have not a thing in common? This is dualism, a philosophy intractable as science.

There is a third way of thinking, and this one leads to a paradigm shift. Your consciousness is the primary fabric of reality, and matter (including the brain and the object you are observing) exists within this fabric as quantum possibilities. Your observation consists of choosing from the possibilities the one facet that becomes the actuality of your experience. Physicists call this process *the collapse of the quantum possibility wave.*

Once you recognize that your consciousness is not your brain but transcends it, once you recognize that you have the power to choose among possibilities, you are ready to act on Joe Dispenza's ideas and suggestions. It will help additionally to know that the "you" that chooses is a cosmic you, a state of consciousness available to you in non-ordinary situations. You reach such states when you have a creative insight. In those times, you are ready to make changes in your brain circuits. Dr. Dispenza shows you how.

There is another reason that I think Dr. Joe Dispenza's book is a welcome addition to the growing literature of the new paradigm of science: he emphasizes the importance of paying attention to emotions. You may already have heard the phrase *emotional intelligence.* What does that mean? First of all, it means that you don't have to fall prey to your emotions. You do because you are attached to them; or as Joe Dispenza would say, "You are attached to the brain circuits connected with the emotions."

There is a story that when Albert Einstein was leaving Nazi Germany for America, his wife became very concerned that she had to leave behind so much furniture and other household items. "I am attached to them," she complained to a friend. To this, Einstein joked, "But my dear, they are not attached to you."

This is the thing. Emotions are not attached to you; because you are not your brain, you don't have to identify with your existing brain circuits.

With regard to the concept of emotional intelligence, some writers are a little confused. They talk about emotional intelligence and how you can develop it, but they also insist that you are nothing but the brain. The problem in thinking that way is that the brain is already set up in a hierarchical relationship with the emotions. Emotional intelligence is possible only if you can change this existing hierarchy, only if you are not part of that hierarchy. Joe Dispenza recognizes the primacy of you, your consciousness, over your brain, and by doing so, he gives you some useful advice about emotional intelligence, about how to change your existing brain circuits and hierarchies.

Gandhi's wife was once asked by a journalist how Gandhi could accomplish so much. "Simple," said the wife. "Gandhi is congruent in regards to his speech, thought, and action."

All of us want to be good accomplishers; we want to fulfill the meaning and purpose of our lives. The crucial challenge is how to achieve synchrony between speech, thought, and action. Put another way, the challenge is to integrate thought and emotion. I believe that the evolution of consciousness demands this from us right now. Recognizing this, Joe Dispenza has provided indispensable knowledge on how you can integrate your feelings and thinking.

I met Dr. Joe for the first time at a *What the Bleep Do We Know!?* conference. This movie, as you may know, is about a young woman who is struggling to change her emotional behavior. In a scene of catharsis (played beautifully by actress Marlee Matlin), the woman looks at her image in a mirror and says, "I hate you." In that moment she frees herself to choose among quantum possibilities of change. She goes on to transform her brain circuits, creating a new state of being and a new life.

You can change your brain circuits, too. You have that power of quantum choice. We have always had the tools to do this, but only now have we become aware of how to use them. Dr. Joe Dispenza's book, *Evolve Your Brain,* will help you use your power to choose and to change. Read this book, use its ideas in your life, and realize your potential.

—*Amit Goswami, Ph.D.*
Professor of Physics, University of Oregon,
and author of *The Self-Aware Universe*

CHAPTER ONE

BEGINNINGS

But strange that I was not told
That the brain can hold
In a tiny ivory cell
God's heaven or hell.

—OSCAR WILDE

I invite you to have a single thought, any thought. Whether your thought was related to a feeling of anger, sadness, inspiration, joy, or even sexual arousal, you changed your body. You changed you. All thoughts, whether they be "I can't," "I can," "I'm not good enough," or "I love you," have the same measurable effects. As you sit casually reading this page, not lifting a single finger, bear in mind that your body is undergoing a host of dynamic changes. Triggered by your most recent thought, did you know that suddenly, your pancreas and your adrenal glands are already busy secreting a few new hormones? Like a sudden lightning storm, different areas of your brain just surged with increased electrical current, releasing a mob of neurochemicals that are too numerous to name. Your spleen and your thymus gland sent out a mass e-mail to your immune system to make a few modifications. Several different gastric juices started flowing. Your liver began processing enzymes that were not present moments before. Your heart rate fluctuated, your lungs altered their stroke volume, and blood flow to the capillaries in your hands and feet changed. All from just thinking one thought. You are that powerful.

But how are you capable of performing all of those actions? We can all intellectually understand that the brain can manage and regulate many diverse functions throughout the rest of the body, but how responsible are we for the job our brain is doing as CEO of the body? Whether we like it or not, once a thought happens in the brain, the rest is history. All of the bodily reactions that occur from both our intentional or unintentional thinking unfold behind the scenes of our awareness. When you come right down to it, it is startling to realize how influential and extensive the effects of one or two conscious or unconscious thoughts can be.

For example, is it possible that the seemingly unconscious thoughts that run through our mind daily and repeatedly create a cascade of chemical reactions that produce not only *what* we feel but also *how* we feel? Can we accept that the long-term effects of our habitual thinking just might be the cause of how our body moves to a state of imbalance, or what we call disease? Is it likely, moment by moment, that we train our body to be unhealthy by our repeated thoughts and reactions? What if just by thinking, we cause our internal chemistry to be bumped out of normal range so often that the body's self-regulation system eventually redefines these abnormal states as normal, regular states? It's a subtle process, but maybe we just never gave it that much attention until now. My wish is that this book will offer a few suggestions for managing your own internal universe.

Since we are on the subject of attention, now I want you to pay attention, become aware, and listen. Can you hear the hum of the refrigerator? The sound of a car passing by your home? A distant dog barking? How about the resonance of your own heart beating? Just by shifting your attention in those moments, you caused a power surge and voltage flux of electricity in millions of brain cells right inside your own head. By choosing to modify your awareness, you changed your brain. Not only did you change how your brain was working moments before, but you changed how it will work in the next moment, and possibly for the rest of your life.

As you return your attention to these words on this page, you altered blood flow to various parts of your brain. You also set off a cascade of impulses, rerouting and modifying electrical currents to different brain areas. On a microscopic level, a multitude of diverse nerve cells ganged up chemically to "hold hands" and communicate, in order to establish stronger long-term relationships with each other. Because of your shift in attention, the shimmering three-dimensional web of intricate neurological tissue that is your brain is firing in new combinations and sequences. You did that of your own free will, by changing your focus. You quite literally changed your mind.

As human beings, we have the natural ability to focus our awareness on anything. As we will learn, how and where we place our attention, what we place our attention on, and for how long we place it ultimately defines us on a neurological level. If our awareness is so mobile, why is it so hard to keep our attention on thoughts that might serve us? Right now, as you continue to concentrate and read this page, you might have forgotten about the pain in your back, the disagreement you had with your boss earlier today, and even what gender you are. It is where we place our attention and on what we place our attention that maps the very course of our state of being.

For example, we can, in any given moment, think about a bitter memory from our past that is only tattooed in the intimate folds of our gray matter and, like magic, it comes to life. We also have the option of attending to future anxieties and worries that do not readily exist until they are conjured up by our own mind. But to us, they are real. Our attention brings everything to life and makes real what was previously unnoticed or unreal.

Believe it or not, according to neuroscience, placing our attention on pain in the body makes pain exist, because the circuits in the brain that perceive pain become electrically activated. If we then put our full awareness on something other than pain, the brain circuits that process pain and bodily sensations can be literally turned off—and presto, the pain goes away. But when we look to see whether the pain is gone for good, the corresponding brain circuits once again activate, causing us to feel the discomfort return. And if these brain circuits repeatedly fire, the connections between them become stronger. Thus by paying attention to pain on a daily basis, we are wiring ourselves neurologically to develop a more acute awareness of pain perception, because the related brain circuits become more enriched. Your own personal attention has that much of an effect on you. This could be one explanation to how pain, and even memories from our distant past, characterize us. What we repeatedly think about and where we focus our attention is what we neurologically become. Neuroscience finally understands that we can mold and shape the neurological framework of the self by the repeated attention we give to any one thing.

Everything that makes us up, the "you" and the "me"—our thoughts, our dreams, our memories, our hopes, our feelings, our secret fantasies, our fears, our skills, our habits, our pains, and our joys—is etched in the living latticework of our 100 billion brain cells. By the time you have read this far in the book, you have changed your brain permanently. If you learned even one bit of information, tiny brain cells have made new connections between them, and who you are is altered. The images that these words created in your mind have left footprints in the vast, endless fields of neurological landscape that is the identity called "you." This is because the "you," as a sentient being, is immersed and truly exists in the interconnected electrical web of cellular brain tissue. How your nerve cells are specifically arranged, or neurologically wired, based on what you learn, what you remember, what you experience, what you envision for yourself, what you do, and how you think about yourself, defines you as an individual.

You are a work in progress. The organization of brain cells that makes up who you are is constantly in flux. Forget the notion that the brain is static, rigid, and fixed. Instead, brain cells are continually remolded and reorganized by our thoughts and experiences. Neurologically, we are repeatedly changed by the endless stimuli in the world. Instead of imagining nerve cells as solid, inflexible, tiny sticks that are assembled together to make up your brain's gray matter, I invite you to see them as dancing patterns of delicate electric fibers in an animated web, connecting and disconnecting all the time. This is much closer to the truth of who you are.

The fact that you can read and comprehend the words on this page is due to the many interactions you have had throughout your life. Different people taught you, instructed you, and essentially changed your brain microscopically. If you accept this notion that your brain is still changing as you read these pages before you, you can easily see that your parents, teachers, neighbors, friends, family, and culture have contributed to who you are presently. It is our senses, through our diverse experiences, that write the story of who we are on the tablet of our mind. Our mastery is being the fine conductor of this remarkable orchestra of brain and mind; and as we have just seen, we can direct the affairs of mental activity.

Now, let's change your brain a little further. I want to teach you a new skill. Here are the instructions: Look at your right hand. Touch your thumb to your pinky finger, and then touch your thumb to your index finger. Next, touch your thumb to your ring finger, and then touch your thumb to your middle finger. Repeat the process until you can do it automatically. Now do it faster and make your fingers move more rapidly without mistake. Within a few minutes of paying attention, you should be able to master the action.

To learn the finger movements well, you had to rise out of your resting state, from relaxing and reading to a heightened state of conscious awareness. Voluntarily, you perked up your brain a little; you increased your level of awareness by your intentional free will. To succeed in memorizing this skill, you also had to increase your brain's level of energy. You turned up the dimmer switch to the light bulb in your brain that is constantly on, and it got brighter. You became motivated, and your choice to do this made your brain turn on.

Learning and performing the activity required you to amplify your level of awareness. By increasing blood flow and electrical activity to different areas in your brain, you could stay more present with what you were doing. You kept your brain from wandering to any other thought so that you could learn a new action, and that process took energy. You changed the way the arrangement of millions of brain cells fired in diverse patterns. Your intentional act took will, focus, and attention. The end result is that you are once again neurologically changed, not only by thinking a thought but also by demonstrating an action or a new skill.

In a moment, I want you to close your eyes. This time, instead of physically demonstrating the finger exercise, I want you to *practice* doing that same action in your mind. That is, remember what you did just moments before and mentally touch each finger the way I asked you to earlier: thumb to pinky finger, thumb to index finger, thumb to ring finger, and thumb to middle finger. Mentally rehearse the activity without physically doing it. Do it a few times in your mind, and then open your eyes.

Did you notice that while you were practicing in your mind, your brain seemed to imagine the entire sequence just as you actually did it? In fact, if you paid full attention to what you were rehearsing in your mind's eye by focusing on mentally practicing those finger actions, you fired the same set of nerve cells in the same part of your brain as if you were actually doing them. In other words, your brain did not know the difference between your doing the action or your remembering how to do the action. The act of mental rehearsal is a powerful way you can grow and mold new circuits in your brain.

Recent studies in neuroscience demonstrate that we can change our brain just by thinking. So ask yourself: What exactly do you spend most of your time mentally rehearsing, thinking about, and finally demonstrating? Whether you consciously or unconsciously fabricate your thoughts and actions, you are always affirming and reaffirming your neurological self as "you." Keep in mind that whatever you spend your time mentally attending to, that is what you are and what you will become. My hope is that this book will help you to understand why you are the way you are, how you got this way, and what it takes to change who you are through your intentional thoughts and actions.

You may ask at this point, What is it that allows us to voluntarily modify how the brain works? Where does the "you" exist, and what allows you to turn on and off different brain circuits that then make you aware or unaware? The "you" I'm talking about operates and lives in a part of the brain called the frontal lobe, and without the frontal lobe, you are no longer "you." In evolution, the frontal lobe has been the last part of the brain to develop, just behind the forehead and right above the eyes. You hold the image of yourself in the frontal lobe, and what you hold in this special place determines how you interact in the world and perceive reality. The frontal lobe controls and regulates other, older parts of the brain. The frontal lobe navigates your future, controls your behavior, dreams of new possibilities, and guides you throughout life. It is the seat of your conscience. The frontal lobe is evolution's gift to you. This brain region is most adaptable to change and is the means by which you evolve your thoughts and actions. My desire is that this book helps you to use this newest, most recent part of your brain's anatomy to reshape your brain and your destiny.

Evolution, Change, and Neuroplasticity

We humans have a unique capacity to change. It is via the frontal lobe that we go beyond the preprogrammed behaviors that are genetically compartmentalized within the human brain, the recorded history of our species' past. Because our frontal lobe is more evolved than that of any other species on earth, we have tremendous adaptability, and with it come choice, intent, and full awareness. We possess an advanced bit of biotechnology that allows us to learn from our mistakes and shortcomings, to remember, and to modify our behavior so that we can do a better job in life.

It is true that a lot of human behavior is genetically preset. All life forms are preordained to be what they genetically express, and we must agree that a lot of who we are as human beings is predetermined by our genes. Yet we are not condemned to live out our existence without contributing some form of an evolutionary gift to future generations. We can add to our species' progress here on earth because unlike other species, we theoretically have the hardware to evolve our actions in one lifetime. The new behaviors we demonstrate will provide new experiences that should be encoded in our genes—both for now and for posterity. This leads us to consider: How many new experiences have we had lately?

The science of molecular biology is beginning to investigate the concept that, given the right signals, our genes are as equally changeable as our brain cells. The question is this: Can we provide the right type of stimulus to the cells of our body, either chemically or neurologically, to unlock their gigantic library of unused latent genetic information? In other words, by managing our thoughts, feelings, and reactions, can we intentionally make the right chemical elixir to drive the brain and body from a constant state of stress to a state of regeneration and change? Can we escape from the limits of our biology and become more evolved human beings? It is my intent to show you that both theoretically and practically, there is a true biology to change—that is, by maintaining a change in your mind.

Is it possible for us to abandon the old model that implies that our genes create disease? Can we speculate beyond the most recent credo, which states that the environment turns on the genes that create disease? Is it possible that by managing our own internal environment, independent of the external environment, we can maintain or change our genes? Why is it that when two factory employees, working side by side for 20 years, are exposed to the same carcinogenic chemical, one manifests cancer, the other does not? Surely, there must be an element of internal order at work in this situation, one that supersedes the continuous environmental exposure to harmful chemicals known to genetically alter tissues.

A growing body of knowledge points to the effects of stress on our bodies. Living in stress is living in a primitive state of survival common to most species. When we live in survival, we limit our evolution, because the chemicals of stress will always drive our big-thinking brain to act equal to its chemical substrates. In effect, we become more animal-like and less divine. The chemicals of stress are the culprits that begin to alter our internal state and pull the trigger of cellular breakdown. In this book, we examine those effects on the body. It is the redundancy not of acute stress but of chronic long-term stress that weakens our bodies. My goal is to educate you about the effects of stress on the body, creating a level of self-awareness that causes you to stop and ask yourself, Is anyone or anything really worth it?

So often it seems as if we cannot shake those internal states of emotional turmoil. Our reliance on these chemical states drives us to experience confusion, unhappiness, aggression, and even depression, to name a few. Why do we cling to relationships and jobs that logically no longer work? Why does changing ourselves and our conditions in life seem so hard? There is something in us that causes us to act this way. How do we manage to endure it day after day? If it is the conditions of our jobs that we dislike so much, why don't we just find other ones? If it is something in our personal life that causes us to suffer, why don't we change it?

There is a sound answer for us. We choose to remain in the same circumstances because we have become addicted to the emotional state they produce and the chemicals that arouse that state of being. Of course, I know from experience that change of any type is difficult for most people. Far too many of us remain in situations that make us unhappy, feeling as if we have no choice but to suffer. I also know that many of us choose to remain in situations that produce the kind of troubled state of mind that plagues us for our entire lifetime. *That* we choose is one thing, but *why* we choose to live this way is another. We choose to live stuck in a particular mindset and attitude, partly because of genetics and partly because a portion of the brain (a portion that has become hardwired by our repeated thoughts and reactions) limits our vision of what's possible. Like a hostage onboard a hijacked flight, we feel as though we are strapped into a seat on a destination not of our choosing, and we fail to see all the other possibilities that are available to us.

I remember when I was growing up, my mother used to refer to one of her friends as the kind of person who wasn't happy unless she or he was unhappy. Not until the last few years, when I've intensely studied the brain and behavior, did I really understand on a fundamental, biochemical, and neurological level what she meant. This is one of the reasons I wrote the book.

The title *Evolve Your Brain* may have appealed to your belief in human potential, and it's probable you are interested in improving yourself. Another likely reason you picked up this book is that, to one degree or another, you are unhappy with the circumstances of your life and you want to change. Change is a powerful word and it is completely feasible, if you choose it.

When it comes to evolution, change is the only element that is universal, or consistent, to all species here on earth. Essentially, to evolve is to change, by adapting to the environment. Our environment as human beings is everything that makes up our lives. It is all of the complex circumstances that involve our loved ones, our social status, where we live, what we do for a living, how we react to our parents and children, and even the times we live in. But as we will learn, to change is to be greater than the environment.

When we change something in our life, we have to make it different than it would be if we left it alone. To change is to become different; it means that we are no longer who we used to be. We have modified how we think, what we do, what we say, how we act, and who we are being. Personal change takes an intentional act of will, and it usually means that something was making us uncomfortable enough to want to do things differently. To evolve is to overcome the conditions in our life by changing something about ourselves.

We can change (and thus, evolve) our brain, so that we no longer fall into those repetitive, habitual, and unhealthy reactions that are produced as a result of our genetic inheritance and our past experiences. You probably picked up this book because you are drawn to the possibility that you may be able to break out of routine. You may want to learn how you can use the brain's natural capacity of *neuroplasticity*—the ability to rewire and create new neural circuits at any age—to make substantial changes in the quality of your life. Evolving your brain is what this book is about.

Our ability to be neuroplastic is equivalent to our ability to change our mind, to change ourselves, and to change our perception of the world around us; that is, our reality. In order to accomplish that feat, we have to change how the brain automatically and habitually works. Try out this simple example of your brain's plasticity. Take a look at Figure 1.1. What do you see? For most people, the first

Figure 1.1

thing that comes to mind is a duck or a goose. It's pretty simple, right?

In this example, the familiar form of the picture in front of you causes your brain to recognize a pattern in the shape of some type of bird. Just above your ears, the temporal lobes (the brain's center for decoding and recognizing objects) lock into a memory. The picture activates a few hundred million neurological circuits, which fire in a unique sequence and pattern throughout specific parts of your brain, and you are *reminded* of a duck or goose. Let's just say that the memory imprinted in your brain cells of what a duck or a goose looks like matches the picture before you, and you are able to recall the word "goose" or "duck." This is how we interpret reality all the time. It's sensory pattern recognition.

Now let's get neuroplastic for a moment. What if I told you to no longer see a bird, but to see a rabbit instead? For you to accomplish this feat, your frontal lobe would have to force your brain to "cool off" the circuits that are related to birds and to reorganize its circuitry to imagine a rabbit instead of a feathered creature with an undying affection for water. The ability to make the brain forgo its habitual internal wiring and fire in new patterns and combinations is how neuroplasticity allows us to change.

Just like the example in Figure 1.1, to break out of a habit of thinking, doing, feeling, perceiving, or behaving is what allows you to see the world—and see yourself—differently. And the best part of this experiment in plasticity is that your brain permanently changed; it neurologically tracked a new way to fire off circuits, by making new neurological patterns work in a different fashion. You changed your mind by altering the brain's typical firing pattern and by strengthening new chains of brain cell connections, and thus who you are changed as well. For our purposes, the words *change, neuroplasticity,* and *evolution* have similar meanings. The aim of this book is for you to see that change and evolution are all about breaking the habit of being the "you."

What I've discovered in studying the brain and its effects on behavior for the last 20 years has made me enormously hopeful about human beings and our ability to change. This is contrary to what we have long thought. Until recently, the scientific literature has led us to believe that we are doomed by genetics, are hobbled by conditioning, and should resign ourselves that the proverbial thinking about old dogs and new tricks has scientific validity.

Here is what I mean. In the evolutionary process, most species that are subjected to harsh environmental conditions (predators, climate/temperature, food availability, social pecking orders, procreation opportunities, and so on) adapt over millions of years, by overcoming the changes and challenges in their external surroundings. Whether they develop camouflage or faster legs to outrun the meat eater, changes in behavior are reflected in physical, genetic biology through evolution. Our evolutionary history is innately encoded within us.

Therefore, exposure to diverse and changing conditions causes certain more adaptable creatures to begin to acclimate to their environment; by changing themselves on an innate level, they ensure their continuity as a species. Over generations of trial and error, the repeated exposure to difficult conditions causes those biological organisms that do not become extinct to slowly adapt, eventually change, and finally alter their genetics. This is the slow, linear process of evolution inherent to all species. The environment changes, the challenges are met, behavior and actions are altered to adapt, genes encode the changes, and evolution follows by recording the change for the future of the species. The organism's lineage is now more suited to endure the changes in its world. As a result of thousands of years of evolution, the physical expression of an organism is equal to or greater than the conditions of the environment. Evolution stores the enduring memories of generations untold. Genes encode the wisdom of a species by keeping track of its changes.

The prize of such efforts will be inborn behavior patterns such as instincts, natural skills, habituations, innate drives, ritualistic behaviors, temperament, and heightened sensory perception. We tend to think that what is genetically dealt to us becomes an automatic program we can't help but live by. Once our genes are activated, either by the timing of some genetic program or by the conditioning of the environment (nature versus nurture), we are wired to behave in certain distinct ways. It is true that our genetics have a powerful influence on who we are, as if we are living by some unseen hand that is leading us to predictable habits and innate propensities. Therefore, overcoming challenges in the environment means that we not only have to demonstrate a will greater than our circumstances, but also must break old habits by releasing the encoded memories of past experiences that may be dated and that no longer apply to our current conditions. To evolve, then, is to break the genetic habits we are prone to and to use what we learned as a species as only a platform to stand on, from which to advance further.

To change and evolve is not a comfortable process for any species. To overcome our innate propensities, alter our genetic programs, and adapt to new environmental circumstances requires will and determination. Let's face it, changing is inconvenient for any creature unless it is seen as a necessity. To relinquish the old and embrace the new is a big risk.

The brain is structured, both macroscopically and microscopically, to absorb and engage novel information, and then store it as routine. When we no longer learn new things or we stop changing old habits, we are left only with living in routine. But the brain is not designed to just stop learning. When we stop upgrading the brain with new information, it becomes hardwired, riddled with automatic programs of behavior that no longer support evolution.

Adaptability is the ability to change. We are so smart and capable. We can, in one lifetime, learn new things, break old habits, change our beliefs and our perceptions, overcome difficult circumstances, master skills, and mysteriously, become different beings. Our big brains are the instruments that allow us to advance at such an enormous pace. For us as human beings, it seems that it is just a question of choice. If evolution is our contribution to the future, then our free will is how we initiate the process.

Evolution, though, must start with changing the individual self. To entertain the idea of starting with yourself, think of the first creature—say, a member of a pack with a structured group consciousness—who decided to break from the current behavior of the whole. On some level, the creature must have intuited that to act in new ways and to break from the normal behavior of the species might ensure its own survival and possibly, the future of its kin. Who knows? Entire new species might even have been created this way. To leave behind what is considered normal amidst social convention and to create a new mind requires being an individual—for any species. Being uncompromising to one's vision of a new and improved self and abandoning one's prior ways of being may also be encoded in living tissue for new generations; history remembers individuals for such elegance. True evolution, then, is using the genetic wisdom of past experiences as raw materials for new challenges.

What this book offers is a scientifically based alternative to the model of thought that told us our brains are essentially hardwired with unchangeable circuitry—that we possess, or better put, that we are possessed by, a kind of neuro-rigidity that is reflected in the inflexible and habitual type of behavior we often see exhibited. The truth is that we are marvels of flexibility, adaptability, and a neuroplasticity that allows us to reformulate and repattern our neural connections and produce the kinds of behaviors that we want. We have far more power to alter our own brain, our behavior, our personality, and ultimately our reality than previously thought possible. I know these truths because I have seen for myself and have read about how certain individuals have risen above their present circumstances, stood up to the onslaught of reality as it presented itself to them, and made significant changes.

For example, the Civil Rights movement would not have had its far-reaching effects if a true individual like Dr. Martin Luther King, Jr., had not, despite all the evidence around him (Jim Crow laws, separate but equal accommodations, snarling attack dogs, and powerful fire hoses), believed in the possibility of another reality. Although Dr. King phrased it in his famous speech as a "dream," what he was really promoting (and living) was a better world where everyone was equal. How was he able to do that? He decided to place a new idea in his mind about freedom for himself and a nation, and that idea was more important to him than the conditions in his external world. He was uncompromising in holding fast to that vision. Dr. King was unwilling to alter his thoughts, his actions, his behavior, his speech, and his message in response to anything outside of him. He never changed his internal picture of a new environment in spite of his external environment, even if it meant insult to his body. It was the power of his vision that convinced millions of the justness of his cause. The world has changed because of him. And he's not alone.

Countless others have altered history through comparable efforts. Millions more have altered their personal destinies in a similar way. We can all create a new life for ourselves and share it with others. As we learned, we have the kind of hardware in our brain that allows us certain unique privileges. We can keep a dream or ideal in our mind for extended periods of time despite external environmental circumstances. We also have the capacity to rewire our brain, because we are capable of making a thought more real to us than anything else in the universe. Ultimately, that is the point of this book.

A Story of Personal Transformation

I want to tell you a little bit about an experience I had 20 years ago that inspired me to investigate the power of the brain to alter our life. In 1986, I was 23 years old, had opened my own chiropractic practice in Southern California less than half a year earlier, and was already seeing more than a full patient load every week. My practice was in La Jolla, a hotbed of weekend warriors and world-class athletes who trained feverishly and took care of their bodies with the same fervor. I specialized in treating them. While still attending chiropractic college, I had studied sports medicine extensively in continuing education seminars. After I graduated, I found a niche and filled it.

I was successful because I had a lot in common with these driven patients. I too was driven, and I was focused. Like them, I felt I could meet every challenge and succeed. I'd managed to graduate with very good grades a year and a half ahead of schedule. Now I was living the good life, with an office along the beach on La Jolla Boulevard and a BMW. You know, the California image.

My life consisted of working, running, swimming, cycling, eating, and sleeping. The physical activities were a part of triathlon training—the eating and sleeping were necessary but often neglected functions. I could see the future spread in front of me like a banquet table featuring one delicious choice after another.

For the first three months of that year, I'd been focused on a goal—a triathlon in Palm Springs on April 12th.

The race didn't start off well. Because twice as many entrants showed up than were expected, the organizers couldn't let everyone start at the same time; instead, they split the field into two groups. By the time I arrived at the staging area to check in, one group was already standing calf-deep in the lake, tugging at goggles and caps, getting ready to start.

As one of the volunteers used a marker to put a number on my leg, I asked a race official when my group was scheduled to start. "In maybe twenty minutes," he said. Before I even had a chance to say thanks, a starter's gun went off across the lake. He looked at me and shrugged, "Guess you're starting now."

I couldn't believe it, but I recovered instantly, set up my gear in the transition area, and sprinted barefoot a half a mile around one end of the lake to get to the start. Though I was a few minutes behind the rest of my group, I was soon among the main pack and their tangled mass of churning limbs. As I stroked along, I had to remind myself that the race was against the clock and we still had a long way to go. A mile later, I splashed through the shallows, every muscle taut and taxed from the exertion. I was feeling good mentally, and the bike portion of the race (in this case, 26 miles) had always been my strength.

I ran to the transition area and hopped into my riding shorts. In a few seconds, I was running with my bike toward the road. Within a few hundred yards, I was really clipping along, quickly passing a host of riders. I eased back onto the seat to make myself as aerodynamic as possible and just kept churning my legs. My progress the first ten miles was rapid and exhilarating. I'd seen the course map and knew that an upcoming turn was a bit tricky—we'd have to merge with vehicular traffic. I eyed the course spotter, gave the brakes a few short squeezes to scrub off some speed, and after I saw a volunteer waving me on, I shifted to the biggest gear, hoping to keep momentum going.

I was no more than 20 feet around the curve when something flashed in my periphery. The next thing I knew, I was flying, separated from my bike by a red SUV traveling at 55 mph. The Bronco ate my bicycle, and then it tried to eat me. I landed squarely on my butt, and then bounced and rolled uncontrollably. Thankfully, the driver of the vehicle realized something was wrong. When she stopped abruptly and jammed on her brakes, I continued to roll almost 20 feet on the pavement. Amazingly, all of this took place in about two seconds.

As I lay on my back listening to the sounds of people screaming and a hornet's-nest buzzing of bikes passing by, I could feel warm blood pooling inside my rib cage. I knew the acute pain I was feeling couldn't be from soft tissue injury like a sprain or a strain. Something was seriously wrong. I also knew that some of my skin and the road surface had traded places. My body's innate intelligence was beginning to take over as I surrendered into the pain. I lay on the ground, trying to breathe steadily and stay calm.

I scanned my whole body with my mind, making sure my arms and legs were still present and moveable—they were. After 20 minutes that seemed like four hours, an ambulance raced me to John F. Kennedy Hospital for evaluation. What I remember most about the ambulance ride is that three technicians were futilely trying to find my veins for an IV drip. However, I was in shock. During this process, the body's intelligence moves large volumes of blood into the internal organs and away from the limbs. Also, I could tell I was bleeding quite a bit internally—I could feel the blood pooling along my spine. There was very little blood in my extremities at the time; essentially, I became a pincushion for the technicians.

At the hospital I was given blood tests, urine tests, X-rays, CT scans, and a gamut of other tests that took almost 12 hours to complete. After three unsuccessful attempts to remove gravel from my body, the hospital attendants gave up. Frustrated, confused, and in pain, I thought this must be some bad dream I had created.

Finally, the orthopedic surgeon, the hospital's medical director, performed his orthopedic and neurological examination. He could determine no neurological defects. Next, he rattled my X-rays into the viewer. One in particular caught my attention—the lateral thoracic view, a side view of my mid-spine. I saw the vertebrae: T-8, T-9, T-10, T-11, T-12, and L-1 clearly compressed, fractured, and deformed. He gave me his diagnosis. "Multiple compression fractures of the thoracic spine with the T-8 vertebra more than 60 percent collapsed."

I thought to myself, It could be worse. I could easily have had my spinal cord severed and been rendered dead or paralyzed. Then he put up my CT scans, showing several bone fragments on my spinal cord around the fractured T-8 vertebra. I knew what his next statement would be. As a matter of fact, we could have said it together. "The normal procedure in cases like this is complete thoracic laminectomy with Harrington rod surgery."

I had seen several videotaped laminectomies performed in surgical settings. I knew it was a radical surgery in which all the very back parts of the vertebral segments are sawed off and removed at each corresponding segment. The surgeon employs a toolbox of carpenter's blades and mini circular saws to cut away the bone and leave a smooth working surface. Next, the surgeon inserts the Harrington rods, which are orthopedic stainless steel devices. These attach with screws and clamps on both sides of the spinal column to stabilize the severe spinal fractures or abnormal curvatures that are the result of a trauma. Finally, new bone fragments are collected from scrapings of the hip bones and packed over the rods.

Without reacting, I asked the doctor how long the rods would have to be. "Eight to twelve inches, from the base of your neck to the base of your spine," he said. He then explained to me how he thought the procedure was really quite safe. In parting, he told me to pick a day within the next three days to have the surgery. I waved good-bye and thanked him.

Still not satisfied, though, I asked for the best neurologist in the area to visit me. After his examination and X-ray study, he bluntly told me that there was a greater than 50 percent chance I would never walk again if I decided against surgery. He explained that the T-8 vertebra was compressed like a wedge—smaller in the front of the column and larger toward the back of the column. If I stood up, he warned, the spine could not support the weight of my torso and my backbone would collapse. Apparently, the abnormal angle of the T-8 vertebra would alter the normal weight-bearing capacity of the spinal segments. According to this specialist, the deformity created a structural imbalance that would cause the spinal bone fragments to move into the spinal cord area and cause instant paralysis. The paralysis would manifest below the fracture of T-8.

I would be paralyzed from the chest down. The doctor added that he had never heard of a patient in the United States opting against the surgery. He mentioned some other options that doctors in Europe had at their disposal, but he knew very little about them and couldn't recommend them.

The next morning, through a fog of painkillers and sleeplessness, I realized I was still in the hospital. As I opened my eyes, I saw Dr. Paul Burns, my old roommate from chiropractic college, sitting right in front of me. Paul, who practiced in Honolulu, had received word of my condition, left his practice to fly to San Diego, drove to Palm Springs, and was there for me when I awoke that morning.

Paul and I decided that it would be better to transfer me by ambulance from Palm Springs to La Jolla's Scripps Memorial Hospital, so that I could be near my home in San Diego. The ride was long and painful. I lay strapped into a gurney, the ambulance's tires transferring every imperfection in the road into a jolt of pain somewhere on my body. I felt helpless. How was I ever going to get through this?

When I arrived in my hospital room, I was immediately introduced to the leading orthopedic surgeon in Southern California at that time. He was middle-aged, successful, good-looking, very credible, and sincere. He shook my hand and told me there was no time to spare. He looked into my eyes and said, "You have twenty-four degrees collapsed kyphosis (an abnormal forward curvature). The CT scans show the cord to be bruised and touching up against the bone fragments that were pushed backwards from the volume of the vertebral segment's columnar shape. The bone mass of each vertebra had to go somewhere when it was compressed, and the normal column shape of each vertebra became more like a tumbled stone. You could be paralyzed at any minute. My recommendation is immediate Harrington rod surgery. If we wait more than four days, a radical surgical procedure will be necessary, in which we open the body from the front, cut the chest open and also the back, placing the rods on both sides, front, and back. The success rate for the more radical option is about 50 percent."

I understood the reason that this decision had to be made within four days. The body's innate intelligence directs strings of calcium to be laid down in the bone to begin the healing process as soon as possible. If we waited longer than the four days, the surgeons would have to work through and around that natural healing process. The doctor assured me that if I chose to have surgery in less than four days, I could be walking in a month to two months and back in my practice seeing patients.

Somehow I just couldn't hastily agree and mindlessly sign away my future.

By this time, I was in tremendous conflict and I was really quite floored. He was so sure of himself, as if there were no other options. I asked him though, "What if I decide not to have the surgery?" He calmly replied, "I do not recommend it. It will take three to six months for the body to heal before you will possibly be able to walk. The normal procedure is strict bed rest in the prone position during the whole time of recovery. Then we would have to cast you in a full body brace and you would be required to wear it constantly for six months to one year. Without the surgery, it is my professional opinion that the moment you try to stand up, paralysis will ensue. The instability of T-8 will cause the forward curvature to increase and sever the spinal cord. If you were my son, you would be on the operating table right now."

I lay there accompanied by eight chiropractors, all of whom were my closest friends, along with my father, who had flown in from the East Coast. No one said a word for a long time. Everyone waited for me to speak. I never spoke. Eventually, my friends smiled, either embraced my arm or patted me on the shoulder, then respectfully filed out of the room. As everyone left, save my father, I became acutely aware of the unanimous relief my friends felt to know that they were not in my position. Their silence was too deafening for me to ignore.

What followed during the next three days was the worst of human suffering: indecision. I repeatedly looked at every one of those diagnostic films, reconsulted with everyone, and finally decided that one more opinion couldn't hurt.

The next day I waited with anticipation until the last surgeon arrived. Immediately, he was practically attacked by my colleagues, who had 25 questions apiece. They disappeared for 45 minutes to consult with the doctor, and then returned with the X-rays. This final doctor said basically the same thing as the others, but offered a different surgical procedure: six-inch rods to be placed in the spine for one year. Then they would be removed and permanently replaced with four-inch rods.

Now I had the additional option of two surgeries, instead of one. I laid there in a trance watching his lips move as he talked, but my attention was now somewhere else. I really didn't want to pretend that I was interested in his prognosis by unconsciously nodding to ease his discomfort. His voice began to recede further and further away as time passed. As a matter of fact, there was no perception of time at this point. I was entranced and my mind was far from that hospital room. I was thinking about living with a permanent disability and, quite possibly, continuous pain. Images of patients that I had attended over my years of residency and practice who opted for Harrington rod surgery earlier in their life rifled through my mind. They lived every day of their life on addictive medications, always trying to escape a brutal torment that never really left them.

I began to wonder, though. What if I had a patient in my office that I x-rayed and attended with similar findings as mine? What would I tell him? Probably to proceed with the surgery, since it was the safest option if he wanted to walk again. But this was me, and I could never imagine living with such a handicap while being partially dependent on others. The thought made me feel sick in the deepest part of my gut. That natural immortality that comes with youth, great health, and a particular station in life began to escape me like a brisk breeze moving down an open corridor. I felt empty and vulnerable.

I focused again on the situation at hand. The doctor loomed over me, all six feet, two inches and 300 pounds of him. I asked him, "Don't you think that placing Harrington rods in the thoracic spine and most of the lumbar spine would limit the normal motion of my back?" Without even skipping a beat, he responded by assuring me "not to worry," because according to him, there was normally no movement in the thoracic spine and therefore my normal mobility would be unaffected by the rods.

Everything changed for me in that moment. I had studied and taught martial arts for many years of my life. My spine was very flexible and super-mobile. During part of my undergraduate studies and throughout most of my time at chiropractic college, I had disciplined myself to do three hours of yoga a day. Every morning, I woke up before the sun at 3:55 a.m. and participated in intense yoga classes before my classroom work started. I have to admit that during yoga practice, I learned more about the spine and the body than all of the hours spent in anatomy and physiology classes. I even had a yoga studio that I taught at and managed in San Diego. At the time of my injury, yoga was part of a physical rehabilitation program for my patients. I knew that there was far more flexibility in that part of the spine than this latest doctor thought.

I also knew from experiencing my own body that I had quite a bit of motion in my thoracic spine. The issue now became a question of relativity. As the doctor and I spoke, I glanced at Dr. Burns, who had studied yoga and martial arts with me while we were in college. My colleague moved his spine in six different serpentine planes while standing behind the surgeon's back. Witnessing this demonstration, I realized that I already knew all the answers to the questions I was asking, because I was an expert on the spine, both from my formal education as well as what I had personally experienced.

The Inner Doctor at Work

I also knew that on some level, I trusted that the body heals itself. This *is* the chiropractic philosophy, that our innate intelligence gives life to the body. We simply have to get our educated mind out of the way and give a greater intelligence a chance to do what it does best.

Holistic practitioners understand that this innate intelligence runs through the central nervous system from the midbrain and the other lower subcortical regions of the brain to the body. This happens all day, every day, and that process had already been healing me. In fact, it was giving life to everything I did and keeping every process running, from digesting my food to pumping my blood. I wasn't always aware of those processes. Most of them took place in the background, in a subconscious realm, separate from my conscious awareness. Even though I had an educated, thinking neocortex that thought it was making the decisions for my body, in truth, the so-called lower centers of the brain had already started the healing process. I simply had to surrender to the intelligence that was already and always actively working within me, to let it work for me. However, I also reminded myself that my body was performing these tasks at a rudimentary level—the subconscious realm works at healing, but only to the extent that our genetic programming allows it to. I needed to aim for something more than that.

I now recognized that I was looking through a different window than the four surgeons; I lived in a realm totally unknown to them. I began to feel in control again, principled.

The next day, I checked out of the hospital. A very upset surgeon told my father I was mentally unstable from the trauma and urged him to seek a psychological evaluation for me. But something inside of me just knew I was making the right choice. As I left the hospital, I held on to one thought: My knowledge of the immaterial power and energy within me that is constantly giving life to my body would heal me if I could make contact with it and direct it. As most chiropractic physicians would say, "The power that made the body, heals the body."

Transported by ambulance, I arrived at the house of two close friends of mine. For the next three months, my room was a beautiful A-frame: multi-windowed, sky-lit, bright, and spacious, as opposed to the dim stuffy hospital quarters. I began to relax and let my mind expand without looking back at my choice. I had to focus only on my healing, and not let any other thoughts and emotions rooted in fears or doubts distract me from my recovery. My decision was final.

I decided I needed a game plan if I was to heal this injury completely. I would eat only a raw-food diet, and only small amounts. In this way, the energy required to digest large cooked meals would be preserved for healing. Next to sex, and severe stress, digestion uses up the largest amount of the body's energy. Also, by having the enzymes already in the nutritional matrix of live raw foods, it would hasten my digestion and take less energy for the body to process and eliminate.

Next, I spent three hours a day, morning, noon, and evening, in self-hypnosis and meditation. I visualized, with the joy of being totally healed, that my spine was fully repaired. I mentally reconstructed my spine, building each segment. I stared at hundreds of pictures of spines to help me perfect my mental imagery. My focused thoughts would help direct the greater intelligence already at work to heal me.

When I was in undergraduate school and in chiropractic college, I had become fascinated with the study of hypnosis. This interest was triggered by having two roommates who frequently sleepwalked and sleeptalked. I witnessed a lot of these incidents. They piqued my curiosity about the powers of the subconscious mind and eventually about hypnosis itself. I read every available book on hypnosis. My interests were also self-motivated—I wanted to be able to go to class, never take any notes, and remember everything. For two years, on the weekends and during many evenings, I attended a school called Hypnosis Motivation Institute in Norcross, Georgia. By the time I graduated from chiropractic school, I had studied over 500 hours in clinical hypnosis developed by the "father of modern hypnosis," John Kappas, Ph.D.

While I was still in chiropractic college, I became licensed and certified as a clinical hypnotherapist, and I developed a part-time, private hypnotherapy practice at a holistic healing center outside Atlanta, Georgia. Although back then I did not understand how the mind works in the same way I do today, I did directly witness the power of the subconscious mind when working with several different health conditions. For example, after inducing an altered state in my patients, I saw an anorgasmic woman experience a clinical orgasm without physical touch, a 20-year smoker completely quit in one session, and a client with chronic dermatitis and rashes completely heal his skin in one hour.

I therefore began my recovery regimen with the simple idea that the healing of my injury was completely possible because I had personally witnessed the ability of the subconscious mind. Now it was my turn to put it to the test.

I also set up a schedule for people to visit me twice daily for one-hour segments, once in the morning before lunch and once before dinner. I had them place their hands over the broken part of my spine. Friends, patients, doctors, family, and even people I didn't know contributed by intentionally laying their hands on my back and sharing the healing effects of their energy.

Finally, I realized that in order for the proper amounts of calcium to be laid down in those broken bones, I needed to apply some gravitational stress on the damaged segments. As a bone develops or heals, the natural force of gravity acts as a stimulant to change the normal electric charge of the outside of the bone, so that by polarity, the positively charged calcium molecule will be drawn to the negatively charged surface of bone. This concept made total sense to me. But nowhere in any literature could I find such reasoning applied to the treatment and management of compression fractures.

That absence of previously published research didn't stop me, though.

I instructed a friend of mine to build an incline board, with a base for my feet to rest on and to give me support. Each day, I slowly and carefully rolled from my bed onto the board, and I was brought outside. I was placed on an angle of two degrees above horizontal to start conservatively stressing my spine. Each day we increased the angle. By the sixth week, I was at 60 degrees, pain-free. This feat was amazing, considering that I was not supposed to be out of bed for three to six months.

Six weeks went by, and I felt strong, confident, and happy. We hired a doctor to run my office, and I managed it by phone.

I decided after a certain point that mobility, not immobility as the medical profession prescribes, would be an asset to my recovery. The time had come to start swimming. I reasoned that water would decrease the weight of gravity on my spine and allow me to move freely. The house I was living in had an indoor/outdoor pool that was ideal. I was placed in a very tight wet suit and carried in a lounge chair toward the semiheated pool. My heart was racing as fast as my mind was. I hadn't been in a vertical position for so long. At first, I just floated horizontally in the lounge chair, but I gradually moved into the vertical position for the first time, holding onto a swing built for my support. I just floated there rigidly, rising and falling in the waves my movement created. By floating upright in the water instead of standing, I actually decreased the weight my spine bore by lessening gravity. This allowed me to be vertical with minimal pressure on my healing spine.

From then on, I swam every day, initially just paddling with my feet. Within a few days, I was swimming like a fish, exercising all my muscles. I loved the new freedom of swimming, floating vertically in the pool, and even playing a little. If only the surgeons could have seen this! My body responded amazingly.

At eight weeks, I began crawling on dry land. I felt that if I imitated the movements of an infant, I could develop similarly and eventually stand. To regain and maintain mobility, I practiced yoga daily to supply continuous stretching of my connective tissue. Most of the postures were done lying down.

At nine weeks, I was sitting up, taking baths, and finally using the toilet. Ah yes, the simple things!

That explains what I did with my body. But I had another crucial experience that influenced my mind, and the eventual positive outcome of my choice. By week six, I was getting a little antsy. Lying in the sun or in bed all day sounds great, if you are doing it voluntarily and can easily get up from that prone position any time you want. Obviously, that wasn't my case. I was looking for whatever kind of mental stimulation I could find. Concentrating all day on the spine and its individual components wasn't possible—or desirable. I needed brain breaks.

One day, during that first six weeks, I saw a book sitting alone on a bookshelf. I was intrigued by its mysterious blank cover so I asked a friend who was over at the time to hand it to me. I flipped the white book over several times in search of its title but couldn't find one. Its author was Ramtha, and it was published by a group affiliated with the Ramtha School of Enlightenment (RSE). I opened *Ramtha: The White Book*[1] and began to read, unaware of how influential this book would be to me.

I had been raised a Catholic, but I wasn't what anyone would consider a particularly religious or even spiritual person. I believed in the body's innate intelligence. I knew that there was a force animating each and every one of us, and I knew that force/intelligence was far greater than anything we humans possessed. I held that there is a spiritual element within everyone but was not drawn to a rigid, hierarchical kind of church or any dogma. I believed that humans are far more capable than we know. I couldn't say that I was a formal believer in any one kind of spiritual practice. I certainly didn't belong to a church that had any kind of denomination attached to it, but I did trust in something tangible, real, and actively at work in my life.

Thus I was in one sense predisposed to be more open-minded than most about what I was soon to read in *Ramtha: The White Book*. I started reading it out of curiosity, but even after the first few pages, the subconscious part of me had nudged my intellect, telling me to pay attention to what I was reading. The words were making sense on a lot of levels. By the time I got to the part in the book that explained how thoughts and emotions create our reality, the idea of superconsciousness, I was completely hooked. I finished it 36 hours later. I was a man in the middle of changing, and the book greatly accelerated the rate of my change.

Ramtha: The White Book was the perfect catalyst, crystallizing much of what I had been thinking about and experiencing for most of my adult life. It answered many questions I had about human potential, life and death, and the divinity of human beings, just to name a few. The book validated many of the decisions I had made, particularly my risky choice to forego surgery. It challenged the boundaries of what I knew to be true intellectually, and it raised me to the next level of awareness and understanding about the nature of reality. I understood better than ever before that our thoughts affect not only our body but also our entire life. The concept of superconsciousness was not only the science of mind over matter, but also the idea of mind influencing the nature of all reality. Not bad for a book that was just sitting on an empty shelf collecting dust!

For a long time, I had been interested in the unconscious, my experiences with hypnotherapy being the most obvious component of that interest. But through the teachings of Ramtha, my exposure to the idea of superconsciousness helped me understand that I was responsible for everything that happened in my life—even my injury. My body had gone from being in a 100 mph fast lane to a dead stop. There were bound to be some effects from that, but most important, I began to see the perfection of my whole creation. I was more profoundly affected by this slowdown than I could have ever imagined—I had to rethink everything that I knew. As a result, I was enriched.

I made a deal with myself. If my body was able to be healed and I could walk again without being paralyzed or in pain, I was going to spend a major portion of my life studying this phenomenon of mind over matter and how consciousness creates reality. I became more interested in learning how to consciously and thoughtfully control my future. That's when I made the decision to enroll at the Ramtha School of Enlightenment, to become more involved in the teachings.

At nine and one-half weeks, I got up, and then walked right back into my life. At ten weeks, I returned to work, seeing patients and enjoying my freedom.

No body cast, no deformity, no paralysis. At twelve weeks, I was lifting weights and continuing to rehabilitate. I had been fitted for a body cast six weeks after the accident, but I only wore it once, when I first began walking, for about one hour. At this point in my recovery, I didn't need it.

It is now more than 20 years since the date of my injury. I find it interesting that although 80 percent of the American population complain of some type of back pain, I have hardly ever had pain in my spine since my recovery.

I often wonder, if I hadn't made the choice for my own natural healing, where I would be today. Some of you may ask, was it worth the risk? When I glance back to imagine the consequences of making a different choice in my past, I quietly exalt in my present freedom. During that brief time in my life, I think I became more inspired about the process of healing the mind and the body than I could have ever imagined if I had opted for conventional surgery.

In all honesty, I truly don't know if what I experienced was a miracle. But I made good on my promise to explore as fully as possible the phenomenon of spontaneous healing. *Spontaneous healing* refers to the body's repairing itself or ridding itself of disease without traditional medical interventions like surgery or drugs.

Through 17 years as a student and the seven years I spent as a teacher at the Ramtha School of Enlightenment, I have gone well beyond the original boundaries of that inquiry. I have been inspired and enriched by those experiences. This book would not be possible without the learning and experiences I had at RSE. *Evolve Your Brain* then, is an attempt to put together an accurate account of my own education and experiences, some of the teachings of Ramtha, as well as my own research.

For the last seven years, Ramtha has at times gently nudged me in the direction of sharing this information, my experiences, and my personal research; at other times he has wheedled, cajoled, and pushed me in this direction. This book represents my coming to terms with all the various influences in my life, having a firmer grasp now on the scientific concepts than I did seven years ago, and having committed myself to giving back in whatever proportion to what I have been blessed to receive. Truth be told, *Evolve Your Brain* could not have been written seven years ago—the research that is so fundamental to the scope of this book simply was not ready. I was not ready. I am today.

I also know that my choice many years ago to forego surgery has led me to where I am now. My research, my scientific interests, and my livelihood are centered around healings of all types. I have spent the last seven years looking into how believing in a single thought, independent of the circumstances, calls upon a greater mind and takes people to an immense and wonderful future. When I lecture on all the ingredients it takes for a person to turn around his or her condition, I truly feel blessed that I can contribute to the layperson's understanding of the brain and of the power our thoughts have to shape our life.

Aside from dealing with physical ailments, this book is also intended to address another kind of affliction besides physical pain—emotional addiction. In the last several years, as I've traveled widely, lectured, and conducted independent research into the latest evidence in neurophysiology, I've come to understand that what was once theory now has practical applications for us to heal our own self-inflicted emotional wounds. The methods I suggest are not a pie-in-the-sky, wouldn't-it-be-wonderful, self-help miracle cure. Be assured, this book is grounded in cutting-edge science.

We've all experienced emotional addiction at some point in our life. Among its symptoms are lethargy, a lack of ability to focus, a tremendous desire to maintain routine in our daily life, the inability to complete cycles of action, a lack of new experiences and emotional responses, and the persistent feeling that one day is the same as the next and the next.

How is it possible to end this cycle of negativity? The answer, of course, lies in you. And in this case, in a very specific part of you. Through an understanding of the various subjects we will explore in this book and a willingness to apply some specific principles, you can heal yourself emotionally by altering the neural networks in your brain. For a long time, scientists believed that the brain was *hardwired,* meaning that change is impossible and that the system of responses and tendencies you inherited from your family is your destiny. But in fact, the brain possesses elasticity, an ability to shut down old pathways of thought and form new ones, at any age, at any time. Moreover, it can do so relatively quickly, especially compared to the usual evolutionary models in which time is measured in generations and eons and not in weeks.

As I'm beginning to learn and as neuroscience is beginning to acknowledge:

• Our thoughts matter.

• Our thoughts literally become matter.

CHAPTER TWO

ON THE BACK
OF A GIANT

We must deliver ourselves
with the help of our minds . . .
for one who has conquered the mind,
the mind is the best of friends;
but for the one who has failed to do so,
the mind will remain the greatest enemy.

—BHAGAVAD-GITA

We've all heard the expression "mind over matter" used in the context of a person overcoming an obstacle. Someone could easily use it in the context of my recovery from my accident, discussed in chapter 1. Generally, we use that expression without giving it much thought—it simply means that someone decided to do something and didn't let conventional thinking or obstacles get in the way of achieving the goal he or she had in mind. It truly involves will. You probably believe you are capable, in some circumstances, of using this force of mind to affect changes in the physical, mental, or emotional realms.

For example, suppose that, as a kid, you had a fear of heights. You and your friends went on a camping trip, and near your campsite was a lake with a rocky outcropping at its edge. Everyone else was having a great time jumping and diving off the bluff into the water. You were content to swim around, enjoying the water's cooling effects, until someone—likely one of your older friends or siblings—had to point out to everyone that you were the only one to not take the leap of faith. Even the youngest kid on the trip had taken the plunge. Eventually, goaded on by their teasing and to escape the constant splashing of water in your face, you climbed out of the water and made your shivering way up onto the outcropping.

The sun burning your shoulders, the wind chilling your skin into goose flesh, you stood blinking past the water dripping off your hair. All the while, your mind was racing, telling you, "No way." Your teeth alternately chattering and grinding against one another, you took a tentative step back from the edge. The hooting and catcalls intensified. You looked down and the chief tormenter had turned into your cheerleader, his "C'mon" no longer a taunt but a mantra. Fueled by a jolt of adrenaline that quivered your bladder and buckled your knees, you staggered out and away from the edge and into space.

You came up sputtering, and then whooped in triumph, knowing that something fundamental had changed inside you. All the doubts, fears, and uncertainties were left behind. They were back there on the flat rock, rapidly evaporating like your footprints. All the imagined horrors had dissipated, leaving a new, more positive reality in their place.

I use this somewhat commonplace example on purpose. Literally and metaphorically, many people are crippled by something that prevents them from reaching the heights of their existence, something that keeps them from experiencing the freedom and exhilaration of a life unencumbered by fear or doubt.

I'm sure that at some point in your life, you've had your own mind-over-matter experience. I'd had several in my life, but none was as provocative as my healing from the injuries I'd sustained in that triathlon. I'd always been interested in pushing myself, in improving myself, and I'd always been fascinated by the potential the human mind and body possessed. I was especially interested in what happened when mind and body truly worked in unison. Of course, I knew that mind and body weren't really separate, but I'd often wondered which of the two was really driving the so-called bus. Which was really in control? Were we genetically predetermined to suffer from certain diseases and afflictions of the body and mind? Were we totally subject to the whims of our environment?

An Introduction to Change

Once I experienced for myself the power of the mind and body working together, I wondered whether others had experienced something similar. I knew that many people had defied conventional medical wisdom before me, and I wanted to investigate the concept of healing more fully. I didn't have to wait very long to find suitable subjects for my informal study of the phenomenon.

Dean: A Wink and a Nod

When I first saw Dean sitting in my waiting room, he smiled and winked at me. On his face he had two tumors the size of very large lemons. One was under his chin on the right side, and the other growth was on his forehead on the left side. During my examination, Dean explained that he had leukemia. I asked him what medications and therapies he used to keep the disease under control. "None, never," he replied. I continued my examination, trying to focus on what I was doing but wanting to ask him dozens of questions. I had healed from an injury, but this was clearly different. Leukemia, especially untreated acute myelogenous leukemia, was a debilitating and painful disease. It was not an injury the body could simply heal over time, like a broken bone.

The doctors who diagnosed Dean had given him six months to live. Right then, Dean said, he had made himself a promise to see his son graduate from high school. That pivotal moment had occurred 25 years earlier. Now, beaming at me across the examination table, Dean announced that in a few months, he was going to his youngest grandchild's high school commencement. I was amazed.

After our first encounter, Dean returned to my office for a couple of follow-up visits. One day, after I finished treating him, I finally had to ask, "How did you do it? You should have been dead 24 years ago, but with no medications, no surgeries, no therapies, you are still alive. What's the secret?" Dean smiled broadly, leaned across the examining bench to bring his face close to mine, pointed to his forehead, and said, "You just have to make up your mind!" He shook my hand firmly, turned to leave, and then gave me one more wink.

Sheila: The Past as Precursor and Curse

Sheila suffered from a host of debilitating symptoms including nausea, fevers, constipation, and severe abdominal pain. Her doctor's diagnosis was chronic diverticulitis—a painful inflammation or infection in small pouches that develop in the intestine. Although Sheila received medical treatment, she continued to experience ever more frequent, acute episodes.

One day, Sheila learned about the connection between unhealthy emotions and physical ailments, and it prompted her to look at her life in a new way. Even as an adult in her thirties, Sheila considered herself a victim of her childhood. Her parents had divorced when she was young. She was raised by her mother, who worked a lot and had left Sheila alone much of the time. Having grown up without most of the material possessions and social experiences that other children enjoyed, she felt cheated.

When Sheila decided to pay attention to her emotions, she had to admit that they qualified as unhealthy. Day in and day out for 20 years, she had been thinking and saying that because her childhood was tough, she could never do anything worthy or personally satisfying. She had constantly reminded herself that her existence was futile, that she could never change, and that her parents were to blame for all of the misfortune in her life. Now, the realization dawned on her that throughout most of her waking hours during all those years, her thoughts had been a repetitive litany of blame, excuses, and complaints. Since medical intervention had not provided a permanent cure, Sheila began to explore the possibility that the grudge she carried against her parents might directly relate to her disease. She became aware of all the people and situations in her life that allowed her to think and behave as a victim, and she recognized that she had been using these people and circumstances to excuse her own unwillingness to change.

Gradually, by exercising consistent awareness and self-will, Sheila surrendered her old thought patterns and the feelings connected to those repetitive, victimizing thoughts. She taught herself to give up the part of her identity that was related to negative thoughts about her childhood, and she forgave her parents. Sheila no longer had any reasons to suffer and as a result, she became happy.

Her symptoms began to ease. Within a short time, all the physical symptoms associated with her illness disappeared. Sheila had healed herself of a debilitating disease. More important, she had also freed herself from the chains of her self-imprisonment.

A Search for Similarities

Over the last seven years, I have been investigating cases of people who have experienced spontaneous remissions and healings from serious diseases. The information I have collected and the stories these individuals shared during our interviews are truly amazing. They showed substantial clinical changes in health conditions like benign and malignant tumors, heart disease, diabetes, respiratory conditions, high blood pressure, high cholesterol, varicosities, thyroid conditions, dental problems and gum disease, poor vision, musculoskeletal pain, and rare genetic disorders for which medical science offers no solution, to name a few.

These men and women recovered when no conventional or alternative treatments had been effective in reversing their conditions. Each individual healed his or her own body. When I examined these case histories from a therapeutic standpoint, I could not find any common, consistent behavioral factor that could explain their recoveries.

Various therapies they had tried had altered their conditions to some extent but did not take them away completely. For example, some submitted to radiation and/or chemotherapy, but their cancer persisted or quickly returned. Others underwent routine or experimental surgery, which provided some relief of their symptoms, but didn't resolve their problems. Many had been on medications for years to treat conditions such as high blood pressure, without experiencing significant or lasting changes. Some patients took part in clinical trials of experimental drugs, but this produced no healing. Vitamins or special dietary regimens did not restore their health. A few reported that fasting somewhat relieved their symptoms, but yielded no permanent recovery. Alternative therapies had also failed. In certain cases, counseling helped to reduce some of their stress, but produced no cure.

Many of the subjects had discontinued any therapies they were using when these proved ineffective. Some never sought medical or alternative intervention at all. What had these formerly ill persons done that resulted in the restoration of their health?

After analyzing the information from my interviews, I suspected that from a scientific standpoint, these spontaneous healings were more than a fluke. If something happens one time, we call that an incident. If the same type of event takes place a second time for no apparent reason, we might label it a co-incident (second incident) or *coincidence*—a surprising occurrence of two events that seems to have happened by mere chance, but gives them the appearance of being causally related.

But if the same type of event transpires a third, fourth, or even a fifth time, we must rule out the possibility of a coincidence. Something must be consistently happening to produce these reoccurrences. In light of such repetition, we can employ the reasoning that for every effect there must be a cause. Presuming that there might be a cause and effect relationship at work here, I wondered: If the effect we're talking about is the spontaneous restoration of health, what *caused* the physical changes in all of these individuals?

I started to speculate that since these subjects could not attribute their recoveries to any treatment or therapy directed at affecting the body, perhaps some internal process in the mind and brain had produced their clinical changes. Could the mind really be that powerful? Most doctors acknowledge that a patient's attitude affects his or her ability to benefit from medical treatment. Could it be that for these people, healing their illnesses was solely a matter of changing their minds?

I also contemplated whether a scientifically verifiable relationship existed between what was occurring consistently in these case histories and the human mind. If we applied the scientific method to evidence from cases such as these, might we discover some process that had occurred in the mind—and therefore, in the very tissues of the brain—to produce these healings? Could we repeat that process to produce the same effect? Would studying spontaneous healings help us to uncover scientific laws that could explain the mind-body connection?

Intrigued by my exposure to the Ramtha School of Enlightenment (RSE, see chapter 1), with the concept of mind over matter being its very credo, I used this line of questioning as the starting point in my endeavor to study spontaneous remissions and healings, and their possible relationship to the function of the mind. I was predisposed to believe they were related, since I understood that it was truly quite possible that the mind could heal the body of any condition. As a matter of fact, some of the people that I interviewed over the years were RSE students who were taught how to heal their own bodies.

The Nature of Miracles

At times, I found the healings difficult to accept. Yet these types of incidences/coincidences have been going on for as far back as history has been recorded. When such events happened in antiquity, explanations were usually rooted in a culture's religious beliefs. Whether we look to Christian scripture, Buddhist texts, Islamic sacred writings, Egyptian tablets, or Judaic scrolls, many civilized cultures have believed in and reported on the spontaneous restoration of health.

Throughout centuries past, when something happened that was outside the realm of that society's scientific understanding, people often termed the event a "miracle." A *miracle*, according to Webster's International Dictionary, is an "effect or extraordinary event in the physical world that surpasses all known human or natural powers and is attributed to some supernatural cause."

If we examine historical records, we see that events were described as miracles when they took place outside the boundaries of a culture's secular beliefs and beyond its social, scientific, or political conventions. Imagine that a man jumps out of an airplane, his parachute opens, and he lands safely in a field. This would have seemed miraculous two centuries ago. Like other unfathomable events of the day, it would have been attributed to the action or intervention of a supernatural power—whether deity or demon.

Fast forward to the present. A woman develops a terminal disease with a prognosis of six months to live. After six months, she returns to her doctor for a checkup. The doctor examines her and performs a series of diagnostic tests, including advanced imaging scans. To his surprise, no clinical, objective signs of the disease persist. By all objective measures, the person has been cured.

If we label this type of recovery as a miracle, we might miss a deeper truth. Once a society comprehends the causes, workings, and effects of an event, it no longer gives that experience a supernatural context. Myth and folklore have always served this purpose—they offer an explanation of natural phenomena. Every culture has its own creation myth, for example, and many cultures, Christian and non-Christian, tell a flood story as well. Today, we understand that our inability to explain an occurrence may be due to our own lack of knowledge, individually and as a culture. Many events we once considered miraculous we now redefine as natural happenings. Is there a plausible explanation, then, for spontaneous healings?

There is an interesting component to the miraculous. A person who pursues so-called miraculous experiences or results, exploring ideas beyond society's current beliefs, might reasonably consider acting counter to medical, social, or even religious conventions. Imagine that a man is diagnosed with high blood pressure and elevated cholesterol. His allopathic (conventional) doctor gives him a prognosis and treatment plan, possibly including medications, dietary restrictions, an exercise regimen, and a prescriptive set of do's and don'ts. If the client responds, "Thanks, Doc, but I'll handle this on my own," the doctor would likely conclude that the patient is risking his health by not taking the standard route. Anyone who embraces the hope for a miraculous outcome in his life may have to storm the fortress of conventional beliefs and risk being considered misguided, irrational, fanatic, or even insane.

But if there were a method to understanding the hows and whys of so-called healing miracles, those who seek to experience them would no longer be deemed foolhardy or unstable. If we could access information on how to accomplish these feats, and experience that knowledge for ourselves by practicing the specific science involved, our efforts to produce miraculous results should meet not with resistance, but with support.

The Four Pillars of Healing

It became clear to me, after years of interviewing people who had experienced spontaneous remissions and healings, that most of these individuals had four specific qualities in common. They had experienced the same coincidences.

Before I describe the four qualities common to these cases, I would like to note some of the factors that were not consistent among the people I studied. Not all practiced the same religion; several had no religious affiliation. Not many had a background as a priest, rabbi, minister, nun, or other spiritual profession. These individuals were not all New Agers. Only some prayed to a specific religious being or charismatic leader. They varied by age, gender, race, creed, culture, educational status, profession, and tax bracket. Only a few exercised daily, and they did not all follow the same dietary regimen. They were of varying body types and fitness levels. They varied in their habits pertaining to alcohol, cigarettes, television, and other media. Not all were heterosexual; not all were sexually active. My interviewees had no external situation in common that appeared to have caused the measurable changes in their health status.

Coincidence #I: An Innate Higher Intelligence Gives Us Life and Can Heal the Body

The people I spoke with who experienced a spontaneous remission believed that a higher order or intelligence lived within him or her. Whether they called it their divine, spiritual, or subconscious mind, they accepted that an inner power was giving them life every moment, and that it knew more than they, as humans, could ever know. Furthermore, if they could just tap into this intelligence, they could direct it to start working for them.

I have come to realize that there is nothing mystical about this greater mind. It is the same intelligence that organizes and regulates all the functions of the body. This power keeps our heart beating without interruption more than 100,000 times per day, without our ever stopping to think about it. That adds up to more than 40 million heartbeats per year, nearly three billion pulsations over a lifetime of 70 to 80 years. All this happens automatically, without

care or cleaning, repair or replacement. An elevated consciousness is evidenc-
ing a will that is much greater than our will.

Likewise, we give no thought to what our heart is pumping: two gallons of
blood per minute, well over 100 gallons per hour, through a system of vascular
channels about 60,000 miles in length, or twice the circumference of the earth.
Yet the circulatory system makes up only about 3 percent of our body mass.[1]
Every 20 to 60 seconds, each blood cell makes a complete circuit through the
body, and every red blood cell makes anywhere between 75,000 and 250,000
round trips in its lifetime. (By the way, if all of the red blood cells in your bloodstream were lined up end to end, they would reach 31,000 miles into the heavens.) In the second it takes you to inhale, you lose three million red blood cells,
and in the next second, the same number will be replaced. How long would we
live if we had to focus on making all this happen? Some greater (more
expanded) mind must be orchestrating all of this for us.

Please stop reading for one second. Just now, some 100,000 chemical reactions took place in every single one of your cells. Now multiply 100,000 chemical reactions by the 70 to 100 trillion cells that make up your body. The answer
has more zeros than most calculators can display, yet *every second,* that mind-
boggling number of chemical reactions takes place inside of you. Do you have
to think to perform even one of those reactions? Many of us can't even balance
our checkbooks or remember more than seven items from our shopping lists, so
it's fortunate for us that some intelligence smarter than our conscious mind is
running the show.

In that same second, 10 million of your cells died, and in the next instant,
almost 10 million new cells took their place.[2] The pancreas itself regenerates
almost all its cells in one day. Yet we give not a moment's thought to the disposal
of those dead cells, or to all of the necessary functions that go into *mitosis,* the
process that gives rise to the production of new cells for tissue repair and
growth. Recent calculations estimate that the communication between cells
actually travels faster than the speed of light.

At the moment, you are probably giving some thought to your body. Yet
something other than your conscious mind is causing the secretion of enzymes

in exact amounts to digest the food you consumed into its component nutrients. Some mechanism of a higher order is filtering liters of blood through your kidneys every hour to make urine and eliminate wastes. (In one hour, the most advanced kidney dialysis machines can only filter 15 to 20 percent of the body's wastes from the blood.) This superior mind precisely maintains the 66 functions of the liver, although most people would never guess that this organ performs so many tasks.

The same intelligence can direct tiny proteins to read the sophisticated sequence of the DNA helix better than any current technology. That's some feat, considering that if we could unravel the DNA from all the cells of our body and stretch it out end to end, it would reach to the sun and back 150 times![3] Somehow, our greater mind orchestrates tiny protein enzymes that constantly zip through the 3.2 billion nucleic acid sequences that are the genes in every cell, checking for mutations. Our own inner version of Homeland Security knows how to fight off thousands of bacteria and viruses without our ever needing to realize that we are under attack. It even memorizes those invaders so that if they enter us again, the immune system is better prepared.

Most marvelous of all, this life force knows how to start from just two cells, a sperm and an egg, and create our almost 100 trillion specialized cells. Having given us life, it then continually regenerates that life and regulates an incredible number of processes. We may not notice our higher mind at work, but the moment we die, the body starts to break down because this inner power has left.

Like the people I interviewed, I have had to acknowledge that some intelligence is at work in us that far exceeds our conscious abilities. It animates our body every single moment, and its incredibly complex workings take place virtually behind our back. We're conscious beings, but typically, we pay attention only to events that we think are important to us. Those 100,000 chemical reactions every second in our 100 trillion cells are a miraculous expression of the life force. Yet the only time they become significant to the conscious mind is when something goes wrong.

This aspect of the self is objective and unconditional. If we are alive, this life force is expressing itself through us. We all share this innate order, independent of gender, age, and genetics. This intelligence transcends race, culture, social standing, economic status, and religious beliefs. It gives life to everyone, whether we think about it or not, whether we are awake or asleep, whether we are happy or sad. A deeper mind permits us to believe whatever we want, to have likes and dislikes, to be allowing or judgmental. This giver of life lends power to whatever we are being; it bestows on us the power to express life in whatever way we choose.[4]

This intelligence knows how to maintain order among all of the cells, tissues, organs, and systems of the body because it *created* the body from two individual cells. Again, the power that made the body is the power that maintains and heals the body.

My subjects' illnesses signified that, to some extent, they had gotten out of touch or distanced themselves from part of their connection with this higher order. Maybe their own thinking had somehow directed this intelligence toward illness and away from health. But they came to understand that if they tapped into this intelligence and used their thoughts to direct it, it would know how to heal their bodies for them. Their greater mind already knew how to take care of business, if they could only make contact with it.

The abilities of this innate intelligence, subconscious mind, or spiritual nature are far greater than any pill, therapy, or treatment, and it is only waiting for our permission to willfully act. We are riding on the back of a giant, and we're getting a free ride.

Coincidence #2: Thoughts Are Real; Thoughts Directly Affect the Body

The way we think affects our body as well as our life. You may have heard this concept expressed before in various ways—for example, in that phrase "mind over matter." The people I interviewed not only shared this belief but also used it as a basis for making conscious changes in their own mind, body, and personal life.

To understand how they accomplished this, I began to study the growing body of research on the relationship between thought and the physical body.

There is an emerging field of science called *psychoneuroimmunology* that has demonstrated the connection between the mind and the body. I can describe what I learned in these simplistic terms: Your every thought produces a bio-chemical reaction in the brain. The brain then releases chemical signals that are transmitted to the body, where they act as the messengers of the thought. The thoughts that produce the chemicals in the brain allow your body to *feel* exactly the way you were just *thinking*. So every thought produces a chemical that is matched by a feeling in your body. Essentially, when you think happy, inspiring, or positive thoughts, your brain manufactures chemicals that make you feel joy-ful, inspired, or uplifted. For example, when you anticipate an experience that is pleasurable, the brain immediately makes a chemical *neurotransmitter* called *dopamine*, which turns the brain and body on in anticipation of that experience and causes you to begin to feel excited. If you have hateful, angry, or self-deprecating thoughts, the brain also produces chemicals called *neuropeptides* that the body responds to in a comparable way. You feel hateful, angry, or unworthy. You see, your thoughts immediately do become matter.

When the body responds to a thought by having a feeling, this initiates a response in the brain. The brain, which constantly monitors and evaluates the status of the body, notices that the body is feeling a certain way. In response to that bodily feeling, the brain generates thoughts that produce corresponding chemical messengers; you begin to *think* the way you are *feeling*. Thinking cre-ates feeling, and then feeling creates thinking, in a continuous cycle.

This loop eventually creates a particular state in the body that determines the general nature of how we feel and behave. We will call this a *state of being*. For example, suppose a person lives much of her life in a repeating cycle of thoughts and feelings related to insecurity. The moment she has a thought about not being good enough or smart enough or enough of anything, her brain releases chemicals that produce a feeling of insecurity. Now she is feeling the way she was just thinking. Once she is feeling insecure, she then will begin to think the way she was just feeling. In other words, her body is now causing her to think. This thought leads to more feelings of insecurity, and so the cycle perpet-uates itself. If this person's thoughts and feelings continue, year after year, to generate the same biological feedback loop between her brain and her body, she will exist in a state of being that is called "insecure."

The more we think the same thoughts, which then produce the same chemicals, which cause the body to have the same feelings, the more we physically become modified by our thoughts. In this way, depending on what we are thinking and feeling, we create our state of being. What we think about and the energy or intensity of these thoughts directly influences our health, the choices we make, and, ultimately, our quality of life.

Applying this reasoning to their own lives, many interviewees understood that many of their thoughts not only did not serve their health, but also might be the reason their unhappy or unhealthful conditions developed in the first place. Many of them had spent nearly every day for decades in internal states of anxiety, worry, sadness, jealousy, anger, or some other form of emotional pain. Thinking and feeling, feeling and thinking like that for so long, they said, is what had manifested their conditions.

From this, they reasoned that to transform their physical health, they had to address their *attitudes*: groups of thoughts that are clustered in habitual sequences.[5] One's attitudes create a state of being that is directly connected to the body. Thus, a person who wants to improve his health has to change entire patterns in how he thinks, and these new thought patterns or attitudes will eventually change his state of being. To do this, he must break free of perpetual loops of detrimental thinking and feeling, feeling and thinking, and replace them with new, beneficial ones.

Here's an example: Developing one digestive ailment after another and living with constant pain in his spine finally prompted Tom to examine his life. Upon self-reflection, he realized that he had been suppressing feelings of desperation caused by the stress of staying in a job that made him miserable. He had spent two decades being angry and frustrated with his employer, coworkers, and family. Other people often experienced Tom's short temper, but for all that time, his secret thoughts had revolved around self-pity and victimization.

Repeatedly experiencing these rigid patterns of thinking, believing, feeling, and living amounted to toxic attitudes that Tom's body just "couldn't stomach."

His healing began, Tom told me, when he recognized that his unconscious attitudes were the basis for his state of being—for the person he had become. Most of those whose case histories I studied reached conclusions similar to Tom's.

To begin changing their attitudes, these individuals began to pay constant attention to their thoughts. In particular, they made a conscious effort to observe their automatic thought processes, especially the harmful ones. To their surprise, they found that most of their persistent, negative inner statements were not true. In other words, just because we have a thought does not necessarily mean that we have to believe it is true.

As a matter of fact, most thoughts are ideas that we make up and then come to believe. Believing merely becomes a habit. For example, Sheila, with all her digestive disorders, noticed how often she thought of herself as a victim without the capacity to change her life. She saw that these thoughts had triggered feelings of helplessness. Questioning this belief enabled her to admit that her hardworking mother had done nothing to prevent or dissuade Sheila from going after her dreams.

Some of my subjects likened their repetitive thoughts to computer programs running all day, every day, in the background of their lives. Since these people were the ones operating these programs, they could elect to change or even delete them.

This was a crucial insight. At some point, all those I interviewed had to fight against the notion that one's thoughts are uncontrollable. Instead, they had to choose to be free and to take control of their thinking. Everyone had resolved to interrupt habitual negative thought processes before they could produce painful chemical reactions in their body. These individuals were determined to manage their thoughts and eliminate ways of thinking that did not serve them.

Conscious thoughts, repeated often enough, become unconscious thinking. In a common example of this, we must consciously think about our every action while we are learning to drive. After much practice, we can drive 100 miles from point A to point B and not remember any part of the trip, because our subconscious mind is typically at the wheel. We've all experienced being in an unaware state during a routine drive, only to feel our conscious mind reengaging in response to an unusual engine sound or the rhythmic thump of a flat tire. So if we continually entertain the same thoughts, they'll start off as conscious ones, but they'll ultimately become unconscious, automatic thought programs. There is a sound explanation in neuroscience for how this happens. You'll understand how this happens from a scientific standpoint by the time you finish reading this book.

These unconscious ways of thinking become our unconscious ways of being. And they directly affect our lives just as conscious thoughts do. Just as all thoughts set off biochemical reactions that lead to behavior, our repetitive, unconscious thoughts produce automatic, acquired patterns of behavior that are almost involuntary. These behavioral patterns are habits and most surely, they become neurologically hardwired in the brain.

It takes awareness and effort to break the cycle of a thinking process that has become unconscious. First, we need to step out of our routines so we can look at our lives. Through contemplation and self-reflection, we can become aware of our unconscious scripts. Then, we must observe these thoughts without responding to them, so that they no longer initiate the automatic chemical responses that produce habitual behavior. Within all of us, we possess a level of self-awareness, which can observe our thinking. We must learn how to be separate from these programs and when we do, we can willfully have dominion over them. Ultimately, we can exercise control over our thoughts. In doing so, we are neurologically breaking apart thoughts that have become hardwired in our brain.

Since we know from neuroscience that thoughts produce chemical reactions in the brain, it would make sense, then, that our thoughts would have some effect on our physical body by changing our internal state. Not only do our thoughts matter in how we live out our life, but our thoughts *become* matter right within our own body. Thoughts . . . matter.

Out of their belief that thoughts are real, and that the way people think directly impacts their health and their lives, these individuals saw that their own thinking processes were what had gotten them into trouble. They began to examine their life analytically. When they became inspired and diligent about changing their thinking, they were able to revitalize their health. A new attitude can become a new habit.

Coincidence #3: We Can Reinvent Ourselves

Motivated as they were by serious illnesses both physical and mental, the people I interviewed realized that in thinking new thoughts, they had to go all the way. To become a changed person, they would have to rethink themselves into a new life. All of those who restored their health to normal did so after making a conscious decision to reinvent themselves.

Breaking away often from daily routines, they spent time alone, thinking and contemplating, examining and speculating about what kind of people they wanted to become. They asked questions that challenged their most deeply held assumptions about who they were.

"What if" questions were vital to this process: What if I stop being an unhappy, self-centered, suffering person, and how can I change? What if I no longer worry or feel guilty or hold grudges? What if I begin to tell the truth to myself and to others?

Those "what ifs" led them to other questions: Which people do I know who are usually happy, and how do they behave? Which historical figures do I admire as noble and unique? How could I be like them? What would I have to say, do, think, and act like in order to present myself differently to the world? What do I want to change about myself?

Gathering information was another important step on the path to reinvention. Those I interviewed had to take what they knew about themselves, and then reformat their thinking to develop new ideas of who they wanted to become. Everyone started with ideas from their own life experiences. They also delved into books and movies about people they respected. Piecing together some of the merits and viewpoints of these figures, along with other qualities they were contemplating, they used all this as raw material to start building a new representation of how they wanted to express themselves.

As these individuals explored possibilities for a better way of being, they also learned new modes of thinking. They interrupted the flow of repetitive thoughts that had occupied most of their waking moments. Letting go of these familiar, comfortable habits of thought, they assembled a more evolved concept of whom they could become, replacing an old idea of themselves with a new, greater ideal. They took time daily to mentally rehearse what this new person would be like. As discussed in chapter 1, mental rehearsal stimulates the brain to grow new neural circuits and changes the way the brain and mind work.

In 1995, in the *Journal of Neurophysiology,* an article was published demonstrating the effects that mental rehearsal alone had on developing neural networks in the brain.[6] *Neural networks* are individual clusters of neurons (or nerve cells) that work together and independently in a functioning brain. Neural nets, as we will affectionately call them, are the latest model in neuroscience to explain how we learn and how we remember. They can also be used to explain how the brain changes with each new experience, how different types of memories are formed, how skills develop, how conscious and unconscious actions and behaviors are demonstrated, and even how all forms of sensory information are processed. Neural networks are the current understanding in neuroscience that explains how we change on a cellular level.

In this particular research, four groups of individuals were asked to participate in a five-day study that involved practicing the piano, in order to measure the changes that might take place in the brain. The first group of volunteers learned and memorized a specific one-handed, five-finger sequence that they physically practiced every day for two hours during that five-day period.

The second group of individuals was asked to play the piano without any instruction or knowledge of any specific sequence. They played randomly for two hours every day for five days without learning any sequence of notes.

The third group of people never even touched the piano, but were given the opportunity to observe what was taught to the first group until they knew it by memory in their minds. Then they mentally rehearsed their exercises by imagining themselves in the experience for the same length of time per day as the participants in the first group.

The fourth group was the control group; they did nothing at all. They never learned or practiced anything in this particular experiment. They never even showed up.

At the end of the five-day study, the experimenters used a technique called transcranial magnetic stimulation along with a few other sophisticated gadgets, in order to measure any changes that took place in the brain. To their surprise, the group that only rehearsed mentally showed almost the same changes, involving expansion and development of neural networks in the same specific area of their brain, as the participants who physically practiced the sequences on the piano. The second group, which learned no piano sequences at all, showed very little change in their brain, since they did not play the same series of exercises over and over each day. The randomness of their activity never stimulated the same neural circuits on a repetitive basis, and thus did not strengthen any additional nerve cell connections. The control group, the ones who never showed up, evidenced no change at all.

How did the third group produce the same brain changes as the first group without ever touching the keyboard? Through mental focusing, the third group of participants repeatedly fired specific neural networks in particular areas of their brain. As a result, they wired those nerve cells together in greater measure. This concept in neuroscience is called *Hebbian learning*.[7] The idea is simple: *Nerve cells that fire together, wire together.* Therefore, when gangs of neurons are repeatedly stimulated, they will build stronger, more enriched connections between each other.

According to the functional brain scans in this particular experiment, the subjects that were mentally rehearsing were activating their brain in the same way as if they were actually performing the endeavor. The repetitive firing of the neurons shaped and developed a cluster of neurons in a specific part of the brain, which now supported the pattern of conscious intent. At will, their thoughts became mapped and plotted in the brain. Interestingly, the circuits strengthened and developed in the absolute same area of the brain as the group that physically practiced. They grew and changed their brain just by *thinking*. With the proper mental effort, the brain does not know the difference between mental or physical effort.

Sheila's experience of curing her digestive illness illustrates this process of reinvention. Sheila had resolved that she would no longer revisit memories of her past and the associated attitudes that had defined her as a victim. Having identified the habitual thought processes she wanted to release, she cultivated a level of awareness where she had enough control to interrupt her unconscious thoughts. She therefore no longer fired the same associated neural networks on a daily basis. Once Shelia gained dominion over those old thought patterns and no longer fired those neurological habits of thinking, her brain began pruning away those unused circuits. This is another, related aspect of Hebbian learning that we can sum up as follows: *Nerve cells that no longer fire together, no longer wire together.* This is the universal law of "use it or lose it" in action, and it can work wonders in changing old paradigms of thought about ourselves. Over time, Sheila shed the burden of old, limited thoughts that had been coloring her life.

Now it became easier for Sheila to imagine the person she wanted to be. She explored possibilities that she had never considered before. For weeks on end, she focused on how she would think and act as this new, unknown person. She constantly reviewed these new ideas about herself so that she could remember who she was going to be that day. Eventually, she turned herself into a person who was healthy, happy, and enthusiastic about her future. She grew new brain circuits, just like the piano players have done.

It is interesting to note here that most people I interviewed never felt like they had to discipline themselves to do this. Instead, they loved mentally practicing who they wanted to become.

Like Sheila, all the people who shared their case histories with me succeeded in reinventing themselves. They persisted in attending to their new ideal until it became their familiar way of being. They became someone else, and that new person had new habits. They broke the habit of being themselves. How they accomplished this brings us to the fourth credo shared by those who experienced physical healings.

Coincidence #4: We Are Capable of Paying Attention So Well That We Can Lose Track of Relative Space and Time

The people I interviewed knew that others before them had cured their own diseases, so they believed that healing was possible for them too. But they did not leave their healing up to chance. Hoping and wishing would not do the trick. Merely knowing what they had to do was not enough. Healing required these rare individuals to change their mind permanently and intentionally create the outcomes they desired. Each person had to reach a state of absolute decision, utter will, inner passion, and complete focus. As Dean put it, "You just have to make up your mind!"

This approach requires great effort. The first step for all of them was the decision to make this process the most important thing in their life. That meant breaking away from their customary schedules, social activities, television viewing habits, and so on. Had they continued to follow their habitual routines, they would have continued being the same person who had manifested illness. To change, to cease being the person they had been, they could no longer do the things they had typically done.

Instead, these mavericks sat down every day and began to reinvent themselves. They made this more important than doing anything else, devoting every moment of their spare time to this effort. Everyone practiced becoming an objective observer of his or her old familiar thoughts. They refused to allow anything but their intentions to occupy their mind. You may be thinking, "That's pretty easy to do when faced with a serious health crisis. After all, my own life is in my hands." Well, aren't most of us suffering from some affliction—physical, emotional, or spiritual—that affects the quality of our life? Don't those ailments deserve the same kind of focused attention?

Certainly, these folks had to wrestle with limiting beliefs, self-doubt, and fears. They had to deny both their familiar internal voices and the external voices of other people, especially when these voices urged them to worry and to focus on the predicted clinical outcome of their condition.

Nearly everyone commented that this level of mind is not easy to attain. They had never realized how much chatter occupies the untrained mind. At first they wondered what would happen if they began to fall into habitual thought patterns. Would they have the strength to stop themselves from going back to their old ways? Could they maintain awareness of their thoughts throughout their day? But with experience, they found that whenever they reverted to being their former self, they could detect this and interrupt that program. The more they practiced paying attention to their thoughts, the easier this process became, and the better they felt about their future. Feeling peaceful and calm, soothed by a sense of clarity, a new self emerged.

Interestingly, all the subjects reported experiencing a phenomenon that became part of their new life. During extended periods of introspection on reinventing themselves, they became so involved in focusing on the present moment and on their intent that something remarkable happened. They completely lost track of their body, time, and space. Nothing was real to them except their thoughts.

Let me put this in perspective. Our everyday, conscious awareness is typically involved with three things:

- First, we are aware of being in a body. Our brain receives feedback on what is happening within the body and what stimuli it is receiving from our environment, and we describe what the body feels in terms of physical sensations.

- Second, we are aware of our environment. The space around us is our connection to external reality; we pay attention to the things, objects, people, and places in our surroundings.

- Third, we have a sense of time passing; we structure our life within the concept of time.

However, when people inwardly focus through serious self-reflective contemplation, when they are mentally rehearsing new possibilities of who they could become, they are capable of becoming so immersed in what they are thinking about that, at times, their attention is completely detached from their body and their environment; these seem to fade away or disappear. Even the concept of time vanishes. Not that they are thinking about time, but after such periods, when they open their eyes, they expect to find that just a minute or two has elapsed, only to discover that hours have gone by. At these moments, we don't worry about problems, nor do we feel pain. We disassociate from the sensations of our body and the associations to everything in our environment. We can get so involved in the creative process that we forget about ourselves.

When this phenomenon occurs, these individuals are aware of nothing but their thoughts. In other words, the only thing that is *real* to them is the awareness of what they are thinking. Nearly all have expressed this in similar words. "I would go to this other place in my mind," one subject said, "where there were no distractions, there was no time, I had no body, there was no thing—nothing—except my thoughts." In effect, they became a no-body, a no-thing, in no-time. They left their present association with being a somebody, the "you," or "self," and they became a nobody.

In this state, as I was to learn, these individuals could begin to become exactly what they were imagining. The human brain, through the frontal lobe, has the ability to *lower the volume to,* or even shut out, the stimuli from the body and the environment, as well as the awareness of time. The latest research in functional brain scan technology has proven that when people are truly focused and concentrating, the brain circuits associated with time, space, and the feelings/movements/sensory perceptions of the body literally quiet down.[8] As human beings, we have the privilege to make our thoughts more real than anything else, and when we do, the brain records those impressions in the deep folds of its tissues. Mastering this skill is what allows us to begin to rewire our brain and change our life.

WHAT IS ATTENTION?

Some of the most recent findings in neuroscience suggest that to change the brain's architecture, we have to pay attention to the experience in a given moment. Passive stimulation of our brain circuits, without our paying attention to the stimulus and without putting awareness on what is being processed, causes no internal changes in the brain. For example, you might hear a family member vacuuming in the background while you read this book. But if this stimulus is not important to you, you will not attend to it; instead, you will continue reading. What you are reading in the moment is most important to you; therefore, your attention is selectively activating different circuits in the brain while other unimportant data are being filtered out.

So what is attention? When you pay attention to any one thing, you are putting all your awareness on whatever you are attending to, while ignoring all other information that might be available for your senses to process and your body to feel. You can also hinder random, stray memories. You inhibit your mind from wandering to thoughts about what's for dinner, memories of last Christmas, and even fantasies about your coworker. You restrain your mind from acting or doing anything other than what you have set as an important intention. You really could not survive without this ability to select certain things for attention. Your ability to select a small fraction of information for attention depends on the brain's frontal lobe.

As the frontal lobe allows you to place sustained attention on any one thing, such as reading these pages, it turns off other brain circuits that have to do with modalities like hearing, tasting, moving your legs, feeling your butt on the couch, feeling the pain in your head, and even feeling bladder fullness. Therefore, the better you are at paying attention to your internal mental imagery, the more you can rewire your brain and the easier it is to control other circuits in the brain that process familiar sensory stimulation. In other words, attention is a skill!

Other Commonalities

Although not as fundamentally important as the four elements previously covered, several other minor points of intersection emerged among the experiences of my interviewees. I'll limit the discussion here to two. The first is that these subjects knew, on some deeper level and to a great degree of certainty, that they were healed. They didn't need any kind of diagnostic test to let them know this (even though many of them underwent tests proving they were healed).

The second commonality is that several doctors thought their patient's choice to forego conventional methods to be insane. Equally, the cured patients' medical doctors didn't believe them when they first revealed what they knew to be true. In some ways, the doctors' response is understandable. In others, it is deeply regrettable. However, most doctors, when reviewing the changed objective finding, frequently said, "I don't know what you're doing, but whatever you're doing, keep doing it."

The New Frontier in Brain Research

Investigations into spontaneous healings, ignited my intent to learn all I could about the brain. There has never been a more exciting time than the present to pay attention to what neuroscientists are learning about this remarkable organ. Some of the recent findings on how the brain facilitates thought may lead to knowledge that we can apply to create positive new outcomes in our body and in our life.

Most of us who went through school 20 or more years ago were taught that the brain is hardwired, meaning that we are born with nerve cell connections in our brain that predestine us to display predispositions, traits, and habits inherited from our parents. Back then, the prevailing scientific view was that the brain is unchangeable, and that our genetic predispositions leave us with few choices and little control over our destiny. Certainly, all humans have portions of our brain that are hardwired in the same ways, so that we all share the same physical structures and functions.

However, research is beginning to verify that the brain is not as hardwired as we once thought. We now know that any of us, at any age, can gain new knowledge, process it in the brain, and formulate new thoughts, and that this process will leave new footprints in the brain—that is, new synaptic connections develop. That's what learning is.

In addition to knowledge, the brain also records every new experience. When we experience something, our sensory pathways transmit enormous amounts of information to the brain regarding what we are seeing, smelling, tasting, hearing, and feeling. In response, neurons in the brain organize themselves into networks of connections that reflect the experience. These neurons also release chemicals that trigger specific feelings. Every new occurrence produces a feeling, and our feelings help us remember an experience. The process of forming memories is what sustains those new neural connections on a more long-term basis. Memory, then, is simply a process of maintaining new synaptic connections that we form via learning.[9]

Science is investigating how repetitive thoughts strengthen these neurological connections and affect the way in which our brain works. In addition to what we've already discussed about mental rehearsal, some other intriguing studies have shown that the process of mental rehearsal—thinking over and over about doing something without physically involving the body—not only creates changes in the brain but also can modify the body. For example, when test subjects visualized themselves lifting weights with a particular finger over a certain period of time, the finger they had imagined lifting with actually became stronger.[10]

Contrary to the myth of the hardwired brain, we now realize that the brain changes in response to every experience, every new thought, and every new thing we learn. This is called *plasticity*. Researchers are compiling evidence that the brain has the potential to be moldable and pliable at any age. The more I studied new findings on brain plasticity, the more fascinated I became to learn that certain information and skills seem to be the ingredients for selectively changing the brain.

The brain's plasticity is its ability to reshape, remold, and reorganize itself well into our adult life. For example, expert violinists show a remarkable enlargement in the somatosensory cortex—the brain region assigned to the sense of touch. But this holds true only for the fingers in the left hand, which moves about the neck of the instrument (compared to the fingers of the right hand, which hold the bow). Scientists compared the two halves of the brain that controlled the violinists' sense of touch coming from both sides of the body. It became apparent that the compartment of the brain assigned to the left-hand fingers of the violinist had become larger in size than the normal-sized compartment for the fingers of the other hand.[11]

As late as the 1980s, the notion prevailed that the brain is fixed and hard-wired into neatly organized compartments; neuroscientists now understand that the brain is continuously reorganizing itself throughout each person's daily life.

There is also interesting evidence to dispel a long-held myth about nerve cells. For decades, scientists have thought that nerve cells were unable to divide and replicate themselves. We have heard that the number of neurons we are born with is fixed throughout our lifetime, and that once nerve cells are damaged, they can never be replaced. These beliefs are now being challenged. In fact, recent studies suggest that the normal, healthy adult brain can generate new brain cells. This process is called *neurogenesis*. Research over the last few years has shown that when mature nerve cells are damaged in a particular part of the brain called the hippocampus, they are naturally capable of repairing and regenerating.[12] Not only can certain damaged parts of the brain be restored, but new evidence now suggests that a fully mature adult brain can produce additional nerve cells everyday.

Learning to juggle may actually cause specific areas of the brain to grow, according to a study published in the journal *Nature* in January 2004.[13] We've known from functional brain scans that learning can cause changes in brain activity, but this particular study demonstrated that *anatomical* changes can occur as a result of learning something new.

German researchers at the University of Regensburg recruited 24 people who were non-jugglers and divided them into two even groups. One was assigned to practice juggling daily for three months. The control group did no juggling.

Before and after the first group learned to juggle, the scientists conducted brain scans on all the volunteers using magnetic resonance imaging (MRI). In addition, rather than limiting their investigation to changes in brain activity, the researchers used a sophisticated analysis technique called voxel-based morphology to detect structural changes in the gray matter of the neocortex. The thickness of our gray matter reflects the total number of nerve cells in our brain.

Subjects who acquired the skill of juggling had a measurable increase in gray matter in two separate areas of the brain that are involved in visual and motor activity. The scientists documented an increased volume and higher density of gray matter in these areas. The study suggests that the adult brain may have some ability to grow new nerve cells. Dr. Vanessa Sluming, a senior medical imager at the University of Liverpool, England, commented that, "What we do in everyday life might have an impact not just on how our brains function but on the structure at a macroscopic level." It is interesting to note that those people who later stopped juggling had their enlarged brain areas return to normal size within three months.

Even meditation has shown promising results in changing not only how the brain works, by altering brain wave patterns, but also by growing new brain cells that are the product of inner mindful attentiveness. Studies published in November 2005 in the journal *NeuroReport* demonstrated increased gray matter in 20 participants, all with extensive training in Buddhist Insight meditation.[14] Here is the best part of the study: Most of the participants were average, normal people with jobs and families, who meditated only 40 minutes a day. You don't have to be a holy man or woman to make more brain cells. Researchers in the study also are suggesting that meditation may slow age-related thinning of the frontal cortex.

According to research by Fred Gage of the Salk Institute for Biological Studies, La Jolla, California, mice that lived in enriched environments where they could stimulate their minds and their bodies showed a 15 percent increase in their total number of brain cells, compared to mice in conventional rodent surroundings. Furthermore, in October 1998, Gage and a group of Swedish researchers demonstrated for the first time that human brain cells have regenerative capabilities.[15]

Out of Injury, Hope

Research with stroke patients is providing some of the most exciting evidence of the brain's potential to change. When a cerebrovascular accident—a stroke—occurs in the brain, the sudden decrease in the supply of oxygenated blood damages neurological tissue. Many times, a stroke injury to a specific part of the brain associated with a leg or an arm leaves a patient without motor control of their limbs. The traditional thinking has been that if a stroke patient shows no improvement within the first week or two, their paralysis will be permanent.

Numerous studies are now exploding this myth. Stroke patients who were technically past the recovery period—even patients in their seventies who had been paralyzed for up to 20 years—have been able to regain some motor control that they had not had since their strokes, and they were able to maintain these improvements long-term. In certain research experiments in the late 1970s at the Department of Neurology at Bellevue Hospital in New York City, up to 75 percent of the subjects achieved total restoration in the control of their paralyzed arm or leg. Repetition was the key to their ability to rewire their brain.[16]

With the proper instruction, the subjects diligently practiced focusing their mind while mentally moving a paralyzed limb. They received mental feedback through sophisticated biofeedback machines. When they became able to reproduce the same brain patterns when thinking about moving their affected limbs as they did when moving their well limbs, they began to reverse their paralysis. Once similar brain patterns were produced when initiating movement to the affected limb, the volunteers were able to increase the strength of the neurological signal to their paralyzed arm or leg, which made it move to a greater degree. Independent of age and the duration of injury, their brain showed an amazing ability to learn new things and restore the body to a higher level of function, just by applying mental will.

The Brain: The Matter of Mind and the Intertwined Mystery

The positive results that stroke patients have achieved might make you wonder what increased attention and daily training could do to enhance the brain in healthy individuals, given the proper knowledge and instruction. This is one of those situations where one question leads to another, which leads to yet another, but we'll start with this: If the physical structure of the brain is damaged, what does that say about the condition of the mind? You've probably heard of people identified as savants, who suffer some affliction of the brain, yet possess a mind capable of astounding feats. Ultimately, the question we must ask is this: What is the mind, and what is the relationship between the brain and the mind?

As the organ having the greatest number of neurons gathered together, the brain facilitates thought impulses, both consciously and subconsciously, and acts to control and coordinate both physical and mental functions. Without the brain, no other system in the body can operate.

Sir Julian Huxley, a British biologist during the early part of the 1900s and author of several writings relating to evolution, must have foreseen the question, "Is the brain a good enough explanation for describing the mind?" His answer is paramount in the history of biology. "The brain alone is not responsible for mind," he said, "even though it is a necessary organ for its manifestation. Indeed, an isolated brain is a piece of biological nonsense as meaningless as an isolated individual."[17] He knew that there must be another component to the mind.

From the time I was a freshman in college, I always found it fascinating to study the mind. My biggest quandary as an undergraduate was that certain fields of psychology attempted to use the mind to know and observe the mind. This was somewhat troubling to me, because it seemed like conjecture to study the mind without studying the organ that produces mind. It is like watching a car run but never looking under the hood to see what is making it run. Studying behavior is essential for our observations, but I often wondered, if we could actually observe a living, functioning brain, what would we learn about what was *really* happening with the mind?

After all, the brain of a deceased person can tell us only so much. Studying the lifeless anatomy of the brain in order to gather information about how it works is like trying to learn about how a computer operates without turning it on. The only tool we have for truly understanding the mind has been to observe the workings of the living human brain.

Now that we have the technology to observe a living brain, we know from functional brain scans that the mind is the brain in action. This is the latest definition of mind according to neuroscience. When a brain is alive and active, it can process thought, demonstrate intelligence, learn new information, master skills, recall memories, express feelings, refine movements, invent new ideas, and maintain the orderly functioning of the body. The animated brain can also facilitate behavior, dream, perceive reality, argue beliefs, be inspired, and most important, embrace life. In order for the mind to exist, then, the brain must be alive.

The brain is, therefore, not the mind; it is the physical apparatus through which the mind is produced. A healthy, functioning brain makes for a healthy mind. The brain is a bio-computer that has three individual anatomical structures with which it produces different aspects of mind. The mind is the result of a brain that is coordinating thought impulses through its various regions and substructures. There are many diverse states of mind, because we can easily make the brain work in different ways.

The brain facilitates the mind as an intricate data-processing system, so that we have the ability to gather, process, store, recall, and communicate information within seconds, if need be, as well as the capacity to forecast, hypothesize, respond, behave, plan, and reason. The brain is also the control center through which the mind organizes and coordinates all the metabolic functions necessary for life and survival. When your bio-computer is turned on, or alive, and it is functioning by processing information, the mind is produced.

According to our working neuroscientific definition, the mind, then, is not the brain; it is the product of the brain. The mind is what the brain does. We can be aware of the machine in operation (the mind) without being the machine (the brain). When the brain is animated with life, the mind is processed through the brain. Essentially, the mind is the brain, animated. Without the brain, there is no mind.

ADVANCES IN IMAGING TECHNOLOGY

Until recently, our potential to understand the brain had certain limits, imposed by the 80-year-old technology of the electro-encephalogram (EEG). The EEG provided graphic representations of brain performance, but no imagery to see a living brain. Today, however, scientists can measure brain activity, moment by moment. They can view the structure and activity of the living human brain in unprecedented detail, thanks to a revolution in neuroscience and the EEG over the past 30 years. Enhanced by computer technology, the EEG can now provide a three-dimensional representation of a functioning brain.

Even more important in revolutionizing the field of cognitive neuroscience are the latest advances in functional imaging. This technology is based on various principles of physics, from changes in local magnetic fields to the measurement of radioactive emissions. A host of new imaging technologies is literally producing volumes of information about the working brain (and the rest of the body as well). As a result, neuroscientists can now study the immediate physiological actions of brain matter, observing the specific, repeatable patterns of a functioning brain.

First of the new technologies, introduced in 1972, was computed tomography (CT), also called CAT scanning. A CT brain scan takes a picture or snapshot of the inside of the brain to see whether there is abnormal tissue within the brain's structural components. CT scans merely capture one moment in time; therefore, they only tell us what anatomical structures exist, what structures are missing, what areas are injured or diseased, and whether there is additional anatomical material that should not be present in the brain. Accordingly, CT scans do not tell us anything about how a brain works, but only why it may not be working normally.

We now know that the brain generates numerous chemical mechanisms that are too minute to be visualized and can be measured only by their effects. Only by visualizing a working brain, which CT scans do not permit, can we see these chemical effects in action.

Positron emission tomography, or PET scanning, is useful in examining the biochemical activity in a functioning brain. The PET device uses gamma rays to construct images that indicate the intensity of metabolic activity in the part of the brain, or other body part, under observation. In this case, we can now observe the workings of the brain over time.

Functional magnetic resonance imaging (fMRI) is a radiographic technique that can also take an image of the living brain and show which brain regions are active during any particular mental activity. Although fMRIs do not really show brain activity, they provide a huge clue as to what parts of the brain are working, via the local metabolic action of the nerve cells as they consume energy and oxygen in different regions of the brain.

Single-photon emission computed tomography, nuclear medicine's SPECT scan, uses multiple gamma-ray detectors that rotate around the patient to measure brain function. Functional brain images produced by SPECT can correlate certain patterns of brain activity with neurological illnesses or psychological states. Once again, like fMRIs, SPECT scans are a valuable tool in measuring how the nerve cells of the brain metabolically consume energy when those cells are activated.

These last three functional scanning techniques go way beyond the snapshot technology that demonstrates the still life of the brain, seen in typical CT scans. Instead, brain functional scans are like a motion picture of the entire neurological activity of the brain during a period of time. This is advantageous, since a working brain will reveal more about the normal and abnormal activity of the mind. Functional brain scans have allowed us to examine and observe the brain in action or at work. By using functional brain technology, we are studying the mind more accurately than ever before in the history of neuroscience. Researchers have been able to detect repeated patterns in the brain scans of individuals with similar afflictions or injuries, thus helping doctors with the appropriate diagnosis and treatment.

A Meditation on the Mind

Let's look at a recent investigation into the relationship between the brain and mind. In the proceedings of the National Academy of Sciences in November of 2004, an article surfaced to validate that mental training through meditation and single-minded focus can change the inner workings of the brain.[18] Simply stated, the article demonstrated that it is quite possible to change the way the brain works, thereby changing mind.

In the study, Buddhist monks with considerable expertise in meditation were asked to focus on specific states of mind such as compassion and unconditional love. All the subjects were connected to 256 electrical sensors for a sophisticated scan to measure brain wave activity. During their single-minded focus, their brains became more coordinated and organized in processing mental activity than the brains of a control group, who could not even come close to demonstrating brain wave patterns comparable to those produced by the expert monks. Some of the monks, who had practiced meditating for up to 50,000 hours, displayed frontal lobe activity and overall brain wave activity that are connected to higher mental functioning and heightened awareness. In fact, they could change the way their brain worked, on command.

The results showed frontal lobe activity was dramatically elevated in the monks compared to the control group. In fact, the monks who had meditated the longest showed levels of one kind of electrical brain impulses, called gamma waves, that were higher than researchers had ever seen in a healthy person. These particular brain wave states are typically present when the brain is making new circuits.

The left frontal lobe is the area in the brain that correlates with joy. In one Buddhist monk, his activity was so enhanced in the left frontal region, the scientists performing the study said that he must be the happiest man alive.

"What we found is that the longtime practitioners showed brain activation on a scale we have never seen before," stated Richard Davidson, Ph.D., from the University of Wisconsin, who headed the experiment. He added, "Their mental practice is having an effect on the brain in the same way golf or tennis practice will enhance performance." In a later interview, Dr. Davidson said, "What we found is that the trained mind, or brain, is physically different than the untrained one."[19]

From this experiment, we see that if one can improve how the brain works, we are essentially changing the mind. Let's ponder the implications of this study for a moment. If the brain is the instrument of conscious and subconscious thought impulses, and the mind is the end product of the brain, then who or what is doing the changing of the brain and the mind? The mind cannot change the mind, because the mind is the result of the brain. The mind cannot change the brain, because the mind is the brain's product. And the brain cannot change the workings of the mind, because the brain is only the hardware through which the mind operates. Finally, the brain cannot change the brain, because it is lifeless without some force at work influencing the mind.

If the brain and the mind can be made to work better by practice, and a mindful skill can be developed to change the internal workings of the brain, then who or what is doing the changing of the brain and the mind? The answer is that elusive thirteen-letter word, *consciousness*. That concept has confounded scientists for many years. However, in the last ten years, scientists are beginning to include consciousness as a factor in many of the theories directed toward understanding the nature of reality.

Without getting too mystical or philosophical, consciousness is what gives the brain life—it is the invisible life essence that animates the brain. It is the unseen aspect of self, both aware and unaware, both conscious and subconscious, using the brain to capture thoughts, and then coalescing them to create the mind.[20]

Mind, Matter, and More

When I took neuroanatomy in graduate school and Life University for my doctorate in chiropractic, I dissected countless numbers of brains. I quickly saw that without life, the brain is just a piece of matter, an organ that, when unanimated, cannot think, feel, act, create, or change. Even though the brain is our most important organ—active and necessary for everything we do, how we think, how we behave, what we feel—it needs animation. It is the organ of intelligence, but it's just an organ. In other words, the brain cannot change itself without an operator.

The brain is the organ of the central nervous system that has the greatest number of nerve cells or neurons clustered together. When neurons are in great number, we have intelligence. Neurons are extremely tiny; about 30,000 to 50,000 would fit on the tip of a pin. In one part of the brain called the neocortex, the home of our conscious awareness, each nerve cell has the possibility of linking with 40,000 to 50,000 other nerve cells. In another area known as the cerebellum, every neuron has the potential to connect with up to a million other neurons. To view these two types of neurons, see Figure 2.1.

As a matter of fact, the brain consists of some 100 *billion* neurons that are connected in a myriad of three-dimensional patterns. As we already learned, the diverse combinations of these billions of neurons linked together and firing in unique sequences make up what scientists call *neural networks*.

When we learn something or have an experience, nerve cells team up and make new connections, and that literally changes us. Because the human brain affords so many possible connections between neurons, and because neurons can communicate directly with each other, the brain is able to process thought, learn new things, remember experiences, perform actions, demonstrate behaviors, and speculate on possibilities, just to name a few. It is the central processing unit of the body. Therefore, the brain is the instrument we physi-

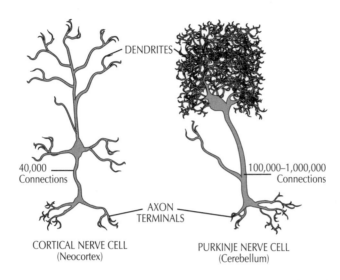

DENDRITES

40,000
Connections

100,000–1,000,000
Connections

AXON
TERMINALS

CORTICAL NERVE CELL
(Neocortex)

PURKINJE NERVE CELL
(Cerebellum)

Figure 2.1

The difference between the possible number of dendrite connections in the neurons of the neocortex and the cerebellum.

cally use to consciously evolve our understandings in life and to subconsciously support our very life.

Think of consciousness as what inhabits and occupies this bio-computer called the brain. It is like the electrical current that runs a computer and all its programs. The brain has hardware systems built in and software systems that consciousness is upgrading or routinely using.

Consciousness enables us to think, and at the same time, to observe our thinking process. We typically think of consciousness as our awareness of self and our perception of the world around us. However, there is another type of intelligence within us, one that consistently gives life to us, moment by moment, without any need for our help. Doctors of chiropractic call this *innate intelligence,* and it resides equally in all things. In fact, this philosophy states that our innate intelligence facilitated through the physical brain is just an expression of universal intelligence in a body.[21]

Therefore, from what I learned both as a chiropractor and as a student at

RSE, it seems that there are two elements to our consciousness. One aspect, which we will call *subjective consciousness,* maintains our individual free will and enables us to express ourselves as a thinking self, with our own traits and characteristics. The individual, subjective part of us, this element of consciousness encompasses our unique qualities, including the abilities to learn, remember, create, dream, choose, and even *not* choose. This is the "you" or the "self."

Subjective consciousness can exist both in the body and independent of the body. When people have an out-of-body experience during which they are completely aware, yet can see the body lying in bed, it is subjective consciousness that is aware in the experience, independent of the body. Therefore, subjective consciousness is not the body, but it uses the body. It is our self-conscious identity. For the most part, throughout our life, it is localized within the physical body.

The other element of consciousness is the intelligent awareness within us that gives us life every day. Let's term this *objective consciousness* or the *subconscious.* This is a system of awareness separate from the conscious mind. It is subconscious, but it is incredibly intelligent and mindful. It is also separate from the thinking brain, but it operates via the other parts of the brain to keep our body in order. With objective consciousness running the show, the brain processes millions of automatic functions every second on a cellular level and an aggregate level as well, of which we are not consciously aware. These are the aspects of our health and life that we take for granted every day, the systems that control our heart, digest our food, filter our blood, regenerate cells, and even organize our DNA. It takes a great and unlimited consciousness to be responsible for all these functions.

This objective intelligence knows so much more than what our personality self knows, even though we think we know it all. This is a universal, fundamental aspect of every human being, independent of age, gender, education, religion, social status, or culture. Few ever stop to acknowledge its power, will, and intelligence.

In fact, this aspect of consciousness is what gives life to *all* things. It is a real intelligence, with quantifiable energy or force that is innate to all things. It is objective and constant. It has been called Zero Point Field, the Source, and universal intelligence. It is the Source that collapses the quantum field into all physical form. Literally, it is the life force. Quantum physics is just beginning to measure this field of potentials.

As human beings, we possess both elements of consciousness. We are consciously aware as a subjective consciousness, and we exist because we are connected to the force of life that is an objective consciousness. We have free will to choose the quality of life we desire, and at the same time, a greater intelligence is giving and allowing us the animation of life in every second. In fact, science now understands that everything physical (including you and me) is just the tip of an immense iceberg. The question is, what is the field that holds it all together, and how do we make contact with it?

The brain has the equipment, so to speak, to facilitate both these levels of consciousness. The brain without consciousness is inert and lifeless. When consciousness is facilitated through the human brain the end result is called *mind*.[22] Mind is a working brain, a brain in action. Mind comes into being when an operating brain is animated with life. There is no mind without the physical expression of life through a functioning brain.

Mind, then, is the product of consciousness manipulating the subtle and diverse neural tissues of the brain. Since both of these specific levels of consciousness animate the brain to create mind, we must possess two different arrangements at work in the brain. We have conscious mind and subconscious mind embroidered in two diverse brain systems.

Accordingly, the brain has two distinct, generalized systems with appropriate hardware to facilitate two types of consciousness. Our conscious awareness is based in the neocortex. The "crown" of our brain, the neocortex is the seat of free will. This is the conscious thought center of the brain, where everything an individual learns and experiences is recorded, and where information is processed. The arrangement of how brain cells are connected together in the neocortex distinguishes you from other individuals and makes you unique. If you look at Figure 2.2 you will see the neocortex.

You have the ability to be consciously aware of yourself, your actions, your thoughts, your behavior, your feelings, your environment, and your mind, and to

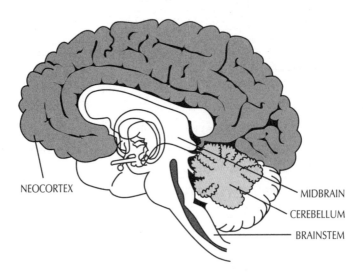

Figure 2.2
Split view: one-half of the brain depicting its major regions.

express thoughts and ideas. The invisible qualities of self-reflection, self-contemplation, and self-observation define your subjective experience of self. When we speak in terms of a person losing consciousness or regaining consciousness, we mean that he or she is leaving or returning to a level of "being": self-aware, awake, and possessing a conceptual memory of self. All this is managed by the *neocortex,* the new brain.

Let's talk a bit more about the conscious and subconscious aspects of mind. Conscious mind affords us the ability to process conscious thoughts and information. This mind is self-knowledgeable, self-conceptual, self-realizing, and self-perceiving. It is what we refer to as the self: the "you." Using its free will, the conscious part of us can place its attention on any one thing. This is the privilege of being human. In the chiropractic science and philosophy, it is called the educated mind and it is processed in our newest brain region, the neocortex.

The parts of the brain that function under subconscious control are the midbrain, the cerebellum, and the brainstem. For the most part, these regions have no conscious centers. However, they do operate under the higher intelligence that I've spoken of, which not only keeps the body in order but also handles an infinite to-do list. This greater mind knows how to maintain health so that we can enjoy all the other benefits of life. Figure 2.2 shows the subconscious realms of the human brain.

To summarize, then, the brain is the organ with the greatest number of neurons organized together. Where there is the greatest number of neurons, there are the greatest levels of intelligence. Consciousness uses the brain to mindfully process learning and experiences into electrochemical impulses called thoughts. The mind, then, is the product of the brain in action. The mind operates when the brain is "alive" and facilitating consciousness. Consciousness has two specific qualities:

- Objective consciousness is the life force, the Source, and the Zero Point Field. You and I are connected to that field, which affords us life through the midbrain, the cerebellum, and the brainstem. This is the subconscious mind.

- Subjective consciousness, situated in the neocortex, is the explorer, the identity that learns and evolves its understandings for a greater expression of life. This is the conscious mind.

In Figures 2.3A and 2.3B, a simple graph describes the two operating systems of the brain.

Once we understand how the brain works to create mind, we can go beyond the comfortable boundaries of what we already know. When we can unite our conscious mind to that infinite mind with unlimited potential, we will have access to a world of new possibilities. Consciousness is the only element that makes sense of how we can change the brain and mind. It is that intangible aspect of our self that influences the brain to produce mind. The time that we are truly conscious, attentive, aware, and present is when we change how the brain works, to create a new level of mind.

When we can use the conscious mind together with the subconscious mind, we will be able to modify our hardware and upgrade our operating systems. At that moment of merging consciousness, the brain can be rewired.

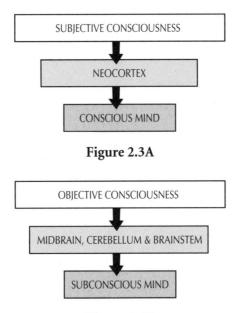

Figure 2.3A

Figure 2.3B
The two operating systems of the brain.

The aim of *Evolve Your Brain* is to raise questions and provide information that may help you comprehend how the human brain, mind, and consciousness interact to create your health and your experience of life. Simple step by simple step, this book puts together a working model for understanding the marvelous organ called the brain. Along the way, we will also explore some of the evidence that neuroscience has uncovered about how our brain processes many levels of mind and how we can rewire the brain. You can literally change your mind. When you understand that, you can look forward to seeing that change reflected in your health, your life, and your future.

In the next chapter, we begin by learning about nerve cells, how they function and connect to each other, the different branches of the nervous system, and how the distinct sections of the nervous system function in diverse ways to keep us alive and maintain health. Once we comprehend the basics, we can begin to expand our understanding of how we are wired to be who we presently are. Then we can begin to look at how we can change our mind.

CHAPTER THREE

NEURONS AND THE NERVOUS SYSTEM: TRAVELING THE ORIGINAL INFORMATION SUPERHIGHWAY

*The simplest schoolboy is now familiar
with truths for which Archimedes
would have sacrificed his life.*

—ERNEST RENAN

iven that the brain is a part of the body, and that water comprises a
significant part of the body, it should come as no surprise that the
brain is made up of about 75 percent water. In terms of solid material, strictly speaking, the most numerous cells in the brain are *glial cells,* from
the Greek word *glia,* meaning glue. For the most part, glial cells serve a supportive role in the brain, both structurally and functionally, but they also fulfill a
number of purposes that scientists are still endeavoring to understand.

Aside from water and glial cells, our brain primarily consists of nerve cells
called *neurons.* (Up until this point, we have been calling them brain cells.) In
many ways, neurons are the most specialized cells and the most sensitive type of
tissue of all biological systems. They process information and pass it on to other

neurons, thus initiating specific actions in other parts of our brain and body. Most significantly, neurons are the only cells in the body that communicate directly with one another; they send messages back and forth in the form of electrochemical signals or impulses.

Not only are neurons the most significant cells that make up the brain, they also are the most fundamental component of our nervous system: the intricate network of structures, consisting of the brain, spinal cord, and nerves, that controls and coordinates all the functions of our bodies. The unique way that nerve cells communicate is what makes the nervous system so specialized and different from any other bodily system.

The brain has the greatest cluster of neurons in the entire body. A tiny slice of brain tissue the size of a grain of sand contains about 100,000 neurons. They are packed so tightly that a pebble-sized chunk of tissue from the human brain contains about two miles of neuron material. Your entire brain contains some 100 *billion* neurons, each one a fraction of a millimeter in size. To give you an idea of how many neurons this is, if you were to count to 100 billion, second by second, you would be counting for nearly 3,171 years. If you could stack 100 billion pieces of paper, the stack would be 5,000 miles high—the distance from Los Angeles to London.

Other neurons are much longer than the nerve cells in the brain. Some neurons extend from the brain down the spinal cord and run up to three feet in length. Even though neurons vary in length, they essentially function in the same manner.

To illustrate a few of the roles that neurons play in your life, imagine that it is morning, and you are planning the day ahead. As your brain pieces together ideas of what you will need to do during portions of your day, neurons transmit electrochemical information to and from various parts of your brain. Sensory neurons send information to your brain not only about your external surroundings—via sight, hearing, smell, taste, touch, and pressure—but also about your internal environment, including sensations of hunger, thirst, pain, temperature, and so on. Once you decide to get up and take action, motor neurons send electrochemical impulses from the brain through the spinal cord to the body, matching your movements with the mental plan you constructed.

The general method of communication between neurons is the same in all human beings. However, nerve cells are organized in networks or patterns that shape individual behavior and give us those unique differences we all possess.

Components of the Neuron "Tree"

A typical nerve cell resembles a leafless oak tree in winter (some neurons look more like this than others). At the part of the "tree" where the large branches converge inward toward the trunk, we find the nucleus or cell body of the neuron.

The nerve cell nucleus, like the nuclei of all other cells, contains genetic information called *DNA,* which directs the manufacture of proteins necessary for the structure and function of the cell. The DNA in our nerve cells is almost the same as the DNA of any other cell in our body (except for red blood cells, which do not contain DNA). What differentiates one type of cell from another is the active expression of just a few particular genes. When a cell expresses a gene, it makes a specific protein that is related to a specific function. For example, a muscle cell will create specific muscle proteins that make up the structure of our muscle tissue. So what makes a particular cell a nerve cell is that it expresses a DNA sequence that differs slightly from that of a muscle cell or skin cell.

What also differentiates a nerve cell from other cells is its external structure. A neuron has two types of appendages (also known as *neurites*) that extend off the cell body in approximately opposite directions, as shown in Figure 3.1. The trunk of the neuron tree is a long fiber called an *axon;* all neurons have only one axon. Axons range in length from a tenth of a millimeter to two meters. If you look down the axon tree trunk, you see root-like ends called *axon terminals.*

Now, let's look up the axon tree trunk. Imagine the large branches of this tree-like cell body extending outward three-dimensionally in different directions, narrowing into smaller branches that further divide into finger-like twigs. These branches and twigs are flexible, antennae-like extensions called *dendrites.* Like the branches of a tree, each nerve cell has numerous dendrites. Dendrites

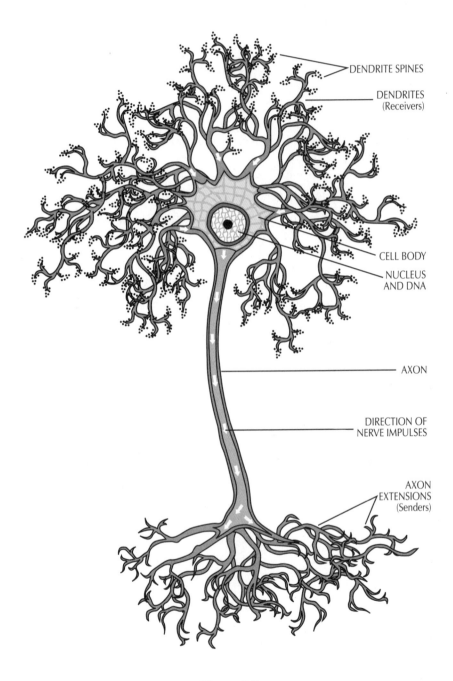

Figure 3.1
A Neuron

terminate in tiny, granular bumps, termed *dendrite spines*. These knob-like extensions are the dendrite's specific receivers of information, and they are important in the learning process. Again, see Figure 3.1.

Actually, all the parts of entire nerve cells are so flexible that they look more like spaghetti cooking in boiling water than like stiff branches on a tree. Live neurons are not rigid but elastic and amorphous.

NEURONS: MANY TYPES, MANY FUNCTIONS

There are different types of specialized neurons, which receive many kinds of stimuli and conduct electrochemical signals to neighboring neurons in specific directions. Neurons are classified by various factors, including their location, shape, the direction in which they conduct impulses, and the number of extensions they possess. For example, *sensory neurons* receive information from both outside and inside the body via our senses, and they send that information to the brain or the spinal cord. *Motor neurons* convey signals from the brain or spinal cord to the body, causing movement or a specific function to take place in a tissue or an organ.

Neurons can be further classified by the number, length, and mode of branching of the neurites, or cellular branches. For example, *unipolar neurons* have only a single neurite that divides a short distance from the cell body into two branches. *Bipolar neurons* have an elongated cell body, from each end of which a neurite emerges. Bipolar neurons, which are less numerous than the other types, have one axon and only one dendrite. *Multipolar neurons* have a number of axon neurites arising from the cell body. They have one axon and several dendrites. Most neurons of the brain and the spinal cord are multipolar neurons. Take a look at Figure 3.2 to compare different types of nerve cells.

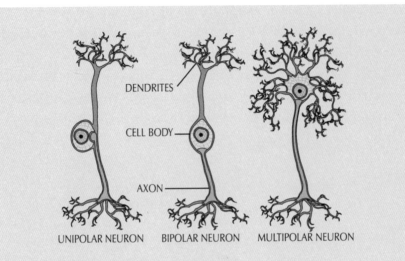

DENDRITES

CELL BODY

AXON

UNIPOLAR NEURON   BIPOLAR NEURON   MULTIPOLAR NEURON

Figure 3.2

Neurons are also classified according to size. *Golgi type I neurons* have a long axon that reaches up to a meter in length. The axons of these neurons form from fibers of the brain and the spinal cord, as well as from the peripheral nerves that exit the spine. If you are interested in the names of such neurons, the pyramidal cells of the cerebral cortex, Purkinje's cells of the cerebellum, and the motor cells of the spinal cord are all good examples.

The most numerous type of nerve cells are short-axon multipolar neurons known as *Golgi type II neurons*. Their short branches usually end close to the cell body, and in some cases, the axon might even be absent. Golgi type II neurons have a sort of star-shaped appearance. These cells are the most common in the cerebellar cortex and cerebral cortex—that is, the small nerve cells that make up the brain's gray matter. Figure 3.2 pictures these Golgi type I and II nerve cells.

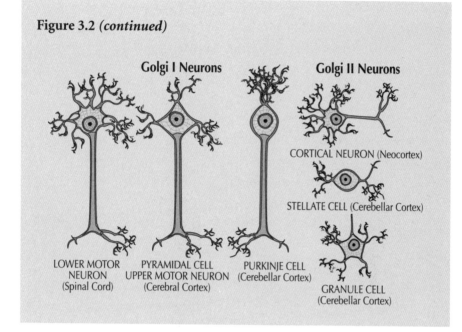

Figure 3.2 *(continued)*

Golgi I Neurons   Golgi II Neurons

CORTICAL NEURON (Neocortex)

STELLATE CELL (Cerebellar Cortex)

LOWER MOTOR NEURON (Spinal Cord)   PYRAMIDAL CELL UPPER MOTOR NEURON (Cerebral Cortex)   PURKINJE CELL (Cerebellar Cortex)

GRANULE CELL (Cerebellar Cortex)

Neurons communicate via their axons and dendrites in a kind of intricate wiring system. Whereas the axon sends electrochemical information to other neurons, the dendrites receive messages from other nerve cells. In terms of our tree analogy, the dendrites (branches) receive messages from the axon terminals (root system) of other trees where they connect, and pass them down the axon (tree trunk) to their own axon terminals (roots), which touch another tree's dendrites (branches), and so on.

That's a very rudimentary look at how this communication takes place. What do I mean by rudimentary? For one thing, we will find it useful at this point to talk about neurons as if they connect through direct contact. The amazing thing is that neurons never actually touch each other. There is always a space between them about one-millionth of a centimeter in width, called the *synapse*. Point A in Figure 3.3 will help you visualize the synaptic space between neurons.

Also for the sake of simplicity, although a neuron can communicate with thousands of other nerve cells in a three-dimensional fashion, I'll begin by describing how one nerve cell (neuron A) passes along a message to another single nerve cell (neuron B). Incidentally, although axon terminals typically send information to another neuron's dendrites, every now and then an axon extension will connect directly to the cell body of a neighboring neuron.

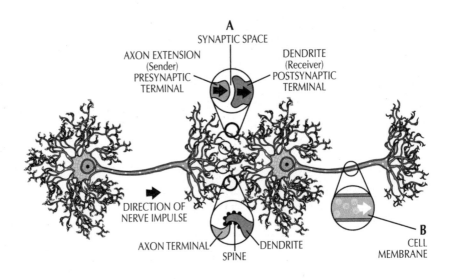

A
SYNAPTIC SPACE

AXON EXTENSION
(Sender)
PRESYNAPTIC
TERMINAL

DENDRITE
(Receiver)
POSTSYNAPTIC
TERMINAL

DIRECTION OF
NERVE IMPULSE

AXON TERMINAL   DENDRITE
            SPINE

B
CELL
MEMBRANE

Figure 3.3
A schematic of the synaptic space, dendrite spines, and the cell membrane.

Nerve Impulses Spread the Message

Imagine that you decide to pick up a pencil. How would your nerve cells transmit this thought and cause your hand to make the necessary movements to pick up the pencil? Let's follow this process (much simplified, of course).

First, you need to understand where and how communication between nerves takes place. The site where this communication is initiated and conducted is a neuron's *cell membrane* or *plasma membrane*. You might think of this as the skin of the nerve cell; this continuous external boundary surrounds every neuron, including the cell body and its extensions. This membrane is so thin—about 8 nanometers, or 100,000th of a meter—that you could not view it with a standard light microscope. Point B in Figure 3.3 shows the nerve cell membrane.

Perhaps you remember the term *ion* from your high school chemistry class. If you recall, an ion is an atom having an electrical charge, because it has either gained or lost an electron in its outer shell. Ions are important to our discussion, because these charged atoms generate the electrical signals by which nerve cells communicate. A neuron's cell membrane allows certain ions to diffuse through it, but it restricts others. The ions that we are most concerned with here are sodium and potassium ions, which have positive electrical charges, and chloride ions, which are negatively charged. When a neuron is in its resting or unstimulated state, the inner surface of its cell membrane has a negative charge relative to its surroundings, because fewer positively charged ions exist inside the cell membrane than outside the cell. But when a neuron is activated or stimulated, more ions instantly move into the neuron through the cell membrane, making the membrane's inner surface change from a negative charge to a positive charge.

This flow of ions lasts only five milliseconds, but it is long enough to propagate an electrical current, called an *action potential,* that travels down the axon. For our purposes, all you need to know about action potentials is that when a nerve cell gets excited, meaning that it reaches a certain threshold of electrical charge, a quick exchange of charged particles takes place, which flow all the way along its membrane to the axon terminals. Following this activity, the ions' positions swiftly revert to their resting state.

Once an action potential is triggered, it is conducted along the nerve cell in a cascading, wavelike effect called a *nerve impulse.* To visualize this, imagine that you are holding the end of a long rope. If you flick it like a whip, you will generate a wave that travels down the entire length of the rope. In a similar fashion, once a stimulus is strong enough to cause a nerve cell to turn on or to fire, this generates a self-propagating electrical impulse, meaning that it can't stop until it has gone all the way down to the end of the axon. The electrical current proceeds down the axon in a single pulse until the entire nerve impulse is discharged. Scientists call this the *all-or-none law* or *Bowditch's law.* In this book, we refer to an action potential in any neuron or set of neurons by using statements such as "when neurons fire," "when neurons are activated," or "when neurons are turned on."

The speed of this transmission in nerve fibers is impressive. An action potential lasting a thousandth of a second can travel down an axon at speeds well over 250 miles per hour. Put another way, this pulse can move at up to 100 meters, approximately the length of a football field, in one second. Once a nerve impulse starts, its intensity or its strength of transmission always stays the same until that transmission ends. Since a nerve impulse travels by means of an electrical current flowing down an axon, can we measure this current?

The exchange of ions inside and outside the nerve cells (an action potential) generates an electromagnetic field. During brain activity, millions of neurons fire in unison, and this produces a measurable electromagnetic field. If you have ever seen EEG technology in action, during which electrodes are placed on a person's scalp to provide a reading of brain activity, you were watching these inductance fields being recorded. Nerve cells firing in tandem throughout the brain can produce different types of electromagnetic fields that signify various states of mind. Using EEG technology, scientists can even correlate increased activity of these electromagnetic fields with specific regions of the brain, related to different thought processes.

We generate electrical impulses in our brain moment by moment, whether we are processing information from our environment, engaging in our own personal thoughts, or sleeping. This is happening in various parts of our brain, in millions and millions of different neurons, every second. In fact, the number of nerve impulses the human brain generates in one day is greater than the number of electrical impulses of all the cell phones on the planet.

Now, let's look more closely at how information moves from one nerve cell to another. As neurons transmit signals in the form of electrical impulses, they must communicate with one another across the gap that separates them. This gap, between the axon terminal (signal sender) from one nerve cell, and the dendrite (signal receiver) from its neighboring neuron, is a *synaptic connection* or *synapse*. (This term originated from a Greek word meaning "to connect" or "to join.") Only thousandths of a millimeter wide, the synaptic gap allows nerve impulses to continue along their routes from one neuron to another without interruption.

The sending side of the gap where the axon terminal ends (depicted as the tree's root system by point A in Figure 3.3) is termed the *presynaptic terminal,* because a signal on this side of the gap has not yet crossed the synapse. The receiving end of the synapse, where the dendrite accepts information, is the *postsynaptic terminal* (the tree's outermost, finger-like branches).

Keep in mind that neurons do not link up in simple chains like railroad boxcars strung together, one after the other in sequence. For one thing, an axon can send information to more than one nerve cell at a time, a process called *divergence.* When this occurs, a message from one nerve cell diverges or spreads to multiple neighboring nerve cells. Potentially, one neuron creates a cascade of information that it may send to a jungle of thousands of other neurons. The process of neuronal divergence is much the same as dropping a pebble in the water and watching the impulse spread out in all directions.

In another process, termed *convergence,* a single nerve cell receives messages at its dendrites from multiple nerve cells, and then converges these different bits of information into one signal, which it passes along via the axon. Imagine our oak tree with its branches (dendrites) spreading out in all directions. Now picture thousands of other trees floating three-dimensionally in midair with their root systems (axon terminals) touching a small part of our original tree's canopy. All those different trees are funneling numerous electrical currents to the one tree, and it is converging all of that information into one single pathway along its trunk to its roots. Convergence occurs when widespread neuronal activity is dovetailed seamlessly together so that all nerve impulses meet at a few single neurons. You can look at Figure 3.4 to view divergence and convergence.

How to Pick Up a Pencil

Okay, our pencil is still laying there. What has to happen for you to pick it up? If you reached for and picked up a pencil, a cascade of action potentials would fire in a whole host of neurons in different areas of your brain to cause the coordinated action of movement in your arms and hands. Following are some of the simple steps in this process, which do not necessarily occur in this exact sequence.

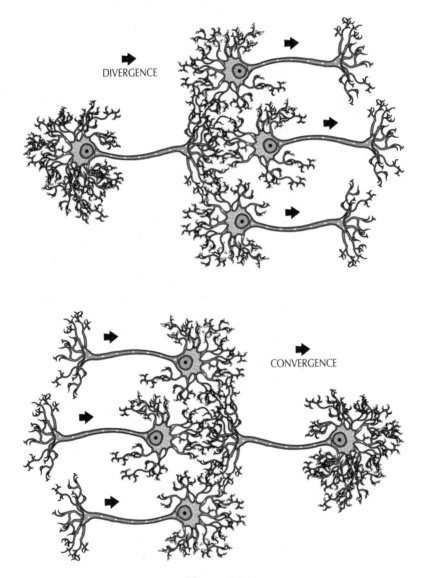

Figure 3.4
Divergence and Convergence

1. Your thought of picking up a pencil creates the first series of action potentials in your brain.

2. Your eyes see the pencil and initiate the second series of action potentials.

3. Your *occipital lobe* (the part of the brain responsible for vision) registers the image of what you see.

4. The *temporal lobe* (responsible for association in conjunction with memory storage and learning) associates the image of what you see with what it remembers about pencils, which then creates another series of action potentials.

5. The *frontal lobe* (responsible for higher mental activities) allows you to maintain your attention while you intentionally reach for the pencil.

6. When you begin to formulate and integrate the movement of reaching for the pencil, the frontal lobe and *parietal lobe* (the motor portion of the brain, also responsible for language mechanisms and general sensory functions) help you initiate the action of movement in your arm, hand, and fingers, and trigger your sensory anticipation of what a pencil will feel like.

7. The *parietal lobe* allows you to feel that you have the pencil in your hand—you can sense its shape, the rougher surface of the wood exposed by sharpening, the softness of the eraser.

8. At the same time, the *cerebellum* (responsible for coordinating voluntary muscular activity) directs the body's fine motor movements to reach out and grasp the pencil. Without the cerebellum, you might take hold of the pencil but send it flying over your head or sweep it to the floor.

Throughout this cascade of action potentials, sodium and potassium ions were rushing in and out of your nerve cells, and this electrochemical activity took place without any conscious awareness on your part. Thank goodness for that!

Nervous as a Jellyfish

The first nerve cells evolved in creatures very similar to the present-day jellyfish. Millions of years ago, the survival of this primitive organism depended on its ability to detect (sensory function) and move (motor function) toward food. It was essential that the jellyfish develop specialized cells that could initiate movement by tissue contraction. But these movements had to be more than just random actions.

The jellyfish needed a system that could guide its movements with some degree of awareness and coordination, so that it could interact more effectively with its environment. Such a system required the ability to receive sensory messages from the environment and to conduct those signals to the cells that had become specialized for producing movement. Essentially, this is what the nervous system does: it senses the environment, and then responds appropriately via movement and action, sometimes voluntarily and sometimes involuntarily.

In other words, the jellyfish needed a rudimentary consciousness or intelligence and a simple nervous system to facilitate a basic level of awareness. Accordingly, this creature developed nerve cells and the sensory and motor functions of one of the earliest nervous systems.

The simple neurological mechanisms that evolved in jellyfish and other primitive organisms were such effective adaptations that they became the norm in evolution. All nerve cells, whether they are from jellyfish, other animals, or human beings, operate under the same basic electrochemical principles for conducting information. Today, we humans behave and respond to our environment using the same processes that evolved in the jellyfish millions of years ago.

How did nature make the quantum leap from the most primitive nervous systems to the human brain? For organisms to develop increasingly complicated, sophisticated, and adaptive behavior, all they needed was to put more of these nerve cells together in diversified ways.

As neurons wire together in increasingly intricate neurological networks, the communication between neurons multiplies exponentially. It's a simple correlation: As communication among neurons escalates, intelligence expands and organisms are able to behave within their environments in ever more advanced and adaptive ways. In essence, we can learn, remember, create, invent, and modify our behavior faster than any other species, due to the size of our expanded brain. Human beings, because of the enormous number of interconnected nerve cells that give our brain both immense size and unsurpassed complexity, are at the top of the chain of command.

Chemical Messengers Make the Connection

Let's look more closely now at how nerve impulses travel from one neuron to another. How do they cross that synaptic gap?

When a nerve impulse travels down a neuron to the very end of the axon, it reaches the presynaptic terminal on the sending side of the synaptic gap. At the presynaptic terminal are minuscule synaptic vesicles, which store chemical messengers called *neurotransmitters*. Neurotransmitters pass important information to other nerve cells across the tiny synaptic space and to other parts of the body, to orchestrate specific functions. Point A in Figure 3.5 illustrates these vesicles filled with neurotransmitters.

Neurotransmitters (for example, serotonin or dopamine) also produce the moods that flavor our experiences. They are the reason that sometimes we do an activity and feel happy, while at other times, when we do the same activity,

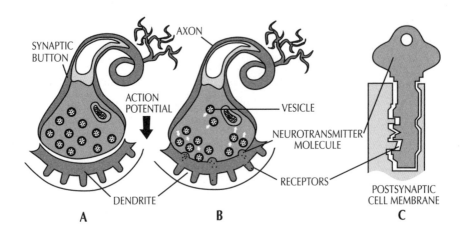

Figure 3.5
The action of the neurotransmitters at the synaptic space.

we have a different set of emotions. If, like most people, you go through many different moods in the course of a day, from being excited or in a positive frame of mind, to feeling depressed, irritable, or fatigued, you have experienced the effects of neurotransmitters. The brain chemistry we create on a daily basis, by our own thoughts, determines how we feel.

Think of the vesicles at the end of the axon terminal as tiny, specially built water balloons, and the neurotransmitters as the fluid in the balloons. Only matching sets of terminals and neurotransmitters can work together. Like a lightning bolt, the electrochemical activity of a nerve impulse causes one or more vesicles to burst, and each one that bursts releases thousands of neurotransmitter molecules. With every nerve impulse, some vesicles erupt, while other vesicles are unaffected, so that certain neurotransmitters are emitted while other chemical messengers are not released.

What determines which neurotransmitters are released? Nerve impulses aren't all the same; each electrical impulse traveling down the neuron has a specific frequency (or magnitude of charge), and each kind of neurotransmitter responds to a different frequency. Thus, a specific electrochemical impulse causes a particular vesicle to burst and discharge a corresponding frequency-specific neurotransmitter.

Imagine these chemical messengers, if you will, as tiny ferryboats crossing a channel and docking on the other side at their proper destinations. At the receiving dendrite, each neurotransmitter docks, or binds, to a specific chemical receptor site, like a key fitting into its matching lock. The shape of the neurotransmitter must match the shape of the receptor. Points B and C in Figure 3.5 demonstrate this lock and key model.

At the point where neurotransmitters dock on the other side, they release their "passengers," which then have specific duties. Individuals that leave the ferryboats may all travel down the same highway, but they have different agendas. Some may go home to rest, some may go to work, some may be on vacation, and some may even police the ferryboat itself.

This is analogous to what neurotransmitters do. They cross the gap between the neuron that releases them and a neighboring nerve cell. On the receiving end of the gap, they cause the release of specific chemicals that influence the activity of the neighboring nerve cell. That, in turn, influences the next receiving neuron, and so on.

The Chemical Electrical Exchange

Have you noticed that nerve impulses start as electrical in nature, then turn chemical, and then become electrical again? In other words, the electrical impulses that neurons generate are transmuted into chemical impulses at the synapse via neurotransmitters. These chemical messages stimulate complex molecular interactions, including ion fluxes, which trigger electrical impulses at the neighboring neuron. When a certain electrical threshold is reached, this activates that adjoining neuron and sets off an action potential that continues the message along the receiving nerve cell.

Not every nerve cell passes along the messages it receives. To illustrate this, imagine that you are trying to cheer up a friend who is very depressed over a lost love. He is stuck in inertia, repeatedly rehashing his woes. Realizing that he needs to forget about his misery, you decide to stimulate him in many different ways.

You take him out for an early dinner, go for a stroll and an ice cream on the boardwalk, accompany him to a movie, and then meet up with friends at a nightclub, where you watch stand-up comedy.

At some point in all this activity, your friend probably reached a threshold at which he became excited enough to forget about his initial resting state.

Nerve cells change from a resting state to an excited state in much the same way your friend did. One form of stimulation sometimes may not be enough, but if you can provide enough stimulation to get them to the point of excitement, they will become excited and stay that way. Once a nerve cell becomes excited at the postsynaptic terminal, it now changes from a receiver of information to a sender of information. Now the nerve cell will spread its excitement.

When neurotransmitters are released at the presynaptic terminal (the neuron's sending point), they generate an electrical response at the postsynaptic terminal of the receiving nerve cell. This electrical impulse has to travel from the (receiving) dendrite to the cell body and down the axon before the neurotransmitter accomplishes its job. Think of neurotransmitters as chemicals that link the communication between neurons so that messages travel throughout the brain.

Usually there must be an abundance of neurotransmitter activity (stimulation) at the postsynaptic terminal (the neuron's receiving end) for the next nerve cell to become excited enough to fire. Small amounts of neurotransmitters from singular nerve cell firings generally do not reach the threshold to produce an action potential on the postsynaptic terminal. It's an all-or-nothing phenomenon, like that moment when your alarm clock goes off—either you get out of bed or you don't, but you can't do both. Different types of neurotransmitters also play a role in whether nerve cells get fired up or ignore the alarm.

Types of Neurotransmitters

Neurotransmitters are found in varying concentrations in specific parts of the brain, based on each area's particular function. Some major neurotransmitters are glutamate, GABA, acetylcholine, serotonin, dopamine, melatonin, nitric oxide, and various endorphins.

Neurotransmitters can perform many different types of functions. They can stimulate, inhibit, or change the activity of a neuron itself on a cellular level. They can tell a neuron to unhook from its current connection or make a neuron stick better to its present connection. Neurotransmitters can signal neighboring neurons to become excited, or they can send a message to the next neuron down the line that will inhibit or completely stop a nerve impulse. They can even change the message as it is being sent to a neuron, so that it sends a new message to all the nerve cells connected to it. Any of these activities can take place in a millisecond.

We have two types of neurotransmitters in the brain and nervous system. *Excitatory neurotransmitters* stimulate or activate nerve transmissions; they change the electrical state of the postsynaptic membrane, allowing the action potential in the next cell to be initiated. These types of chemicals, in the appropriate combinations, enable our mental functions to take place at warp speed.

The major excitatory brain neurotransmitter is *glutamate*. When glutamate is released from a neuron's presynaptic (sending) terminal, it binds to the receptor at the postsynaptic terminal of the next cell. Then it changes the postsynaptic cell's electrical state to make it more likely that an action potential will fire.

Conversely, *inhibitory neurotransmitters* do just what their name says—they inhibit or stop activity in the next cell down the line, and end the excitement on the postsynaptic terminal of the receiving nerve cell. The major inhibitory neurotransmitter is *GABA* (gamma-aminobutyric acid). When GABA is released at the presynaptic synapse it, too, attaches to the corresponding postsynaptic receptors. However, GABA makes it less likely that an action potential will be generated. Without GABA, nerve cells would fire so repetitively that they would become overstimulated, causing significant damage and resulting in major imbalances in the brain.

Neurons can easily associate with, and connect to, many different neurons. They also have the ability to readily turn impulses on and off at will, converge information to a single cell, and diverge electrical activity in a myriad of different directions. Instantaneously, neurons also connect and disconnect from one another at different synaptic spaces.

Based on their complexity, biological science is beginning to comprehend how little we really know about the inner working and interconnectedness of neurons. It stands to reason that because neurons can direct so many functions and easily read on/off patterns in collective ways, they bear little resemblance to the drawings we may remember from our schoolbooks, depicting tiny wires lining up in a tidy fashion. For our purposes, we might picture neurons in terms of the vast, ever-changing network of individual computers communicating at lightning speeds via the Internet. If we can visualize neurons as billions of computers, constantly connecting to and disconnecting from one another, we may begin the enormous task of explaining their intelligence on a microscopic level. Therefore, when I talk about "wiring of neurons," understand that this is a metaphor to help us learn how these superior cells tend to make contact and work cooperatively with each other.

The Water Between Our Ears

As mentioned earlier, some 75 to 85 percent of the contents of our wonderfully complex bio-computer is water. The consistency of a living brain is similar in some areas to a soft-boiled egg, while other areas are dense and rubbery like a hard-boiled egg. No wonder nature has surrounded the brain with a bony cranium to protect its delicate tissues against injury! Water is essential to the brain's electrical means of information exchange. The brain's watery content amplifies its electrical conductivity and allows electrical currents to spread quickly throughout the cranium in a smooth and continuous fashion. This spreading process (divergence) is greatly facilitated by water.

To illustrate why this is true, consider what happens when lightning strikes a pond. If you are in the pond, even if you are a half-mile away from the lightning bolt's point of entry, you can be electrocuted, because the electric current will travel at extremely fast speeds through the water in all directions. In a similar fashion, the water in your brain acts as a conduit to facilitate electrical charges. Water provides the perfect medium for these charged particles to diffuse quickly and freely across the inner and outer environment of the nerve cell.

And Now, the Nervous System

Other parts of the nervous system, besides the brain itself, conduct impulses to and from the brain. These are the *nerves*. A nerve can be one or more bundles of nerve cell fibers branching out into every part of the body, forming part of a system that conveys impulses of sensation, motion, and so on between the brain or spinal cord and all the other parts of the body. Nerves are extensions of the brain. The nervous system serves to connect the environment to the body, the body to the brain, and the brain to the body.

Fundamentally, the nervous system as a whole activates, controls, and coordinates all bodily functions, integrating the vast complexities of living tissue into order and harmony. It regulates the endocrine, musculoskeletal, immune, digestive, cardiovascular, reproductive, respiratory, and elimination systems. Without the nervous system, there could be no life.

To monitor and maintain all these systems, the nervous system constantly communicates with the rest of the body. Through our senses, which are extensions of nerve receptors that allow us to process different types of information about our environment, the nervous system receives information and evaluates conditions both outside and within the body. In addition to hearing, sight, smell, taste, touch, and pressure, the nervous system processes other, internal senses, including hunger, thirst, pain, temperature, and *proprioception* (awareness of the spatial positions of body parts). The nervous system stores the information it receives in the form of memories.

Components of the Nervous System

The nervous system actually consists of several component subsystems, which overlap within the body. The *central nervous system* consists of the brain and the spinal cord. One can think of the spinal cord as an extension of the brain, with billions of sensory and motor impulses traveling up and down the spinal column as if it were a fiberoptic cable.

Our other nervous system is the *peripheral nervous system,* and it includes all the nerves that are outside the brain and the spinal cord. Nerves that carry impulses from tissues and organs to the spinal cord, and nerves that convey signals from the spinal cord to tissues and organs, including our sensory organs, are all included as peripheral nerves. If the spinal cord is comparable to a fiberoptic cable, then peripheral nerves are like wires that extend out from this fiberoptic cable and carry two-way communications between the spinal cord and the arms and legs, the feet and hands, and all the internal organs. In Figures 3.6A, 3.6B, and 3.6C, you can compare the central nervous system and the peripheral nervous system.

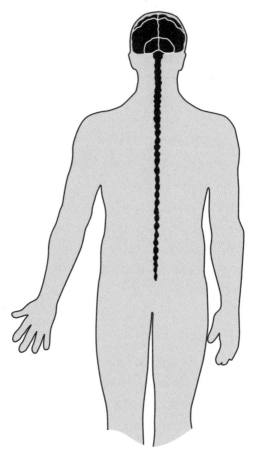

Figure 3.6A
The Central Nervous System

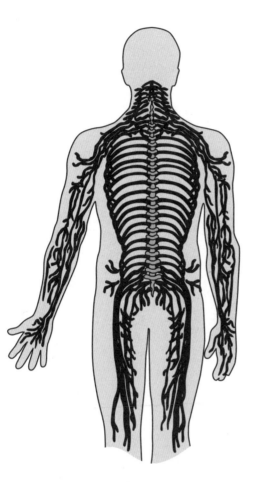

Figure 3.6B
The Peripheral Nerves of the Voluntary Nervous System

Two types of nerves make up the peripheral nervous system. The first type of peripheral nerve is the *cranial nerve* (because it is near the head). There are 12 pairs of cranial nerves, which originate in the brainstem. They carry impulses for many functions, such as smell, vision, the maintenance of equilibrium, glandular secretion, hearing, swallowing, and facial expression (see Figure 3.6C to visualize some of the cranial nerves). The second type of peripheral nerve is made up of the 31 pairs of *spinal nerves,* which emerge from or between the vertebrae on both sides of the spinal column. Each spinal nerve branches out and connects with a specific region of the neck, trunk, or limbs, and is responsible for function, movement, and sensation. Figures 3.6B and 3.6C clarify how some peripheral nerves exit the spine and communicate with muscles and tendons, while other peripheral nerves connect to various organs.

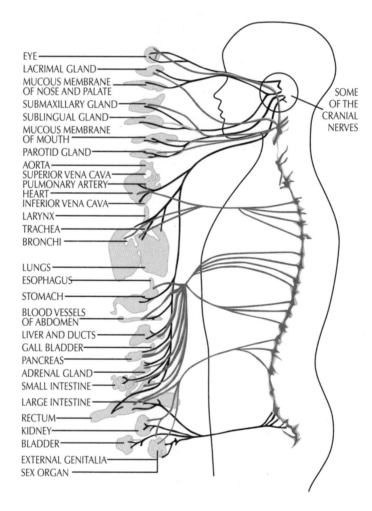

EYE
LACRIMAL GLAND
MUCOUS MEMBRANE OF NOSE AND PALATE
SUBMAXILLARY GLAND
SUBLINGUAL GLAND
MUCOUS MEMBRANE OF MOUTH
PAROTID GLAND
AORTA
SUPERIOR VENA CAVA
PULMONARY ARTERY
HEART
INFERIOR VENA CAVA
LARYNX
TRACHEA
BRONCHI
LUNGS
ESOPHAGUS
STOMACH
BLOOD VESSELS OF ABDOMEN
LIVER AND DUCTS
GALL BLADDER
PANCREAS
ADRENAL GLAND
SMALL INTESTINE
LARGE INTESTINE
RECTUM
KIDNEY
BLADDER
EXTERNAL GENITALIA
SEX ORGAN

SOME OF THE CRANIAL NERVES

Figure 3.6C
The Peripheral Nerves of the Involuntary Nervous System

Our Involuntary, Subconscious Intelligence

Residing within both the central and peripheral nervous systems is the *autonomic nervous system*. This is the body's automatic, self-regulating control system, and its origins are in the midbrain, an area just below our neocortex and one of three major divisions of the brain. The midbrain (see Figure 3.7) is under the neocortex and is the area responsible for the body's automatic functions.

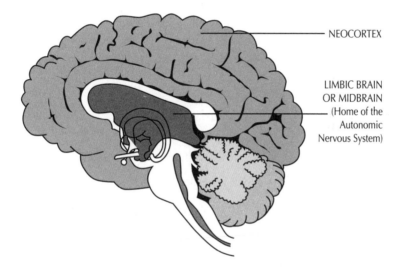

NEOCORTEX

LIMBIC BRAIN
OR MIDBRAIN
(Home of the
Autonomic
Nervous System)

Figure 3.7
Split view of half of the brain.

The autonomic nervous system is responsible for involuntary functions and for *homeostasis,* the continuous balance that the body's innate intelligence maintains. Our autonomic nervous system regulates body temperature, blood sugar levels, pulse rate, and all those millions of processes that we take for granted every day. It is called autonomic (think "automatic") because of all the functions it controls without any conscious effort on our part. For example, we need not intentionally control our heartbeat or deliberately release the enzymes needed to digest our last meal. The autonomic nervous system automatically self-regulates to keep the body in internal chemical order and maintain a normal level of health. We could say that it operates at a subconscious level.

The autonomic nervous system (ANS) has two divisions, the sympathetic nervous system and the parasympathetic nervous system. Figure 3.8 depicts the two branches of the autonomic nervous system.

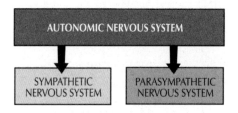

Figure 3.8
The two branches of the ANS.

Because the *sympathetic nervous system* prepares the body for emergencies, this part of the autonomic nervous system is sometimes called the *fight-or-flight nervous system*. When we perceive a threat from the environment, this nervous system automatically activates to get the body ready to either fight or run away. Our heart rate accelerates, blood pressure increases, respiratory rate quickens, and adrenalin is released for immediate action. At the same time, the body's energy is moved away from the digestive tract and toward the arms and legs. The sympathetic nervous system changes the body electrochemically to improve its chances for survival.

Just the opposite functions are the domain of the *parasympathetic nervous system*. This division of the autonomic nervous system conserves and restores the body's energy and resources. When we do not perceive any threat in our environment, the parasympathetic nervous system slows the heart rate, increases energy to the digestive system, relaxes the body, and moves blood flow away from the skeletal muscles of the extremities and into the internal organs to support growth and maintenance processes. Think of our parasympathetic nervous system in relation to how we feel just after finishing a big dinner.

Another part of the involuntary nervous system involves the many different reflexes that occur in response to various external stimuli; the body may employ these reflexes for purposes of survival and immediate action. For example, when the doctor hits your knee just below your kneecap with a rubber hammer, your leg immediately and involuntarily jerks. When you put your hand on a hot pan, it automatically pulls away. If you walk into a bright room after being in a dark room, your pupils contract. These rudimentary, automatic muscular actions are directed by the brainstem and the cerebellum. They are primitive responses that have been encoded through millions of years of adaptation.

Now that we have the foundation for understanding the more instinctive functions of the involuntary nervous system—functions derived from our autonomic or "automatic" nervous system—we can begin to appreciate the importance of all its responsibilities. This is our subconscious nature, and it houses an intelligence, or a mind, that is capable of controlling all the countless bodily functions that happen moment to moment, on a cellular level and on a large scale, without our conscious effort or attention. This amazing, brilliantly designed system automatically sustains our very life, and, when not disrupted, maintains our level of internal order, or health.

Our Voluntary, Conscious Nature

As human beings, we are privileged to have the ability to act voluntarily and consciously. We have the free will to make and to execute choices concerning what we want to think about, what we want to remember, what skills we want to develop, and what actions we want to take. We use our brain and nervous system to exercise voluntary control over our decisions—whether to eat, take a walk, or sit down and read a book—and we control our muscles to carry out those choices. Our desires and actions are derived from our free will. For this reason, we can speak of having a voluntary nervous system, which houses our conscious mind and free will to make and carry out choices that are under our voluntary control. The seat of our free will, the voluntary nervous system, is located in the part of the brain called the neocortex. You can review the neocortex in Figure 3.7.

What makes us human, what provides the source of our human nature, is the interaction between our involuntary nervous system and our voluntary nervous system. On the one hand, the voluntary nervous system is under our conscious control, and it gives us the free will to do what we want to do. At the same time, the autonomic nervous system is controlled by our subconscious intelligence, providing and regulating all those countless electrochemical reactions that give life to our body and support whatever we are doing and feeling. Figure 3.9 provides an overview of the nervous system with its component parts.

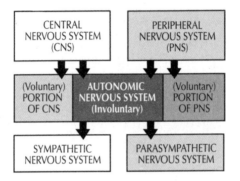

Figure 3.9
The nervous system and all of its divisions.

I hope that you are beginning to appreciate why we began our exploration of the brain by focusing at the cellular level. Our nerve cells have been designed by nature to allow communication to occur exponentially. We can use the same neural connections and pathways in our brain but produce different neurotransmitters each time, to create an infinite variety of thoughts, feelings, actions, moods, and perceptions. This process can inspire actions and reactions, elicit emotions, regulate bodily functions, manifest moods and behaviors, stimulate drives, release hormones, and create the holographic images called thoughts and memories.

Now we can begin to explore the anatomy of *attitude*, building from our simple lesson in neurobiology and brain chemistry. An attitude is a cluster of thoughts strung together, which turn on particular nerve cells in the brain, which then stimulate specific neurotransmitters to make us think, act, and feel certain ways. For example, say you wake up in the morning and wash the dishes that were left from the night before. Your attitude toward the task is a function of these thoughts: "I really got a good night's sleep. I'm so glad I don't have to work today. Man, that pasta we had last night was good, and I'm glad we rinsed these dishes after dinner. I can't believe how blue the sky looks today." Later that evening, when doing the dishes again, your attitude may be comprised of these thoughts: "I don't know why she had to bring that up again. I thought we'd finally settled the issue and now we're back to talking about it again. Why is that damn light buzzing like that? I don't feel like doing the dishes tonight. I'd rather be in bed."

Based on those two different sets of thoughts, you would likely experience quite a contrast between the attitudes you held while performing the same dish-washing task on these separate occasions. We often refer to free will as our ability to express whatever attitude we choose, and it's all associated with our brain and its chemistry. By extension, free will is what makes individual human beings so different from one another. The next time you begin any endeavor, consider how your thoughts affect the chemical dance going on in your brain.

If our brain is the engine that powers us in our daily life, it's a pretty good idea to know how it works and how we can control it, so we can get where we want to go. That's the whole point of this material. Knowledge is power. Power is control. We're working toward the point where we have the ability to take control over our mental/chemical state, our life, and ultimately, our personal reality. The great thing is that our mental/chemical state and our life are so enmeshed that to affect change in one means that the other will change as well.

In chapter 4, I will explain how the brain has evolved to this point in our human history. Then I will also familiarize you with the different landmarks, regions, and substructures of the brain so that you have a better understanding of how you process both your internal thoughts and external reactions. As we tie this all together, it will begin to help you understand more about why you are the way you are.

CHAPTER FOUR

OUR THREE BRAINS AND MORE

*In proportion to our body mass, our brain
is three times as large as that of our nearest relatives.
This huge organ is dangerous and painful to give birth to,
expensive to build, and, in a resting human, uses about
20 percent of the body's energy even though it is just
two percent of the body's weight. There must be
some reason for all this evolutionary expense.*

—SUSAN BLAKEMORE

American author Kurt Vonnegut, in his novel *Galapagos*, uses a refrain to express his disdain for the "so-called" advances in human progress and social and political evolution. He writes, "Thanks a lot, big brain."

While Vonnegut writes of his unhappiness with war, poverty, violence, and so on—results of what our brains produce—many of us don't share his cynicism. When Vonnegut spoke of the "big brain," he didn't mean it literally. Weighing some three pounds and making up about two percent of our body weight, the human brain is six times larger, relative to body size, than that of any other living mammal, with the exception of dolphins. Human and dolphin brains are very close in proportion to body size. But the dolphin brain has not significantly developed or changed in the last 20 million years.

A mystery of human brain evolution has long puzzled many biologists and paleontologists. As animal species evolved, their brain mass enlarged in the same ratio as the lungs, liver, stomach, and the rest of the body's physical structures. About 250,000 years ago, most mammals reached the height of their evolution in brain complexity and mass. Just in the last 250,000 to 300,000 years, as the mammalian brain reached its zenith in size and efficiency, the evolution of our human species diverged from other mammals in several quite unpredictable ways. For one thing, early humans should have reached a plateau in brain development, as other mammals did during the same period. Instead, the human neocortex underwent an enormous leap in overall mass and complexity within a short amount of time.

The Quandary of Brain Growth

Recent findings show that when the human midbrain reached its present-day level of evolutionary complexity (250,000 to 300,000 years ago), our ancestors at that time experienced a 20 percent increase in actual mass of the neocortex, the thinking, reasoning area of the human brain.[1] This sudden acceleration in the volume and density of brain mass appears to have occurred spontaneously and unexplainably, as opposed to the normal, linear course of evolution. Our rapid 20 percent outgrowth of gray matter is responsible for the superiority of the human brain. What caused this explosive brain development, which gave us a neocortex so much larger and denser than that of any other species, remains a mystery.

Also unlike other mammals, when the density of the human neocortex enlarged by 20 percent, the size of the human body increased only by 16 percent. To put this another way, the human body's size increased only 80 percent in proportion to the expansion in mass of the brain, which is quite a deviation from the mammalian body-brain ratio.

Another interesting question comes to mind. Why did the brain expand to such a great degree, while the size of the head, both generally and in relation to the growth of the rest of the body, did not keep pace? The overall volume of the human skull did enlarge to some degree but not proportionally, the way animal evolution would predict. Scientists believe that if the human head had grown at the same rate of increase as the brain, the female pelvis could not have accommodated an infant's enlarged head circumference during birth. Even today, the human birthing process remains risky and difficult due to fetal head size. Back then, an increase in fetal head size without an increase in pelvic size would have accelerated infant and maternal mortality, and humans would have been eliminated as a species. One possible solution that Mother Nature rejected was merely to increase the size of the female pelvis to allow a larger fetal head circumference. We can only imagine what shape females would have evolved into, had there been this increase in the size of the head. With such an increase in pelvic capacity, this probably would have forced early female humans back on four legs.

The Nerf Ball Brain

Nature's solution to the need for a larger brain without a corresponding increase in skull size was simple and elegant. The brain folded in on itself, so that about 98 percent of the neocortex is hidden within the folds. Just as a Japanese fan, when folded, hides its floral patterns beneath the surface, the new, enfolded brain hides most of its gray matter and material. This design, which greatly resembles a walnut, is an efficient way to pack more material into a smaller space.

A few years ago, I was helping my daughter with a school assignment on the brain. We were discussing how the brain's numerous folds maximize mass and minimize the use of space. She was having difficulty understanding the general idea. After she went to school the next morning, I bought 10 Nerf balls that were four inches in diameter. I also found a one-gallon glass jar with a large opening. That evening I asked her to put just two balls in the jar. They took up most of the jar's volume. "No folds, right?" I asked. She nodded. "That's what the brain would look like if it had no folds in it," I said. Then I asked her to stuff all 10 Nerf balls into the jar and put the lid on it. As she did, she began to grin, then to laugh. The contents of the jar now looked like the folds of the brain.

A vital part of the brain's evolutionary leap 250,000 years ago, the brain's folding gradually increased to the level we see today. As my daughter can now tell you, the brain's folding in on itself was an adaptation that gave early humans crucial advantages over other species in their environment. By increasing the potential for early humans to grow in intelligence and in their ability to learn, without compromising the body in other ways, brain folding gave us an evolutionary edge that improved our species' chances for survival.

Brain folding and the evolution of the new brain also gave humankind a potential for mental growth that we have barely tapped, even today. Present-day humans still have almost the same proportional brain mass as we did 250,000 to 300,000 years ago. Once we became a new species of humans with an enlarged new brain, we were no longer limited to traveling the long, linear evolutionary road that the rest of the planet's creatures had to follow. Clearly, however, our species as a whole is not using the full capacity of the new brain.

The Brain: Evolution's Time Capsule

If you want to trace the evolutionary development of humanity, a good place to start is at the very top. The brain serves as a kind of time capsule illustrating humankind's evolutionary development, and evolution has a long memory. We hold the entire course of our evolution inside our skull. If our brain were different today, the history of our species would be different as well.

According to research pioneered by Paul MacLean, M.D., the human brain has three formations, each with a different shape, size, chemistry, structure, and pattern of function that reflect our development during distinct eras. In essence, the human brain consists of three separate sub-brains. MacLean's research suggests that the three brains amount to three interconnected biological computers. Each possesses its own intelligence, its own individual subjectivity, its own sense of time and space, and its own memory, as well as other functions.[2]

The original names given to the three substructures were the *archipallium* (also referred to as the reptilian brain; the R-complex or reptilian complex; and the brainstem in conjunction with the cerebellum or hindbrain), the *paleopallium* (the midbrain, mammalian brain, or limbic brain), and the *neopallium* (the new brain, neocortex, cerebral cortex, or forebrain). For simplicity, we refer primarily to the brainstem and cerebellum together as the *first brain,* the midbrain as the *second brain,* and the neocortex as the *third brain* or *new brain.* At times, I use the different names assigned to each of our three brain systems interchangeably throughout the book. Look at Figure 4.1; this drawing is taken from MacLean's book, *The Triune Brain in Evolution.* You can compare it to the present-day human brain in Figure 3.7. Although each sub-brain does work independently, in humans the whole brain works together to make the sum greater than the parts.

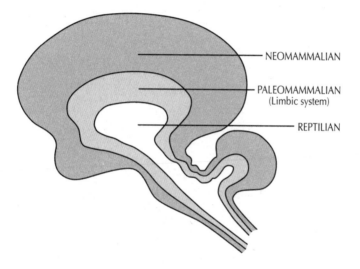

NEOMAMMALIAN

PALEOMAMMALIAN
(Limbic system)

REPTILIAN

Figure 4.1
The Triune Brain

The hierarchal order of these three brains tells us important information about our evolution and the brain's functions. First to evolve, more than 500 million years ago, was the *brainstem,* the junction where the spinal cord connects to the base of the brain. The most primitive brain area, it makes up the majority of brain matter in reptiles and lizards. Scientists of old called this the reptilian brain, because it resembles the entire brain of a reptile.

Attached directly behind the brainstem, the *cerebellum* evolved roughly 500 to 300 million years ago. This part of the first brain is responsible for coordination, *proprioception* (the unconscious perception of movement and spatial orientation), and body movement, both gross and fine. Recent studies suggest that the cerebellum performs additional functions. For example, the cerebellum is closely connected to the frontal lobe, the area of the neocortex responsible for intentional planning.[3] In addition, the cerebellum has been shown to play a dynamic role in complex emotional behaviors.[4] The neurons in the cerebellum are the most densely connected nerve cells in the entire brain. This heightened interconnectivity enables the cerebellum to control many functions without our having to impose our conscious awareness on them.

The midbrain appeared somewhere between 300 to 150 million years ago. This second brain is sometimes called the mammalian brain, because it is most highly evolved in mammals. Wrapping around the brainstem, the midbrain underwent its greatest increase in complexity and development in the last 3 million years and reached the height of its development about 250,000 years ago. This area is home to our involuntary, autonomic nervous system.

Finally, beginning about 3 million years ago, the new brain—with its most important component, the neocortex (*neo* means new or modified) or cerebral cortex—molded itself around the first two brains. That makes this outer shell (which looks like the skin of an orange) the most recent layer and the most advanced brain area to evolve in primates and humans. The seat of our conscious awareness, the new brain houses our free will, our thinking, and our capacity to learn, reason, and rationalize. Figure 4.2 is a cross section of the brain (ear to ear) demonstrating the thickness and size of the neocortex. The gray matter (neurons) as well as white matter (glial cells) of the third brain are also visualized.

The First Brain to Develop: The Brainstem and Cerebellum

The brainstem primarily supports the basic life functions, including the maintenance and control of heart rate and breathing. These life functions are common to all species of animals. The brainstem also has the job of regulating

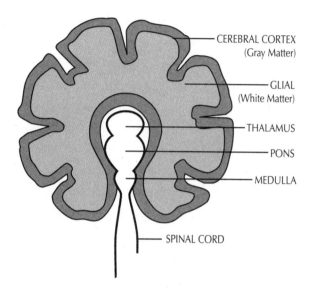

Figure 4.2
Ear-to-Ear Cross Section of the Brain

our various levels of wakefulness and sleep. Both wakefulness and levels of alertness are controlled by the brainstem to a greater extent than by the higher centers of the neocortex.

The cerebellum, or *little brain,* is also part of our first, or reptilian, brain. Its wrinkles and folds give it a distinct appearance. Relatively large compared to other brain structures, it is a three-lobed structure attached to the brainstem at the very back of the skull, underneath the hindmost area of the neocortex.

Recent functional brain scans reveal that the cerebellum is the brain's most active area.[5] Scientists believe the cerebellum is responsible for balance, coordination, proprioception, and the execution of controlled movements. In coordinating movement, the cerebellum performs both a motor (excitatory) function as well as a braking (inhibitory) function.

Certain types of simple actions and responses are learned, coordinated, memorized, and stored in the cerebellum. For example, once a person learns how to crochet, or even ride a bicycle, it requires very little conscious memory to perform this action. After a skill is learned and memorized—wired to the cerebellum—our body can perform the action automatically with very little conscious thought. Hardwired attitudes, emotional reactions, repeated actions, habits, conditioned behaviors, unconscious reflexes, and skills that we have mastered are all connected to and memorized in the cerebellum.

As we have learned, in the neocortex, the average number of connections per neuron is about 40,000. Remarkable as that is, in the cerebellum those neurons called *Purkinje's cells* process between 100,000 to 1 *million* connections per neuron. The cerebellum is the most densely packed area of gray matter in the brain. More than half of all the neurons that make up the human brain are contained in the cerebellum. In fact, the cerebellum is one of the few areas of the brain where brain cells continue to reproduce long after birth. Interestingly, when a baby is rocked or cuddled, impulses are directed to the cerebellum, which actually stimulates his development. This benefit of rocking continues until around age two.

The Second Brain to Develop: The Midbrain

The second brain area to evolve is called the midbrain, because the structures that make up this particular region are located directly in the middle of the brain. One of many terms for this area is the limbic system; *limbus* means forming a border around an edge or ring and pertains to something that is marginal or at a junction between structures. The term mammalian brain also applies, because this region is the most highly developed and specialized in mammals. Situated just above the brainstem, the midbrain in an adult human is about the size of an apricot. As a reminder, check out Figure 3.7 to examine the midbrain's location and size. Also see Figure 4.3, which illustrates and labels most of the brain regions related to our discussion in this chapter.

REGULATORY FUNCTIONS OF THE MIDBRAIN

Although the midbrain occupies only one-fifth of the volume of the brain, its influence on behavior is extensive, which is why it is also known as the *emotional brain*. The midbrain is sometimes called the *chemical brain* as well, because it is responsible for regulating many different internal states.

It is our midbrain that performs all those marvels that we usually take for granted, automatically maintaining and controlling body temperature, blood sugar levels, blood pressure, digestion, hormone levels, and innumerable other processes. The midbrain also adjusts and maintains our internal state to compensate for changes in our external world. Without the midbrain, our metabolism would be like that of a cold-blooded reptile because we could not maintain a sustained internal state to counter environmental temperature changes.

The Midbrain's Four Fs

In addition to these kinds of regulatory functions, the midbrain is responsible for what we can describe as the four Fs: fighting, fleeing, feeding, and fornicating.

Fight-or-flight. We know the midbrain's first two roles as our fight-or-flight response. As you'll recall from chapter 3, the autonomic nervous system originates in the midbrain and includes the sympathetic (fight-or-flight) nervous system, which kicks in when you feel threatened or scared. Imagine that you are taking the garbage out, and you see a bear in the bushes. The moment your neocortex (conscious brain) perceives the threat, this fear-producing external stimulus activates the autonomic nervous system. (In fact, we now know that certain parts of the midbrain sense the external threat even before you are conscious of it.) In turn, your autonomic nervous system automatically triggers your fight-or-flight response to prepare you for activity. This initiates a sequence of automatic internal events. An instant burst of adrenalin prepares your body to flee. Blood flow is directed away from your internal organs to your arms and legs, maximizing your ability to move so that you have the best odds of escaping.

In threatening situations, the midbrain controls your vital functions for preservation of life. These reflexive responses seem to be universal among all mammals because we all share that portion of the brain called the mammalian brain. In other words, when faced with fearful situations, human beings respond physiologically and biochemically almost exactly as would a rabbit or a dog.

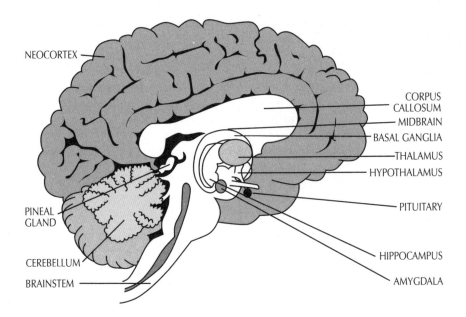

NEOCORTEX

CORPUS
CALLOSUM
MIDBRAIN
BASAL GANGLIA
THALAMUS
HYPOTHALAMUS

PITUITARY

PINEAL
GLAND

HIPPOCAMPUS

CEREBELLUM

AMYGDALA

BRAINSTEM

Figure 4.3

Overview of the Brain

The s*pinal cord* acts as a "fiberoptic" cable that conveys impulses from the brain to other parts of the body and relays messages from the body back to the brain.

The *brainstem* helps regulate primitive functions like breathing, swallowing, blood pressure, levels of wakefulness, and respiratory rate.

The *cerebellum* is responsible for balance, posture, and the body's position in space. It also coordinates movements and facilitates automatic hardwired memories and behaviors.

The *midbrain* acts as the chemical brain, where automatic internal regulation occurs and chemical balance is maintained. It also helps organize signals from the external world with our internal world.

The *thalamus* acts as a junction box to integrate all incoming sensory information (except smell) to various regions of our conscious thinking brain.

The *hippocampus* is responsible for formulating experiences with associated emotional memories, for processing vital information during learning, and for encoding long-term memories.

The *amygdala* works with the hippocampus to generate primary emotions from external perceptions and internal thoughts. It helps to emotionally charge experiences and to warn us about vital sensory information.

The *hypothalamus* chemically regulates the body's internal environment so that homeostasis is maintained. Conditions like body temperature, blood sugar levels, hormone levels, and emotional reactions are regulated here.

The *pituitary* gets its orders from the hypothalamus to secrete hormones in the form of peptides that circulate throughout the bloodstream and activate different glands, tissues, and organs in the body.

The *pineal gland* chemically regulates levels of sleep as well as cyclic rhythms of procreation and mating.

The *corpus callosum* is a band of fibers that connects the two hemispheres of the brain so that they can exchange information.

The *cerebral cortex* is the seat of our conscious awareness and is responsible for carrying our sophisticated functions like learning, remembering, creativity, invention, and voluntary behavior.

The midbrain is also intrinsically involved in emotional reactions that have to do with the survival of the physical body.

Feeding. When you sit down to have a meal, your parasympathetic nervous system relaxes you, conserves your energy, and prepares your body for digestion and metabolism.

Fornicating. If you're interested, when you engage in the fourth F, both the parasympathetic and the sympathetic components of your autonomic nervous system come into play. The former helps you get in the mood (you probably wouldn't feel too sexually aroused if that bear was chasing you), and the latter turns on when you have an orgasm.

To progress your understanding of the limbic brain a little more, let's add a couple more Fs and see how they all relate to the sympathetic and parasympathetic nervous systems. The sympathetic system has its own four Fs: fight, flight, fright, and fornicating (orgasm). The parasympathetic system is responsible for a few Fs as well: feeding, fixing (growth and repair), and fornicating (getting in the sexual state of mind). One system utilizes, releases, and mobilizes energy, while the other system conserves, builds, and stores energy.

STRUCTURES OF THE MIDBRAIN

The midbrain is primarily composed of the thalamus, hypothalamus, pituitary, pineal gland, hippocampus, amygdala, and basal ganglia.

Thalamus. The *thalamus* is the meeting point for almost all nerves that connect one part of the brain to another part of the brain, the body to the brain, and the brain to the body. The thalamus, the name of which is derived from the Greek word meaning "inner chamber," is the oldest and largest part of the midbrain. A collection of nerve cell nuclei that meet at a central junction point, it is made up of two distinct thalamic centers, one on each side of the midbrain. Think of the thalamus as a switchboard or air traffic control tower that can connect any part of the brain and the body. There is not one signal from the environment that does not pass through the thalamus. The sensory organs (ears, eyes, skin, tongue, nose) send messages to the thalamus, which relays them to their final destination in the neocortex/conscious brain.

At the same time, the thalamus can send signals to other areas of the brain so as to alert or inhibit different brain systems. In this way, the thalamus processes sensory information from the external world, identifies and sorts the input into the appropriate category, and transmits this data to the many conscious centers in the cerebral cortex. Depending on the nature of the sensory information or the type of stimulation from the environment, the data is then passed in many different directions throughout the brain (the midbrain, the brainstem, and so on) and body. The thalamus is also the relay system between the neocortex and the brainstem. Thus, this part of the midbrain allows the entire brain to receive a multitude of important data from the external world all at once, so that the brain can readily be introduced to vital information.

Hypothalamus. This area of the midbrain is a chemical factory that regulates your body's internal environment and balances your systems with the external world. The *hypothalamus* (which translates literally to "under the thalamus") is the most important and fascinating part of the midbrain, because it generates the chemical messengers for the entire body. The oldest part of the limbic system, it can affect any organ or tissue in the body.

Unlike the thalamus, which monitors external stimuli, the main job of the hypothalamus is to make chemicals called *neuropeptides* that keep the internal affairs of the body in balance with reference to the external world. The hypothalamus regulates many bodily functions necessary for survival through the process of *homeostasis,* the automatic self-righting mechanism that, like a thermostat, regulates and maintains the body's chemical balance and internal order. The hypothalamus controls and manages bodily functions such as appetite, thirst, sleep, wakefulness, blood sugar levels, body temperature, heart rate, blood pressure, chemical balance, hormonal balance, sex drive, immune system reactions, and metabolism. It also plays the most important role in your experience of emotions. This is the part of the brain that manufactures the chemicals that allow you to feel the way you were just thinking or how you were reacting.

Let's get back to our hypothetical survival situation, an encounter with a bear, to see how the thalamus and the hypothalamus would come into play. When your sensory organs pick up the sight and the sound of an approaching bear, those important messages are sent to the thalamus. The thalamus quickly orients your brain to the danger, ensuring that the warning sensory signals arrive throughout the entire brain nearly at the same time. The thalamus then coordinates your entire body for immediate action. It sends information to the neocortices (the higher conscious brain centers within the neocortex), which make decisions, plan actions, observe the surroundings for quick exits, and the like.

The thalamus also signals the hypothalamus to chemically prepare your fight-or-flight body functions, so that your body has the energy and resources to respond to the threat. For instance, the hypothalamus ensures that your legs are physiologically ready to run, jump, and turn quickly, based on the decision of the conscious brain. On the other hand, you don't need any blood flow to the digestive organs during this imminent threat, so the hypothalamus manages your body's internal state for action rather than for digestion—that is, for fighting and fleeing, but not for feeding (or fornicating).

Pituitary gland. The *pituitary gland* secretes chemicals that activate your body's hormones. Briefly, *glands* are organs or specialized groups of cells that separate certain elements from the blood and secrete them in a form the body can use or eliminate easily. *Hormones* are complex chemicals, produced in one part or organ of the body, that initiate or regulate the activity of an organ or group of cells in another part of the body. The different glandular tissues of the body that secrete various hormones are organs such as the adrenal glands, the thyroid gland, and the reproductive organs, to name a few.

The pituitary is often called the *master gland,* because it governs and controls many vital processes in the body. This pear-shaped gland, which hangs off the hypothalamus like a piece of fruit, helps in manufacturing most of the hormonal signals created by the hypothalamus to communicate with the body's major glands. The hypothalamus sends both chemical and electrical signals to the pituitary so that it can make certain chemicals that turn on various chemical/hormonal states.

Pineal gland. The *pineal gland,* a tiny, pine cone–shaped structure, sits in the back of the midbrain, above the cerebellum. (A common misconception is that, in humans, the pineal is embedded in the brain just above the eyes. Hence it has been termed our *third eye.*) The pineal chemically regulates our cycles of sleep and wakefulness. Think of the pineal gland as the brain's internal clock—it chemically controls patterns of sleep and wakefulness. Photoreceptors in the eyes sense levels of daylight or darkness, then transmit that information to the hypothalamus and, in turn, to the pineal gland. The pineal in humans (and in many other non-nocturnal mammals) then secretes different neurotransmitters that are directly influenced by the amount of light the eyes receive.

Two neurotransmitters are produced in the highest quantities in the human body by the pineal gland. *Serotonin,* the so-called daytime neurotransmitter, prepares the brain to be awake during the hours of daylight. *Melatonin,* the nighttime neurotransmitter, prepares the body to experience restorative sleep during the hours of darkness and plays a role in causing the brain to dream. Thus, if you are reading this book late at night and experiencing sleepiness, the reason (I sincerely hope) is biological. The fact that your eyes' photoreceptors are no longer sensing daylight prompts your pineal gland to transmute serotonin into melatonin.

ANIMALS AND THE PINEAL GLAND

Unlike its embedded location in humans and other primates, the pineal gland sits close to the surface of the skull in many lower life forms, including amphibians, reptiles, fish, birds, and certain mammals. This placement enables the pineal gland to sense the changing amounts of sunlight and darkness that these animals are exposed to during different times of the year, as well as different times of the day.

Thus in many animal species, the pineal directly influences biological cycles that are dependent on the changing seasons, such as migratory patterns, circadian rhythms, reproductive cycles, seasonal bearing of offspring, and even mating rituals.

How does the pineal gland prompt animals to birth their young at certain times of the year? Take, for example, animals that hibernate during the winter, such as bears. During the darker winter months, their pineal glands secrete more of the nighttime neurotransmitter, melatonin, into the bloodstream and the fluid of the brain. Some of this melatonin is absorbed by the pituitary gland. The pituitary responds by producing neurohormones that suppress the activity of the sex organs, decreasing the animals' drive to procreate.

The pineal gland also alters melatonin into a neurohormone called 5-methoxytryptamine, which eliminates sex drive and decreases appetite in some species of hibernating mammals. Their altered brain chemistry also produces a slowdown in metabolic and other body functions, which causes them to sleep throughout the winter.

When spring brings the stimulation of increasing light levels, this heightens production of serotonin and other neurotransmitters, prompting these animals to once again become sexually active and have an increased appetite. As a result, they deliver and raise their offspring during the warmer months, when food supply and other environmental conditions favor their survival.

Hippocampus. The *hippocampus* makes long-term memories. It gets its name from the Greek word for seahorse, which this brain region resembles. We learn from new experiences and form memories thanks to this area of the midbrain.

A sort of clearinghouse for memory, the hippocampus classifies incoming information as having either short-term or long-term importance, and files it accordingly. Memories that move into short-term storage pertain to information that we need immediately but can then forget. Shopping lists, phone numbers that we will call only once, and directions that we will probably never need again are good examples of information that is stored in short-term memory.

In long-term memory, the hippocampus stores information that we may need to access repetitively or at will in the future. Obvious examples are our address, our spouse's name, what type of car we own, and so on. At our annual office party, we may meet numerous people whose names we won't need to remember tomorrow, but it would be wise to store the name of our employer's spouse in long-term memory. The hippocampus stores long-term memories that are involved mostly with our experiences, based on the various types of information our five senses provide.

The type of memory encoding that takes place in the hippocampus is called *associative learning* or *associative memory*. For example, imagine that a child throws rocks at a beehive, and then has the novel experience of receiving multiple stings. In the future, the child will associate bee-provoking behavior, such as rock-throwing, with the sight of the agitated bees pouring out of the hive, the sound of their angry buzzing, the place he stood when he was repeatedly stung, and the feel of those painful stings. The hippocampus will facilitate storage of this sensory information as long-term memory throughout different regions of the neocortex, so that the experience can be encoded as wisdom. With any luck, this child won't have to repeat the experience to make the message clear. The evolution of the hippocampus has permitted many species to repeat behaviors that improve their chances of survival and to avoid repeating actions that threaten their survival.

Let's explore how the hippocampus accomplishes this feat. It keeps a log of facts associated with people, places, things, time, and events. Humans tend to remember experiences better when they are somehow connected to one of these items. The hippocampus creates a memory of personal events associated with things that happen to us at a particular time and place.[6] In this example, people might be the neighbor whose hobby is beekeeping; the place might be the neighbor's property; things might include the rocks the child threw, the bees, and beehives; the time could be a midsummer day; and events would certainly include the throwing of the rocks, the consequence of being stung, and perhaps any subsequent first-aid treatment.

Whenever we have a new experience, the hippocampus, through the combination of all our senses (seeing, smelling, tasting, feeling, hearing), allows us to create a new memory. By connecting all this incoming sensory information, the hippocampus will associate a person with a thing, a place with a time, a person with an event, and so on. The child in our example will file his experience into long-term memory by associating the neighbor (people) with bees (things), beehives (things) with the first-aid lotion his mother applied (smell), the neighbor's property (place) with the experience of getting stung (event), the pain of the stings (feeling) with rocks (things), and so on. Later on, experiencing one of these elements again (smelling the first-aid lotion, for example) will trigger a flood of memories of this experience. But this happens only after about age four. The reason we cannot remember many conscious memories as a very young child is that the hippocampus is not fully developed until after we are four years old.

Associative memories allow us to use what we already know in order to understand or learn what we don't know; in other words, to use what is familiar to us to understand something that is unfamiliar. These memories are the building blocks for us to arrive at greater understandings. When we take new information relating to people, places, things, time, and events and we *associate* this information with our log of past events that we have already experienced through our five senses, we build an associative memory.

One primary function of the hippocampus is closely related to our search for novelty. This is the part of the brain that is responsible for making unknowns, known. For example, if the hippocampus is destroyed in laboratory animals, and then they are given the opportunity to explore new environments, they will ignore unfamiliar areas and return repeatedly to familiar areas of their cage. In fact, new research suggests that our ideas about what motivates learning may not be very accurate. Some scientists are reevaluating their long-held models involving conditioned behavior, in which reward or punishment (pleasure or pain) appeared to provide inducements for animals to learn. Perhaps the animals in such studies, rather than learning, were being trained. Many studies involving the hippocampus suggest that for several different animal species, learning new things is a reward in itself.[7]

Amygdala. The *amygdala,* which means "almond-shaped," is a structure of the midbrain that is responsible for alerting the body in survival situations. It also stores the four highly charged primitive emotions: aggression, joy, sadness, and fear. The amygdala also helps to attach different emotional charges to our long-term memories.

When a life-threatening situation exists, the amygdala gives a rapid, action-oriented assessment of the external environment. It is the most important fear-generating region of the brain. In fact, the amygdala is the part of the midbrain that activates the body to respond even before you are consciously aware of the danger, so we sometimes call this a *precognitive response.* This is why the amygdala is so important for the survival of our species, as well as many animals. It processes incoming sensory information that is vital to survival in a crisis situation and instantaneously alerts the body, bypassing other circuits.

For example, imagine that you are riding your bicycle in the park while listening to your MP3 player, mesmerized by a melody. In an instant, a young child darts out of the bushes and begins to cross your path, right in front of the bike. Your amygdala receives vital information that bypasses your neocortex, causing you to hit your brakes even before you are conscious of your actions. This enhanced precognitive reaction may make the difference between life and death. Because the midbrain is a more primitive area than the neocortex, it makes sense that this mechanism was probably hardwired into our species millions of years ago, long before the development of our newer thinking, reasoning neocortex.

When activated, the amygdala also creates emotions of rage and aggression to help us protect ourselves in potentially threatening situations. Thus, a mother will aggressively defend her offspring or risk her life in any harmful situation, even though the odds are against her.

Recent studies also indicate that the amygdala is associated with the storage of emotional memories and with the perception of certain situations based on those memories. The amygdala brands survival situations as emotionally fearful, so that memories of threatening circumstances can help us avoid similar situations. In humans, highly charged emotional experiences involving anger, fear, sadness, and even joy are encoded by the amygdala for long-term memory. However, the amygdala does not assign any specific region of nerve cells to store memories of these primitive hardwired feelings in order to create or facilitate memory of any single, specific emotion. Researchers cannot point to a particular region of the brain and say that it is where sadness, for example, resides. Similarly, studies involving primates have found no specific areas of the amygdala that produce joy, sadness, rage, or fear.

In an intriguing new study, scientists at the University of Wales worked with a blind patient who seems to possess a sixth sense that allows him to recognize sad, angry, or happy faces. Patient X, age 52, cannot see after having two different strokes, which damaged the brain areas that process visual signals. However, brain scans reveal that when he looks at faces expressing emotion, another part of his brain besides the visual cortex is activated—the amygdala. This small structure responds to nonverbal facial signs (or memories) depicting anger and fear.[8]

Dr. Alan Pegna, in the School of Psychology at the University of Wales, Bangor, headed the research team with colleagues in north Wales and at Geneva University Hospital. They found that Patient X was unable to identify shapes like circles and squares. Furthermore, he could not identify the sex of "deadpan" male and female faces, nor tell the difference between "normal" and jumbled faces. But when the subject was asked to identify the emotions of an angry or happy human face, he accurately did so 59 percent of the time. (Most blindfolded subjects in this type of test are usually successful 50 percent of the time, give or take a percentage point.) This success rate is statistically quite a bit higher than what would be expected by chance, and it consistently applied as well when he was asked to distinguish between sad and happy, or fearful and happy, faces.

From this experiment, the researchers concluded that emotions displayed on a human face are registered not in the visual cortex but in the right amygdala, which sits deep within the brain's temporal lobe. "This discovery is . . . interesting for behavioral scientists as the right amygdala has been associated with subliminal processing of emotional stimuli in clinically healthy individuals," said Dr. Pegna. "What Patient X has assisted us with establishing is that this area undoubtedly processes visual facial signals connected with all types of emotional facial expressions."[9] Having memory stored in this area of the brain, which also triggers instantaneous responses, could explain much about the sensitivity of some individuals.

Basal ganglia. The *basal ganglia* integrate thoughts and feelings with physical actions. Basal ganglia are intricate bundles of neurological networks that are interconnected with the neocortex; they are situated in each hemisphere of the midbrain, directly under the neocortex and above the midbrain's deeper structures.

To illustrate how the basal ganglia function, recall a time when you were learning a skill that involved muscle movements, such as riding a bike. In the beginning, you had to think consciously about what you were doing. Every time you practiced, you reinforced neural circuits in your brain that relayed commands to your body relating to balance, coordination, and so on. After much repetition, these neural networks became hardwired, and your movements in pedaling the bike and keeping your balance became automatic.

At that point, your basal ganglia, along with your cerebellum, took over the coordination of those automatic movements. As you rode, the basal ganglia received sensory information from your environment via the neocortices, plus commands from your neocortex to move your muscles and orchestrate your actions. Your basal ganglia integrated your thoughts and feelings with your physical actions, smoothed out your fine motor movements, and suppressed your body from making random, involuntary movements. In addition to that role, the basal ganglia allows us to control our impulses, to set our idle speed for anxiety, and to contribute to our feelings of pleasure and ecstasy.

To get a clearer picture of the important roles basal ganglia play, consider what can happen when they malfunction. In people with Tourette's syndrome, the basal ganglia fire improperly and fail to coordinate their thoughts and feelings with their actions. These people often lose inhibitory control over their impulses, feel overly anxious, and display uncontrolled behaviors such as erratic motions, twitches, eye blinks, head jerks, and so on.

At one time or another, most of us have been in a situation in which our basal ganglia receive so much input from the neocortex that the threshold of electrochemical charge is too high for the basal ganglia to process. When this happens, the stimulus causes the basal ganglia to act like a breaker in a fuse box and throw the main circuit, so to speak, putting the body into a temporary state of disruption. For example, when we are scared, we may freeze; when we are embarrassed or intimidated, we sometimes become speechless; when we try to speak with someone we find very attractive, our mind occasionally goes blank. (Not that I know any of this from personal experience, I'm just saying . . .)

Just as some cars idle faster than others, some people have overactive basal ganglia. These people are frequently anxious or nervous. Without good cause, they constantly evaluate their environments, anticipate risks, and prepare for potential danger. Their basal ganglia operate in a heightened state—not high enough to throw the body's circuit breaker, but higher than seen in most people. As a result, these people tend to be easily overwhelmed by minor stresses in their lives.

On the other hand, according to the latest functional brain scans, so-called doers usually have basal ganglia that function at a *slightly* more active level than in most people. Their increased basal ganglia activity does what it is supposed to— it processes thought and emotion into immediate action—but *doing* becomes the means for these people to keep their basal ganglia from reaching overload. The increased activity of their basal ganglia produces excess energy, which they release by taking action. If they stop doing, they can experience an energy overload, and the byproduct is nervous anxiety. A simple example of this is when we are sitting with a group of people and someone cannot stop bouncing his leg up and down—his basal ganglia is slightly overactive and is discharging anxious energy.[10]

The Third and Most Recent Brain to Evolve: The Neocortex

The neocortex is the seat of our awareness and of our creativity as a species. It is our thinking, reasoning brain that allows us to learn and remember everything that we experience from our external world, and then modify our actions to do something better, or different, or to repeat an action the next time, if it had a positive result.

When our brain is actively performing one of the so-called higher functions—reasoning, planning, intellectualizing, learning, remembering, creating, analyzing, verbally communicating, among a host of others—our neocortex is at work. Without the neocortex, our senses would still be able to alert us to the fact that we are cold, but we could not proceed further. The neocortex is what allows you to interpret the sensation of being cold and choose among multiple options—remain cold, close the window, put on a sweater (and choose from among a number of sweater options), or turn up the thermostat—and your neocortex would also remember a time you camped in the winter at Mt. Rainier National Park and nearly got frostbite.

HOW DO MALE AND FEMALE BRAINS COMPARE?

Generally, the male brain is larger than the female brain by more than 100 cubic centimeters, about the size of a small lemon. Does this difference have direct cognitive effects? Not necessarily. Although there is still a gender difference in brain volume after scientists compensate for body size, studies attribute some of the variation to an individual's physical dimensions. In a very specific MRI study, which paid equal attention to both brain and body size para-meters, Michael Peters and associates, at the University of Guelph, Ontario, Canada, showed that the difference in brain volume between the sexes dropped by two-thirds after height was included as an additional covariant.[11]

Differences in brain volume between the sexes are distributed quite evenly throughout the major lobes of the brain. The propor-tions of the four major lobes of the neocortex are similar. In both sexes, the frontal lobe comprises about 38 percent of the neocortex (ranging from 36 to 43 percent); the parietal lobe, 25 percent (21 to 28 percent); the temporal lobe, 22 percent (19 to 24 percent); and the occipital lobe encompasses about 9 percent (ranging from 7 to 12 percent) of the neocortex.

This means that there is no sex-specific brain region that con-tributes to an additional share in total brain volume, and that it will be difficult to find a functional sex difference that correlates with dif-ferences in total brain volume. In simple terms, if we were to look at the brains of two individuals, one male and the other female, we would not be able to tell them apart, aside from the size difference, because male and female brains share similar proportions.

In terms of differences between males and females, the brain structure that has probably drawn the most attention over the years is the *corpus callosum*. This band of white matter connects the right and left hemispheres, and some early research suggested that it might be larger in women than in men. When that was first suggested in the early 1980s, many scientists speculated that the larger band in women meant that females had a greater degree of communication between the two hemispheres. This idea seemed to support the myth that in women, the emotional right side of the brain and the analytical left side were more connected and integrated with each other.

It is now known that women do not have a larger corpus callosum than men do. The corpus callosum is actually about 10 percent larger in men than in women, probably because men have larger brains due to their larger body size. There is no substantial anatomical evidence for greater functional connectivity between the hemispheres (as the stereotype would have it) in either men or women.

The source of this myth may be that the corpus callosum does account for a significantly greater percentage of the total white matter in women (2.4 percent in females versus 2.2 percent in males). This fact just might mean that women are able to process the two types of thoughts (emotional and analytical) between the two hemispheres of the brain a lot *faster* than men. If the greater distribution of total fatty *myelin,* or white matter, in the female corpus callosum does account for speedier neurological transmission between the brain hemispheres, this may explain why men are often dumbfounded when observing women's problem-solving abilities in action.

Evolution's most sophisticated achievement to date, as we discussed earlier, the new brain appeared when mammals began their climb up the ladder of evolution. Highly developed in mammals, the new brain reached its greatest level of complexity in humans. Since our new brain is proportionately larger and more complex than that of any other species—comprising two-thirds of our total brain area—it affords us unique characteristics that distinguish us from reptiles, other mammals, and fellow primates.

For the sake of simplicity, I will describe the new brain as having an *inner,* supporting layer, and an *outer* layer. The inner layer of the brain is like the meat of an orange, while the outer layer, called the cortex, is like the rind or skin of the orange. The word *cortex* literally means "bark." As discussed, most of the brain is structured in convoluted folds rather than simple layers. But as my purpose is to build a mental model for understanding the brain, I will occasionally overlook some of the brain's complexities.

Wrapping around the midbrain is that portion of the new brain called the *white matter,* made mostly of nerve fibers insulated by fatty myelin sheathes, as well as *glial cells,* which are neural cells that primarily have a connective tissue supporting function in the central nervous system (see chapter 3). Several types of glial cells exist, performing different functions in the various components of the nervous system. The most important thing to remember about glial cells is that they help facilitate the forming of synaptic connections; that may explain their large numbers. In other words, every time you learn something new and make a new synaptic connection in the brain, a specific type of glial cell called an *astrocyte* is always present, helping with the process. Every neuron has the possibility of making an incredible number of connections to other neurons, and nature may have provided humans with an abundance of glial cells to facilitate so many potential synaptic connections. Researchers have found evidence that glial cells have their own independent communication system, separate from neurons.[12]

The part of the new brain that we will refer to most often is the outer layer, the neocortex or *cerebral cortex,* also called our gray matter. Although it is only about 3 to 5 millimeters thick ($\frac{1}{7}$ to $\frac{1}{4}$ of an inch), this layer is so rich in neurons that, aside from the cerebellum, the neocortex has more nerve cells than any other brain structure.

Like the midbrain, the neocortex is composed of several parts.

THE CORPUS CALLOSUM

The *corpus callosum* is a "fiberoptic" bridge comprised of hundreds of millions of neurons that connect the two hemispheres of the new brain.

As most people are aware, the new brain is divided anatomically into two distinct sections that mirror each other in some degree of anatomical symmetry. If you drew an imaginary line from the middle of the forehead over the top of the head to the center of the base of the skull, you would be dividing the new brain into its two halves. These are commonly known as the left and the right *cerebral hemispheres.* These twin neocortices literally encapsulate the midbrain and the brainstem. Each hemisphere is responsible for controlling the opposite side of the body.

The cerebral hemispheres are not completely separate structures. This thick band of nerve fibers called the *corpus callosum* joins the two halves of the new brain. Figure 4.4 provides a view of the corpus callosum. The corpus callosum is the largest fibrous pathway of neurons in the entire body, totaling approximately 300 million nerve fibers. This large band of white matter possesses the greatest number of nerve bundles anywhere in the brain or the body. Scientists postulate that the corpus callosum evolved along with the new brain, so that its two separate houses could communicate with each other through this bridge. Nerve impulses constantly travel back and forth across the corpus callosum, giving our new brain the specialized ability to observe the world from two different points of view.

The Four Neocortical Lobes

The two cerebral hemispheres are further subdivided into four separate regions known as *lobes*. Thus as part of the neocortex, we have two frontal lobes,

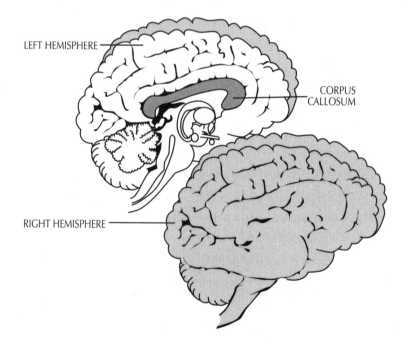

Figure 4.4
The corpus callosum and how it connects the two hemispheres of the neocortex.

two parietal lobes, two temporal lobes, and two occipital lobes. Each of these areas processes different sensory information, motor abilities, and mental functions and is assigned to perform different tasks.

In general, the *frontal lobes* are responsible for intentional action as well as for focusing our attention, and they coordinate nearly all the functions in the rest of the brain (the motor cortex and language center are part of the frontal lobe). The *parietal lobes* deal with sensations related to touch and feeling (sensory perception), visual-spatial tasks, and body orientation, and they also coordinate some language functions. The *temporal lobes* process sounds, perception, learning, language, and memory, and they are the centers that process smell. This lobe also includes a region that facilitates our ability to choose which thoughts to express. The *occipital lobes* manage visual information and are often called the *visual cortex*. Take a minute, if you will, to examine the four lobes of the cerebral cortex in Figure 4.5.

For purposes of building our understanding in a logical way, I'm going to go out of sequence here, and describe the parietal, temporal, and occipital lobes first, then conclude with the most recent achievement of our evolution, the frontal lobes.

The parietal lobes. The parietal lobes are located just above each ear, and they extend to the top center of the head, reaching the midline of the brain. This is the *feeling/sensing* region of the cortex. The parietal lobes process what we feel with our hands and with our bodies, also called tactile and somatosensory perceptions. *Somatosensory* by definition is the information we receive from the body (somato) that we feel (sensory) in the brain. Features such as pressure, temperature, vibration, pain, pleasure, light touch, two-point discrimination, and even the awareness of where our body parts are located without looking at them (proprioception) are all integrated in the somatosensory cortex of the parietal lobes.

The parietal lobes process information from the body received by our peripheral nerves, mainly from our external environment and to a lesser degree from our internal environment. Remember, peripheral nerves are those long nerves that act like communication wires, transmitting information from the

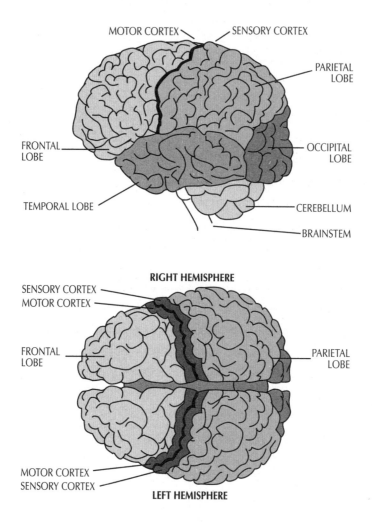

Figure 4.5
A side and top view of the different lobes of the neocortex.

brain to the body and from the body to the brain. In particular, we are discussing the peripheral nerves that are sensory in nature, which receive and process billions of bits of information every second, from all areas of our body, and send it to the brain. These peripheral nerves converge from different areas of the body (hands, arms, legs, toes, feet, lips, tongue), and then connect to the spinal cord, which is the "fiberoptic" cable that passes all the incoming information to the brain—specifically, the somatosensory cortex.

When you have a rock in your shoe, feel a warm breeze on your face, receive a relaxing massage, or have a stomachache, it is the parietal lobe that gathers all that sensory information and determines how it feels and what you should do about it. First, this lobe interprets what type of stimulus it is receiving. Then, it evaluates how a stimulus feels—whether you like it or whether it is a threat to the body. The somatosensory cortex is the region that primarily gauges how you consciously feel under different environmental conditions. Once the sensory cortex processes the information, other regions such as the frontal lobe take over to carry out the brain's primary goal—taking care of the body's survival and maintenance.

Here is an example. The subtlety of a fly landing on your arm instantly catches your attention. The sensory receptors of the arm send an immediate message along the peripheral nerves to the spine, entering through the cervical vertebrae and on to the somatosensory cortex in the side of the brain opposite to the arm. Once your brain interprets the stimulus, the message is then forwarded to the frontal lobe, where it is processed for motor responses. At this point, the whole brain may or may not be involved. You may respond automatically by using your motor cortex to move your arm, shooing the fly away. Or you might think for a moment what to do. Maybe you'll get up, look for some ice cream in the freezer, and get the flyswatter.

The parietal lobes are subdivided and organized into several areas that relate to different regions of sensory experience in the body. Every inch of the body's surface area has a corresponding point on this somewhat narrow slice of cortical neurons. The somatosensory area is like a map of individual clusters of neurons that are somewhat compartmentalized into specific sensory regions that relate to different parts of the body.

In the mid 1900s, a few scientists were learning about how to map these regions by studying animals. Researchers used touch to stimulate different parts of their bodies, identifying the activated neurons in the brain corresponding with the particular region of the body being touched. The initial work using animals to explore the sensory cortex was performed on rats and monkeys by Vernon Mountcastle at Johns Hopkins University.

In humans, these particular sensory areas of the parietal lobes are classically known as the *representation zones,* named during this same period by Canadian neurosurgeon Wilder Penfield.[13] Penfield conducted several experiments using human subjects to determine the precise sensory correlations between particular parts of the brain and specific areas of the body. While performing brain surgery on conscious human patients under local anesthesia, Penfield used a tiny electrode to stimulate different regions of the somatosensory cortex. As he excited the exposed surface of their cortex, he asked the patients what they were feeling. In every case the patients were quick to report particular sensations in the hands, fingers, feet, lips, face, and tongue as well as other body parts. In this fashion, Penfield was able to explore and name the regions of sensory input within the somatosensory cortex.

As Penfield discovered, the entire body surface is outlined or laid out along the sensory cortex in humans and all mammals. There are regions specified for the lips, hands, feet, tongue, genitalia, face, fingers, and so on. In humans, this area has been affectionately called the *homunculus* or "little person." Figure 4.6 shows the homunculus and it illustrates how somatosensory feelings are mapped in the human brain.

Curiously, however, the body as mapped in the sensory cortex looks nothing like an actual human body. Not only is this map peculiarly compartmentalized, but it is also not in direct correlation to the anatomical layout and proportions of the human body. For example, the representation zone for the face is located next to the hand and fingers. Penfield also discovered that the feet are neighbors to the genitals. In the cortex, the tongue area exists outside the mouth area, under the chin. At that time he had no idea why the cortical map is so structurally odd.

Presently, there are two working models that, together, explain this obscure presentation.[14] The first model pertains to the locations of the representation zones. During prenatal growth, the fetus has its arms bent so that the hands are touching the face, and its legs are folded so that the feet are touching its

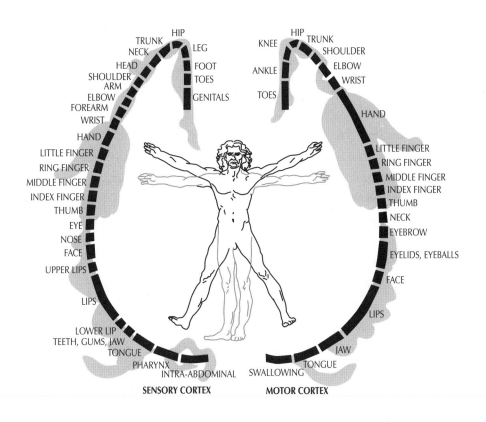

Figure 4.6

An ear-to-ear slice of the neocortex demonstrating a view of both the sensory and motor cortices. The shaded areas are the representation zones that illustrate how the entire body is mapped as a little distorted man called the *homunculus.*

genitalia. Developmentally, the recurring contact in utero between these body parts might produce repetitive firing of sensory neurons within different regions in the developing cortex. This sensory activation of the cortical neurons might trick the parietal lobe into organizing its sensory regions as if these body parts are side by side, when they are merely in constant contact. Thus the first impressions of cortical mapping may lay the foundation for where different sensory regions will ultimately exist within the somatosensory template.

The second working model may explain distortions in the size of individual sensory areas, as compared to normal human anatomy. According to the sensory map, the "little person" lying along the sensory cortex has a huge face with large lips, big hands and fingers with extra-large thumbs, and oversized sexual organs. What is the explanation for this? We can look to these oversized areas of the cortical map for the answer. When I was a child and felt sick, my mother accurately gauged my body temperature by putting her lips on my forehead. This makes sense since human lips are so highly specialized; they possess numerous, densely packed sensory receptors. Similarly, the neurons sensitive to touch on the fingertip of the index finger are 15 times as dense as the touch-sensitive receptors on the leg. There is an immense amount of sensory receptors in the genitals of human beings.

During evolution, the acute sensitivity of our lips, tongue, hands, and sexual organs has been crucial to supporting the survival of our species. In humans, not only are more sensory receptors located in these parts of the body, but additional territory is allocated to them in the brain. The amount of cortical tissue designated to a specific body part reflects not the size of that particular part of the body, but its sensitivity. In simple terms, larger regions are mapped in the sensory cortex because we feel more with those parts of the body. As a result, the body parts of the homunculus appear in a hierarchal order that is directly proportional to how specialized each area of the body is, with regard to sensation, and how much we use that body part to feel.

The same principle holds true for other mammals. In cats, the sensory cortex is regionalized differently than in humans. A feline has a huge cortical area mapped for its nose and whiskers, because those structural organs are associated with its primary means of information processing. Therefore the cat, which explores the world primarily with its nose and whiskers, will have a "catunculus"—a different map of the somatosensory cortex than our human one.

So, the areas of the human body having the densest amount of sensory nerves will have larger real estate in the somatosensory cortex. That is why, comparatively, more territory in the sensory cortex is assigned to the lips than to the back, and more cortical space is designated to the fingers than the entire leg.

Thus, you can better tune your brain into feeling with your hands, lips, and fingers than with other body parts.

Here, too, is a clear demonstration as to why we humans are so driven by sexuality. The map of the feeling body in the sensory cortex of the brain has more real estate devoted to the genitalia than to the entire surface of the chest, abdomen, back, shoulders, and arms put together. We are literally mapped for procreation to ensure the propagation of our species. Interestingly, when epileptic seizures originate in these areas of the sensory cortex, they are usually preceded by intense sexual sensations.

What is most important to remember at this point is that an entire map of how the body feels can be charted in the sensory cortex of the brain, specifically in the somatosensory areas located in the parietal lobes.

The temporal lobes. The temporal lobes are just under the surface of and slightly above each ear. They are responsible for auditory perception—that is, how we process what we hear. The auditory lobes are primarily positioned in this quadrant to process all types of sounds. Within these lobes there seem to be thousands of colonies of neurons related to specific aspects of how we process sounds. Because what we hear is so intricately tied to language, we will define *language* as a series of specific sounds that are produced for intentional communication, and then comprehensively understood. In other words, what arrives at your ears is a stream of continuous sounds carrying an intention or meaning that is called language.

The eardrum vibrates as a result of sound waves hitting it, which produce electrical signals that travel along the auditory nerve to individual compartments in the temporal lobes. The temporal lobes deal with language comprehension, decoding sound into meaning. This trait is assigned mostly to the diversified regions on the left side of the neocortex, unless we are learning a new word or sound or language, and then it is the right temporal lobe that takes over.

There are different clusters of neurons in the auditory cortex that apply to every single *phoneme,* or minimal unit of sound that we use to interpret language. For example, when we hear the sounds *baah, moo,* or *su,* individual modules or compartments within the auditory complex are assigned to process these specialized sounds. As human infants develop through interactions with the environment, different noises that we hear are stored as geographically mapped patterns of diversified sounds, ready for us to access and to process as language. The infant's brain is also busy pruning away unnecessary synaptic connections, to make meaning out of sounds from its environment.

Our brains are nonlinear enough that when we hear a series of sounds, we can immediately understand what is being verbally communicated. Remarkably, as electrical signals from the eardrum activate multiple clusters of neurons in the temporal lobes to fire simultaneously, the combination and sequence, as well as locations of these neural circuits, allow us to gain meaning from the auditory stimuli. There are hundreds of neuron clusters within specific compartments in the temporal lobes that are doing this as we listen to music, watch television, have a conversation at dinner, and even talk to ourselves, out loud or internally.

The temporal lobes are intricately involved in storage of some types of memory and facilitate the making of long-term memories. As we know, this takes place through the hippocampus. When there is damage to both the temporal lobes and the hippocampus, many people cannot form new memories. Scientists who experiment on the temporal lobes using low-voltage electrical stimuli have reported that their subjects experience immediate sensations of *déjà vu* (an uncanny sense of familiarity and memory), *jamais vu* (a feeling that a familiar person or place is unfamiliar), heightened spontaneous emotions, and/or strange spiritual reveries or insights.

The temporal lobes also have a visual association center that links what we see to our emotions and memories. It is the storehouse of many of our visual emotional memories. Once we see something in the external world, our brain uses this association area to process what we see with what we remember and how it may feel emotionally. In other words, the temporal lobes process visual symbols with meaningful feelings.

When this part of the temporal lobes is electrically stimulated, subjects report vivid visual imagery, equally as real to them as their external surroundings. We use the stored database of the temporal lobes when we associate what we know to better understand what we are attempting to learn that is new and unknown. The temporal lobes also help us recognize familiar stimuli that we have already experienced.

For example, let's say I told you that a special type of white blood cell chases and attacks foreign agents, and then ingests them just like a little Pac-Man (if you can remember the old video game from the 1980s). The visual association center in your temporal lobes would bring up the visual memory of the Pac-Man video game, so that you could identify this new concept with what you already have stored in your brain as memory. It would flash pictures representing your accumulated memories of those little munching Pac-Man creatures, and then assemble a three-dimensional memory to help you understand the new idea about white blood cells. Most of the millions of learned associations that you have experienced in your lifetime are stored in the temporal lobes' association cortex, to be activated as needed.

Thus, the temporal lobes are responsible for language, hearing (processing sounds), conceptual thinking, and associative memories. The temporal lobes associate most of what we have learned and experienced via our senses throughout our lifetime to people, places, things, time, and past events in the form of memories. We can associate what we hear, see, feel, taste, and smell, and it is the temporal lobes that facilitate this skill.

The occipital lobes. The occipital lobes are the vision centers. The *visual cortex,* as it is sometimes described, has six distinct regions that process data from the outside world in order for us to see coherently. This complexity stands to reason, because vision is the sense that human beings rely on the most in order to function in the world.

If we were to start at the very back of the brain at the occipital lobe and slice it with a knife like a loaf of bread six times to the temporal lobe, this would give us a good idea of how the visual cortex is organized. These regions are functionally separated so as to process different sensory data about what and how the brain is seeing. Six distinct layers are allocated to interpret visual qualities like light, movement, form, shape, depth, and color.

The *primary visual cortex* (V1) is the first slice of brain tissue located farthest back in the brain. This area of the visual cortex encounters visual information that our eyes see and we consciously process. V1 is organized in such a way that nerve cells are divided up to process different parts of a whole picture. Therefore, when only one small area of V1 is damaged, we have a visual blind spot, because the nonfunctioning neurons cannot process their part of the picture. When this area is completely damaged, normal sight as we know it is lost. Amazingly, when scientists began studying individuals who were blind in the V1 area, these subjects not only perceived movement, but could also perceive the shape of an object.

A completely different area of the visual cortex is organized to exclusively process movement (V5). The nerve cells in this area cannot detect a stationary object; they are stimulated only when an object moves across one's visual field. These cells were discovered when blind people were found to be able to see movements. The first subjects who were ever recorded as having an ability to perceive moving objects without seeing them were soldiers in World War II. Some soldiers who had lost their sight from combat injuries could still dodge grenades and rockets, even though they could not consciously see them. This phenomenon was appropriately termed *blindsight*.[15]

Distinct geographical locations within the visual cortex process other aspects of sight. Some clusters of neurons perceive only color. Generalized forms and edges are perceived in one area, while specific shapes and patterns (such as the shape of a hand) are recognized in another neural region. Still other nerve cells respond to depth perception, angles, and dimension.

As visual information passes from the eyes to the occipital lobe, it is processed in a cascade of nerve reactions from the back of the brain to the front, through these six different regions. This is why a blindsighted person could still interpret reality through his visual field. The information that made it to his primary visual cortex was passed to the adjacent areas, which were activated for further processing. Thus while he could not consciously see an object, he could perceive movement, shape, the direction from whence the object came, and other aspects of vision.

When visual stimuli are all integrated, a picture appears as a "hologram" of what we are seeing. How does this take place? As sensory information is transmitted through the different regions of the visual cortex, there is a hierarchy of data processing, layer by layer. By the time the information has passed through these layers of specialized neurons, which make sense out of light, movement, form, shape, depth, and color, a continuous picture has been created. This image is then distributed to the appropriate associated areas of the brain's temporal lobe, which participate with the visual cortex to make meaning out of the incoming data.

The frontal lobes. If you are asked, "Where do you, as a conscious being, think, dream, feel, focus, concentrate, and imagine?" you will most likely point to the area on your forehead just above the bridge of your nose—the frontal lobe.

The frontal lobe is the resting place of conscious awareness. When we are the most conscious and the most aware, our frontal lobe is at the height of activity. Although the visual cortex, the temporal lobes, and the parietal lobes can serve to create a picture, a concept, or an idea, it is the frontal lobe that willfully keeps an idea on our mind, calling it to the stage for an extended review.

The frontal lobe is also where self-awareness is born. The most highly evolved area in the brain, it is the place where the self can express itself. Because of the frontal lobe, we break from the outmoded view that a human being is merely the byproduct of accumulated sensory experiences. Instead, the frontal lobe allows us to take our emotions and define them into meaning. The prefrontal cortex is the laboratory where we paste together thoughts with their associations to derive new meaning from what we are learning. The frontal lobe gives us the privilege to gain meaning from the external world.

Free will is a major keyword we use to describe the frontal lobe. The seat of our free will and self-determination, the frontal lobe allows us to choose our every thought and action and, in so doing, control our own destiny. When this lobe is active, we focus on our desires, create ideas, make conscious decisions, assemble plans, carry out an intentional course of action, and regulate our behavior. The evolution of the human frontal lobe bestowed on humans a focused, intentional, creative, willful, decisive, purposeful mind, if we will only put it to use.

The frontal lobes are regionally divided into subsections that are responsible for myriad related functions. The back part of the frontal lobes is home to the *motor cortex,* which exists as a neighboring slice of cortical tissue right in front of the sensory cortex. The motor cortex and the sensory cortex are at the dividing line between the parietal lobe and the frontal lobe. If you return to Figure 4.5, you will see the division between the two cortical regions marked by the sensory and motor cortex. (Some references refer to the sensory-motor cortex as one region of the neocortex; however, for the sake of simplicity, I discuss them separately.)

The motor cortex activates all of the voluntary muscles in the body and participates in all our voluntary movements and actions. We activate the motor cortex when we need to take determined actions and control purposeful movements.

Just as the sensory cortex has areas allocated by sensitivity and function, the motor cortex is divided into territories according to structure and function. And like the sensory cortex, the neurological map of the motor cortex displays a quite distorted homunculus. In this homunculus, the face has the hand exiting the crown of the head, and the arm, the shoulder, the trunk, the leg, and the feet are formatted in a disproportional layout, out of sequence with the normal human anatomy. Figure 4.6 shows the diversified subdivisions of the motor cortex parceled into bodily regions. The individual size of compartments is based on necessity, much like the sensory cortex.

In the motor cortex, for example, the real estate apportioned for hand movement is enormous, when compared to the area allocated to moving the neck. As a matter of fact, the hand and fingers take up more space in the motor cortex than the combined areas of the wrist, the elbow, the shoulder, the thigh, and the knee. What is the reason? We use our hands and fingers more than these other body parts, because their specialized structure permits us to be more functionally skilled in our environment. The brain provides enlarged domains to handle the considerable motor demands placed on our hands and fingers.

The frontal cortex also extends all the way back to the temporal lobes, where intentional speech is initiated in the language centers. Thus the frontal lobe is intrinsically connected to voluntary speech articulation, which is seamlessly encoded in the area farthest back in the frontal lobe toward the rest of the brain.

Just in front of the motor cortex is an area called the *premotor cortex* or the *supplementary motor area* (SMA), which is responsible for mentally rehearsed intentional actions—before those actions are actually carried out. This is the planning center for our future actions.

The *prefrontal cortex* is a cortical region related to the crowning achievement of our abilities in the areas of consciousness and awareness. This is the brain area that is most active during our important periods of conscious, deliberate concentration. It is in this compartment that our true uniqueness as human beings exists.

This area allows us to supersede the stimulus-response, action-reaction, cause-effect patterns we unconsciously live by day to day. For example, all the automatic, repetitive programs that have been hardwired in the brain such as brushing our teeth, driving, dialing familiar phone numbers, combing our hair, and so on, are of no interest to the prefrontal cortex. These predictable, recurring behaviors, which stem from what we constantly see, smell, taste, hear, and feel, can be performed quite nicely without the allegiance of the prefrontal cortex.

Test Driving the New, Improved Neocortex

With its enlarged size, the cerebral cortex is what separates us from other species, in our ability to consciously learn and remember by processing data derived from our senses. The neocortex is the seat of your executive mind, your identity, your personality, and your higher brain functions. At this very moment, you comprehend the information on this page by using many different regions of your neocortex. Mapped within the neocortex are the capacities for rational thought, reasoning, problem solving, freewilled decision-making, planning, organization, verbal communication, language processing, and computation, to name just a few.

Scientists have to put their collective neocortices to work to better understand the neocortex. We do know that its development made possible our highly advanced level of adaptability in the world. Early humans with the new, expanded neocortex would have learned faster than other species, and would have had a greater capacity for invention, reason, and ingenuity with which to outsmart predators or overcome other dangerous situations. The neocortex gives us the intellect to create new ideas, develop new behaviors and skills, and invent new tools and technologies. Because of its enormous size, it gathers volumes of learned or remembered information (that is, known information) and it naturally creates new models, ideas, and archetypes to explore or invent—both in the physical world and in our imagination. Thus, we are not limited to evolving in a lengthy, linear fashion. Instead, we can change the course of our species with even one new theory or invention.

Moreover, the advancements the neocortex makes possible are not limited to the need to ensure our survival in the face of harsh or changing environments. Via the neocortex, we create and appreciate music, art, and literature, and we strive to explore and understand both the external world and our internal world. The creative neocortex gives each of its owners an individual, unique personality, and enables humans to live as great thinkers and fabulous dreamers.

How is the human head able to accommodate not only the reptilian brain and the mammalian brain but also the new brain? To reiterate our computer analogy, when our new bio-computer evolved, we gained the world's most powerful processor, the most advanced operating system, the largest hard drive, and the greatest amount of memory. As we mentioned, neurons themselves should never be thought of only as wires that connect to each other. Instead, each neuron should be seen as a complete, individual super-processor system that performs millions of functions daily. By connecting billions of neurons to each other, we now have billions of computer systems working as one incredibly huge computer network, having outstanding memory, storage abilities, and super-high speed, as well as other amazing capabilities. Remember that the number of potential synaptic connections in the human brain is virtually unlimited. When the size of the new brain expanded during evolution, we managed to compress all this processing capability into a bio-computer that is no bigger than a cantaloupe. We have all the machinery to express unlimited potential.

Why do human beings as a whole seem to use only a small fraction of our potential? In our defense, *Homo sapiens sapiens* is a relatively young species, and we have only had a few hundred thousand years to start learning how to use our new brain efficiently. Perhaps we are still novices, and we have barely begun to take our new brain out for a test drive. It's my hope that by reading this book, you'll be better able to push the limits of reality's engine: your brain.

CHAPTER FIVE

WIRED BY NATURE, CHANGEABLE BY NURTURE

*Whatever any man does he first must do
with his mind, whose machinery is the brain.
The mind can do only what the brain is equipped to do,
and so man must find out what kind of brain he has
before he can understand his own behavior.*

—GAY GAER LUCE AND JULIUS SEGAL

Compared to many other disciplines, *neuroscience* (the study of the brain) is in its infancy, with little more than 100 years under its belt. That's not to say, however, that scientists and philosophers haven't been thinking about the nature of the brain, mind, and thought for much longer. As far back as the ancient Greeks, great minds have posited great thoughts about the origin and nature of consciousness. It's only as technology has progressed and we've been able to see how and what parts of the brain function during specific tasks that pure neuroscience has flourished.

We've made great advances in the study of the brain's anatomy and function, yet many crucial questions remain. One of those key questions, *Are we born with a blank slate?* takes us all the way back to Aristotle. According to the renowned Greek philosopher, the brain of a newborn baby was a blank slate or *tabula rasa*. He theorized that humans start out with a brain that has no record of any experiences; it is only a blank tablet with which we begin our journeys in life. He believed that we begin to write on that tablet—to develop who we are—by using our senses to interact with our environment. "There is nothing in the mind that is not first in the senses," Aristotle preached, and that idea prevailed throughout Western civilization for almost 2,000 years.

Apparently, Aristotle spent little time observing newborns. Just minutes after birth, babies turn their heads toward the stimulus of a sound. What makes them behave as though there is something to look at, when they have not yet seen the world? The fact that newborn infants demonstrate amazing perceptual abilities suggests that genetic and biological factors are already mapped as pre-existing patterns of neural circuits within the brain. In other words, humans are born with functional circuits in the brain that can predispose specific behaviors, given the right stimuli.

Another example of the brain's neurologically mapped hardware lies in the language center, which is located on the left side of the brain. When an infant hears her mother speak repeatedly, this auditory stimulus activates prewired tissue in her language center. This universally preclaimed real estate will develop into the home where language will be stored and used.

To be fair to Aristotle, he was correct in observing that we gather information from our environment through the senses, and that the senses play a part in the development of the mind. But from our earlier discussion of the parts of the brain that are already patterned for various aspects of consciousness, we now know that we process those senses within the framework of a brain that is genetically prepatterned. The brainstem, the cerebellum, the midbrain, and even the neocortex all have trillions of prepatterned synaptic connections that have been encoded throughout the history of our species. Instead of a blank slate, the starting point in our lives as human beings includes universally human genetic traits, plus our individual hereditary lineage from our parents. And there is much more to who we are than our genetic potential. The brain may be prewired by genetics, but it is then subjected to the stimulation of the environment through what we learn and experience.

Before we embark on a deeper exploration of how these various influences shape our brain, let's turn to that not-so-blank slate that is the brain of a human child. How does the brain develop, and what can that teach us about ourselves?

Brain Development

More than half of the genes we express as human beings contribute to shaping the complex organ called the human brain. Human brain development does not take place in distinct and well-defined stages, although we can identify several periods of growth acceleration. For now, keep in mind that before a baby is born, one primary force at work in shaping the development of its brain is the baby's genetic inheritance.

On the other hand, we also know that a pregnant woman's external and internal environment play a very strong part in fetal brain development. For example, when an expectant mother lives under extremely stressful conditions, in so-called *survival mode,* her infant is more likely to have a relatively smaller skull circumference, less synaptic connections in the forebrain than average, and even a relatively smaller forebrain and a relatively larger hindbrain.[1] Given what we have already learned, this makes sense. The *hindbrain* is the powerhouse of the brain that regulates survival, and the *forebrain* is the thinking and reasoning, creative brain. But given normal circumstances during the pregnancy, it seems that the genetic program most strongly influences neurological growth and development before birth. After birth, both genetics and the environment interact as the baby's brain continues to develop.

Conception Through Second Trimester

Just four weeks after conception, a human embryo is already producing more than 8,000 new nerve cells every second. That is about a half million neurons made every minute during the first month of life. Over the next several weeks, the neurons begin to make their way to the developing brain, where they will organize into specific locations. Later on in the pregnancy, there are two distinct growth spurts in the fetal brain. The first growth acceleration extends from the second trimester of pregnancy (fourth, fifth, and sixth months) to early in the third trimester. During this time, the brain makes about 250,000 neurons per minute.

During the end of the first trimester and the beginning of the second trimester, the fetal neurons begin to develop dendrites, which establish synaptic connections with neighboring neurons to form vast regions of interconnected neural networks. Every second, an estimated two million synaptic connections form during this critical period of development. If we do the math, the brain is busy making close to 173 *billion* synaptic connections a day during this growth spurt.

While these branches between neurons begin to connect with each other at such a rapid speed, the brain is downloading general tendencies and propensities that have worked for or have been experienced by previous generations. The baby's genetic inheritance guides the formation of the three-dimensional pattern of neurological tissue that becomes its first individual neural patterns. (As we discussed in chapter 3, rather than simply connecting in a linear chain, neurons form synaptic connections similar in shape to the models you've likely seen of atoms.) An innate intelligence begins to form the architecture of the brain, which will support the functions of the brain, mind, and consciousness. Given all those synapses being formed, it's difficult to believe the blank-slate theory.

Third Trimester

The second growth acceleration begins during the third trimester of pregnancy (seventh, eighth, and ninth months), continues after birth and through to approximately six months to one year of age. An enormous increase in the total number of nerve cells occurs during this period. During the third trimester, the fetal brain develops and refines all the structures or regions that make up the adult brain and make the human brain distinct from other species, including all of the folds and valleys described in chapter 4. The brain's initial wiring is firmly established during this second neurological growth spurt. In fact, at this time, the baby possesses more brain cells and synaptic connections than it will ever have throughout her normal adult life. These are essentially the raw materials with which the child will begin her lifelong process of learning and change. The number and health of synaptic connections is more important than the total number of nerve cells. For as we now understand, the density and the complexity of dendrite connections wire the brain for greater development, enriched intellectual and practical learning, accelerated skills, and permanent memory.

Imagine that the fetal brain is like a new business. In the beginning, this company hires scores of unspecialized workers, and nobody seems to be in charge to tell them where to go and what to do. Gradually, though, they start forming connections to other employees. Those connections build into networks of employees who have found specific, useful tasks to perform. The survival of the company depends more on the health of its network groups than on the total number of workers. Those employees who get together the fastest to join these networks are able to stay at the company. However, after about six months, the company starts weeding out employees who have not become part of an established network. This imaginary company also continues to hire many new staffers, but prunes away any workers if their services prove unnecessary down the line.

Just as in this analogy, by the third trimester of fetal brain growth, there are too many random patterns of nervous tissue in place. The developing brain must become more tightly organized into networks of neurons that will be responsible for specific tasks. Just weeks before birth, under genetic control, the maturing neurons of the infant brain begin to compete with neighboring neurons to form circuits of neural networks that are modified to handle specific functions. The idea is simple: groups of neurons that get together the fastest to form a neural network in a specific area are the ones that will remain and build the necessary pattern of synaptic connections. This means that some neurons will die off. As neurons gang up to develop these important patterns, the neurons that did not compete fast enough will die. This neurological survival of the fittest is called *neural Darwinism*.[2]

Because the organization of neural networks begins during pregnancy (and the external environment has little to do with this automatic process), it is easy to see that our inherent genetic mechanisms are at work to shape the growing brain.

Birth to Age Two

After the child is born, some 67 percent of the calories she consumes are used to nourish her growing brain. This makes sense, because five-sixths of the brain's development takes place after birth. In fact, a newborn is in such growth acceleration that she rarely stays awake for more than six minutes at a time. Most of her energy is conserved for growth and development. New genetic synaptic patterns continue to develop at an incredible pace during this stage of development. As neural Darwinism continues, the pruning away of unnecessary synaptic connections continues as well.

After birth, the brain's development is shaped not only by genetics but also by input from the environment. As the infant begins to have experiences, her senses gather vital information from her surroundings. Stimulation from sensory input that she receives repeatedly will cause her brain to develop strong synaptic connections. The young child will pay special attention to the voice of her mother, connecting with the familiarity of the voice she heard for nine months in the womb. As the baby is repeatedly exposed to the same visual and auditory sensory information, she will begin to identify her mother's face with her mother's voice. In this way, the child begins to make some vital associations to recognize her most important means of survival.

The baby's newly awakened and freshly formed synaptic connections start to build a neurological record of her experiences from the environment. Through this process, nerve cell connections in the child's brain begin to form specific patterns to make important neural networks, enabling the brain to organize its many functions, and to store, retrieve, and process information efficiently. We call this *learning*—and the infant's brain is learning at the fastest rate it will ever achieve in its life. For example, from birth, a baby can hear every sound that an adult can hear. However, only words that she repeatedly hears her mother use will construct the foundations of the child's native language. If her mother continually speaks English, the child's native language will be English, even though the child may occasionally hear other people speaking other languages.

Recent scientific studies have demonstrated the crucial role of parental feedback in this process. When one group of babies made cooing or babbling sounds, their parents were instructed to give them immediate feedback in the form of smiles and encouragement. With a second group of babies, their parents were told to smile at them at random moments unrelated to their children's attempts to produce sounds. The babies that received instantaneous feedback progressed more rapidly in their ability to communicate than the infants who received little or no reinforcement from their parents. These results suggest that immediate, consistent parental encouragement plays a vital role in stimulating babies to experiment with making new sounds, and in helping infants neurologically wire (learn) the elements of language.[3]

All along, in a process called *pruning*, the brain is busy pruning away and modifying synaptic connections according to what it begins to know, remember, and recognize. Synapses that are seldom activated will atrophy; eventually they will be eliminated or pruned away. Synapses pertaining to sounds the infant infrequently hears, for example, will be removed. Many parents who have adopted children under the age of two from other countries have been amazed at how quickly these children pick up their new language, while simultaneously forgetting their native language if it is not spoken in their new family.[4]

As a young child's body and brain develop, growth spurts and developmental changes take place at certain critical stages, independent of her environment. These automatic processes are genetically programmed to occur throughout her development. In the child's growing brain, these genetic programs trigger chemical and hormonal signals that cause certain neural nets to develop and activate. In turn, these developmentally enhanced neural nets enable the brain to be ready to process all the stimulation from the child's environment. Accordingly, when a very young infant looks at faces, she may see only black and white patterns and vague shapes. As genetic programs prompt her brain to develop further, her neural circuits become more refined, and the natural outcome is enhanced visual perception.

Simply put, our natural process of development stimulates neural circuits to unfold, quite apart from any environmental stimuli. As genetic influences continue to refine our senses and grow our brain, we are able to process greater amounts of input from our environment, thereby learning more from our world. As every human child enters the world, their growth begins to take shape through this intricate, almost equal dance between genetics and environment— nature and nurture, respectively.

Early Childhood

By the age of two, the human brain approaches its adult size, weight, and number of nerve cells. Most neurons continue to multiply through the second year of life. (In some parts of the brain, such as the cerebellum, nerve cells continue to multiply and divide into adulthood). The greatest number of synapses present in the neocortex also seems to be at two years old. By this age, the circuits of the frontal lobe begin to develop. (However, the frontal lobe does not finish developing under the genetic program until our mid-twenties!) The selective pruning of synapses that began before the age of two now continues to change the brain further, based primarily on repetitive experiences as well as genetic influences. By age three, a child's brain has formed about 1,000 trillion synaptic connections, about twice as many as in a normal adult.

Puberty Through Mid-Twenties

Another growth spurt of neural tissue happens genetically at puberty, as the brain makes another necessary sprint that corresponds to the genetically accelerated growth and changes in the body. For the most part, the corresponding chemical and hormonal changes will cause structural changes in the brain, independent of the environment. During adolescence, for example, nerve cells that have to do with emotional centers in the midbrain (especially in the amygdala) are activated and developed. During this dynamic period, it is common to see the neocortex increase in overall thickness roughly at age 12 in boys and 11 in girls. Also around the age of 11, the brain once again seems to prune away unused neural circuits at an increased pace.

Following this massive explosion of neuron growth, the process of thinning out nerve cell connections continues throughout our mid-twenties. Considering that every time the brain changes, there is an increase in conscious awareness—that is, in our ability to learn, remember, and formulate a sense of self—it makes sense, then, that during this stage of brain development, many teenagers fight so hard for their newly forming beliefs and for their new identities.

At this final stage, a hierarchical order in the maturation of the human brain exerts itself. The first areas to finish developing are the sensory and motor cortices, those areas involved in sight, hearing, feeling, and movement. The parietal lobes then finish their evolutionary stint by mapping some of the final patterns of language and spatial orientation. The last area of the brain to complete its development is the prefrontal cortex, that area responsible for all our executive functions, such as paying attention, formulating and acting on intentions, planning the future, and regulating behavior. This is the part of the brain having the most plasticity, meaning that it has the greatest ability to make new connections and to unhook from past connections. This most newly developed area is what we use to change ourselves.

The completion of frontal lobe development in the mid-twenties is the necessary last ingredient for the brain to reach adult maturity. This stage of brain specialization is what establishes us as adults. During puberty, we have strong sexual drives, powerful emotions, impulsive behaviors, adult fixations, and increased energy levels. However, the control of these elements does not happen until well into our twenties or sometimes later, because it is the frontal lobe that controls and restrains impulses and emotions.

Simply put, we think clearer and better after our mid- to late twenties than we were able to in our earlier years. In a wry observation, Jay Giedd of the National Institutes of Mental Health summed up society's dilemma: "We can vote at the age of eighteen and drive a car. But you can't rent a car until you're twenty-five. In terms of brain anatomy, the only ones that have it right are the car-rental people!"[5]

The brain does not even stop there in terms of its advancement. Until recently, many scientists considered this stage of growth in the mid-twenties as the end of human ability to develop the brain any further. The truth is that we are not as rigid or hardwired as science once speculated. In fact, the human brain is extremely *neuroplastic,* meaning that by persistently learning, having new experiences, and modifying our behavior, we may continue to remold and shape the brain throughout our adult years. This directly contradicts past assertions that the brain is essentially fixed and complete by this stage in our life.

With this basic understanding of how our genetic inheritance and early experiences shape the developing brain, we as individuals can now delve into two more important inquiries in the quest to understand our brain's capacity: What does my brain have in common with the brains of all other humans? How does my brain express the genetic inheritance from my parents that makes me a unique individual?

The Qualities That Make Us Human

Members of any species of animals share similar physical, behavioral, and mental characteristics because of the comparable chemistry and anatomical structure of their brain systems. For example, house cat or show cat, lion or lynx, all cats share certain basic, inborn traits. This is equally true of our own species, *Homo sapiens sapiens.* All normally functioning humans walk upright, are bipedal, and have opposing thumbs. While many animals see the world in black and white, humans see the world in color because we share the same neurological ability to process visual stimuli. We eat and digest food in the same fashion, share common sleep cycles, and have some form of spoken language. Every one of us experiences emotions and displays similar facial expressions when we are sad, angry, or happy. As members of the human species, we inherit the potential to perform complex reasoning. We all display similar physical, behavioral, and mental traits inherent in our species, which is nature's way of enabling us to share common ground as human beings. These, and others, are our long-term genetic traits. In other words, structure and function are related in all species.

The long-term genetic qualities derived from our human heritage ensure that all normal, healthy individuals are born with virtually the same brain chemistry and functional systems. Once again, this provides a clear example of the scientific concept that structure applies to function. Since everyone shares an identical brain structure, we share the same general functions.

As we all share the same general body structure, our human body—through diverse experiences in its environment during our species' evolution—has shaped the overall structure of the brain. Because we share the same sensory organs (our eyes, ears, nose, mouth, and skin are alike); because we process the same sensory pathways, such as pain and pleasure, in a similar fashion (we all experience fire as hot); and because we interact with our environment using identical body parts and voluntary motor functions (we all hold a stick in a similar way because we share opposing thumbs), it makes perfect sense that the body's experiences over eons have molded and shaped the brain, both macro-scopically and microscopically. Every person inherits matching, basic blueprints of physical, emotional, and mental expression that make us a part of the human race. This is our universal birthright.

How did we come to acquire the blueprints that make us human? The brain is truly the memory of the past, shaped by our species' adaptation to its environment over millions of years. Each of our three brains provides us with its own set of long-term genetic traits, developed in response to environmental pressures. For example, as we have seen, hardwired into every human's mammalian brain is an automatic fight-or-flight response system for the survival of the physical body, with a structure and function that is quite similar to that found in most other mammals. This response system evolved in mammals as a long-term genetic trait, because through untold generations, it improved their ability to survive encounters with predators.

Throughout the further evolution of our own species, the neocortex has recorded the totality of our learned experiences through eons of events that it has encoded in its neurological framework. For example, we already said that within the neocortex there are mapped patterns of neurons that are pre-assigned to our ability to use verbal language. This long-term genetic trait is common to all human beings. Everything we have learned that has contributed to our survival and strength as a species has shaped the structure and function of the present-day brain. Every human being inherits long-term genetic memories, encrypted within the nervous system, that are, essentially, the platform of learning that we operate from as contemporary individuals.

In our discussion of long-term genetic traits, we have been focusing on structures and characteristics that all human beings share. Because all humans have hands, for example, there are certain experiences and abilities that all of us have in common. If our hands exemplify long-term genetic traits that make us members of the same species, then our fingerprints epitomize short-term genetic traits that give each of us our individuality.[6]

Traits That Make Us Individuals

When we began our discussion of how the brain develops, we said that both genetics and the environment shape us as individual human beings. Given that all humans have a similar brain structure and share fundamental physical, behavioral, and mental characteristics that we call long-term genetic traits, what causes us to behave and think as unique individuals from the very beginning of our lives? How does the "you" develop? Why does one person have the behavioral traits of being outgoing and aggressive while the next person is shy and anxious? Why do some people excel in verbal skills, others display an aptitude for math, and still others have a talent for physical coordination? Why do we differ from one another in how we perceive the world, what we believe, what subjects interest us, our desires and goals, our emotional states, and how we respond to stress? What factors produce these individual variances, which we will refer to as *short-term genetic traits,* in members of the same species?

Setting aside for now the impact of a person's experiences and environment, these individual expressions of human nature may partially result when one male and one female combine their genetic information in the form of DNA. This reproductive blending of male and female genetic material creates an individual who inherits short-term genetic traits from both parental gene donors. In other words, we will ultimately become like our parents. Ouch!

Actually, we are not born *exactly* like either of our parents, because each of us inherits a unique combination of our parents' genetic material (including some genetic coding from our parents' parents and, possibly, from earlier generations). Thus our short-term gene expression makes every one of us unique. Given the vast complexities of genetic variables, the odds that the same parents would produce a duplicate of any individual (except in the case of identical twins) are next to impossible. Such is the case for all species that exchange their DNA and add the unique genetic makeup of each individual to the gene pool.

To describe in rudimentary terms how this short-term hereditary process works, we inherit specific genes from both parents. Genes manufacture proteins in all the cells of our body. Bone cells make bone proteins. Liver cells make liver proteins, and so on. All our muscles, internal organs, tissues, bones, teeth, and sensory organs replicate their cells based on the combined genetic information we inherit from our parents. For example, we are familiar with obvious physical characteristics that parents pass on to their offspring, such as hair color, height, or bone structure. For the sake of simplicity, we will merely acknowledge that a complex set of variables governs which particular inherited traits you will exhibit or express.

Yet our individual expression lies not in the ways we may physically resemble one or the other of our parents, but in the subtle wiring patterns of our nerve cells. The brain of every human is uniquely patterned according to DNA instructions from our closest progenitors. Each of our parents, having had certain experiences, acquired particular personality traits and skills, and embraced specific emotions, stores this information in their brain in patterns of synaptic connections, or *neural networks*. It seems our parents pass on some of their unique temperments and propensities to us in the form of short-term genetic coding.

In fact, we are likely to inherit certain aptitudes and emotional tendencies that our parents have demonstrated in a general way, independent of whatever form they take. For example, let's say your mother has tended toward the attitude of victimization. If your mother has repeatedly held thoughts of suffering, both mentally and physically; rehearsed her complaining; demonstrated blaming others for everything; and has mastered the art of making excuses, she is more prone to be synaptically wired equal to her most repetitive intentions. Her recurring thoughts, experiences, and consistent rehearsals of victimization have reinforced that neurochemical program. We then can speculate that your mother's neural network of victimization will contribute to who you or another sibling might become. The same could be true, on a more positive note, of the parent who is musically inclined: this parent's neural networks may predispose her offspring to be naturally wired to play a musical instrument. Practicing, demonstrating, and mentally rehearsing, combined with repetitive thoughts and consistent experiences, will microscopically shape the brain in the same way. In fact, it is now known that a part of the left half of the brain called the *planum temporale* is bigger in musicians than in nonmusicians.[7]

Clusters of neurons connect or wire together to form networks, creating possible ways in which we think, behave, feel, and react. From both parents, we inherit genes that specifically direct the production of nerve cells in our brain. When these nerve cells replicate, they fabricate the specific proteins that make up the structure of neurons.

Before we are born, these genes also begin giving the orders to shape the initial patterns in which our nerve cells wire together. Beginning around the sixth month in utero, an infant's brain is following her parents' uniquely combined genetic instructions to lay down patterns of prewired synaptic connections. Through this process, in a most simplistic explanation, her brain's neurons begin to assemble and organize to reflect portions of her parents' combined genetic blueprints. The blueprints of the child's genetic map become a completely unique makeup, allowing the child to express a distinctive combination of short-term traits.

We therefore may inherit some of the emotional and behavioral tendencies of our parents. The most extensively hardwired patterns of neural networks are laid by the most common thoughts and actions, which will then create the most used circuits in the brain. This is how hardwired programs manifest in a lifetime. We tend to think generally similar thoughts, perform related behaviors, and demonstrate comparable emotional states as our parents, because we may have inherited their most practiced thoughts, actions, and feelings. Before you start to blame (or thank) your parents, though, hold off. We still have a lot of information to cover.

Essentially, we seem to inherit some of the neurological wiring of our parents. If so, the sum total of the synaptic connections encompass only gross personality traits, not specific information, and because each person receives a one-of-a-kind genetic inheritance, our genes provide us with a brain that has qualities and characteristics that are different from every other human being. Every person's patterns of nerve cell clusters are unique, allowing each person to think differently from all other people. In essence, the way your brain is wired is who you are as an individual. If your long-term genetic traits are exemplified by the human hand you inherited, in terms of its overall similar structure from person to person, then it is easy to see now that how you are wired individually is like a personal and unique fingerprint. Your own wiring makes you one-of-a-kind.

The Hierarchy of Brain Organization

At first glance, the human brain looks amorphous, lacking any specific pattern or organization. However, attentive observation reveals that the architecture of the neocortex has a definitive pattern of folds, wrinkles, elevations, and valleys that are strikingly consistent in every human being. These structural regions or territories of brain matter correspond to the same particular functions and behaviors in all of us. As discussed in chapter 4, hearing, vision, touch, taste, motor control, sensations of touch and temperature, even music appreciation, to name just a few, are all preassigned to specific, identical regions mapped within the lobes of the neocortex of every human being. As a side note, this law applies to the rest of the brain as well. The midbrain and the reptilian brain, including the cerebellum, are strikingly similar from person to person.

We as human beings generally tend to behave, function, think, communicate, move, and even process sensory data from our environment in a similar fashion. The bottom line is this: because we share the same anatomy neurologically, biologically, and structurally, we will therefore have the various types of genetic data encoded in the exact same regions in the neocortex, and we therefore share relatively similar characteristics common to all of the human species.

As early as 1829, scientists were attempting to correlate specific regions of the brain with functional capacities. Their initial efforts involved analyzing the numerous bumps on the surface of the skull. They would associate a particular protuberance with some innate drive or cognitive ability, naming the areas they mapped after specific traits, such as the organ of mirthfulness or the organ of combativeness. If a particular bump on the surface of the skull was larger in one individual than the next, these early researchers allotted more brain tissue to that area. According to this model, every individual had his or her own, unique map.

Founded by Franz Gall, this archaic mapping system was named *phrenology*. Figure 5.1 shows you a picture of the human head with many regions covering the entire surface area of the skull, which is one of these early attempts at *compartmentalization*.

By the grace of God, phrenology was quickly overturned. Instead, European universities began to study the functioning brain, conducting diverse animal experiments as well as applying low-voltage electrodes to various regions of the living human brain. Neurologists made fast progress away from Gall's model in determining which area of the brain was responsible for which function.

Around the same time, French neurologist Pierre Paul Broca was studying the brains of deceased people who had suffered a particular type of speech loss. He presented at least eight such cases to the scientific community, pinpointing the exact, repeatable damage to the same area of the left frontal lobe. This is still called *Broca's area*. True science was being initiated, but not without the controversy of calling this a more advanced form of phrenology. It wasn't.

We can characterize these regions and subregions of the new brain as mapped, prewired anatomical modules or compartments. Let's go from biggest to smallest so that you can understand how we go from long-term to short-term traits in the new brain: Hemispheres are divided into lobes; lobes are further divided into regions or strips; regions are then diced up into subregions called compartments or modules; and compartments are made of individual columns of neural networks. As we move downward to smaller levels, we tend to become individualized.

Why is the brain organized into subregions and compartments in the first place? As our species developed over millions of years of diversified experiences, certain universal, long-term abilities that proved conducive to survival were encoded in the human cortex in networks of synaptic connections. These com-

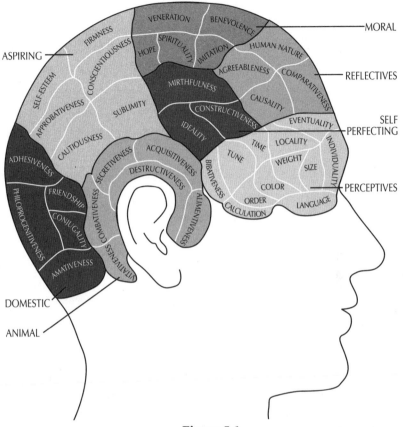

Figure 5.1

A schematic of phrenology demonstrating the archaic attempt to compartmentalize the brain into individual personality traits, based on the external elevations in the surface of the skull.

munities of neurons were nominated to perform specific functions that are common to every human being. Therefore, different geographical parts of the neocortex have become specialized for mental, cognitive, sensory, and motor functions. We all process the numerous kinds of sensory information from our environment in relatively the same specialized neural territories. For millennia, these neural patterns have been genetically passed on to each new generation. Organized into the cortical areas we term *subregions* and *compartments,* these innate, mapped regions serve as the common ground of human experience and the starting place for our own personal evolution.

In this way, humans are wired to perceive the consistent, familiar environmental stimuli that we as a species have been exposed to over millions of years. We have been wired to process certain information in specific compartments of the neocortex so that each new generation of our evolving species can experience what has already been learned, stored, and encoded in our synapses and finally revealed in our genetic expression. This explains why the specific areas of the sensory and motor homunculi exist as premapped areas that relate to our present abilities. It is also why our auditory cortex can process every phoneme, and why vision is uniquely processed as a hierarchy of visual capacities.

From human to human, even the individual compartments that are allocated into different real estate parcels are strikingly similar. Compartments, we now know, are specialized collections of neural networks. They are both universal and individual. What is universal about modules is that we all inherently have almost the same regions of the cortex mapped as data processing centers of information. What is individual is how well we, as diverse personalities, can process, refine, and modify assorted information in the modular sectors of our neocortex, compared to the next person.

The original view of compartmentalization stated that these individual regions within the lobes of the neocortex are delineated by distinct boundaries and engage in very limited interactions with other compartments, no matter how close they are. Every compartment was thought to operate as private neurological property, so to speak. Those views are now dated.

Neurological modules are highly interactive and interdependent, not fixed and rigid as was once thought, because by their very nature, nerve cells are able to connect to and disconnect from other neurons. Because neurons and neural nets can modify their geography, the subregions of the cerebral cortex include both fixed modular zones and changeable modular zones. What makes a module alter its geographical boundaries? The malleability of these zones depends, for the most part, upon our ability to learn and pay attention.

There are some other limitations to the idea of rigid modular compartmentalization. The brain is a highly interactive organ. Given what we are learning so far about our neurons' synaptic plasticity, their ability to reorganize is quite remarkable. Also, the brain is not so linear that injury to one area does not affect other areas. When damage to specific modules of neurological circuits is observed on functional scans, the neighboring modules produce similar, but not identical, cognitive impairments. This provides further evidence that modules operate not as precisely defined, separate units, but as continuous, related elements within the cortex.

In normal, healthy humans, the thought process does not take place in disconnected segments. We experience smooth, connected transitions from one thought or cognitive function to the next, reflecting a continuous movement of neurological activity through the cortex. Imagine picking up a loose sheet on a bed and flapping it to create a three-dimensional wave moving away from the point of propagation. This is a better model of what happens in the new brain.

Nerve cell impulses converge or diverge. When they diverge, they spread outward, using individual modules as a medium to facilitate their activity and enable them to cover greater ground. Because nerve cells have branches that can communicate simultaneously with numerous other nerve cells, many modules may be activated at once. Imagine a cascade of flashing electrical patterns moving diffusely and spreading out three-dimensionally.

Compartmentalization does describe how the brain is organized, but the module concept may not be completely tidy. Modules certainly do exist as distinct units within the neocortex; certain mental and physical functions are localized to individual circuits of synaptic connections within the brain's subregions. However, these subregions and modules are utilized as individual elements that contribute to a whole stream of consciousness. Thinking is not compartmentalized; it is a relatively smooth and continuous process. Thought can be likened to a concert of modules working in unison.

We can now build a greater understanding of how learning and cognitive processing are related. Through learning and experience, we create more integrated nerve cell connections, and those enhanced synaptic patterns can facilitate greater, more diversified thought processes. Encoding new knowledge and experiences in our brain's wired connections is like upgrading a computer's hardware—except that individual human beings are unique in how each person processes cognitive information.

For example, I am in Japan as I write these ideas. I am sure that if we were to examine how my brain processes information based on how I have learned throughout my life, it would be different from the pattern of neurological processing of the typical Japanese person, who writes in symbolic characters, reads language from right to left and top to bottom, and usually speaks more than one language. The same would be true if that person and I both sustained an identical brain injury that damaged the same module in the cerebral cortex. The way I fire neurological patterns in my thinking brain is unique. Therefore, it would be different from the way any other human being fires his or her synaptic patterns.

An uncertainty arose, after scientists had mapped subregions such as the sensory, motor, auditory, and visual cortices with all their associated functions. Their geographic model did not pinpoint where our greater abilities and skills are located. Where do we analyze complex mathematical equations? Where are the nonlinear abstractions of informal logic processed? What region is responsible for divine inspiration? What is the neurological basis for complex intellectual or mental skills? Where, exactly, does the identity exist? How do we learn?

Perhaps the answers to these questions depend not on a linear examination of the individual lobes working independently, but on the holistic way in which the subregions of neural networks coordinate to produce different levels of mind. Many factors govern the various ways in which the brain's subregions blend their efforts; examples include patterns, sequences, combinations, and timing. The key to understanding how different areas of the brain work together to produce the mind is to think of them as components of a symphony orchestra, rather than as individual instruments.

We now have to expand our definition of a neural network. A neural network can be broadened to encompass many different compartments and subregions throughout the brain, firing in unison, to fabricate a particular level of mind. In truth, the sum of the parts is greater than the whole.

Nature Versus Nurture

Scientists have debated the extent to which our brains are sculpted by either our genetic inheritance (nature) or our environment and experiences (nurture). In other words, what determines our destiny: heredity or environment? Your brain at birth is certainly not a blank slate waiting to be written on by life's experiences. Nor are you born with genetics that dictate the way you will behave, act, react, think, feel, and create in a predetermined, unchangeable pattern.

Nature: The Long and Short of It

Our genetic inheritance is a combination of long-term genetic information that is common to all members of our species, plus short-term genetic instructions from each of our parents. The overall shape and structure of the brain and its generalized functions constitute long-term traits that our species developed as an outgrowth of millions of years of evolution. Short-term genetic traits from our parents and from their parents, going back a few generations, give us our individuality.

Both kinds of genetic traits, long-term and short-term, become wired in the brain as it develops before birth and especially during the first year of life. When we speak of certain definitive areas in the brain that are wired, we are referring to fixed, inherited patterns of nerve connections that give us our very personality, facial expressions, coordinated motor skills, intellect, emotional propensities, reflexes, levels of anxiety, internal chemical balance, mannerisms, even creativity and artistic expression.

Both long-term and short-term genetic traits are what nature has given us as an inheritance. We can say it is "our nature."

Nurture: Our Individual Environment and Life Experiences

In addition to our genetic inheritance, what has shaped and molded—in other words, nurtured—the brain over millions of years is what we have learned and experienced from interaction with our environment, how we stored that information, and how the brain has adapted. Nurture also concerns our individual life experiences, which are recorded in the brain. Recent studies have demonstrated the impact of nurture and point out that we are significantly shaped by experiences during our early years of development. In the first decade of life, humans form synaptic connections from the experiences gained through learning and normal developmental lessons. Early experiences also shape the formation of neural networks.

Nature and Nurture Together

The way the brain is wired, then, is a combination of genetic traits and learned experiences throughout life. The brain evolves not via nature or nurture, but by a remarkable interaction of both these processes.

Environmental circumstances can also derail aspects of a person's genetic potential. If a child in utero has parents who are both physicists, he may carry the genetic potential for superior intellectual development. However, should the mother be exposed to a noxious drug during pregnancy or experience high amounts of stress while carrying the fetus, the child's genetic blueprints may be overcome by his unhealthy environment in the womb. Or if a child is malnourished during her first two years of development, she may not develop the intellectual capacity that her genes initially preordained, because inadequate nutrition can adversely affect how the brain develops. On the other hand, if a child is genetically predisposed toward anxiety and timidity, she can be helped to overcome her condition by experiencing a loving family environment or receiving counseling.

Some researchers state that inherited genetic synaptic connections account for only 50 percent of our personality traits.[8] We inherit our parents' knowledge, thought patterns, and feelings as a foundation for who we become. But that is only 50 percent of who we are. The genetic circuits that we inherit are merely a platform for us to stand on to begin our life. In order for the brain to learn new things (keep in mind that learning involves making new synaptic connections), it needs some existing connections with which to make additional new connections. Thus, we began life with our existing inherited connections and the learned memories of past generations, and we use those connections as a foundation to make new ones.

Given that humans are born with certain behaviors, propensities, traits, and talents that are really the wired memories of generations gone by (especially those passed on from parents), it makes sense that we come preloaded with long-term and short-term circuits that define who we are. If nature and nurture are in a constant exchange, then what we experience from the environment only adds to nurturing the "self" as a true work in progress. Every time we learn something new, we forge additional neural connections of our own, we add a new stitch to this three-dimensional tapestry of our neural fabric, and the self is changed.

This is nature's way of generously giving to each individual a true beginning, but with prewired knowledge built in. We are born with a certain amount of prewired learned knowledge already loaded in the brain, so that we can stay abreast of our species' evolutionary development. It is up to us as individuals to add our own synaptic connections, through conscious interactions in our environment. We can add new circuits to our own neural architecture; we can further modify and design a progressive new self. Surely, by this understanding, if we are not learning or experiencing anything new, we are headed for a limited genetic destiny because we will be activating only those circuits equal to the genetic memory of our parents.

Our First Stimuli

It is somewhat ironic that the first environmental stimuli to which a newborn infant is exposed usually are derived from his parents, who share much of the same genetics as their child. From infancy to adolescence, a child will model behavior through social interactions with people in his environment, based on what stimulates him to the greatest extent. This is possible because of *mirror neurons,* a type of neuron in the brain that facilitates imitation of behavior. When a child observes certain traits, actions, emotional reactions, and even mannerisms demonstrated by one or both parents, this can be the right type and amount of information to activate the child's existing, prewired neural patterns and, in doing so, jump-start the child into a more predetermined state of mind that may persist throughout his lifetime. In other words, if you inherit from your parents the neural networks that they have mastered in their own lives, and then use those circuits to build the 50 percent of personality that is based on genetic programs, the other 50 percent of personality that is learned from the environment is most influenced by the people from whom you inherited those programs. Does your individuality stand a chance?

I am certain that this is why, in some ancient schools of wisdom, children were taken from their parents at an early age to study among the mountaintops of the world. The great teachers of the time probably understood that those children had considerable genetic potential, and that if they could teach those children apart from their familial influences, maybe they would have a better chance for greatness.

During the brain's early development and beyond, two broad, simultaneous processes are at work. First, we add new synaptic connections, build new neural nets, and prune away nerve cells and synaptic connections that are unnecessary for our survival and development. Neural organization via this pruning process takes place under genetic programs that have been put into place by natural selection. The external environment plays an equal role in trimming away patterns of nerve cell connections that lack vital meaning or serve no useful purpose to help us function. Both our genetic programs plus information from our environment initiate this refinement. Through nature and nurture together, we cultivate, landscape, and weed our neural garden to meet our needs.

The Wired Brain; the Plastic Brain

Both genetics and experiences are encoded as wired connections in the brain. For most species, this is a criterion for survival. If an animal encounters a predator near the water hole, its ability to hide or employ camouflage may afford it its survival. The next time, this creature may remember to take a different route to the water hole, so that it can avoid the threat it previously faced. By possessing this level of mental flexibility, a species can be less rigid in its patterns of behavior. Moreover, it can adapt to become smarter by encoding its successful behaviors in its neurological framework, so that it may pass on to the next generation what it learns and has remembered. If enough generations of this species behave in a comparable fashion when introduced to similarly dangerous situations, over time, through genetic blending, many of these animals will possess similar genetics. Eventually, the behavior may become a long-term genetic trait, shared by all members of the species.

In humans, as well, the recorded experiences that we call "memory" or "learning" become mapped as the synaptic wiring that reflects who we are. Long-term genetic patterns of neural circuits and structured brain systems that are indigenous to our species are the result of learned, encoded experiences that were passed down individually through the years.

The genetic neural circuitry that we inherit also carries the encoded memories of learned experiences from our lineage. Our parents, grandparents, and even great-grandparents stand as immediate contributors to our prewired genetic brain matter by the ways in which they shaped and molded their brains through life's experiences. (This may give credence to the practice, dating back to antiquity, of a royal family preserving its bloodline.) This is where the influence of culture, creed, and even race can further influence our specific wiring.

Hence our genetic wiring and our wiring from specific lifetime experiences are two ways of accomplishing the same result. Learning allows us to change; evolution allows us to transmute our genes. Learning takes place when nature is nurtured; evolution happens when what is nurtured gives back to nature. This is the cycle of life.

Every time we learn something new, the brain processes the information through the senses and makes new circuits that encode in the neurons the memory of what it has learned. This is important because it emphatically shows that we have the ability to adapt to stimuli from external influences and to change our behavior accordingly.

Neuroplasticity gives our brain the ability to change its synaptic wiring. This is an innate, universal, long-term genetic feature in humans. It affords us the privilege to learn from experiences in our environment, so that we may change our actions to produce outcomes that are more desirable. Merely to learn intellectual information is not enough; we must apply what we learn to create a different experience. If we could not synaptically rewire our brain, we could not change in response to our experiences. Without the ability to change, we could not evolve, and we would be the victim of the genetic predispositions of our ancestors.

Prior to the last 15 years, scientists generally believed that environmental stimuli (nurture) could influence behavior only within the boundaries of inherited, premapped patterns in the brain (nature). We now know that the human brain is plastic enough that it can override genetically programmed compartments or modules mapped for sight or sound and rewire them for new functions, based on the external stimuli that it can process. If an area of the brain is missing out on environmental information because one of the sense organs is not working, another region of the brain will compensate for the lack of stimuli, as long as another sensory organ is functional.

For example, most people have heard that a blind person can develop acute hearing or enhanced tactile perception. What nonscientists might not know is that in the brain of a blind person, the huge area normally assigned as the visual cortex will now process sound and touch.[9] Researchers have also blindfolded sighted individuals for five days, and in as few as two days, fMRIs showed bursts of activity in their visual cortex when they performed tasks with their fingers or even when they listened to tones or voices.[10]

Scientists can also perform a functional brain scan on a sighted person and view the area assigned in the sensory cortex that is mapped for sensations in their fingertips. When we compare scan results from a sighted person to a brain scan of a blind person while he or she is using fingertips to read Braille, much larger compartments in the brain's sensory cortex light up.[11] This signifies that, by consciously paying attention and applying repetition, the brain is plastic enough to begin to reassign new areas to compensate for the change in type of stimuli. The fact that the brain of a blind person will map new dendrite connections in the visual cortex for sound or touch challenges the model of genetic predeterminism. This is a fine example of neuroplasticity overriding a genetic program.

According to the now outdated, limited view of neural organization, wired

compartments were viewed as permanently mapped and organized geographical territories. However, numerous experiments on modular plasticity have
demonstrated how neural circuits that were originally confined to one region
can literally expand their property lines beyond their neurological real estate to
trespass into other neural modules. Typically, there is a trade-off of existing
space to allow for such changes to occur. As one area of neural colonies enlarges
to take on new functional territory, other areas are minimized.

Take, for example, a Braille reader who has been blind for a very long time.
When he reads, he typically uses the index finger of one hand. As he runs his fingertip over elevated bumps on the surface of the paper, his sensory receptors
detect information that his eyes cannot see. The index finger is already rich in
touch receptors and has an associated module in the cortex that is quite large in
comparison to other areas. When we discussed the sensory cortex and the
homunculus (see chapter 4), we said that sensitivity was the main reason the
odd little fellow looked so different from the normal human proportions. Some
modules in the cortex are allotted more room because the body parts that correlate with those assigned areas are more sensitive and carry greater responsibility to detect sensory information from the environment.

Researchers have used functional brain scans to compare experienced and
inexperienced Braille readers in terms of how much of the brain's sensory cortex is turned on when using their index fingers to read. With experienced Braille
readers, scans observed that the module dedicated to the index finger was, when
activated, much bigger than in the inexperienced Braille readers.[12] (As you might
expect, the module of the feeling cortex that had gained in size in skilled Braille
readers was bigger only on the side of the brain that corresponded to the index
finger, right or left, that they used the most.) The repeated stimuli applied to
such a small area of skin on the tip of the forefinger had created a much-
enlarged somatosensory area in the neocortex. In other words, because an experienced reader's mind had repeatedly focused on that one-centimeter space at
the end of his or her finger, the associated module for processing sensory input
from the index finger essentially took over neighboring sensory territory. When
this happens, modules corresponding to body parts that are less extensively used

to gather sensory data, such as the palm of the hand or the forearm, have been shown to lose some of their real estate.

Neural networks designated to a specific module can even take over the job of other preassigned modules. Consider Braille readers who use three fingers, instead of one, to process sensory data. All three fingers at once receive the same sensory stimuli, over and over again. What happens to the modules that were initially assigned by the genetic patterning of the somatosensory cortex? The blind person who reads Braille with three fingers concentrates, focuses, and processes the repetitive stimuli from three fingers all at once, and the brain's sensory map of the body accommodates by molding the web of neurological tissue to facilitate the demand. Whereas each of the three fingers would normally have its own corresponding module of neurons in the sensory cortex, these nerve cells blend together to make one large sensory area covering all three fingers. When three-finger-using Braille readers receive a touch stimulus on just one finger, the nerve cells of the sensory cortex allotted for the other two fingers also fire.[13] The brain cannot tell which finger is being touched, because their separate modules are now integrated as one enlarged area in the subregion of the sensory cortex. *Nerve cells that continuously fire together, will ultimately wire together.*

The synaptic patterns of nerve cells assigned to a specific trait can modify themselves even within the existing modular areas. Neural connections within a module may become so refined and complex that a person demonstrates heightened sensitivities or abilities. For example, when a piano tuner develops his "ear" through repetitive learning and expert instruction—the precise feedback from hearing the proper sounds over and over again—after a period of time, he no longer needs to check his work with instrumentation. The constant repetition of his efforts allows him to hear sounds, with heightened acuity, that others may not even be aware of. The piano tuner who has undergone many years of practice ultimately refines the neural circuits of his auditory cortex to such a degree that they are much more intricately branched compared to corresponding neural circuits in the general population.

We also see neuroplasticity at work when greater-than-normal sensory input extends the usual boundaries of genetically premapped sectors of the brain. In other words, the more we use one of our senses, the larger the portion of the cerebral cortex assigned to process that input. In a typical example, autopsy results demonstrate that people who have worked in small appliance repair or as typists or machine operators develop more numerous and refined neurological networks in the neocortical motor areas that are mapped for hand and finger motion, than they do in areas of the brain related to other areas of the body.[14] In later studies, the same researchers performed postmortem examinations on the brains of subjects of differing ages. Their research demonstrated that the more education a person had, the greater were the complexity, intricacy, and number of synaptic connections in the language area of the brain.[15] What we learn, and how we remember what we learn, shapes who we are. As Buddha put it, "All that we are is the result of what we have thought."

The Hardwired Myth Further Broken: Neural Plasticity Reorganizes Compartments

We now know that much of the cortex is organized and mapped into specific, defined compartments for perceptions like feeling, as well as all the other senses and abilities. Because most of the brain's neurons are wired up and formatted by the time we are toddlers, it stands to reason that throughout the rest of our lives, the neuron webs of our sensory and motor cortex should be securely fastened into a permanent place, rigidly dedicated to well-defined modules for a lifetime of predetermined service. But that's not necessarily true.

There is a congenital condition known as *webbed finger syndrome* or *syndactyly,* in which individuals are born with fingers that are connected together. In severe cases, it is impossible for these people to move one finger without moving all their other fingers as a group. They must use their hands without the dexterity of having individual finger control; most of the pleasure of having five fingers has been reduced to a few gross hand motions, predominantly simple gripping.

If we were to look at the sensory or motor map of the brain in individuals with this condition, would it be the same as that of a normal person? No. In webbed finger syndrome, because the hand and fingers function as a single unit, the brain never creates separate property boundaries for each finger, and so the brain devotes just one area to the entire hand and fingers. During a functional brain scan on a person with syndactyly, when the subject moves one finger, all her fingers move together, and thus a much larger parcel of brain motor cortex lights up than would be seen in a person without this anomaly. In other words, when people with webbed fingers move their fingers and hands, the entire areas in the brain for hand and finger movement light up. The nerve cells related to the fingers all fire together and, therefore, they wire together.

Is the brain plastic enough to change if the hand condition could be altered in these individuals? If the organization of the brain was solely in place due to genetic factors, then there should be little change if the fingers could be separated. Several years back, surgeons created a technique to separate the fingers of people born with webbed finger syndrome, so that their fingers could move independently. When this corrective surgery was performed, guess what happened in the brain?

As it turns out, the brain changed very nicely to adapt to the new functions the fingers of the hand now possessed. Within weeks after surgery, the brain assigned each finger its own individual piece of neurological real estate. As the functions of the hand and fingers were altered, a subject's brain mapped the change as well.[16] The model of preassigned compartments, strictly organized and unchangeable in the brain, was challenged. As a result of the increased ability of each finger, new neurons fired in different sequences and patterns. The nerve cells that once fired together in tandem, when the fingers were all connected, now began to fire independently. When each finger had a new level of dexterity, the brain's neurons related to overall hand motion now reorganized into specific compartments for each finger. The nerve cells assigned to the connected fingers no longer fired together and, therefore, no longer wired together.

What does this mean for us? Maybe our brain stays the same throughout our adult life because we tend to do the same type of things in the same, routine ways, and this constantly sends the same type of stimulation to our brain. If we change the way we do things, the brain will change as well.

Hardwired by Nature

By hardwired, we mean that qualities are fixed and in place when we are born, ready to be triggered or activated either by our genetics or in response to our environment. Hardwired neural networks are automatic programs; once they are turned on, they require little or no conscious effort to run. Equally, once hardwired programs are activated, they require enormous conscious effort and will to turn off, if it is even possible.

In addition, when we say a particular function is hardwired, this denotes that there is either very little possibility of changing the brain's preexisting circuitry for that function, or it will take a tremendous effort to change. Hardwiring can also mean that if that particular neural wiring has been damaged, there is little hope for repair. If the wiring is injured, severed, or broken, or if the wiring never occurred in the first place, change is very difficult or, in some cases, impossible. But while it is true that the brain is hardwired to a great measure, and that different areas of the brain are more hardwired than others, research already mentioned in the preceding chapters has proven that, in fact, given the right instruction and feedback, the brain's wiring is much less fixed than we once thought.

The brainstem and cerebellum (first sub-brain), and the midbrain (second sub-brain) are more hardwired than the neocortex. Because our first and second sub-brains evolved earlier, they house older memories that have essentially become permanent circuits. Their neural clusters have stronger synaptic connections, because these patterns have been around longer and have been used most often. These neural circuits are perpetuated for use by future generations, because they have worked so well for so long. Because the neocortex is the newest brain for most species, including humans, it has fewer hardwired programs. The frontal lobe is the least hardwired of all, since it is our most recent neurological development.

The neocortex is most malleable because it serves as the stage of conscious awareness, memories, and learning. It facilitates our ability to think, act, and choose differently, and it records what we have consciously learned as well. This is the area where we grow new synaptic connections and modify existing neural networks. In this way, the neocortex is constantly being rewired.

Selection and Instruction

Just as neuroscientists have explored how genetics (nature) and our environment (nurture) impact the brain, a related debate has unfolded on how the processes of selection and instruction similarly interact to affect how we express who we are.

The term *selection* describes how we develop by using *neural circuits* that already are in place in our brain. (Neural circuits means those billions of neurons in the neocortex that are arranged in hundreds of thousands of inherited, prewired, mapped synaptic patterns that direct most human behavior.) In other words, we select from among premapped patterns that have already been learned and recorded by our progenitors.

The premise of selection is that we develop when these preexisting neural patterns become activated, by either genetic or environmental cues. For example, when a normal, healthy baby reaches a certain stage of development, he begins to crawl. The baby needs no cue from his environment to initiate this process. A genetic program in the baby's brain triggers one or more prewired neural networks, which cause the baby to crawl. After a while, crawling then activates other preexisting neural patterns, which prompt the baby to pull himself up, take his first teetering steps, and progress to walking.

Selection and activation of prewired synaptic circuitry is also triggered by environmental signals. For example, a newborn baby's brain is already selectively wired for vision, sound, movement, feeling, and other sensory abilities. However, these preassigned areas of neural networks need a signal from the environment to activate them. If you recall our earlier example, when a newborn baby hears a noise, this cue from his environment triggers him to turn his head toward the source of the sound. He looks to see what is causing the sound, because he already has the neural circuitry to process hearing and vision.

If selection is all about using neural networks that are already in place, then *instruction* is the process whereby we develop new circuits or modify existing ones. Instruction describes how we learn from and experience our external world, and then organize synaptic connections to match what we are learning. Instruction is our ability to be neuroplastic enough to further refine our neural architecture. We do this by repeating new or old thoughts, memories, actions, skills, and behaviors. What we repetitively do, how we do it, what we learn, how we think, and what we experience all create and modify the neural tissue that make up who we are. A newer, more aware mind is created by making additional new circuits in the brain. Our thoughts and actions are always reflected in the brain in the form of modified neural circuits.

For example, if you had been instructed for years on how to play the violin, learning new skills and then refining them, the preassigned neural nets in your brain that are responsible for dexterity and motor skills would likely become more densely and intricately connected. Instruction fabricates more intricate and dense synaptic connections and can expand into the real estate of neural parcels.

An accurate description of how we develop must involve both selection and instruction. Simply put, we're born with premapped neural patterns that we select, either genetically or environmentally. We can instruct those selected areas to become more modified and refined, by learning, modifying behavior, or having new experiences.

As you just saw, we have a preassigned area already in place in the sensory cortex for neural networks that process hand and finger movement (selection), but we can enhance those circuits via learning and repeated practice (instruction). We start life with genetically inherited neural patterns, and then we activate and modify those circuits through the environmental instruction we receive in the form of new experiences.

We already develop through selection and instruction, but these processes offer some intriguing implications for our future growth. Among the preassigned neural networks we inherit at birth are *latent* (as yet unused) areas of brain tissue. We know this because during brain surgery on an adult patient,

millions of neurons can be cut away without ever altering the patient's personality and sensory function. We can reasonably infer that in an adult patient,
genetic cues would have long since completed their job of activating preexisting
neural patterns, such as we observe in a crawling baby. Thus, the neurons that
surgeons trim away with no obvious consequences may indicate that every
human brain contains latent, wired patterns of nerve cells.

Do these latent neural nets represent undiscovered regions of human
potential? Could selection turn on these latent areas? Might these neural
areas be activated, developed, and refined, given the proper knowledge and
instruction? Could we occupy or activate these areas so that we can reach a new,
greater level of mind? If so, we could be looking at our evolutionary future, and
our brain may be a record of that future, not just the past.

CHAPTER SIX

NEUROPLASTICITY: HOW KNOWLEDGE AND EXPERIENCE CHANGE AND EVOLVE THE BRAIN

*Every mutation thru a new
combination of genetic factors that provides
the organism with a new opportunity of coming to
terms with the conditions of its environment signifies
no more or no less that new information about this
environment has got into that organic system.
Adaptation is essentially a cognitive process.*

—KONRAD LORENZ, PH.D., *THE WANING OF HUMANENESS*

O ver time, philosophers, psychologists, and neuroscientists have all attempted to formulate theories of learning, behavior, and personality development. From Aristotle's *tabula rasa* to Skinner's behavioral modification to recent research using functional brain scans to study a living brain, our understanding of the brain and the underlying processes that help it develop has evolved a great deal.

Recently, many people have tried to better understand how the brain operates by comparing it to a microcomputer. However, this model falls short of reflecting the reality of the brain in one crucial dimension—it does not reflect how changeable and malleable the brain and its synaptic connections really are.

For many years scientists labored under the false conception that the brain was essentially hardwired (complete in its development) by the time we reached a certain age. Although no one could put a precise finish line on the development of our neural circuits, it was generally thought that all our wiring was complete by the time we were in our early to mid-thirties.

Accordingly, doctors used to think that if the adult brain's circuits suffered damage from a stroke, other illness, or accident, the affected tissues could never be restored or repaired. However, if a person suffered brain damage at a young age, when the brain was still developing, doctors held out some hope that the brain could restore some of the functions that had been lost. Note that functions, but not structures, of the brain were thought to be recoverable to a degree.

Even today, the language we use to describe the brain and how it operates— wires, circuits, networks, compartments, and so on—reflects this lingering idea that the brain is a somewhat rigid instrument. In many ways, our limited ability to craft more suitable analogies and metaphors does a disservice to the brain and to our current understanding of how malleable, changeable, flexible, and adaptable the brain really is.

We often use the expression, "I've changed my mind." Until recently, science hasn't supported the contention that this change is a literal possibility. Only in the last 30 years or so has research revealed demonstrable proof that the adult brain continues to grow and change, forming new synaptic connections and severing others. We now know that the brain's plasticity is behind this ability to form new connections. In the last five years, research in this field of study has exploded. We are only just beginning to understand the brain's ability to change both functionally and structurally. Now we know that we are able to change not only our mind, but also our brain. We can do this throughout our life, and at will.

Evidence of the Brain's Neuroplasticity

In previous chapters, we introduced the concept of neuroplasticity and some of its terminology. We spoke of glial cells, and one particular type of glial cell called an astrocyte. Let's revisit these cells for a moment, to learn how science has solved one mystery about the brain—the preponderance of the brain's white matter. We know that glial cells exist in the brain's white matter, but why do their numbers outweigh gray matter by almost tenfold? Research has shown that glial cells not only enhance the speed of neurological transmission, but also help to form synaptic circuits. This process is critical in learning, changing behaviors, and storing long-term memory.[1]

For that reason, astrocytes are catching everyone's attention in neuroscience. Apparently astrocytes, which make up nearly half the brain's cells, increase the number of functional synapses between neurons throughout the brain and central nervous system.

In their research published in *Science* magazine in 2001, Ben Barres, M.D., Ph.D., and his colleagues from Stanford University School of Medicine, California, cultured and analyzed neurons with and without the presence of glial cells. The scientists demonstrated that without glial cells, fewer synaptic connections were made between normal neurons. Moreover, the connections that were made seemed to be functionally immature. Also, there was a sevenfold increase in the total number of functional synaptic connections when astrocytes were present. Their analysis clearly indicated that astrocytes are absolutely needed for the maintenance of synapses, and demonstrated that when glial cells are present, synaptic connections between neurons are almost guaranteed.[2]

The investigators concluded, "Glia may play an important and unexpected role in *adult neural plasticity* underlying learning and memory." This research, as well as studies by other scientists, is beginning to prove that astrocytes facilitate synaptic connections during learning. Because there are so many more possible connections between neurons than just the number of neurons themselves, and because astrocytes are always present when we make new circuits, it makes sense that nature has provided an overabundance of astrocytes, so we can learn at an accelerated pace. Essentially, who we are in terms of the "self" is just the accumulation of our total synaptic connections. Therefore, when we add new synaptic circuits to the "self" by learning, who we are is literally changed.

Seeing in Tongues

What neuroscience is now learning *about* learning, and how it all relates to neuroplasticity, may seem like the stuff of science fiction. For example, Paul Bach-y-Rita, M.D., a neuroscientist at the University of Wisconsin at Madison, may be proving that the brain can be completely rewired compartmentally. Dr. Bach-y-Rita says that our senses are literally interchangeable. At his research lab in Milwaukee, using sensitive feedback devices, he teaches people to see successfully with their tongue. We do not see with our eyes, we see with our brain, he states. The senses are, therefore, just inputs that provide information to our brain. He believes that we can modify the connections in our brain so much that we can begin to swap which sensory organ is processing which sensory experience in the brain.[3]

The tongue has more tactile nerve receptors than any other part of the body except for the lips; hence the tongue is sometimes called *the curious organ*. (Our experience with dental work shows how much the tongue likes to probe its territory.) Working with blindfolded volunteers, Dr. Bach-y-Rita connects a video camera to a subject's head. Input from the camera is shunted to a laptop, which reduces the images to 144 pixels and sends this information via electrodes to a grid that rests on the tongue. As visual images are transferred to the tongue in this way, blindfolded people begin to process this input and provide their brain with information about where objects are located in their environment. With repeated effort and concentration, for example, most subjects can successfully catch a ball that is rolled on the table toward them, nine out of ten times. Not bad.

When one area of the brain is damaged, reports Dr. Bach-y-Rita, other areas can be taught to process the stimuli of the sensory organ that is impaired. One subject, a 16-year-old girl blind since birth, is a lead singer for her high school

choir. She began using the device in order to learn the movements of the conductor and keep time with his cadence. She learned the gestures within a half
hour and eventually began to "see" his movements across the room. This might
not qualify as true sight; nevertheless, she began to perceive or process what was
felt with her tongue as feeling/visual pictures in her brain.

In another experiment, working with leprosy patients who had lost all
sense of touch in their extremities, Bach-y-Rita created gloves that had trans-
ducers on each finger, which connected to five points on their foreheads. When
his subjects touched something, they began to "feel" the relative pressure on
their foreheads. In a matter of moments, the subjects were able to distinguish
between different types of surfaces, and they forgot that their foreheads were
doing the feeling.

Whether the brain is rewiring itself in order to repair damaged neural
pathways, modify existing circuits, or develop new neural nets, research continues to reveal its remarkable ability to adjust and adapt. Most pertinent to us is
this: we don't have to suffer a stroke, participate in a tongue compartmentalization experiment, have webbed fingers, or spend 10,000 hours in meditation in
order to employ the brain's neuroplasticity. In fact, all we have to do is to learn
and experience.

Of course, "learning and experiencing" only begin to describe the process. As
we move on, we'll examine the role that focused attention and repeated practice
play in the development of new neural connections that change the brain structurally. For now, however, our focus is on how we use knowledge and experience
to evolve our brain. To prepare for that exploration, we will take a moment to
consider two other concepts necessary to understand how learning takes place:
how the neurons in our brain wire, and the role of genetic inheritance.

A Hebb Start on Learning

Scientists have taken many approaches to the subject of learning. Our primary focus here is on the electrochemical impulses that are responsible for our
acquiring new knowledge and experiences and storing them in the brain. Simply
put, when we store information in our brain for later retrieval, we have created

a memory. How this process takes place has been the subject of much debate, but one theorist has presented us with the most plausible explanation to date.

In the 1970s, Donald Hebb, Ph.D., a Canadian neuropsychologist, presented a theory of learning and memory based on the nature of synaptic transmissions in the central nervous system (see chapter 2). According to Hebb, when we learn new information, we change the relationship between neurons.

Think of two inactive neighboring neurons (these could also be clusters of neurons) that are not linked in any way other than location. When neuron A is activated or turned on, an electrochemical response flashes across the brain (think of a thunderstorm generating a diffuse form of lightning). This affects the inactive neighboring neuron B, and it becomes easier to make a new synaptic connection between them. When two neighboring neurons are triggered at the same time on several occasions, the cells and synapses between them change chemically. Their chemically altered state means that when one fires, it will be a stronger trigger to the other. Over time, the connection between them grows so strong that they fire simultaneously in a shared response, instead of at random. They tend to gang up in a more lasting and enriched relationship and in the future, they will fire off in tandem much more readily than before. Eventually, neurons that fire together, will wire together. Figure 6.1 displays Hebb's model.

For this to happen, we need to turn on a neuron or a cluster of neurons already synaptically wired in our brain. Then, if a neuron is alone and unstimulated, it will be easier for it to make a new synaptic connection with the group of neurons next door that is already firing in excitement.

Imagine that you want to learn to ride a motorbike. If you have ever ridden a bicycle, you already have clusters of neurons that wired together earlier in your life when you learned to balance on two wheels. When you start to ride the motorbike, those prewired clusters that still store your experience with balance start to fire, and you remember how to balance and what direction to lean as you turn corners. Although operating the motorbike will require you to learn ways of changing speed, braking, etc., that are different from your bike riding days, you will find that it is easier to master the motorbike than it would be had you

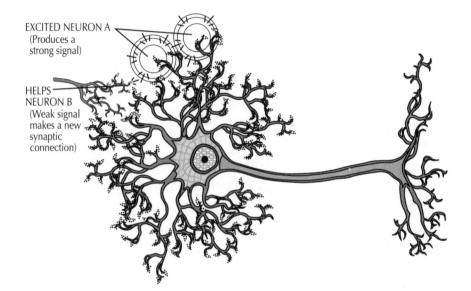

EXCITED NEURON A
(Produces a
strong signal)

HELPS
NEURON B
(Weak signal
makes a new
synaptic
connection)

Figure 6.1

According to Hebb's model, the strong helps the weak. When Neuron A fires (strong signal) and becomes excited, Neuron B (weak signal) will become more easily excited, and the strength of the synaptic connection at Neuron B will be enhanced. Once Neuron A helps to strengthen the connection with Neuron B, the next time they fire, they will turn on more readily in tandem and wire together more strongly.

never ridden a bicycle, because the most important part of the new experience is familiar to you.

The "fire together, wire together" principle explains how we can incorporate new knowledge and experiences into our brain. *Learning* is the new relationship created between neurons, and *remembering* is keeping that relationship socially alive. It becomes easier for us to remember, or produce the same level of mind from what we learned, because the next time the neural network of synapses fire, it will include the new connection and they will all fire together more strongly and easily. Neural networks develop as a result of continuous neural activation.

If Hebb's theory is true, then we need to have a known (stronger signal) already in place in order to learn something that is unknown (weak signal). We must use existing circuits that represent what is familiar to us—what we have already learned and synaptically wired in place—to learn something that is unfamiliar. Hebbian learning states that it is easiest to make a new connection in the brain by turning on a few existing circuits; once these are activated, we can add a new stitch to the living tapestry of connections.

Association is how we accomplish this process. When we learn by association, we draw upon what we have already learned, remembered, and wired in the brain so that we can add a new connection. As we turn on existing circuits, those circuits will be closely related to the new subject we are attempting to learn.

At birth, then, we need prewired circuits already in place in our brain, to build on in order to form new circuits. And so, contrary to Aristotle, we are not born with a blank tablet upon which the environment makes its mark. We now know that synaptic connections are forming at a formidable rate even while embryos are developing in the uterus. We are born with preloaded synaptic connections in the form of existing memories, which serve as the building blocks from which we begin to build our life. But where do the memories originate that enable us to begin learning immediately after we are born?

The Gene Factor: The Long and Short of It

As we learned in chapter 5, the synaptic patterns we inherited genetically (activated through selection or instruction) allow us to function in our environment. Without many of them, our survival would be in jeopardy. For example, we arrive in this world with a predisposition to cry when in distress—whether that distress is due to hunger, thirst, cold, excessive heat, or whatever other sensory experience we are having. All healthy members of our species are born with relatively similar universal compartments in the neocortex, and our brains are generally formatted with specific traits and behaviors that we share as human beings. These are *universal long-term genetic traits,* and they are common to the entire human race.

Another source of those neural connections we are born with is, of course, the genetic inheritance from our nearest ancestors—parents and grandparents. Consequently, we are born with unique patterns of synaptic connections demonstrated by certain *short-term genetic predispositions*—not just for height, weight, and the color of our hair and eyes, but for behaviors and attitudes as well. We carry with us some of the emotional baggage or blessings of our ancestors. Often, the traits that hindered our parents are passed down to the next generation, and then to the next. This may give new meaning to the expression, "The sins of the father are visited upon the sons."

It doesn't serve us, though, to think of our lineage as a vicious circle perpetuating bad habits and the like. It's true that the apple doesn't fall very far from the tree, but that doesn't mean that it can't roll to another location. That's the basic premise of this book, after all. It's true that our genetically prepatterned memories provide a foundation for us to begin life. Whether they are activated by the environment or by some genetic program, these memories begin to build a child's developing identity; they serve as the raw materials to form the "self." However, science now understands that our genes are not necessarily our destiny. We inherit about 50 percent of our neural networks; the other 50 percent we gain through our own knowledge and experiences.

In spite of our long-term commonalities, then, we are each an individual, one of a kind. When we shift our focus away from the gross level of cerebral lobes and compartments and view the brain at a cellular level, this is where our neuroplasticity helps us to have more individualized identities. How these segregated bundles of neural nets are wired, and the specific synaptic connections that comprise them, make us truly unique. Hebb's theory tells us that the number of connections, the patterns of how they are connected, and even how strong the connections are within the neural networks explains how we will express the mind as the individual self in the neocortex.

Our individuality is only partly shaped by those who contributed their DNA to us. You are not a clone rolling off an assembly line, or even a composite version of everyone in your lineage who came before you. Although you may share some traits with your earliest ancestors, much of what you inherit is from your parents, and was shaped, after their own births, by the experiences they have had in their lives. Also, keep in mind that you are a combination of the genetics of two people. Perhaps your father's pessimism is offset by your mother's optimism.

We've all probably caught ourselves at one time or another doing or saying something and then realizing, "I'm starting to sound/act just like my mother/father." I don't know about you, but this realization scared the heck out of me. What are the chances that you will ultimately behave and act just like your parents? This is a legitimate, important question.

If conscious awareness only activates our genetically prepatterned neural network of synaptic connections, we probably will think the same thoughts, feel the same feelings, and act just like our parents at different points in our life. Those inherited synaptic circuits will become so strongly wired by their repetitive firing that we'll be naturally predisposed by our genetic propensities to be of the same mind as our mother and father. Whether we have inherited the wiring for anger, victimization, or insecurity from the genetic code of our lineage (because our parents have remembered, practiced, and mastered those circuits to produce the same repeatable experiences), if these cells continue to fire together, then they will develop stronger and more intricately refined synaptic connections.

Our consciousness tends to live in the part of the brain where those familiar circuits hold the reins. People often operate as if they have only one option for behavior. We've all heard folks say, "Hey, that's just me. That's just who I am." More correctly, given what we know about the role genetics plays, they should say, "Hey, this is just me choosing to activate the circuits I have inherited from my mother and father. Because my brain possesses neuroplastic qualities, I've developed some of my own neural nets. But for now, I'm choosing to go with what has been present from the beginning. That's just who I am."

After studying this phenomenon, I began to realize that, theoretically, if we don't make any new synaptic connections in our life, we can rely only on our inherited synaptic connections, and that leads to a mind expressing only our genetic predispositions.

How can we add, instead, to what we are given? How can we add to the trillions of possible combinations, sequences, and patterns of synaptic connections to upgrade the hardware of our brain? Mathematically, based on potential combinations and permutations, if we just add a few synaptic connections to the existing matrix, we will add many new possible directions in which our brain can fire in novel, sophisticated sequences and patterns.

Our genetic inheritance is not the end-all, but only the initial deposit of our neurological capital. In order to evolve ourselves (and our species), we must be able to add to and modify what we were initially given. Our ability to express a greater sense of self results from adding our own synaptic connections in response to our environment, and utilizing our brain's plasticity. Both play a crucial role in helping us form these connections.

The Way Out of the Genetic Trap

If we choose to rely solely on our inherited circuits, we develop the habit of *being* our genetics. What is the alternative? There are two ways we make new synaptic connections in the brain. The first is to learn new things; the second way is to have new experiences. Every time we learn new knowledge or information, the brain changes. When we embrace a novel experience, the brain also records it as a new pattern of neurological circuits.

Therefore, if we seldom learn new things and have hardly any novel experiences throughout our lifetime, the fewer the synaptic connections we will make. For the most part, our conscious awareness will be limited to using those initial neural networks from our genetic lineage with which to produce the mind. According to Hebb's model, when we fire the same genetically inherited circuits over and over again, then we wire ourselves to live out only our predetermined genetic destiny. Put another way, if we repeat the same familiar, predictable, routine, and automatic actions, thoughts, habits, and behaviors, our brain will remain at status quo. And if we accept the "fire together, wire together" theorem, then it will only make sense that those connections will become more hardwired by the repeated activation of the same neural nets. We will not evolve our brain to any large degree.

The way out, in order to escape our genetic propensities, is to continually learn new information and have new experiences.

To Evolve, Learn New Knowledge

Typically, when we have acquired new knowledge, we say, "I learned something new today." What do we really mean when we say we know or have learned something? Generally, this means that we have been exposed to factual data, have committed that information to memory, and can recall it when necessary or when asked. What this means neurologically is that we have organized a series of synaptic circuits into a neural network, which stores that concept. The mere process of learning a new idea and storing that fact as a memory in the brain leaves a mark of that thought in our living neurological tissue.

In the early 1970s, psychologist Endel Tulving called storing knowledge in the brain in this manner *semantic memory*.[4] Semantic memories pertain to information that we come to know intellectually but have not experienced. In other words, we may understand new information as a concept but have not yet experienced it with our senses. What we have learned has been given life only in our mind, not in our body. I call this the *text method* of making connections because it is devoid of experience. Semantic memories are just facts recorded in the brain, information stored as intellectual or philosophical data. The knowledge exists as a possibility, not a reality.

Therefore, think of learning new knowledge as philosophically embracing someone else's learned experiences. This is information that another person has learned or realized, but that we have not yet applied in our own life. Semantics are just facts that we can recall or remember.

For example, we can read about a concept like *déjà vu*. We can understand that it is the perception that people have when they believe that they are experiencing a previous event or fragment of time. If we commit that definition to memory, by forming the necessary neural circuitry that enables us to capture and recall it, we have a semantic memory of that concept. However, when we ourselves experience the sensations of *déjà vu*, that definition suddenly seems flat and not a true representation of the experience.

We all know people who are *book smart,* meaning that they have a great deal of semantic memories stored away in his or her neocortex. However, not all semantic memories involve the kind of information that might help a contestant on the game show *Jeopardy!* Take phone numbers, for instance. If two people exchange phone numbers, but neither has anything with which to write the information, they would each have to commit the number to semantic memory immediately. We can't experience a phone number, so the act of memorizing that number resides almost entirely in the domain of semantic memory.

However, relying exclusively on semantic memory can put us in jeopardy. It is hard for many of us to retain semantic memories for a long time; that is why this type of memory gets labeled *short-term memory*. We don't experience this information fully. When someone tells us his phone number, we use our sense of hearing to listen to the seven digits being spoken, but if that's all we do—listen, and then repeat it—we are relying on just that one sense. We often fail to form an intricate enough neural network to make it easy to recall that phone number a few minutes, hours, or days later.

Most memories that we learn intellectually in the form of knowledge are apt to be short-term memories; they are available to us for a while, then seem to vanish forever unless someone or something reminds us of that learned memory.

Mapping What We Learn

As we put our attention on new ideas and mentally hold those pieces of information in place long enough, we synaptically encode this knowledge in the neocortex. The purpose of this action is so that we can apply, analyze, and understand new concepts.

When we read a book or listen to a lecture, we learn by associating the new data with familiar information. When we integrate this knowledge as a new thought, it is as if a three-dimensional map is laid down in the brain. The new dendrite connections that form to process and store the knowledge we just learned function as pathways laid down by our conscious awareness, so that we can remember that data at a future time. Neural nets that are associated with that information will now turn on in just the right sequence, order, and combination to remind us of that knowledge. To "re-member" is to "re-mind," and it is our conscious awareness that will animate those newly formed circuits to produce the same level of mind. Our brain's fundamental plasticity makes this all possible.

According to the "fire-together, wire-together" credo, it may take repeated re-minding to create a semantic memory. To make any new synaptic connection more lasting takes repeated activation. Once we memorize information, it has a designated place in our brain for our conscious awareness to activate and revisit, so that we can use what we intellectually learned. The brain is now geographically patterned for the recording of a thought.

For example, say that we have never owned a dog but are contemplating getting a puppy. If we read a book on raising cocker spaniels, we can learn about the breed, its genetic background, the personality of the dog, its life expectancy, and so on. As we look at illustrations in the book, our synaptic patterns will also imprint those pictures as memories associated with our new ideas about cocker spaniels.

As long as we hold an intent to memorize the information, each time we learn something about cocker spaniels, new patterns of connections are made with neighboring neurons. These neighboring neurons may have a limited associative memory of dogs (because we never owned one), yet the brain will build on whatever dog-related knowledge and experience it has in its existing synaptic patterns. In Hebbian terms, the strong signals firing the synaptic connections of what we already know about dogs are helping to fire the weak signals of neighboring neurons; we are trying to make connections regarding what we don't know but are just learning about cocker spaniels.

When we then think about what we just learned regarding cocker spaniels, we actually fire those patterns and reinforce what we learned. We remember, process, and mentally rehearse our new knowledge, strengthening those neural connections to prepare ourselves for the experience of owning the new dog. We now have an integrated concept, a cocker spaniel neural net. (Our subsequent experiences with actually owning the dog will enrich this neural net even more.)

As we now see, a *neural network* is literally millions of neurons firing together in diverse compartments, modules, sections, and subregions throughout the entire brain. They team up to form communities of nerve cells that act in unison as a group, clustered together in relation to a particular concept, idea, memory, skill, or habit. Whole patterns of neurons throughout the brain become connected through the process of learning, to produce a unique level of mind.

Growing the Brain

Our ability to educate ourselves actually grows the brain, making additional synaptic connections. In a recent article in the *New York Times,* Anders Ericsson, Ph.D., a psychology professor at Florida State University, discussed his work in trying to discover what factors determine whether a person is good at a particular task. Ericsson's early experiments dealt with memory. He asked subjects to listen to a series of random numbers, memorize them, and then repeat them in the order in which they were heard. After 20 hours of training, one of his test subjects was able to improve from remembering seven digits to 20 digits. After about 200 hours of training, the subject was able to listen to and recall 80 digits![5]

Ericsson was surprised to learn that memory was more of a cognitive (thinking) exercise than an intuitive one. He had presumed that genetics played a major role in how well one person can memorize, versus another. The initial differences in memory ability his subjects displayed, however, were overcome by how effectively each person encoded the information. The deliberate practice he put his subjects through involved setting goals, obtaining immediate feedback, and concentrating on technique. Memorizing these numbers was purely an endeavor in semantic learning, and practice (resulting in the repeated firing of those neural sequences used to store numbers) resulted in the subjects' improved performance.

The Power of Attention

The key ingredient in making these neural connections from semantic data, and in remembering that data, is focused attention. When we mentally attend to whatever we are learning, the brain can map the information on which we are focusing. On the other hand, when we don't pay complete attention to what we are doing in the present moment, our brain activates a host of other synaptic networks that can distract it from its original intention. Without focused concentration, brain connections are not made, and memory is not stored. In other words, we make no long-lasting synaptic connections.

Moreover, the stronger a person's concentration, the stronger the signals that are sent to the associated neurons in the brain, leading to a more pronounced level of firing. Attention creates heightened stimulation, which exceeds the normal threshold of neural firing, and it therefore incites new teams of neurons to unite.

Professor Michael Merzenich, Ph.D., of San Francisco, the world's leading researcher on brain plasticity, has observed that sculpting of the brain's neural connections happens only when attention is paid to a stimulus.[6] All types of stimulation should grow new brain circuits, but if we don't pay attention or attend to the stimulation, the neurons will never form strong, lasting connections. It takes attention to what we are learning and presence of mind to focus the brain on desired inputs, so that we can fully activate the appropriate circuits.

Let's assume right now, as you read this chapter, that your attention is completely occupied. Instead, stop for a moment and listen to sounds around you. While you were reading, your attention excluded all the other external stimuli, and you may have been unaware of the sound of the computer running or the clock ticking. By not noticing any sounds around us, the brain has no need to make any synaptic connections other than the connections it has its active attention on. Through paying attention, or employing *focused concentration,* we create longer-lasting memories. In so doing, we make learning more effective.

To Evolve, Have New Experiences

In addition to learning, the second way we make synaptic circuits in the neocortex is through our experiences. Experience enriches the brain and, for that reason, it makes the strongest, most long-lasting synaptic connections.

You've likely heard the expression that "experience is the best teacher." Whoever coined this phrase probably didn't have the same understanding of brain physiology and chemistry as we do today, but the statement rings true beyond the commonplace use the phrase gets. If the goal of any learning is the ability to recall the information at a later time, then experience—in the form of episodic memories associated with known information stored in the neo-cortex—goes the distance for us.

University of Toronto psychologist Endel Tulving has called this type of learning *episodic memory* because this mode of memory is all about our personal experiences. Events we experience that are associated with people and things at specific places and times, he claimed, are more likely to be stored as long-term memories. He reasoned that unlike facts or intellectual information, episodic memories involve the body and the senses as well as the mind. They require our full participation.

Episodic memories are how we learn from experiences. For example, we can consciously link the recollection of a time and a place with a person and a thing—or any combination thereof. These patterns of experience are then embroidered in the neurological framework of the neocortex. The brain stores these episodic memories differently, through a different neurological process, than with semantic memories.

We have a much easier time storing our more sensory experiences in long-term memory than we do with semantic learning. With just the least little trigger, I can remember Brian M. and his habit of sitting next to me in chemistry class with his hand twirling a pencil through his permed blonde hair, and I can recall smelling the lingering sulfurous remnants of some experiment, and seeing the toothpick-and-Styrofoam-ball models of the atom that hung from the fluorescent fixtures. And how could I ever forget the time that Bobby O.'s score on one of the Scantron tests failed to "beat the monkey" (the number on the grading curve that our fiendishly cruel chemistry teacher Mr. A. assigned to a monkey arbitrarily filling in circles). How I hated those agonizing moments I spent waiting, sitting on that metal and wood stool, until Mr. A., with his thin reedy voice, read my own score out loud.

As you can tell from this example, even though it has been years since I was in a high school chemistry class, I still remember much about it (although I've disguised the names to protect the innocent and the not so innocent). Why is that? The key is the gut-wrenching, jaw-clenching dread I experienced every time Mr. A. read those test scores. When we associate a memory with a strong emotion, we create a more long-term memory than if we simply learned a fact and stored it semantically. In fact, chemistry—the biochemistry of neuron function—is partly responsible for how those memories are stored and retained long-term.

Through our five senses, we record all the incoming data from our diverse experiences in the brain's synaptic wiring. The senses provide the raw data that allows us to form episodic memories. If knowledge feeds the mind through the brain, then experience feeds the mind through the body. When we are in the midst of a new experience, all our senses become engaged in the event. What we are seeing, smelling, hearing, tasting, and touching/feeling sends a synchronous crescendo of sensory stimuli through five different pathways to the brain all at once. When that data reaches the brain, jungles of neurons fire and reorganize, and there is an enormous release of chemical neurotransmitters at the synaptic space as well as in other brain regions. New synaptic neurological patterns begin to shape the brain to map that experience as new memories in the form of neural nets.

The release of different brain chemicals produces specific feelings; consequently, the end product of every experience is a feeling or an emotion. Feelings are chemical memories. Therefore, we can remember experiences better because we can remember how they felt. So whether we are remembering the pain of waiting for our father to come home from work because we got in trouble in school, or the pleasure of the picnic where we met our future spouse, those feelings and emotions associated with a past event are what seal the memory with a particular chemical signature called a feeling.

The combination of what we experience with what we feel naturally forms lasting memories branded within us. That is why most of us remember exactly where we were when we learned of the 9/11 attacks on New York City and the Pentagon. We can remember a lot about that day because we remember how we felt. The experience brought with it a striking set of feelings tied to memories of events, people, things, the time in our life, and the particular place we were when we saw or heard the news.

Feelings are what allow us to record our sensory experiences through our neural circuitry and brain chemistry. When we remember an experience, we feel the exact same way we did at the time of the event. When we either consciously or unconsciously activate the associated neural networks of any experience (memory), the circuits we fire create the same, corresponding chemicals in the brain. These chemicals then signal the body. As a result, when we recreate a memory, we reproduce the same feeling in the body connected to the initial event. The body then will experience what is neurochemically recorded in the brain as a feeling. Episodic memories are remembered as feelings, and feelings are always related to experiences.

Tulving reasoned that there are only a handful of elements that are known in our external world. And because our sensory experiences involve all of the knowns (think "nouns" or "items," as he called them) that are familiar to us, they include the events related to people and things, at specific places and times. Episodic memories always tie a person with a place, a thing with an event at a specific time, or a person to a time in our life, to name a few. Tulving noted that these autobiographical memories are based on our perceptual, sensory experience of the environment, and they tend to be stored and retrieved differently than semantic memories.

Nearly everything we learn, experience, and remember is associated with a whole host of associated bits of information and feelings stored in our neocortex. Does the following experience sound familiar? You are driving, and when a song comes on the radio, you remember all the lyrics and begin singing along. Perhaps then you start thinking about the former lover you lived with at a certain time in your life. Then you begin to laugh when you remember your semi-serious arguments about your favorite band kicking ass versus being pretentious to the extreme. Then you tear up, thinking about the cat the two of you adopted as a stray, and how its sudden disappearance seemed to predict your relationship's demise. Any number of other emotions and experiences start running through your head, and the memory of events related to other people and things, at specific times and places, comes to mind, just from a song that jogs a memory of some prior experience.

Let's go one step further to illustrate how episodic memories manage to formulate intricate neural patterns. What if you meet someone for the first time at a cocktail party, while visiting a friend in New York? She approaches you with beautiful curly hair, green eyes, a radiating smile, and bright white teeth. Your brain begins to log this visual information because you are paying attention to all the stimuli. Then you notice that she looks like a friend from high school, and immediately associate the memory of your high school friend with this new acquaintance. Next, she says in a melodious voice that her name is Diana and that she is a singer on Broadway.

As a result of this simple encounter, your brain associates what it is seeing (Diana's physical appearance) with what it is hearing (Diana's beautiful voice and her name). At the same time, your brain associates the visual image of Diana with your memory of a former classmate. Next, she reaches out her hand. Her skin is soft, but her handshake is firm and strong. Now the feeling or sensory pathways in your brain become further involved in the experience. The firm handshake connects to the memory of a high school friend, which connects to the name Diana, which now connects to the sound of her voice.

But what happens next secures the experience as memorable. As she smiles and looks into your eyes, your heart begins to race. You *feel* something. As she leans over to ask if you are okay, you notice that she is wearing jasmine, your favorite scent. As you try to compose yourself and clear your throat, she reaches for a glass of champagne on a passing tray in order to help you. She takes a glass herself and toasts to your health. You take a big gulp of the worst champagne you ever tasted. Now all your senses are involved in the experience.

The new experience with this person is beginning to wire a new and memorable neural network. All your senses have gathered the raw materials to associate what you visually saw with what you verbally heard with what you physically touched with what you sensually felt with what you pleasurably smelled with what you adversely tasted. And all these sensory stimuli are now connected to a neural net that was already wired in your synaptic network—the episodic memories of someone from your past. The result is that you have memorable feelings related to this event.

Let's say now that it's a year later. You never saw Diana again after that encounter and had not thought about her since. Then your friend from New York calls you on the phone and as you are talking, she mentions Diana. You pause and think, saying out loud, "Diana, Diana . . . ," and your friend says, "You know, curly hair, great smile?" And then it hits you. "That's right, cocktail party, Manhattan, 1999, green eyes, firm handshake, tall and slender, smells like jasmine, sweet voice, lousy champagne . . . I remember." It took only a few associative stimuli to activate the past neurological connections, and once they became activated, you remembered the experience.

SEALING THE DEAL WITH EMOTION

In an experiment, two unrelated groups of people were asked to view several movies. The control group was allowed to view the shows without restrictions. The second group was instructed to observe the shows without any emotional or sensory response. At the end of the experiment, both groups were asked to answer questions designed to test their memory.

Every member of the control group, which experienced emotional responses from the stimuli of the movies, remembered the details of each movie to a much greater degree. The other group, which was asked simply to observe the movies from a detached state, demonstrated that their memories of the past events were lessened.

These findings suggest that in the first group, the sensory stimuli from the environment (the movie) reinforced the connections in the neural nets of the brain as if the sensory experiences gained the brain's complete attention. The additional neurotransmitters that

the brain made from becoming emotionally involved apparently activated and further stimulated those networks to fire with greater intensity. A heightened ability to fire synaptic patterns makes for better
memory.[7]

The Importance of Episodic Memory

Our evolutionary success is based on our ability to learn from experiences,
and then to adapt, change, or modify our behaviors at the next similar opportunity. What we learn through experience molds the soft, neuroplastic tissues of
our brain. For example, scientists isolated laboratory rats into three different
environments. In the first environment, a rat was placed in solitary confinement,
having no interaction with any other rats, limited stimulation, and little food and
water. In the second environment, a rat was placed in a standard laboratory
group cage with a running wheel and two other rats. The third environment was
set up as an *enriched environment*. These rats were caged with some of their siblings and offspring, and they had a host of toys with which to interact. All three
groups lived in these environments for months. At the end of the experiment, the
rats had their brains surgically removed and examined microscopically.

When scientists evaluated the rats from the enriched environment, the
rodents' brains had significantly increased in size, had increased in the total
number of neurons compared to the brains of the control groups, and showed
a measurable increase in brain neurotransmitters, which are directly proportional to the number of synaptic connections between neurons.[8] Therefore, the
enriched surroundings did exactly that; they enriched the development of neurons and their connections in the cerebral cortex by increasing the brain's total
experiences. Interestingly, the rats in the enriched environment also lived longer
and had less body fat. Upon further examination of the enriched group's brains,
scientists observed an increase in the number of *dendrite spines,* which are the
docking points to which other nerve cells connect. Figure 6.2 illustrates the dendrite spines of a neuron.

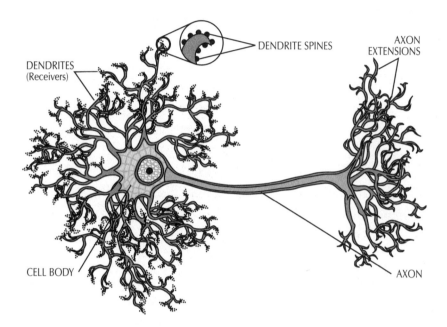

Figure 6.2

A nerve cell with dendrite spines. The thorn-like projections serve as receivers for various synaptic connections. The total number of dendrite spines tends to increase when a living organism is exposed to an enriched environment. Because enriched environments offer more novel and diversified experiences, it is postulated that new experiences create more synaptic connections and, therefore, more intricate and enriched connectivity in gray matter.

This same process also applies to human beings; we, too, produce additional synaptic connections in response to new environmental stimuli. In fact, as we embrace enriched and novel experiences to make new synaptic connections, our potential for brain growth expands exponentially, because we start with an enlarged cerebral cortex. Larger brain volume allows a greater number of neurons, which equals a greater number of potential connections and a greater propensity for learning. Diversified experiences leave new road maps in the neocortex that will then be accessed as stronger, more long-lasting memories. And the more enriched the novel experience, or the more the brain becomes experienced at any one thing, the more the brain's neural networks become interconnected, modified, enriched, and intricate.

Knowledge and Experience United

6.022 x 10^{23}. That's Avogadro's number. I didn't have to look it up. I even knew that the name, Avogadro's number, is just an honorary name attached to the calculated value of the number of atoms, molecules, and so on in a gram mole of any chemical substance. Besides learning it in Mr. A.'s chemistry class, I also came across it in undergraduate and graduate chemistry classes. I don't use the number every day (in fact, not at all anymore), but it's lodged in a neural net along with Mr. A., Brian M., Bobby O., and that darned test-taking monkey. But there's more to this than just having an emotion linked to that information. I did have to use 6.022 x 10^{23} on a few occasions in my time as a student. The combination of experience with a linked emotion and repetition were crucial in securing this concept in the soft tissues of my brain.

Knowledge and experience work together in another way as well. When we learn new knowledge and memorize that novel information, we then have the ability to be more prepared for a new experience. Without knowledge, we enter an experience without the understanding of how to interact in the midst of the experience.

Knowledge, then, is often the precursor of experience. This is really the root of formal education. We often move from classroom instruction to field experience, whether we are going to school to be a nurse; a heating, ventilation, and air conditioning system installer; a repair person, or any one of hundreds of other careers.

Sound pedagogical principles support this notion of instruction and practice. We have to read and study a lot of information in order to turn all the new knowledge into routine memories, so that we know how and why we will be doing certain procedures. How we apply that knowledge is the action of semantic memories, so that we can further prepare ourselves for reinforcing them as episodic memories.

The volumes of stored intellectual data that we learn over time, in the form of hundreds of thousands of new neural networks, can be activated in another way. To personalize and try out what we philosophically learn reinforces those semantic circuits and creates long-term memories from our new experiences. The semantic brain circuits are in place, waiting to be used. We can rely on our neurologically mapped information because we already know what to do to perform a specific result. If there were no circuits present in us for any of the above-mentioned specialties, more than likely we could not know what to do in given situations.

We learn knowledge so that we can demonstrate what we have learned. Learning new knowledge prepares us for a new experience, and the more knowledge we have, the better prepared we are for that experience. Knowledge and experience work together to form the best, most refined neural connections in our brain. In the process, we take advantage of the plasticity of the brain. Although an outside agency can add new circuits to a computer, only the brain can create new wiring patterns for itself.

All that information we learned and memorized is absolutely necessary to prepare us for the experience of being a nurse or an air-conditioning specialist. The next step is to engage in practical experiences; we need to apply, demonstrate, and personalize the information so that our brain can process what we learned to make more enriched connections. This is how we evolve our understanding and evolve our brain. As we get our body involved in these new experiences of practical application, the five pathways of the senses are sending feedback, reinforcing the brain's initial circuits that were fabricated from memorizing a lot of intellectual data. In this way, episodic memories begin to pattern the framework of new neurological connections.

The memories we are creating are associated with what we experience through our senses by interacting with different people and things at different places and times. As we remember how to do certain procedures, we can do them better or even differently, the next time we participate in a similar situation.

For instance, you might remember how to treat duodenal ulcers because you remember that man (person) you became friends with during Christmas of 1999 (time) from Norway (place), and he seemed to suffer so greatly that you never forgot about a specific medication (thing) that gave him such relief. Your experience thus enriched what you intellectually learned at school. Knowledge without experience is philosophy, and experience without any knowledge is ignorance. The interplay between the two produces *wisdom*.

CYCLING: JUST LEARNING ABOUT IT

Suppose that, last year, you sat on your couch munching on Power Bars while rooting on riders in the Tour de France. It's a grueling race, so all those extra calories seemed necessary, but at the end of the 22 days, you noticed your clothes were fitting a little too tightly. You decided to take up the sport. Problem is, you never learned to ride a bike. What to do?

You read a book about cycling. In this process, you intellectually learn semantic information about different bike models, riding techniques, maintenance, and repairs. You might even learn about this mystical thing called balance. If you diligently study the information, it will be stored as philosophical memory in your brain. This will create new synaptic connections in the form of semantic memories.

Then you watch a Lance Armstrong video. Finally, you ask your brother for tips. As you observe him demonstrate his skill, your brain is busy paying attention so that you will remember his instruction when it is your turn to take a shot at it. All this different data is now in the form of mapped synaptic patterns of comprehended ideas.

The information you have learned about the art of bicycle riding is still the wisdom from someone else's experience and, therefore, everything you have learned is still philosophy to you. However, your brain is now mapped and prepared for this new experience. Above all, the more knowledge you have acquired, the more prepared you will be for the experience.

The Ride Experienced: Applying What You Learn

When you get on the bicycle and actually ride it, you will invariably have new experiences. You could experience falling, balance, pedaling, shifting gears, even riding with no hands. You could have the feeling of pain when you fall and skin your knee, or while you are pedaling up a steep hill for 30 minutes. You could experience the feeling of relief when you reach the top of the hill and start to accelerate down. During all these experiences, your senses send enormous amounts of information from your body and the environment through those five sensory pathways to your brain, which records the new experiences as episodic memories. All of these experiences are neurologically and chemically encoded by the senses, and you now have new feelings that are associated with the act of riding a bicycle. The increased cascade of chemicals from the sensory experience of riding a bike for the first time make a new emotion, and that feeling reinforces the memory of riding.

In each situation, as the opportunity presents itself, you rely on what you had semantically learned and mapped in your neocortex during your period of study, as the resource for new or unfamiliar situations.

The process of three-dimensionally interacting with your body in the environment integrates all your intellectual text knowledge with an emotional-sensory experience. The more you experience the ride with your body, the more your synaptic connections are reinforced, because a host of neurotransmitters now pattern those connections more strongly.

Your conscious awareness can now activate all the neural networks of synaptic connections associated with pedaling two-wheeled vehicles, to produce the memory and understanding of how to ride a bicycle. Everything you have learned and mapped as new knowledge, as well as new experiences, is readily available. You have evolved your brain.

From Experience and Knowledge to Wisdom

Intellect is knowledge learned, and *wisdom* is knowledge experienced. When a sensory experience is connected to an episodic memory, we can at last understand the concept of wisdom. Wisdom is having an experience that we understand in its full meaning, because we had the experience and learned from the novelty of that experience. This is one of the great things I learned from the teachings of Ramtha (see chapter 1). He always urges his students to apply philosophy to experience so that wisdom is gained from the experience. This concept is what we can attribute to evolution. Figure 6.3 shows the progression of knowledge to evolution.

Knowledge, then, can be described as someone else's known experiences and the wisdom that he or she can communicate. When we take semantic understandings communicated by someone else and internalize them by analysis, reflection, contemplation, and our own critique, we begin to make synaptic connections in the brain. These newly wired connections will be a network of neurological tissues just waiting to be activated by the experience of living with that new knowledge. Once we are able to take that intellectual information and personalize it by demonstrating what we learned in our environment, we now have a true example of a new experience, with new emotions, producing new wisdom.

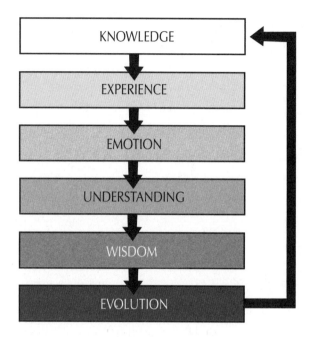

Figure 6.3

This chart is one interpretation of how human beings evolve. Knowledge is the precursor to experience. When we learn new information and apply what we learn by modifying our behavior, we create a new and more enriched experience. Because emotions are the end product of experience, the result of our intentional actions should produce a new experience with a new emotion. When we consciously understand how we created that new experience based on the memory of what we learned and did, we are now embracing wisdom. Wisdom is the conscious understanding of how we can create any experience at will. Wisdom can also result when we learn from an undesirable experience by understanding what we did to produce that outcome, so that we no longer recreate that event over again. Evolution is the wisdom from understanding the feelings we have created, based on what we have learned, demonstrated, and then experienced.

Experience as Teacher

We don't always learn first and experience later. I remember as a young child convincing my brother that we did not need to take any lessons before we went skiing for the first time. I told him that all we needed to do was to keep our skis together and push with our poles as fast as we could, as many times as we could, so that we could go straight down the mountain. My instructions were about two minutes long, and I told him to make sure that he stayed in the tucked position until we reached the bottom. As you can imagine, the day was filled with some unpleasant surprises. We realized in a matter of moments, while traveling down the expert slope (as far as we knew, a black diamond meant something only in poker), that we had no idea how to stop. That was just the beginning. We had no idea that there were any details for us to consider before we started—minor details such as moguls, quick turns, cliffs, trees, ice patches, sky lifts to get on and off, proper clothing to wear, weather conditions, and other skiers. We were engaged in a novel experience, completely lacking in knowledge. We had none of the neural architecture and synaptic connections that other skiers created from the proper learning and instruction. The lessons we learned that day were all through experience, but most were facilitated by the sensory pathways of feeling pain, experiencing cold, and embracing fatigue. The next day, we took lessons.

Learning: The Law of Association

Fortunately for my brother and me, our second-day ski instructor was wise. He asked us if we knew how to ride a bike, if we could skateboard, or if we'd ever water skied before. Although I didn't realize it then, he was using the *Law of Association* to help us learn a new skill.

I've already used this law to help you learn. When I said that a nerve cell looks like an oak tree, I referenced something familiar. Immediately, your brain sorted through all its stored knowledge and experience to come up with a matching bit of information. Our brain does this so well and so often that it makes a Google™ search look like a search through the old card catalog drawer in a university library, or a search through the bookshelves. There—I just did it again. I associated one experience you may have had (old-fashioned library search) with another (the brain) while referencing a third (a Google search).

The way in which we learn and memorize information joins neurons together to form stronger connections by the Law of Association. Hebb's theory helps explain how associative learning takes place. When weak inputs (new information we are attempting to learn) and strong inputs (familiar, known information already wired in the brain as a neural net) are fired at the same time, the weaker connection will be strengthened by the firing of the stronger connection.

When we are learning, we use past memories and prior experiences, things we already know (already wired synaptic connections), in order to build or project a new concept. If we are learning a new bit of information but we have no clue as to what a word means, it is because we have not learned it; we have no synaptic circuitry related to that bit of information. But we can associate other bits of information relative to that new word in the form of other neural nets, and by doing so, we will turn on enough neural network activity in the vicinity to cause gangs of neurons to become electrically activated. Once they become excited, we can add that new word in the form of a synaptic connection to the existing set of hot circuits that are already firing. Remember, it's easier to make a new connection to circuits that are electrically excited.

For example, when I mention the word "malleus," you might produce a weak signal in your synaptic firing because you do not know what that word means. You have no synaptic wiring to process that word. But, what if I say that the malleus is the little bone that looks like a hammer on a drum in the inner ear. What if I explain that when sound waves vibrate the eardrum like the waves created from a pebble thrown in a lake, the waves hit the drum and the hammer moves, which then transfers impulses in the form of sound to be decoded by the brain. According to Hebb's model, those statements just caused the existing circuits in your brain to fire. The concepts of hammer, bone, drum, waves, and ear were all strong stimuli because they are already wired and, therefore, your brain can turn on those neural circuits. I created a level of mind related to all this mapped information, which then allowed you to make a new connection at that activated neural network. Simply stated, by the Law of Association, we use what we know to understand what we don't know. We use existing brain circuits to make new brain circuits. Take a look at Figure 6.4 to help you understand how we learn through association to create a new level of mind.

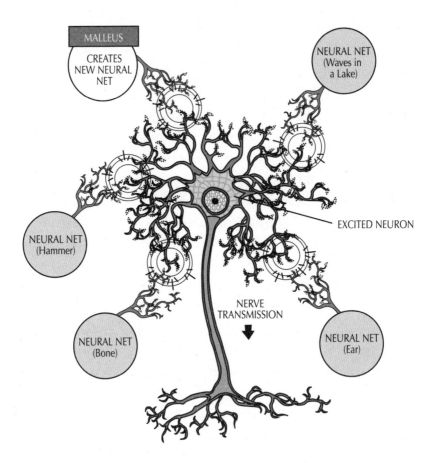

Figure 6.4

An example of associative learning: when we turn on different neural networks of known information in the brain, it is easier to make a new synaptic connection, according to Hebb's model.

An entire concept that is unfamiliar to us can be easily integrated into our preexisting neural nets when we use the Law of Association. Here's a real-life example: In his late sixties, Joe M. had to learn to use a computer for the first time. As a volunteer in his local CASA/GAL (Court Appointed Special Advocate/ Guardian ad Litem) program, he was appointed to serve as an advocate for several abused and neglected children. Every six months he had to email an update to the court on how each child was getting along in their foster home and at school, and include Joe's recommendations for services the child might need. Joe had to keep all previous reports for future reference. His wife Elaine also became a CASA volunteer with her own clients and her own set of computer files.

The problem was, the couple didn't know the first thing about how to create and manage computer files. They couldn't get the hang of saving the original report as a template and using the "File Save As" command to make duplicate reports that they could safely update. They didn't even know how to keep his files separate from hers. They had consulted computer how-to books and had tried many times to understand these procedures, but remained stymied. In other words, they couldn't form any new and lasting synaptic connections, because they were not able to turn on any existing hardware in their brain to which they could relate.

When Joe and Elaine turned for help to my computer-savvy friend Sara, she used the Law of Association and a few standard office supplies to explain the concept of computer file management in terms these former business owners would easily understand. She began by comparing Windows Explorer to a physical file cabinet, and "My Documents" as a drawer in that cabinet. She created computer folders that she named "Joe's Files" and "Elaine's Files," and told the couple to think of these as one standard green hanging folder for each of them. Under "Joe's Files," she created and named a computer folder for each of Joe's young clients, likening these to manila file folders. Then, since knowledge combined with experience is the best way to learn, she asked Elaine to perform the same procedure on the computer for her own clients.

Most important, Sara used association to demonstrate the difference between the "File Save" and "File Save As" commands. She labeled a sheet of paper as "Joe's

CASA report template" (drawing lines for the child's name and the report date), then "saved" it by simply putting it into an actual hanging folder. She labeled a few manila folders with the first names of Joe's clients. Then she took the template sheet, xeroxed it while saying "File Save As," and asked Joe to take the copy, label it with a child's name, and put it in the appropriate manila folder. She then had Joe "save" the original template back into the hanging folder.

By now, the light bulbs had come on for both Joe and Elaine. They each took a turn doing all the same procedures with the computer. They didn't even need a physical demonstration to get the hang of "dragging and dropping" their mixed-up computer files into the appropriate folders. Associating the previously mysterious workings of their computer with familiar, routine office procedures that were already established as neural nets had made the unknown, known. Through diligent practice and with the welfare of children to motivate them, Joe and Elaine have continued to build up their computer file neural net. Truly, their experience demonstrates that our neuroplastic brain can learn new skills at any age.

But association is not the only way we form new neural nets or reinforce existing ones.

Remembering: The Law of Repetition

If we learn by association, we remember by repetition. In the beginning, it takes a tremendous amount of conscious awareness for us to use focused concentration to redirect habitual thinking. But as we keep doing it, over and over, neurons begin to bond with each other. If we can repeatedly think, act, demonstrate, or experience any one thing without our mind wandering to different thoughts, our brain will make stronger, more intricate synaptic connections to facilitate that new level of mind.

Professional athletes practice their moves thousands of times, day after day, week after week, under the tutelage of coaches. They don't want to have to think about every complexity of their golf or baseball or tennis swing—in fact, they want just the opposite. By constantly practicing, they teach their muscles, or better put, develop the memory in their muscles, until they find that elusive zone in which the mind can step aside and let the body do the work. This is the *Law of Repetition* in action.

As any parent knows, children are learning machines. Sometimes they learn too well. For example, when our child first learns to walk, we're thrilled but also worried. Suddenly, her mobility exposes her to a host of potential dangers. As a child's mobility increases, doesn't it seem as though a parent's vocabulary shrinks? The word *no* seems to crop up a lot more. "No, don't touch that." "No, stay away from those stairs." "No, get back here." Imagine mom or dad's surprise when, a few weeks into this new "no" world, little Sarah says "no" when asked to put the television remote down. Where do we think she learned it? How much repetition did she hear, in just a short time, for her to associate the word said in a specific tone with the concept and with the power that word has in her environment?

As I sit here writing this, I'm reminded of how awkward it felt when I first learned how to type. Just finding the home row and positioning my fingers felt funny. Learning the location of every key was a time-consuming and often frustrating experience. But the more I practiced, the easier the skill became. You can probably think of a dozen skills you've learned over time that have now become natural to you. And by "natural," I don't just mean easy. A new skill becomes automatic, then subconscious, and then, when we've truly mastered that particular skill, it becomes unconscious; that is, we don't think about it at all.

Once we engage our conscious awareness in a thought or an experience and repeatedly think about it, continuously demonstrate it, and repetitiously enact it, the neurons in our brain start to fire, to try to hook up with each other, and attempt to form a more lasting, long-term relationship. After repeatedly firing, the neurons begin to release chemicals at the synaptic level, which allow them to team up and create a stronger set of connections.

These *neurotrophic* chemicals—in particular, one called *neural growth factor*—cause the synapses between neurons to form long-term relationships. Like a gardener's fertilizer, these chemicals prompt dendrite connections to flourish, to grow additional, more enriched connections between them, and thus connect to each other to form lasting, more hardwired bonds. As nerve cells become hardwired, whatever we are learning becomes more automatic, more common, more natural, easier, and more of an unconscious process. Whether we're driving a car, typing, riding a bicycle, knitting, or doing many other activities, the more we repeat an action, and the more we reinforce a thought, the stronger the neurological connection will be.

Attention is crucial to this process. As long as we pay attention to whatever we are learning, and then repeat over and over whatever thought we are enacting, the neocortex can begin to pattern new connections in new networks, so that we can have a lasting map that is accessible in the future. If, however, we move our mind to something else in the moment we are attempting to develop new connections, the brain cannot begin to map and pattern our efforts, because the mind has left the scene and gone to a different neural pattern.

Just as with any relationship, neurons need to communicate, or fire together, a lot in the beginning, so that they can develop a more sustained relationship. Ultimately, they can turn on just by being around each other. Now we are strengthening a neurological network that is wired together with that thought, action, skill, idea, feeling, or concept. Whatever we are embracing, the conscious action starts to become simpler, easier, more natural, more familiar, more routine, more effortless, more automatic, and more subconscious, until it becomes unconscious.

If we can imagine Michelangelo's creation painting, where God's hand is reaching for Adam's hand in an effort to make contact, we will begin to see that nerve cells do the same thing: when we strive for something new, to make known what is not yet known, neighboring neurons will reach out to make a lasting union. As we fire these synaptic connections time and time again, there comes a moment that the nerve cells hook up. If Hebb's theory on learning can be summed up by the statement, "Nerve cells that fire together, wire together," then the Law of Repetition adds this additional element: "Neurons that repeatedly fire together, wire together more strongly." Our brain is constantly changing. Wiring is being abandoned and resurrected in new sequences and patterns. Our ever-evolving brain is changed by learning new information and having new experiences, which are processed through association and reinforced through repetition.

Neural networks, then, are just gangs of neurons that fire together and then wire together when we learn new information by association and remember what we learn by repetition. The end result of associating any new concept, idea, thought process, memory, skill, behavior, or action with known data and repeating it over and over again will form a new community of related neural synaptic connections or a new neural net in the brain.

Each time we activate that new neural network, we are essentially producing a new level of mind. If mind is the brain in action or the brain turned on, then new neural networks are making new levels of mind. And most important, one whole neural net can scan acres of neurological real estate to connect different compartments, modules, subregions, substructures, and even lobes to fire in infinite possible combinations.

Dual-Brain Processing, or
How Novel Information Becomes Routine

The brain is wired to learn new things, both at the microscopic level of neurons and synaptic connections (Hebbian learning), and on a macroscopic level, as we will see below, when we discuss how the two halves of the brain process novel information and store it as routine memories.

The two hemispheres of the neocortex are not mirror images of each other. The right frontal lobe is wider than the left frontal lobe. The left occipital lobe is wider than the right occipital lobe. This double asymmetry is widely known as the *Yakovlevian torque,* named after its discoverer, Harvard neuroanatomist Dr. Paul I. Yakovlev.

There is also an asymmetry in the biochemistry of the hemispheres. For example, the left hemisphere has an abundance of the neurotransmitter dopamine, while the right hemisphere has more of the neurotransmitter norepinephrine. The right hemisphere also has more receptors for the neurohormones for estrogen.

You might be thinking at this point that if the two neocortices differ in structure and chemistry, they must have somewhat different functions, and they do.

The left hemisphere (let's abbreviate it as L.H.) used to be considered dominant in comparison to the right hemisphere (R.H.). Not only did the L.H. seem to be the more active, but some neurologists deemed it superior based on its more advanced abilities to process language, to reason using analytical thinking, and to participate in linear symbolic logic. In contrast, the R.H. was initially thought to lack distinct functions.

Moreover, damage to the right hemisphere often seems incidental. Most adult patients with damage or impairments to the R.H.—that is, those who have lost the ability to control the left side of the body—may appear to be fairly unaffected in terms of cognitive abilities. This initially led some neuroscientists to assign a minor role to the R.H. But as research continued, it became apparent that R.H. damage does produce measurable changes in the brain and the body. For example, many subjects who experience R.H. strokes seem to be unaware that there is any problem with their body at all—even if they are paralyzed to the point of dragging one leg. This is called *unilateral neglect,* a state in which a person is perceptually unaware of and inattentive to one side of the body.

One puzzling situation has led to many new understandings about the role of our two hemispheres. When a young child suffers damage to the right hemisphere, this is considered extremely serious, whereas damage to the left hemisphere is usually regarded as less critical in children. This supposition is exactly opposite to the way that physicians generally regard hemisphere damage in adults. With adult patients, many surgeons think twice about operating on the L.H., where the language center and many other specific functions are housed. Surgeons may be more comfortable with operating on an adult's R.H., because there has seemed to be a greater margin for error.

Since children are still in the early process of learning language, it might make sense that damage to their left hemisphere would tend to be benign, because not many synaptic connections would be mapped there yet. But this does not explain why damage to the right hemisphere is so devastating in children. Is it possible that the R.H. is more active in children, then as we become adults, the left lobe becomes the more active hemisphere? If this is so, what would cause this transference, and what purpose would it serve? These were the thoughts of neuropsychologist Elkhonon Goldberg, Ph.D.[9]

As Kids Become Adults,
Could Hemisphere Roles Switch?

Goldberg observed that as children, we are exposed to enormous amounts of novel information, whereas as adults, we operate much of the time by performing routine tasks and using information that has long been familiar to us. He wondered whether the transition from childhood to adulthood involves a broad transfer of functions and information from the R.H. to the L.H. In 1981, Goldberg published a theoretical paper that linked the R.H. to cognitive novelty and the L.H. to cognitive routine. He posited that the right side of the neocortex is most active in processing new, unknown concepts and the left side is most active in processing familiar, known traits. As an individual develops from youth to adulthood, the introduction of new stimuli might be processed in the right side of the cortex, and then be transferred and stored as familiar information in the left side of the cortex. This could explain why right-hemisphere damage is so significant in children, and why left-sided injury is more devastating to adults. In both cases, the injury sites affect the most active area of the brain.

Goldberg's hypothesis was actually a simple reflection of how we tend to learn as an advanced species. That is, just like Hebb's microscopic model of learning between neurons, we are wired on a large scale to draw upon known patterns of information to better understand new and unknown information. It would make sense that we are equipped with a large brain consisting of a right hemisphere that is skilled at processing novel information, and a left hemisphere that is equally skilled at processing routine, familiar, automatic patterns of information and behavior. Our learned relationship to familiar stimuli builds a storehouse of habitual skills that provides a springboard to our ability to learn novel concepts. The plasticity that sets us apart as a species is our ability to use familiar concepts and wire them to unfamiliar concepts.

We also know from Hebb's model that when we encounter new information or experiences, we learn by associating the new stimuli with stored memories (known, familiar data) in the form of preexisting synaptic patterns. In this way, we create new, more enhanced synaptic circuits to build greater models of understanding.

In the early stages of learning, we are faced with novelty. Learning continues through our ability to be present and attend to the new information. Next follow moments during which we review and internalize the new stimuli, as we begin to make it familiar or known. By the end of every learning process, the newly acquired information is known and familiar; if we have learned a behavior or a task, it may now be routine, even automatic. Our ability to process unknown to known, unfamiliar to familiar, novel to routine is the very way in which we proceed in our individual evolution.

If the mind draws from familiar internal representations (known ideas) to speculate and to create new internal representations (unknown ideas), could the right hemisphere be the place where we process novel experiences, serving as the stage where we invent new ideas for future experience? Could the left hemisphere be our storehouse for information and actions that have become familiar?

If true, this paradigm would begin to redefine our model of the brain's hemispheres, which many standard neurological texts describe as being completely separate in function. For example, it would now make sense why the language center has long been thought to be located in the left hemisphere. Since language is a routine, automatic function for most of us, it is predominantly L.H. dominant. The idea that the right hemisphere is responsible for spatial relationships can now be understood as well. When test subjects learn spatial representations by being exposed to those novel puzzles that cognitive neuroscientists use, these subjects initially process their spatial experiences in the R.H. *because of* their novelty.

Dual-brain processing, the shift from the processing of novel information in the right hemisphere to its mapping as routine in the left hemisphere, is consistent with all types of learning, according to a study by Alex Martin, Ph.D., and associates at the National Institutes of Mental Health. Using PET scans, they studied blood flow in functioning human brains during exposure to novel tasks involving words and objects. Every time that the subjects were introduced to a new task, a specific area in the R.H. was particularly active. As participants learned different types of information, so that the subject matter became familiar or routine, activation in the R.H. decreased. As the task was practiced by repeated exposure to the new word or object, a specific region in the L.H. became more activated. In all subjects, there was an obvious shift in the way novel information became processed as routine.[10]

In fact, numerous studies have demonstrated that humans learn through dual-brain processing.[11] In experiments that put subjects in novel situations requiring complex problem solving, increased brain activity was seen to begin in the right frontal lobe. As participants learned the solutions to problems, their left frontal lobe displayed heightened neurological activity.

It seems that the transformation of novel information from the right hemisphere to routine information in the left hemisphere takes place regardless of the nature of the type of information being learned. The neurological circuits located in the R.H. are especially skilled at learning a new task quickly, while the synaptic networks in the L.H. are more skilled at perfecting a task—given sufficient motivation and diligent practice.

Making the Unknown, Known

It is important to understand that we are talking about degrees of activity within neural circuits. The general activities of the right and left hemispheres, observed in the novel-routine model, show definite trends or patterns that correlate with an active mind. As we can begin to understand at this point, each individual has their own ability to process information and to learn, based on how difficult a task may appear to them. That is why the movement of activity from right cortex to left cortex in novel-routine processing can occur in minutes or hours or years, depending on the complexity of the task and the skill of the person involved.

Initially scientists speculated that the functions handled by the right hemisphere were more creative, intuitive, spatial, nonlinear, meaning-oriented, emotional, and abstract than the activities of the left lobe. According to our model of dual-brain processing, this is correct. When we are creative, we are embracing novelty. When we are intuitive, we are projecting unknown possibilities. When we are nonlinear and abstract, we are not in routine or fixed in a pattern of familiarity. When we are searching for meaning in reference to our own identity, we are projecting new ideas in relationship to old concepts to advance the wisdom of self. This is how the right brain is mapped to function.

For example, the myth that music is processed in the right brain only holds true for those people who are unskilled in music. Most of us that are nonmusicians, because of its novelty, will process music on the right side of the brain. Functional brain scans show that skilled musicians listen to and process music in the left side of the brain because of the established neural nets in place from learning and experiencing.[12]

Given the nature of our anatomical duality, we can now say that the right hemisphere is a fair equal to the left. We are given a brain that is structurally wired to learn new tasks and perfect them. Making known what is not known is the mandate that is preprogrammed within the macroscopic and microscopic hardware of our human brain.

Before we move on, I want to summarize what we've learned so far:

1. By learning new information (semantic memories) and having new experiences (episodic memories), we make new synaptic connections and evolve our brain's hardware.

2. We learn by association. We use what we already know to understand the unknowns we encounter. When we fire neurological networks that are already developed from our knowledge and experience, that part of the brain is now receptive to making new synaptic connections for even greater understanding. This is Hebb's "fire together, wire together" model of learning.

3. We remember by repetition. When we put our full attention on what we are learning and practice it repeatedly, firing these synaptic connections time and time again, *neurotrophic* chemicals are released that cause the synapses between neurons to form long-term relationships. "Neurons that repeatedly fire together, wire together more strongly."

4. We have hardware in our brain that enables us to learn—to make the unknown, known—on both the Hebbian level of neurons (microscopic) and on the level of dual-brain (macroscopic) processing.

CHAPTER SEVEN

PUTTING KNOWLEDGE AND EXPERIENCE INTO PRACTICE

*The greatest discovery of my generation is
that man can alter his life simply by
altering his attitude of mind.*

—WILLIAM JAMES

In this chapter, I discuss how the Laws of Repetition and Association work in combination to form memories; examine the role that our senses and emotions play in determining the strength of the neural connections we form, and lastly, examine how our common thoughts form our personality. The emphasis here is on how we can use the Laws of Association and Repetition, our semantic and episodic memory, and the unique properties of our neocortex to best advantage. We can control these many functions, and one key to this process is our ability to focus and our willingness to use repetition.

To reinforce what I've discussed in the preceding chapters, I want to briefly take a closer look at Hebb and his model of learning. Here was Hebb's hypothesis: when two connected neurons at a synaptic junction are repeatedly triggered at the same time on several occasions (either by learning new knowledge or by experience), the cells and the synapses between them change chemically, so that when one fires, it serves as a stronger trigger for the other to fire as well. The once-unstimulated neurons become partners, and in the future, they will fire off in tandem much more readily than before. This "fire together, wire together" principle is called *Hebbian learning,* and the chemical change in the nerve cells and synapses is called *long-term potentiation* (LTP).[1] Long-term potentiation means that nerve cells at the synaptic level develop a long-term relationship. Long-term potentiation is how the brain's neural nets tend to become more "glued together" and wired.

To make this as simple as possible, when we are learning new information, we combine different levels of mind to make a new level of mind. Learning occurs when we fire different neural nets relating to similar concepts all together in unison, to construct a more expanded understanding. By using what we know as building blocks, various neural nets are triggered, then turned on, and they begin to fire in a holistic pattern. Once those circuits are turned on, we can make a new circuit to the cluster of neurons that is activated. In other words, it is easier for us to make a new addition in any part of the brain when circuits are alive, turned on, and electric.

The totality of the diverse circuits in combination with a new additional circuit begins to build for us a new model of understanding. The more we produce the same level of mind, the easier it is to remember what we learned. Due to the increased strength at the synapse, that new information is then mapped in the brain. The repeated activation of the synapse allows the neurons to fire more readily and easily.

If the postsynaptic terminals (receiving end; already wired information) of a neuron are firing because other neurons that are connecting to the same nerve cell are influencing it, the presynaptic terminals (sending end; new information) can easily make a new connection to a circuit that is electrochemically animated. The presynaptic nerve cell attempting to make a connection will get triggered by the existing circuits already firing. As a result, it will be easier for the presynaptic nerve cell to create a union with another nerve cell that is already activated. This model explains how we use what we know (postsynaptic nerve cells) in an attempt to make a new connection (presynaptic nerve cell) and learn what we don't know. Figure 7.1 shows a dendrite with several dendrite spines receiving strong signals from the presynaptic terminals to the postsynaptic terminals.

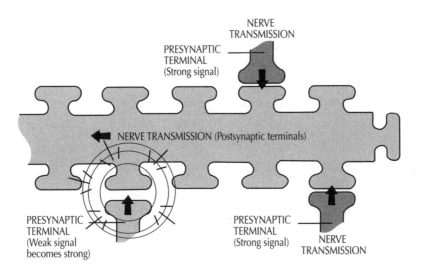

Figure 7.1

A dendrite showing a strong signal helping a weak signal at the synaptic space.

The Strong Helping The Weak

Did you ever work with electromagnets and iron filings in science class? Until the magnet is turned on, the little pieces of iron just sit there. After an electric current is run through the magnet, those iron filings race across the surface and attach themselves to the magnet. That's how the strong signal of known information works to attract the weak signal of unknown information. The key, then, is to turn on the brain and those appropriate synaptic connections so that they can go to work attracting and helping to fire the neurons needed. Once an existing neuron or neural net is activated, like the iron filings being drawn to the magnetic source, the neuron that is attempting to connect to existing circuits will quickly rush to the site where there is electrochemical activity and become immediately bonded.

Most of what we've talked about has been learning new knowledge and building bigger understandings. The same principle that applies to semantic knowledge also works when we learn from experience and have formed episodic memories (discussed in chapter 6). Now let's talk about learning from experience.

Let's say that we are out camping and fishing with our best friend (person) near our favorite water hole (place) at dusk in the summer (time) with the new fishing rod we received for our birthday (thing). Then we are stung by a host of angry hornets (event providing strong stimulus). We will associate the campsite (place providing weak stimulus) with where we were stung by the hornets (strong stimulus), and we probably will modify the situation or our behavior the next time we go camping.

Simply said, we now have made a new connection, because a strong-enough sensory stimulus (pain caused by the hornets) caused an elevated level of neurological firing (producing a new memory) from a relatively weak stimulus (fishing with a new rod together with our friend on a normal summer evening at dusk). The strong stimulus activated the firing of the weak stimulus. Therefore, the next time we are camping (weak stimulus), our neurons will now fire as a stronger active signal, based on our past experience. We'll think twice about the wisdom of our site selection and be extra vigilant. A new memory has been formed. That's called learning.

When we associate from experiences that are episodic in nature, our senses associate at least two independent bits of information together in order to make meaning from what we have processed. In essence, the association of episodic experiences is how, through natural evolution, most species have learned, altered their tendencies, and adapted.

Humans are not the only ones who learn from experience in this way. If a dog finds a piece of food, it smells the food to determine whether this is something that it wants to ingest. It will begin to quickly associate what it sees with what it smells. If the animal now tastes the food, the flavor and texture give the brain more raw materials for memory.

Now let's say that the dog leaves the scene to rest and starts to get violently ill. The animal will naturally associate what it saw, smelled, tasted, and ate with the way it felt from the experience of that food. As a result, it will remember the next time it smells anything at least vaguely similar. It made an important memory. That experience is ingrained as a valuable lesson for the survival of that animal. The animal's choice to behave differently in the future, given similar circumstances, is an example of how plasticity influences evolution.

Being Aware of Memories Being Formed

One of the reasons episodic memories stay with us for so long—we are able to recall them for such a long time after the experience—is that our senses were intimately involved in their formation.

When we associate or identify a sensory experience together with our past memories, that act of identification is, in and of itself, an event that forms the new memory. We know that any experience we embrace from our external world will cause a change in our internal chemistry, because a flood of sensory information reaches our brain, producing new chemical reactions, which, in turn, alter our body chemistry. Therefore, when we associate what we are presently experiencing as a novel moment with what has been synaptically wired in the mind and brain through the feedback from our body, this act of association is the exact event that forms the connection into a memory. In a sense, we *remember our re-membering* (rewiring, reconnecting) of the moment. We become aware of all the various stimuli; we tie them together, and in that elevated moment of awareness, we store this information by identification. The stronger the initial sensory stimuli (and, therefore, emotional components of the experience), the greater the chance we will remember the event and the formation of its memories.

I know a person who was in New York on September 11, 2001, working in an office building about a mile from where the Twin Towers stood. Everyone in the office was gathered in a conference room that faced south toward the burning buildings. In the room sat a television, on which they were watching the coverage of the unfolding tragedy. Above the television was a window through which they could also see the buildings and what was transpiring. This person was keenly aware of the odd sensation of simultaneously watching events unfold in person and on television.

His attention was first captured by what seemed to be sparklers or flashing bits of light spraying out from the tower as he watched through the window. It was a brilliant early fall morning, and the display seemed beautiful—until the top of the building pitched to one side and he recognized that it was collapsing. He told me that every hair on his body literally stood on end. Every gasp and cry of the people in the room, the television broadcasters' shouts of surprise, the closeups of the plume of smoke and dust rising, all immediately imprinted in his memory, and he knew that he would never forget any of those sights, sounds, and sensations. The feelings that were created from that startling experience assaulted his brain through multiple sensory pathways and combined with where he was, when he was there, what he was doing, and whom he was with on that day. He was keenly aware of those memories being processed and stored as the events unfolded.

Essentially, because the incidents of 9/11 were so far removed from his normal routine that day, my friend became highly aware that the sensory information he was engaged in from his *external* world was producing a distinct change in his *internal* world. When he connected the change in how he felt internally with what he was experiencing externally, that process was the distinct event that, in itself, at that exact moment, made a lifetime memory. We could say that experiences from our external environment produce internal change because our brain chemistry changes, which affects our body chemistry.

Of course, it is not only when we experience or witness such a dramatic historical event that we form vivid, long-term memories. Whenever we identify any change in our normal internal chemical state that is influenced by any stimulus from our external environment, we have made an episodic memory. When external cause and internal effect, outward stimulus and inward response are united, we create a neurological moment of connection called an episodic memory. We record a moment based on how we felt.

Another principle also applies here. Once an event is embraced by our senses, the more novel or new the experience is, the stronger the signal to the brain. The stronger the signal, the more likely the memory is to be stored long-term. What determines the strength of the signal? The extent to which we consider the event to be new, unpredictable, out of routine, uncommon, and unfamiliar. It is the novel combination of cumulative sensory information that pushes the familiar threshold of the nervous system and bombards the brain with an abundance of new inputs. The release of chemical neurotransmitters at the synaptic spaces of that particular forming neural network produces the feelings associated with that experience. This is what makes lasting synaptic connections.

Once the chemical signature of the neural net has been recorded and established as an episodic memory, every time we trigger that neural net to bring forth the memory of the experience, there will be a feeling connected to that event. The reason is simple. All memories include a feeling (or feelings) that is the chemical signature recorded from some past experience. As we willfully, consciously, and mindfully activate the memory of the event gone by, the moment we remember, we release the same neurotransmitters within that neural network and, therefore, create the same feelings. The same activated neural net related to a prior experience will produce a level of mind with its share of chemicals, which will make the body feel like it did when the experience actually happened. This may explain why some people keep talking about "the good old days." Perhaps they just want to relive the feelings of their past moments of glory because in their present moments, nothing new or stimulating is happening. They want to be released from their tedium and boredom.

Because our memories of past events are always linked with emotions (emotions are the end product of experience) and are primarily tied to events related to people and things at specific times and places, our episodic memories are filled with the feelings of past associations of known external experiences. We tend to analyze all experiences based on how they feel.

Miracle Chemicals

Let's face it: unless we received some kind of pleasurable sensation—sexual excitement, security, diversion from other painful experiences, and so on—we wouldn't stay in a relationship with someone else for very long. (For now, we'll discount those people who need to feel bad in order to feel good.) As you probably know, most of what we feel is due to chemicals in our brain and in our bloodstream. And a less-romantic notion of attraction and romance tells us that the main reason we fall in love with another person is neurochemically based.

Neurons are really no different from us in this sense. They are chemically activated beings. Once we repeatedly fire a series of neural connections (Law of Repetition), there comes a moment when the individual neurons of the brain release a chemical to make those connections become wired. The chemical synaptic enhancer involved is called *neural growth factor* (NGF). When it is released, NGF travels not in the same direction as the nerve impulse, but instead, it travels *in the opposite direction* from the far side of the receiving dendrite and crosses the synaptic gap to the sending axon extensions. If you review Figure 7.2, it shows how neural growth factor crosses the synaptic space in the reverse direction as the flow of nerve transmission.[2]

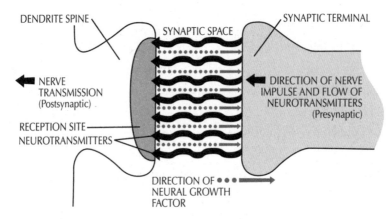

Figure 7.2

The flow of neural growth factor traveling in the opposite direction of nerve transmission.

When neural growth factor moves in the opposite direction as the nerve impulse, it fosters the growth of extra terminals on the other bank at the axon extension. As a result, longer, larger, and more numerous docks are built between neurons, for an easier and a more holistic transport of information.[3] Figure 7.3 illustrates how neural growth factor influences neurons to manufacture additional synaptic connections.

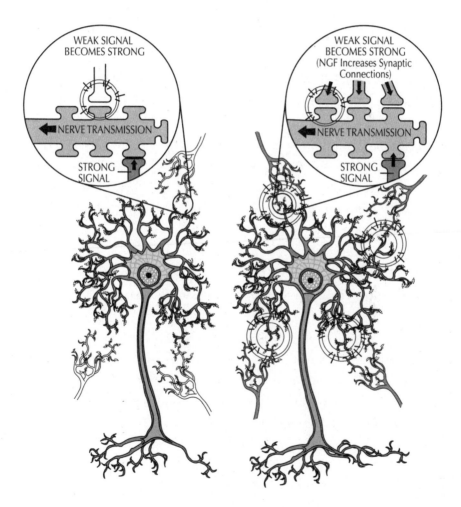

Figure 7.3
When a strong signal helps a weak signal, NGF facilitates stronger and more numerous synaptic connections.

Neurons are greedy little creatures who want and need neural growth factor. They can get it only when enough nerve cells fire together, thus producing a large enough burst of current at the end of the presynaptic terminal, forcing nerve cells to wire together. Groups of neurons firing together will suck up the neural growth factor in order to gain new synaptic recruits. They will even steal it from nerve cells that are not firing. It's almost as if once they get a taste for it, they have an insatiable desire for it.

Another name for neural growth factor molecules is *neurotrophins*. These miracle chemicals actually help neurons grow new synaptic connections and survive. Neurotrophins are like a fertilizer that causes one neuron tree receiving a signal from another neuron tree to release a strong potion that will cause new branches to form from the sending nerve tree, in order to make new and more sophisticated connections between them.

People who perform intricate hand motions, such as surgeons or harpists, have more synaptic connections in the motor cortex in their brain. They repeatedly fire the circuits related to the motor control of their fingers and, as a result, they produce more intricate and refined neural wiring compared to the average person. The neurotrophic chemicals that are released at the synaptic level allow this enhanced wiring to occur. Neurotrophins help the less activated, weak-signaled cell knocking on the door of the already active, strong signaled cell to receive a boost. Neurotrophic chemicals allow lonely neurons to join a lively party.

Action potential is another name for nerve cells that fire. Chapter 3 discussed the idea that an action potential of a nerve cell travels from the presynapse to the postsynapse, and the neurotransmitters that are released in the space between them flow in the same direction as the action potential. Remember, neurotrophic chemicals do the opposite. When there is an action potential between two neurons that causes them to fire, these molecules will swim upstream against the current from the postsynaptic terminal to the presynaptic terminal. The reason is clear: the stronger cell that is already turned on is attempting to receive a new message to help the weaker cell to become attracted to it and make the connection. Therefore, the more active cell will send help in the form of a fertilizer-like chemical that will enhance new neuron sprouts in the form of additional dendrite branches, and will also synaptically bond the new connections together in a long-lasting relationship. Consequently, this potion will even help the weaker cell make additional connections with the stronger cell if necessary. Please refer once more to Figure 7.3.

Chemistry and Repetition

Hebbs' model also explains the cellular mechanics of the Law of Repetition. In order for long-term potentiation to be complete, we must experience repeated firings at the synaptic level, over and over again, until the stimulus is great enough to cause the two cells to finally team up. Once nerve cells repetitiously fire in an attempt to unify, a strong enough action potential must be presented to initiate the production of these neurotrophic chemicals. Once they are produced, then we are beginning the process of making synaptic connections more wired. This is why we may need to experience something a few times or repeatedly review new information to finally learn the lesson.

There are only two ways that we make neural growth factor in the brain—when we learn and memorize new information by repetition, and when we have novel experiences. The repeated action of learning semantic knowledge with attention and awareness initiates a strong enough signal to make new intellectual data that we never experienced before form long-lasting and more numerous synaptic connections. The key ingredient here is focused attention. By paying complete attention to our task, we produce a strong enough signal to form that new synaptic connection. In doing so, we have created a more refined memory. The more numerous synaptic connections formed in the brain, the greater the working mind at that level. When we turn on that particular neural network, we will have more enriched machinery to process more enhanced mind. We can therefore perceive more information from our environment, demonstrate a skill with greater ease, or learn more readily, because we paid attention to the stimulus to make more circuits.

A Wine Example of a Neural Net

Many people like to drink wine. A few people develop their sense of taste well enough to be considered wine connoisseurs. As is true in most cases, a connoisseur is made and not born—at least not completely. We may have inherited certain proclivities, but that doesn't mean that we can spring into the world with a fully formed palate that is able to distinguish a shiraz from shampoo.

During the course of our life we have to experience (which means taste) a lot of different wines to refine our palate. Simply drinking wine repeatedly won't get us to that level of expertise. We need to acquire a bit of knowledge from someone who has already had enough experience to attain the level of familiarity and taste precision that we aspire to. We must pay close attention to their instruction. We also need to stay focused during the experience of drinking wine, to discern the subtle differences in taste and bouquet that distinguish the different varieties, vintages, and other variables. And it bears repeating that we do need to drink numerous different wines, tasting them over and over again to practice the skills we've learned and to develop a breadth of experience, so that we can compare unknown tastes to known tastes. We will naturally find ourselves using the Law of Association to create connections between familiar words such as dry, oak, acid, and full bodied, and the various types of wines. In doing all of these things, we are forming a complex and more refined understanding that involves not only the taste and smell of the wines, but their color, clarity, and other characteristics. All of those sensory impressions, as well as each bit of data that we learn about various wine-producing regions, soils, vintages, vintners, and varietals, become collectively gathered in intricate clusters of neurons that comprise our concept of wine and wine tasting, or what we may call our "wine tasting neural net."

Remember, in chapter 6 we said that knowledge is the precursor to experience. These new series of circuits will become the foundation that prepares us for a new experience. In our example of wine tasting, prior to the instructive process we were not wired to know or appreciate that these subtle elements ever existed in wine. Once the neural net has been prepared and constructed in a more refined manner, all we have to do is apply that information we learned and pay attention to what we are experiencing, so that we can perceive more information about wine. The moment we pay attention and look for semantic knowledge and associations with the experience, we will form an episodic memory. Learning is rendered complete because philosophy is transformed and deepened into a richer understanding of reality through a more profound sensory experience. Now our neural net of wine tasting has been more richly refined.

When we have a novel experience, the newness of the experience consumes all of our awareness in the moment and produces enough of an electrochemical rush to make a signal strong enough to produce neural growth factor (NGF), which helps to form a more long-term connection as a memory. Who among us can forget our first kiss with a lover? Whether it was a passionate lip lock or a paltry peck, chances are we recall that moment. Hopefully, it was one of those quiet, romantic moments on the beach in Tahiti with a fragrant tropical breeze, an Impressionist's dream of a sunset as a backdrop, and the soothing sound of the sea as a soundtrack. Each of those sensory impressions will have added to the embroidery of the neural net we formed.

The Formation of Neural Networks

Did you ever notice that when you've had something happen out of the ordinary—whether it is a car accident, meeting a new person whom you found attractive, or having a mystical experience—you can't stop thinking about that event? In a sense you are preoccupied; it's almost as if those memories from the past (good or bad) have invaded and taken up residence in your brain. The reason you focus on those inputs is simple. To make that memory stick, you had to repeatedly think about it and solidify that experience into a long-term memory—that is the process of learning. Each time the thoughts were repeatedly fired in your brain, you were wiring those particular circuits into a more enduring memory. By repeatedly thinking about that experience, you were associating it with other memories—both of experiences and of knowledge you previously acquired. This process seems natural to us, because in evolution, it is essential for all species to remember in order to modify any prior behavior.

Therefore, when we utilize the Law of Association by learning new concepts and couple it with the Law of Repetition, we will form what we have been casually referring to as a neural network. Whether we are developing new concepts in our mind, learning new information, having new experiences, repeating the same experiences, or practicing a skill, the process of associating what we know in order to understand what we do not know, and then repeating the thought process again and again, will cause neurons to pattern together as a neural community. The end product of this activity is a new neural network.

Putting Ideas Together

We demonstrate our willful intent when we choose to focus our attention. Often, we are at the mercy of environmental stimuli that come at us willy-nilly through our senses. When we take charge and actively choose on which of these inputs to focus, we are being "willful" in the best sense of the word. When we are focused, we learn through the principle of associating one concept with another. The brain actually reflects that *idea* by associating one neural net with another.

For the sake of example, suppose you are learning about a new object called an apple. If there is a neural net in your brain for the color "red," and there is also a neural net in your brain for a "round" form, you can simply mold them together as a new idea. If I ask you to imagine this round object as red, your mind will create a new understanding that will formulate an image of a round red circle. If I then say that an apple is about the size of a baseball, your brain will piece together from its associative memory the idea of round circle with an object about the size of a baseball. Therefore, you understand from your past knowledge base that this new object is three-dimensional like a baseball. As all three neural nets are integrated or connected, you conceptualize a new idea called "apple."

Once I verbalize the word "apple" in describing it to you, your brain hears the new name and associates it with the internal representation of what your mind has created, based on what I told you it looked like. Once you can hear the word, then you will connect that sound called "apple" (in the form of a new synaptic link) with the new pattern of synaptic firing and with the memory of apple encoded in your neurological fabric. You will now remember that "apples" are round red things that are the same size as baseballs.

What makes this process possible is the way in which the sensory organs integrate all the incoming information into order and meaning. Our senses provide the raw materials for us to gather information from the environment by association. What we see, smell, hear, taste, and feel are all used as different pathways of information, and they are seamlessly pasted together, through association, throughout whole different areas of the brain to enhance our memory. What we experience via our senses becomes what we can draw upon to formulate and strengthen our connections.

Different areas of the neocortex store and process sensory information. Sight is processed in the visual cortex (occipital lobe); hearing is facilitated in the temporal lobe; and touch and feeling are mapped in the parietal lobe. We then make meaning of all this incoming data by associating an experience processed through one sense with the same processed through another, such as what we are seeing with what we are hearing, or what we are tasting with what we are feeling. As the neocortex assigns meanings to different sensory inputs that we are experiencing, the association cortex of the temporal lobe assembles these inputs as associative memories.

Therefore, the image of an apple is organized in the visual cortex, but it then has to be connected to the word associated with the object, as well as what it tastes like and feels like. Eventually we have a whole experience of an apple logged as important sensory information that we can relate to. There is now an established neural net for apple, and it is the result of the cumulative individual neural networks coming together to form an enlarged series of neural patterns, giving us a more holistic meaning of the concept of apple.

The Importance of Repetition

If we modify our existing hardware every time we make a new connection, and can maintain that modification for a long enough time, we can now turn on a completely new series of neural connections, even when only one or two new synaptic connections have been made. If we are able to fire these new circuits to turn on the brain in a new sequence, pattern, and combination, we essentially have created a new level of mind. Remember that the mind is the brain in action, and when we make the brain work differently, we are making a new level of mind.

Once the permanent tracks of a thought or experience are left in the brain, it will take only a familiar stimulus from our environment or a thought from our past to activate these networks, allowing them to automatically fire in unison. Their activation creates a memory that is now related to a particular experience or set of learned knowledge. We are reminded of that person, place, thing, time, or event, and we begin processing a series of automatic thoughts, mapped in our brain, that are associated with our past experience related to each one of those things. Those thoughts are automatic because, as the Law of Repetition tells us, they have formed a neural network that functions without too much involvement of our conscious mind.

The thoughts do not necessarily have to be true, correct, healthy, accurate, or even constructive, but we think they are because we wired them there in the first place. The more often we fire those established neural networks, the stronger the synaptic connections become, thus the easier it is for us to activate them and the easier it gets to attach new concepts to that network. This makes the patterns and sequences of those firings more complex and organized. In so doing, we are literally changing our mind, altering the architecture of its connections and increasing the amount of physical space devoted to a concept.

How Our Environment Shapes Our Thinking

As we experience different stimuli from our external world, all the sensory data the brain and the mind are processing causes a host of different neural networks to create mindful internal representations of what is in our external world. This allows us to recognize everything we could possibly know in our external environment. On a daily basis, the bombardment of various sensory information activates the circuits in our brain to think equal to our encounters with our immediate environment. In other words, the environment is making us think.

Let's say you decide to take your lunch and eat it on a bench in a city park. As you are sitting there, you notice a man who reminds you of your college roommate's boyfriend. He has the same blocky jaw, icy blue eyes, and one untamed lock of curly hair that scythes across one eye. Suddenly, you're not in that park anymore eating an egg salad sandwich. You're back in Dooley's, a campus bar, and the smell of stale beer, cigarette smoke, and Charlie perfume all hang heavy in the air. The sunlight through the bar's smudged window casts your roommate in silhouette, and you can only make out her features when the tip of her cigarette glows orange and illuminates her mascara-stained face. She caught her boyfriend sitting in the stairwell of their apartment building the night before, drinking and laughing with another woman. The jerk. You shake your head sadly, still angry that he could have hurt your friend like that.

Then you think of your last lover, how he unceremoniously dumped you one day out of the blue. Two days later, you saw him walking arm in arm with another woman. You felt like someone had sliced through your stomach and all of your insides spilled out onto the sidewalk. Suddenly, you're back to sitting in the park, and it feels like someone is pressing his full weight against your back and shoulders. What's the use in sitting out here even on a nice day like this one? Nothing's going to change. You're always going to be the one sitting alone.

What had started as a pleasant lunchtime diversion descends into a recital of the automatic, unconscious, routine, familiar, common, habitual thoughts that plague you. You're cursed. You ruin every relationship. Men are so unreliable.

How you got from point A (seeing someone who reminded you of someone else) to point B (feeling unloved and unworthy) is a journey that many people take on a daily basis. One of the key words to consider here is "reminded." If you think carefully about this word in the context of the example of seeing a person who looked like someone from your past, you can see that you originally had in "mind" an entire complex of events related to people and things at a specific time and place tied to that original image. All it took was a simple nudge for this complex of beliefs, memories, and associations to be called up as a stream of consciousness that the brain produced. That neural net is always ready and at our disposal; it is one of the easy, common, natural, familiar modes of thinking to which we have instant access.

Neural Networks and Automatic Programs

Don't get me wrong, having a great memory can serve you well. From the simplest acts, like remembering a lock's combination, to more involved activities, like how to use a compass to orient ourselves in the woods, triangulate our position, and then return to our car, we constantly use a combination of semantic knowledge and experience that we've associated and experienced to navigate our way in the world. The more often we utilize this *"infoperience,"* the more solidly it is wired in the brain, the easier it is to recall (re-mind), and the easier it is to add new bits of infoperience to our existing connections and form a neural net.

However, when we are processing the same thoughts repeatedly every day, the mind that is created from the same stimulation of the exact same neural networks will become automatic, unconscious, routine, familiar, common, and more habitual. We begin to habitually and automatically think about ourselves in the same way. We therefore become neurosynaptically wired equal to our prior experiences in our environment. The neural networks we form from our repeated thoughts, actions, behaviors, feelings, emotions, skills, and conditioned experiences are now etched in the brain's hardware, and they become an effortless, unconscious response stimulated by our environment. The more we repeatedly think and feel unconsciously, the more we become unconscious.

As with the example of seeing someone who resembled a friend's ex-boyfriend, it may take only one thought, stimulated by an external cue, to turn on an associative pattern of firing related to the thought or stimulus that activated that particular circuit. Once the thought activates a specific neural circuit, it runs as an automatic thought program or as a particular stream of consciousness. The more frequently we are exposed to the same environmental stimuli, the more we wire ourselves to the same things in our external world. The pains of ending a romance just might be breaking those neurologically habitual thought patterns that were developed by constant activation.

Essentially, when we respond to the daily stimuli of the environment that we already know from past interactions, we are using the same circuitry to define ourselves in our world. We are thinking from past associations and not from the present moment. The experiences in which we previously engaged are encoded in our brain, and, therefore, they have a feeling associated with the memory. In the present, we remember a past experience, and how we felt back then is how we are feeling now.

Most people spend a great deal of their day unconsciously feeling and thinking from past memories. They do this because they have hardwired those experiences by repeatedly thinking of them and by associating many other experiences with them. If we can accept that our unconscious thinking creates unconscious feelings, derived by interactions in our environment through the activation of different hardwired neural nets, we can see that we are no greater than our feelings.

It makes sense that if most people maintain the same environment for long periods of their lives (where nothing new is happening or there is no change), the repeated stimuli will therefore produce the reactivation of associative neural networks, which will become more developed, strengthened, and refined. As a consequence of that lack of novelty in their environments and experiences, they have become hardwired to their own worlds. No wonder change is so difficult.

With a Flip of a Switch

When we respond to any input, a neural net in the brain becomes activated by one of the sensory organs and automatically plays the thoughts and associative memories connected to that time in our life. In other words, the events related to persons and things at particular times and places are all associated with that neural net of a past experience, that episodic memory. We were consciously reminded of that time, because our consciousness moved to that part of the brain where an old set of circuits laid dormant for years, and turned it on. Once consciousness moved to that cluster of neurons, it caused a pattern of neural networks to fire in a specific order, sequence, and combination. As the brain turns on to create the mind, we are consciously reminded of that memory.

Our Common Thinking

When we frequently think the same thoughts over and over again, the Law of Repetition states that the continuous firing of these thought patterns in the brain will actually create our everyday thoughts. These are the thoughts that we think most often, and are, therefore, more deeply etched in the brain's neural networks. These thoughts appear as the voices we hear in our own mind that tell us what to say, think, act, feel, emote, or respond with. But they're all based on our memories encoded with the past.

Everyday thoughts take no effort to think about. We are producing the same mind on a daily basis, because we are firing the same neural networks in the same patterns, combinations, and sequences. As we process thought in the brain and repeat it over and over by firing *repetitive* inputs, the nerve tracts that are turned on will, just like muscles, develop and strengthen their connections.

In addition, the nerve tracts will become thicker and more pronounced because they have been utilized. Imagine that thousands of people are traveling from one city to the next along the same road. It has become the most common road, and it is busy and full of daily use. The only solution to facilitate the increase in demand is to make the pathway wider, so that the road has the available capacity to allow transportation and communication.

Nerve cells respond in much the same way. They become thicker and more prominent as they carry more electrical messages from one area to the next, and nerve tracts have to expand their once-slender pathways to open up to more expanded communication. The Law of Repetition makes stronger, more long-lasting connections that are also facilitating thicker, more developed neuron branches for expanded communication.

As we frequently utilize the same neural networks, they modify themselves so that communication gets easier. If communication takes less effort on a synaptic level, we develop more integrated systems. More refined hard-wired systems of neurons create more programmed activity. Eventually, our common thoughts are the most synaptically wired thoughts stored in our neocortex.

Therefore, if we continually remember a thought from our past associations, we will ultimately strengthen the synaptic connections related to that thought process. As a result, the same thought fired in the brain daily will cause that same thought (or thoughts) to fire more.

According to Hebb's model, thinking the same thoughts on a daily basis wires us to be prone to think about the same thoughts with less effort. Hebb probably would say that a weaker and weaker signal will be required to activate the same nerve cells to fire. The more we think certain ways about things, the more prone we are to think the same ways about those things, because we are reinforcing the neural architecture to make it easier to think the same way the next time, according to Hebb's model. So the more we think about the same things, the more we'll think about those same things.

In other words, playing the same programs in our mind, time and again, will cause those programs to run more automatically each time. Our brain will require less of a stimulus from our conscious awareness for it to turn on to produce that mind. As we continuously re-mind ourselves of what we already know, less conscious awareness is needed to turn on that mind. If our conscious awareness, or our free will, becomes less consciously aware of our mind when we are firing these automatic unconscious thoughts, how present are we in that moment? How awake or alive are we really?

Our routine thoughts are our most hardwired thoughts because we practice and attend to them so well. They form the basis of what we commonly call the *personality*.

The Development of Personality

Our personality is a set of memories, behaviors, values, beliefs, perceptions, and attitudes that we either project into the world or hide from the world. The personality is formed in the same way as our neocortex. That makes sense, because the neocortex is the seat of the personal identity. We inherit genetic predispositions in the form of synaptic patterns, including those that form the core of our personality, as a developing fetus and infant. We have a propensity to inherit emotionally based thoughts, actions, traits, and attitudes from both our parents, because we inherit their memories in the form of repeated or mastered experiences, which all have feelings attached to them. But the environment is also constantly acting on us as a means of forming the person, the identity, the image of ourselves, that is essentially who we each are, the "you" or the "self."

The Laws of Association and Repetition are at work in our early development and throughout our lifetime. They act together to form neural nets in our neocortex that shape our personality self, derived from the neural nets we inherited from our parents and ancestors, from all of our sensory experiences, and from the knowledge we've gained throughout our life. This is our autobiographical self. Our identity is our unique set of neural networks, with specific synaptic wiring that is as individual as the features on our face.

Were you raised as an only child? Or were you raised in a family with ten children? Were you brought up by one parent or both parents? Were they Buddhist, Christian, Muslim, Jewish, atheist? What were your family's political beliefs? Were your parents Republicans, Democrats, Communists, or Socialists? Was your family rich or poor? What part of the world do you come from? In how many countries have you lived throughout your lifetime? What type of cultural experiences have you have? What types of food do you enjoy? Are you a vegetarian, an omnivore, or do you practice macrobiotics? What cultural, religious, and social traditions do you live by?

We are, synaptically, the sum total of what we have learned, experienced, and genetically inherited; however, that is not the end-all of our development. According to all that neuroscience has taught us, we are so much more than the hardware of our brain. What particular types of thoughts we continuously attend to, the corresponding circuits in our brain we turn on, how we repeatedly fire diverse neural networks, and what patterns of the mind we keep active by our own free will determine who we will neurologically become. It is our mind that is the only product of our animated microscopic hardware. The brain and the mind are not static; they are forever changing, based on the operator. It really comes down to which circuits we use: the repeated intensity of our intention and attention, what memories we embrace, what actions we demonstrate, what thoughts we think, what feelings we keep alive, and what skills we practice keep our self wired to be who we are. Our freedom of choice determines what mind we want to make or change from the hardware of our own individual brain. Can we willfully fire new combinations of neural networks by changing our mind, and make those patterns as automatic as any other neural habit we are responsible for creating?

Surely, a child who has been loved and encouraged throughout her life would have a different neural network in her personality than the person who was physically beaten every day after school. Furthermore, these two likely have a different definition of love. One person might see love as giving, supporting, and inspiring, while the other could perceive love as unwanted attention from abusive parents. Neither is right or wrong. They are wired differently, based on the diverse exposure to their personal environmental experiences. The feelings that are the result of their accumulated past experiences give each of them the ability to remember their past in their own manner. They perceive reality in their unique ways, because they are wired to perceive it differently.

The *self* then becomes the combination of specific patterns of neurological connections that have been left in the brain as learned memories from our past. The accumulation of a lifetime of information stored as memories is assembled in a medley of different synaptic combinations to make us who we are today. We can fire different patterns of neural networks in a host of different combinations, which then allows us to process a myriad of unique thoughts, ideas, concepts, memories, actions, opinions, facts, behaviors, personality traits, judgments, likes/dislikes, and skills.

We then keep the identity of the "self" alive by firing those connections, and thus reinforce and reaffirm who we are as individuals. Therefore, the way we maintain our personal identity is through our association with people, places, things, time, and events. Each of these elements reflects a bit of our known information, already stored as a specific neural network, and we reaffirm who we are by remembering ourselves in reference to those known associations.[4]

For example, when you meet a new person for the first time, the majority of the conversation is based on prior experiences through their association to people, places, things, time, and events. Most conversations start off like this. The new acquaintance says, "Where are you from (place)?" You respond by saying, "I am from San Diego." She says, "San Diego? I lived in San Diego!" Then you say, "When did you live there (time)?" And you say, "I lived in San Diego from 1984 to 1988." She replies, "That's funny, I lived there from 1986 to 1990." Then you say, "Really? Where exactly did you live (place)?" And she responds, "I lived in Mission Beach." You laugh out loud and say, "I lived in Pacific Beach. The town right next door." She says, "Did you know Peter Jones (person)? He is from Pacific Beach." You say, "I met Peter Jones at my best friend's wedding in 1986 (event). I was in the wedding party, and he was one of the drivers of the wedding cars. I remember because they had old 1950s classic cars in the wedding brigade (things)."

When you meet someone for the first time, you begin by displaying all the different neural networks from your past personal experiences to define your own personality. You both will mutually fire all your neural programs to check out whether you have any neural nets in common. The person you meet sounds like this: "I know these people. I own these things. I've been to these places. I lived here during this time. I have had these experiences." And in astonishment you say: "I know those people. I've done those things. I've been to those places. I own those things. I lived in those cities, during that time, and I have had all those similar experiences! Hey, I like you! We have a lot in common!" Which really translates into, "My neural net matches your neural net. We can relate to each other." And you have a relationship based on past experiences and their related feelings. Now, just as long as no one changes, the relationship might work.

This is how you maintain your own, personal working identity. Because you know yourself in relationship to these known things, this remembering process only makes more habitual who you are, and makes it harder to neurologically be anything else.

People who don't reaffirm who they are—who don't have a cohesive, repetitive central core of so-called personality traits—are said to suffer from mental illness. Consequently, the repetitive firing of those neural nets that construct who we are serves a valuable function and also differentiates us from other people.

Let's bring this idea to life. Imagine those lightning storms that we talked about in earlier sections, firing in different areas of the neocortex. When any aspect of our personality is turned on, what makes us different from the next person is not only that we are uniquely wired, but also the combinations, sequences, and patterns of the way in which we fire our synaptic connections. Every person has his or her own individual signature of neural firing based on individual wiring. And each lightning storm is different than the next. Everyone has their own neurological weather patterns. We know this to be true because on functional brain scans, most people produce the same signature of thought processes without much change in cerebral activity.

If a person thinks every day about how little money they have, the neural networks that have to fire for them to process those thoughts repetitively will be easily activated and ultimately strengthened by those natural laws we discussed. The thoughts that they revisit every day become the effortless way in which they can think about the same issue the same way. This unconscious process creates their neurological signature about money within the intimate folds of their neo- cortex. They have thicker nerve pathways with stronger and more numerous synaptic circuits, which then allows the anatomy of their repetitive thoughts to match their most conscious mind—or should we say their unconscious mind.

If a person has strong personality traits—for example, if they are extremely outgoing or overly organized—theoretically, he or she will have more developed neural networks associated to those characteristics. If the unique idiosyncrasies of a personality have been repeatedly activated, used, and fired in a designated neu- ral network, they will become more strongly wired. The corresponding neural net- work associated with these individual personality traits will have more synaptic connections that are more intricately connected, integrated, and enriched. They will develop to become an easy, simple, routine, natural way to think and be.

Making Changes

We can say, then, that when we fire a specific pattern of neural combinations that we have developed over time in the personality, the common way in which we fire the individual system of connections becomes the template of who we are neurologically. According to my scientific research of the brain and the information I have interpreted from what I learned at RSE, this template can be referred to as *the box of the personality*. It's not a literal box or compartment in the neocortex; instead, it is the most common arrangement of neural synaptic wiring that the mind uses within the myriad of synaptic circuits that defines our identity. It is the limit of the way the mind has come to be neurologically wired.

The problem lies in the fact that this frame of mind, by definition, delineates the only way we can think within the parameters of the way we have become wired. Within that box of the personality are a finite host of different "minds" we can produce predictably at will.

The "you" and the "me," then, can only habitually fire neural patterns common to the ways in which we individually process thoughts. We develop hardwired habits of being ourselves. When the combination of neural nets have become common, they will become the most natural ways in which we think, feel, remember, behave, talk, espouse knowledge, and execute various skills based on our own philosophy or experiences.

To think outside of the box would mean to fire different sets of synaptic connections in a different combination and order, which are not as hardwired as the ones we most commonly use. If the mind is the brain in action, then to create a new frame of mind would mean to rearrange how we use the existing circuits in our brain.

To *think inside the box* is to cause our mind to fire in the most regular way in which we fire our own pattern of neural circuits, based on what we know and remember. To *think outside the box,* then, is to force our brain to fire synaptic patterns in different orders and arrangements to make a new level of mind, based on what we do *not* know. To accomplish this feat, we have to break the neural habits of common thinking that have become the permanent, long-lasting circuits we have reinforced daily. We have to stop our most natural way of thinking. This will repattern our brain out of its neurological habit of firing, and make a new sequence of circuitry and new footprints. This is, by definition, our working understanding of neuroplasticity.

How we can break out of this prison is the subject of the remaining chapters in this book. We are the ones responsible for the habit we have formed of being ourselves. That also means that we have the power to change or modify that habituated self. It will take great will to change the habit of being ourselves. The wonder of it all is that we possess the power to alter our neural networks, and we can effectively alter our neural nets and literally change our minds. With just a little more information, we can break from the shackles of our own making.

CHAPTER EIGHT

THE CHEMISTRY OF SURVIVAL

If we lack emotional intelligence,
whenever stress rises the human brain switches
to autopilot and has an inherent tendency to do more
of the same, only harder. Which, more often than not,
is precisely the wrong approach in today's world.

—ROBERT K. COOPER, PH.D.

e all experience fear, anxiety, depression, hunger, sexual desire, pain, anger, and aggression. Although we may express them outwardly in different ways, scientists are now able to observe, through functional brain scans, how those states of mind are produced within the structures of the brain. That said, how, why, and to what extent we express, experience, or perceive these emotions creates our own distinct personality or individual self.

Because we are all wired similarly, yet differently, and because the mind is the most subjective reality of all (think of how much we differ in our personal views, opinions, and perceptions), we can understand why, in the past, brain research was considered a less objective natural science. We can measure traits, behaviors, abilities, actions, and overall function, but we need correlations to repeatable patterns of mind.

Scientists can now study brain *physiology* objectively, because they can observe the structures and functions of a living brain. Researchers can anaesthetize subjects, insert tiny probes in parts of their brain, and ask the subjects questions to determine which function that part of the brain performs. In much the same way, scientists can attach electrodes to the outside of a person's brain and ask the same questions to map the areas of the brain responsible for particular tasks.

Processing New Information

How the brain works and how humans process new information is another matter. Until the advent of functional brain scans a few years ago, scientists had no way of observing the brain at work, actually engaged in producing the mind. Now they can. Imaging technologies allow doctors and researchers to see how various parts of the brain are activated.

Like most research, these scanning efforts were initially directed toward identifying problems or anomalies. Nevertheless, just as the study of stroke victims enabled researchers to learn a great deal about how adaptable the brain is and the degree to which its plasticity aids us, functional brain scans have begun to usher in new eras in psychology and neuroscience.

Haven't you thought, at one time or another, "What is going on with my head today?" What you were really wondering was why you were having an off day in terms of being able to learn, store, or retrieve new information, or to cope with a situation. Of greater consequence, and likely of more importance to you now that you understand how you learn, is the question of how you can overcome yourself—your own mind.

The Routine Response

Our environment dictates most of our responses. Our routine, which is natural, easy, familiar, automatic, and second nature, is dominated by our reaction to the stimuli we take in from our surroundings. Over time, those neural circuits are reinforced to such a degree—by association initially, and then through repetition—that they truly do become hardwired. In many ways, we are no longer really "thinking" when we act based on what these programmed neural networks initiate.

We act unconsciously most of the time because after neural networks become hardwired, we become less conscious of their activity. Most often, it only takes one thought, or one small stimulus from the environment, to initiate a programmed set of responses and behaviors. When that program is running, our actions become automatic, routine, and most important, unconscious. We no longer have to think consciously with any level of awareness about how to act, how to feel, what to say, and even what to think. Our responses feel natural and normal because we have rehearsed them so well and for so long.

Let's face it: most of us are lazy. Okay, that's probably an overstatement. But keep this in mind: both the body and the brain are wonderful energy conservers. Neither wants to act in a way that will deplete its stores of energy. Common thoughts take no effort to engage in—in fact, they are like our car engine at idle. We are sitting in mental "park" or "neutral," not going anywhere.

We can remember these common thoughts so easily and so well because our continuous effort to refire the same neural pattern keeps the same pattern of synaptic connection intact. We are producing the same mind on a daily basis because we are firing the same neural networks in the same routine patterns, combinations, and sequences. That's why it is so easy to be the way that we are. Behaving habitually takes no effort at all—no conscious awareness means no free will need be exerted.

If our personality is the sum total of the automatic neural networks we've inherited and developed, and those networks run like computer programs, then when we initiate a habitual thought, those programs will run without any willful effort on our part. We have stopped consciously thinking and are responding with a preprogrammed set of hardwired actions and behaviors. These are based on past associations with our environment and are developed through repetitive experiences.

That Same-Old, Same-Old Life

Given that process, can we see how "asleep" we are when we continuously respond to our external environment in the same ways? As we go through our life, working at our job, interacting with our spouse of 20 years, driving our kids to school, mowing the lawn, even living in the same home next door to the same neighbors, is it any wonder we fall prey to the same neural habits? Most important, we have to recognize that how we think about our present and our future is dictated by how our past has programmed us. Has our life become just a series of unconscious, knee-jerk reactions?

For example, when we woke up this morning and got ready for work, chances are we followed the same routine we do every other day of our working life. Not only did we follow the same general order of activities—relieve ourselves, brush our teeth, shower, dress, listen to the morning traffic report, drive to the coffee shop, order the same beverage and breakfast, follow the same route to work, park in or near the same spot—but within that larger routine, we probably also performed most of the tasks following a standard set of steps. Of course, it's important to take the top off the toothpaste tube before we begin using it, but we probably started brushing on the same side of our mouth, at the rear with the molars, switched to the other side after the same number of brushing strokes as every other day, and so on. The same likely was true of how we dried ourselves after we showered; we automatically performed our own customary routine—toweling our hair lightly, patting our face dry, working the upper left arm and armpit next, switching to the right, drying our chest, grabbing the towel with both hands to saw the towel across our back, putting our left leg up on the edge of the tub, toweling it dry, and then switching to the right leg.

Every day, thousands of times in our lifetime, we perform these repetitive actions. Hundreds of times a day, we engage in behaviors that require little or no focused concentration on our part. At one time, they required our attention to learn, but after we memorized them and became skilled at the actions, we had other things to think about. These tasks are easy, common, natural, familiar, and routine; they truly are second nature to us. All of these are examples of our hardwired neural networks in action.

One of the marvelous things about the brain is that it is capable of taking over for us. In one sense, these routines are a marvel of efficiency and proficiency. Humans are masters of multitasking; while we are performing these routine functions, our mind is busy elsewhere. Yet, isn't there some drawback when we consider that in the first half hour of each day, we go through those experiences as though we are lobotomized? How many people truly take advantage of the kind of autopilot we have, using that time to seek out new experiences and learn new things? It's usually just too much of a hassle to turn off the autopilot function, become conscious, and try doing something differently.

Also consider what happens when that "elsewhere" our mind can go becomes as routine as the actions we are performing subconsciously. What are the consequences, when not just our behaviors but also our beliefs, values, attitudes, and moods fall into the same unconscious, unthinking, utterly predictable pattern? What happens when that self-imposed box of our own mindset changes from being a comfort zone to a prison or a dungeon? How do we escape from the trap we've set for ourselves, simply by being ourselves?

What keeps people trapped inside the same frame of mind is that the most commonly fired, and therefore most hardwired, automatic neural nets are the result of our own thinking. These are the sequences, combinations, and patterns of neurons that we fire the most.

If we return to the oak tree analogy from chapter 3, these hardwired neuron clusters have the thickest trunks, the most entwined branches and root systems. They are the most refined and enriched networks we have, and they have been produced through the interaction of our internal thoughts and external reactions. What defines the "box" of our personality, and any box for that matter, isn't simply what it contains. We have to take a look also at the frame or the boundary of that box, at what defines what is inside and what is outside.

Life Inside the Box

The very boundaries of the box are our feelings. Because we remember experiences and associate them with feelings, this should come as no surprise. What we keep inside the box and what we keep outside of it is primarily based on this assessment: is the input something that will feel familiar, predictable, routine, or comfortable?[1]

Consider this notion of comfort for a moment. If the box of personality contains our personal identity, and our identity is comprised of the actions, beliefs, perceptions, and values that essentially add up to who we are, then anything that is not habitually, automatically, naturally, easily us is a source of discomfort.

For example, imagine that you are at a party where people are drinking and talking, and you're enjoying yourself. After a while, someone turns up the music a bit, some of the furniture gets pushed to the walls, and people start to dance. You're having a good time watching everyone else, but then the dancing turns into one of those awful solo spotlight things you've seen at weddings, where everyone takes a turn showing off their moves.

You're not a dancer. You never have been. You never developed the skills or rhythm. You've always felt self-conscious about how you look while dancing, because you never know what to do with your hands and arms. Suddenly, you go from gregarious to withdrawn. You'd rather have people notice that you're not dancing (and, potentially, make a big deal out of it), than have people notice your "bad" dancing. You're used to fitting in and fading into the background a bit, and this level of attention is not what you bargained for. You can't bring yourself to dance, because of the level of discomfort you'd feel. After several people attempt to get you out there on the dance floor, you decide to leave the party.

What just happened? Someone in your environment approached you and asked that you step outside the boundary of your box, and you couldn't make that choice. That action was outside your comfort zone, so you dismissed the opportunity and retreated to the safety of another series of neural nets that made you feel comfortable—your sense of yourself as a bit of a social outcast.

We determine what experiences we want to engage in, based on how well we can predict the familiarity of the feelings those experiences will trigger.

For example, I once traveled to South Africa for a conference. After one of the sessions, a group of us went out to eat together. Someone noticed that the restaurant offered crocodile as one of the appetizers. I'm generally pretty receptive to culinary adventures, but at first, I wasn't going to try it. After a few of my dinner mates urged me (dared me/teased me) to try the croc, I thought, what the heck? When the server set the plate down in front of me, all eyes were on me. I cut into the thick chunk of meat, stabbed it with my fork, and popped it into my mouth. I chewed thoughtfully, and with "Well? How was it!" expressions painted on the faces of everyone around me, I announced, "Tastes like chicken." The moment they heard that, everyone was eager to jump in to embrace the novel experience, because they could now predict what the new food would taste like, based on a familiar memory of the past. Once the chicken neural net was activated, it was easy for the others to feel courageous, because it was within the realm of the box of their familiar experiences and feelings. I wondered, if I had said that it tasted like a cross between salamander and gecko, how eagerly everyone might have responded.

If neural nets and synaptic connections are like footprints left by past memories, then we have to stop our most natural way of thinking and feeling (and feeling and thinking) to repattern the brain. This gets the brain out of its neurological habits of firing and allows it to make new sequences of circuitry— new footprints. This takes will and mental effort.

To think outside the box, then, is to force our brain to fire synaptic patterns in different orders and arrangements than usual. The box of our personal identity has become natural to us, because we have trained our brain to think the way in which it has been neurologically mapped. Instead of making any new connections (by learning through association and repetition with increased conscious attention), we rely on what we have mapped in the brain as familiarly known past information, and not really much more. What has become neurologically mapped in the brain, therefore, causes us to think and feel equal to, and no greater than, how we are mapped.

Is thinking inside the box such a bad thing? It's really not bad in the strictest sense, but it limits our ability to evolve, progress, or modify our behavior.

On the other hand, is thinking inside the box a good thing? After all, haven't our most common neural networks become the ones that we use most often *because* they are the ones that are most successful? That question is a good one, and the answer is an emphatic "No!" for most people. For the basics like walking, typing, driving, eating, or tying our shoes, yes, living inside the box is a good thing. But the larger reason that this kind of thinking is self-limiting is based on what happens to the brain in survival mode.

Survival Mode

Very far back in our genetic past, we, and most other mammals, lived in an environment that posed a great number of threats to our very survival. Life was harsh, brutish, and short. We were very much subject to the whims of nature and needed to be alert to any potential threat—from a predator, from an enemy, or from nature. Being alert to these threats kept us alive and kept our genetic lineage intact. It is not too far of a stretch to say that those of us alive on the planet today are the beneficiaries of an ancestral heritage that was either very alert or very lucky—or most likely both.

Times have changed, and the kinds of threats to our survival have changed in both type and degree. Although some may argue that early humans did not have to worry about nuclear annihilation or the threat of organized terrorist cells, I think we can all agree that they faced more imminent dangers than most of us do: starvation, illness, predators, and the like. What hasn't changed is that much of the hardwiring that was necessary for us to survive that harsh existence, most of those networks and regions of neurological memory, are still active in our brain. Remember that nerve cells that fire together, wire together. Over time, through repetition and association, the neural networks that helped keep us alive—what we commonly refer to as the fight-or-flight response—have been fired for hundreds of thousands of years.

Those instinctual responses are about as hardwired as anything else in our brain. In fact, they are stored away in our limbic system or midbrain, beneath the neocortex. This involuntary system is what facilitates the mind that operates our body, brain, and entire being without our conscious awareness. It is what maintains our internal order "independent" of our conscious mind.

Briefly, when a survival response is initiated through the sympathetic nervous system (SNS), it increases heart rate and blood pressure, reduces the amount of blood flow to the digestive organs, increases blood flow to the extremities for action, mobilizes sugars in the bloodstream for energy, releases hormones that give the body a rush of energy, turns on the brain to become super-aware, dilates the pupils and clears the lenses to facilitate seeing greater distances, and dilates the bronchioles, allowing greater oxygen transfer in the lungs. All those changes enable the body to flee or fight, heightening our awareness and our level of preparedness for physical action.

If you remember, the parasympathetic system (PNS) does the opposite. It slows down our body's responses, decreases heart rate and blood pressure, slows down respiratory rate, increases blood flow to the skin and to the digestive tract, constricts the pupils and the lenses, etc. Think of these processes as our rest and digest response.

The SNS uses energy for immediate emergencies; we can think of the SNS as a gas pedal. The PNS conserves energy for long-term projects such as repair and growth; like a clutch, it allows us to coast and conserve vital energy.

One of the main jobs of the neocortex, apart from its intellectual, cognitive, problem-solving, self-awareness, learning, and communicative skills, is to use all five senses to stay conscious and aware of the external world. Aside from its innate abilities (to learn, reason, analyze, concentrate, dream, remember, use language, invent, and embrace abstractions), it has the propensity to be aware of the environment through all our senses. When the neocortex is not learning or processing data for higher thinking and reasoning, it shifts into its inherent nature and engages mechanisms to constantly evaluate the external environment, gathering important information to determine which stimuli or inputs from the environment could be potentially dangerous or threatening. All creatures use their sensory receptors to interact with the external world to both survive and evolve. The rule is simple: when we are threatened, the body comes first.

When the neocortex functions in survival, it consciously assesses the environment with all the sensory organs. It scans all the potential situations in that moment to decide whether our chemical continuity in the body will be maintained. Like an octopus, it has its tentacles reaching in all directions to ensure safety. Based on this primitive reflex, we tend to move toward what is comfortable and pleasurable and away from what is painful or uncomfortable. The body stands a greater chance of surviving in a comfortable situation than in an uncomfortable one.

In evolution, this reaction was wired into most mammals when they faced challenging situations dealing with cold or heat, pain or pleasure, exerting energy or conserving energy, being at the top of the pecking order or being the outcast or the bottom feeder.

To have our awareness on the environment and the body at all times is a good definition of survival. It is when we anticipate a future time based on our memory of a past time. In all species that have a neocortex, it looks, it listens, it smells, it feels, and it tastes in order to associate what it presently is paying attention to with some past memory of what it recognizes as familiar and known.

Remember, the bigger the neocortex, the greater the ability to learn and remember. Therefore human beings have a better ability to predict, prepare for, or expect a future moment. When the neocortex notices interruptions in the familiar external environment through its internal representations, it immediately gets prepared for activity. That way, it can be ready to respond, and then afterward, return to its state of balance.

Therefore, if we are not living in the present moment but in an anticipatory state of mind, we are, in a sense, projecting the mentality of survival. We are utilizing the circuits of the learned database in the neocortex and are processing the mind within the very boundaries of the box of our personal identity. Our attention will be on what is predictable, common, familiar, routine, and known. We are comparing our present state of internal balance with a projection of a potential feeling we may experience in a future time—and to upset our current state of internal chemical continuity with any threatening situation (known or unknown) can initiate a survival response. Therefore, we are already living in a state of survival, because our very thoughts reconstruct the mind of survival. When we are experiencing this protective state of mind, we are essentially prepared to react with a certain set of primitive responses that include doing anything to protect "the self," which we identify as our body.

Detecting a Pattern

The neocortex looks for patterns of familiar stimuli so that it knows what to anticipate and how much it needs to be prepared for what might happen. Therefore, it is always using what is scientifically termed *pattern recognition:* we use our neural nets of associative memory to match what we've learned and experienced with some stimulus from the external world. Once any one or all of our senses perceive the trigger from our environment, that stimulus will activate an associative memory mapped from past experiences as a neural net in the neocortex.

In addition, when we experience a change in our environment, the body responds immediately. For example, if we enter a dark room, our pupils instantly dilate. This is known as the *orienting response* or *orienting reflex*. Not only does this response kick in when we experience a change in the environment, but it is also initiated when we encounter something novel.

If there is a match between the external input and the internal representation, and that match is recognized as a known memory that poses no threat, the neocortex can decide that the body will be safe. Then the body can relax, and its awareness can move to the next future potential coming from the external world.

Survival is always about being ready for or expecting the next moment based on our past moments; it is never solely about the present moment. If the neocortex experiences pattern recognition between an external stimulus and a neural net corresponding to a familiar predator or known danger from our memory, the moment that the stimulus is perceived, the brain will begin to respond with natural, primitive survival mechanisms.

The survival response will cause the brain to activate the fight-or-flight autonomic nervous system. When this happens, all the blood flow and energy that was once in the neocortex moves to the midbrain, in order to prepare the body with enough energy to react to the threatening stressor. We no longer think or reason; we react. Now the body is prepared to address the threat by either staying for a good fight or running like hell. Fight or flight is our only option. In most cases, many species will react by moving away from the predator or the discomforting stimulus. Fleeing is often a better option than fighting.

Some fears are well recognized: when facing a huge bear on a camping trip, no one would question our fight-or-flight response. But what if you are at a wedding with a friend, and one of the guys sitting at your table gives you the creeps? You keep elbowing her to tell her that you want to leave. Your friend is pleasantly ignoring you as she carries on a conversation with a few handsome men. During the conversation, you are quiet, detached, and almost unfriendly. Finally, as the two of you go to the ladies' room, your friend grabs you by the elbow and says, "What is wrong with you? Why are you being so antisocial and rude?" Finally, you respond by admitting, "I don't know. The one guy to my left reminds me of my ex-husband, and he makes me totally uncomfortable."

In this case, we can say that the external stimulus of the gentleman sitting next to you triggered the associative neural net of your memory of your ex-husband. As a result you responded, based on a past familiar association, to a person you do not yet know, as if he were your ex-husband. The external pattern of his face, voice, or other recognition brought up the internal representation of a familiar memory, along with a host of chemical feelings related to the neural network of your ex-husband, and it made you uncomfortable enough to want to flee the scene. You used your past memory to determine your present moment. You based your assessment of the situation on a feeling. Why? Because all our memories have a feeling associated with them. Survival is really an emotional mode of operating.

The Unknown Can Make Us Uncomfortable

In survival mode, even more than feeling that we have seen someone who reminds us of an unpleasant person, place, event, or thing, what we really strive to avoid is the unknown. When we can't associate something with a neural net we've developed through heredity, learning, or remembering, we're often distressed. This distress is tied to the idea of discomfort. The brain and the body are hardwired to achieve homeostasis, or internal balance. In survival, the unknown always threatens that balance. And when that balance is compromised, we become uncomfortable. Comfort, familiarity, and predictability are what we are hardwired to desire and achieve in survival.

So, in addition to initiating a flight-or-fight response when we perceive a known past threat, we also can go into that mode when there is a break in the continuity of a familiar circumstance. For example, if something is rustling in the bushes, the neocortex puts all of its attention on the external world and pays attention to what may be a potential threat. If we cannot match the unfamiliar stimuli with a pattern of what we know from past neurologically mapped experiences, this external cue will be addressed as an unknown, and the brain will send a message to the body through the fight-or-flight nervous system to be prepared for danger. In other words, when the external world is no longer a familiar pattern, we are preeminently wired to be prepared for whatever that may bring.

As in all other species, we have a built-in defense mechanism to protect ourselves from unknown stimuli. Unknown situations turn on our automatic reactive midbrain, with all of its survival instincts, and we respond just like all other life forms. Fear or aggression tends to be the dominant responses in survival. When we respond with these elements, we are executing our natural animal tendencies. Most important, our heightened awareness is on the body, the environment, and time.

In the animal kingdom, this fear or reaction to the unknown is a means of preservation. Anything out of the ordinary alerts a particular species to pay attention and be prepared. For example, when a deer sees a logging machine moving through the forest, it immediately reacts by running from this unknown stimulus. Its large, brightly colored, loud, smelly appearance is an unknown assault to the animal's senses, and in a moment, that unfamiliar stimulus causes the creature to increase its level of environmental awareness. It smells the diesel smoke belching out of the machine, hears the rumble of its motor, and the piercing beep, beep, beep of its reverse indicators, and feels the ground tremble as a tree crashes to the earth. So many new sensory inputs are coming its way that the deer turns tail and runs. Because the inputs are unfamiliar, the deer can't predict what the object might do next, so it flees the scene. This mechanism is inherent in most life forms.

In humans, we have the same mechanisms for survival. We fear the unknown. We become chemically prepared for what our brain cannot neurologically or chemically predict. And the unfamiliar or the unknown turns on our survival responses. Most often, that survival response will result in fleeing. The principle is "better safe than sorry."

Therefore, if we are afraid of the adventure of the unknown, chances are that we are living in a state of mind that replicates survival. In survival mode, if we can't predict how an experience will feel (because we lack any related past memories that have already been experienced as a set of feelings), we will avoid engaging in that experience. How, then, can we ever experience anything truly unknown without fear?

Avoidance happens many times when people have had supernatural, religious, or paranormal experiences. For example, if during sleep a person finds herself for the first time floating above her body, separate from her physical self, in that moment of awareness she may not have the neural equipment to associate this experience with anything that is vaguely familiar, except maybe for death. Because she has no pattern to match what is presently happening, immediately she reacts with terror, and the sympathetic nervous system turns on. Once that occurs, since the body is a primary focus, awareness will move back into the body, and she will wake up. She sits up panting and scared and thinks maybe she was dead or was, at the very least, dying. The experience was so unknown and new to her that because there was nothing internally to match this moment with, the body became threatened, and the experience ended.

Now, if that person learns about out-of-body experiences by reading a few books, she may begin to make enough important new synaptic connections to form a new neural network, so that if it happens again, she will be more prepared for the experience without feeling the threat of survival. She can then surrender to the unknown experience. Knowledge removes the fear of survival.

Modern-Day Survival

Survival takes many forms with our large neocortex. With the complicated life of contemporary man, the meaning of survival has been modified. Unlike other life forms whose main concerns are food, shelter, protection against predators, procreation, birth, and safety from the elements of nature, our concerns have been altered because we have adapted differently as a result of our advanced society. Survival concerns still matter to us; however, they have become much more complicated.

Presently, survival still means, at its base level, the attraction of the opposite sex (or same sex, for that matter), adjusting to external threats, overcoming pain, attaining social status, having a place to live, providing food and comfort, ensuring a future, protecting and educating our offspring, to name a few. We have modified our concerns a bit due to social structures and technology. Sitting in traffic jams, paying mortgages and health insurance, bickering with a spouse about credit card debts, having employment conflicts, saving for retirement, reacting to political views, and worrying about Social Security can seem to be more realistic problems in our modern world.

Taken to its most basic level, though, when we react to the external world, no matter the stimulus, we respond in the same way with the same neurological systems. When we are threatened and in survival mode, we react with a set of circuits related to the past habits, behaviors, attitudes, and memories that are either genetically wired or are wired by our experiences.

Therefore, our interpretation of external threats or stressors has been changed to meet the demands of our current living situations. However, at the most simplistic level, survival is still survival, and our reaction to external pressures or perils will always be the same. A good rule of thumb is that survival usually means the following:

- Sexual procreation for the continuation of the species
- The avoidance of pain and predation for the immediate survival of the body and its offspring
- Dominance through power and through control of the environment for securing the greatest evolutionary opportunity[2]

With our enlarged neocortex and complicated social mores, we have only modified these three primitive survival responses to dress up basic animal traits. Still, when we modify our behavior to the most basic of human conditions, most of our motives revolve around these factors.

Dancing with the Environment

When the neocortex is busy evaluating the environment to determine the status of the external world, in order to make sure it can predict its next moment, this state of vigilance causes us to lean toward our innate survival tendencies. Being prepared has its roots in survival. When the neocortex anticipates potential dangers, and when our awareness is pointed toward the environment and the state of the body at a future time, our neocortical function is altered. It is no longer being used for learning or higher thought processes. Instead, it is remembering and recognizing past familiar situations and linking them to the present situation. When we remember, we activate existing brain circuits that have been developed from past experiences. It is the chemical substrates of the survival response that activate existing neural circuits for us to automatically think this way. By turning on circuits repetitively, we are turning on a stress reaction by our thoughts alone.

The Neurology and Chemistry of Stress

Living in *stress* is living in survival—they are one and the same. Stress is when our body moves out of normal homeostatic balance. When we react to something, the body produces numerous chemical changes that alter the normal physiological-chemical order. A *stressor* is anything that disrupts the normal chemical balance of the body. And the *stress response* is what the body does to reestablish normal homeostatic balance.

I'm sure you know people who always seem to be stressed—even if they didn't insist on telling you all the time about how stressed they are, you'd still be able to figure it out on your own. Other people may seem placid and smiling on the outside, but inwardly are a simmering cauldron about to boil over. Still others have an inner and outer peace that can lead us to believe that they have minimized their stress levels. Regardless of our experience with others and with our own stress levels, it's time to take a different approach to the subject.

In short, it is important to understand that how we react to our environment, or how we think in response to some past or future moment that may be stressful, is responsible for most of the maladies, both physical and emotional, from which we suffer. It's that simple. When we repeatedly (chronically) place ourselves in a high-stress mode, or when we are hyper-vigilant in looking for stressors that may affect us at some future moment, we engage the body's emergency response to stress all the time. What with continually being on high alert or in emergency mode, our body doesn't have the time or the resources necessary to repair and regenerate itself.

Remember chapters 1 and 2, when we talked about the body's innate intelligence and its ability to help us heal? Well, when we are constantly engaged in the stress response, that intelligence gets silenced. In addition, our body is in a constant state of trying to catch up, but it can't.

In one scenario, we may be loudly arguing with our spouse, or madly dashing around trying to fit a day's worth of errands into an hour. At such times, a stressor in the *present* moment has us mashing a figurative gas pedal to the floor, to produce the adrenaline that is the primary chemical released during the stress response.

In another type of situation, no current stressor can be seen. We might be sitting in a chair or lying in bed, not even moving, and yet we are under stress just the same, worrying about tomorrow's job interview or how we are going to pay next month's property taxes. At such times, we are anticipating a *future* stress that we'll need to resolve. Now we have the brake on plus that gas pedal is mashed to the floor, because that future stress is flooding our body with adrenaline and other stress hormones.

In either case, we are depleting our body's systems until the point at which they break down. We know this breakdown by other terms: illness, injury, and overload.

We respond to stress via two pathways. The first one is called the neurological response; the second pathway is termed the chemical response.

The Neurological Response: The Fast Track

A quick overview of the neurological process that constitutes a stress response proceeds like this:

1. The first response is the most immediate. In it, the autonomic nervous system turns on in response to something real or imagined in our environment.

2. The automatic nervous system passes along information directly through the spinal cord and spinal nerves to the peripheral nerves that are most readily connected directly to the adrenal glands.

3. Once this lightning bolt of information reaches the adrenal glands, they produce adrenaline (also known as epinephrine) that goes immediately into the bloodstream.

This first/immediate response takes place in a flash. It produces an adrenal hit that results in a radical altering of our chemical makeup, plus a number of other physiological responses. The body shuts down or limits nonessential functions like digestion, and the blood is diverted from internal organs to the muscles to prepare them for action. We are in a state of heightened awareness and energy. We are ready either to fight or to flee. This whole process takes place in a matter of seconds. Figure 8.1 shows the fast track.

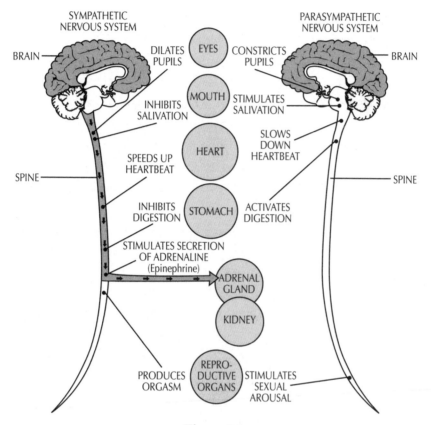

Figure 8.1

The action of the sympathetic and parasympathetic nervous system on various organs in the body.

The Chemical Response: The Slow Track

Just like the neurological stress response, the chemical response of stress can be triggered by a mere internal thought as well as a reaction to something outside of us. Here is how this process transpires: when we have a reaction to a stressor (that is, a thought in anticipation of the presence of a stress or in memory of a past stress), our brain fires diverse neural nets through diverse systems. Those neural nets send a signal to a part of the midbrain called the hypothalamus. The hypothalamus is a kind of factory that takes in chemical raw materials and assembles them to produce peptides. A *peptide* is a chemical messenger that signals the body to turn on in some fashion.

In the stress response, the peptide made from the hypothalamus is called *corticotrophin releasing hormone* (CRH). Once CRH is released, it delivers a chemical message to the pituitary gland. When the pituitary gets the signal from the hypothalamus, it makes another chemical peptide called *adrenocorticotropic hormone* (ACTH). The new chemical message is now "acceptable" to the receptor sites located on the cells of adrenal glands in the body.

The chemical message from the pituitary (ACTH) makes its way to the adrenal glands, and it stimulates its cells to produce various chemicals called *glucocorticoids,* which further change the internal order of the body. Glucocorticoids are steroid hormones secreted by the adrenal glands in much the same way as testosterone and estrogen, which are made in the sex glands. Just

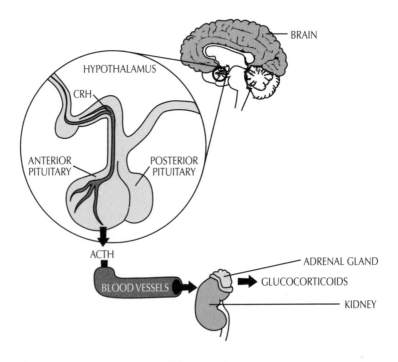

Figure 8.2
The hypothalmic-pituitary-adrenal axis.

as in the neurological response, similar physiological changes are occurring in the body in response to the presence of these chemicals that are being released. The slow-track chemicals are made through the hypothalamus-pituitary-peripheral gland axis, and their activity takes minutes or hours to transpire.

One of the ways to think of the two different responses is that the first is more immediate and direct, like the express lanes on an interstate. The second involves more "exit" and "entrance" ramps and consequently is akin to the local lanes. They both get us to Survival City, but one (relatively speaking) does it much faster. Figure 8.2 illustrates the slow track.

Stress Defined

When we are living in survival mode, our neocortex becomes attuned to functioning as a kind of radar sweeping the environment. When it perceives a threat, we are immediately on alert. We move into a heightened state of antici-pation (or even expectation) that something potentially harmful could (or will) happen. Unlike most other vertebrates, we can signal this response by our reac-tion to the environment or just by expectation, through thought alone.

Whenever we are in the presence of a stressor or we anticipate being in the presence of one, and any of our normal levels (blood pressure, heart rate, pupil dilation, chemical balance, and the like) change, we're experiencing stress. As we can imagine, based on our understanding of homeostasis and the body's innate desire to return to a state of order, the body will always react in response to that stress by releasing high amounts of adrenaline and glucocorticoids. All the changes in the chemical balance in the body during the stress response are due to the release of adrenaline and glucocorticoids from our adrenal glands.

Humans share this response with many other life forms, but because of our enlarged brains with their huge memory bank (that is, because we're so smart) and our evolved social structures, we experience very different types of stress-inducing stimuli, environments, and behavioral responses. As humans, we're subject to three categories of stress: physical, chemical, and emotional/psychological.

- *Physical stress* includes events like a car accident, a fall, an injury due to overexertion, and exposure to harsh environmental conditions such as extreme cold or heat, lack of sleep, and lack of food or water.

- *Chemical stresses* are an increasing concern for many people today. In our environment, we are exposed to a host of toxins, allergens (including certain foods), pollutants, and many other chemical stresses.

- *Emotional/psychological stresses* include concerns about time, money, career, and loss of a loved one.

An important thing to remember is that when we are exposed to any of the three categories of stress, the body will respond to each type in the exact same fashion as with an autonomic reaction (see chapter 3 for more on the autonomic nervous system).

For the most part, all other species, except for some social primates, experience stress as primarily a physical threat to their survival: predators, starvation, lack of mates, and disabling injuries primary among them. We, too, have physical stress, as well as chemical stresses that can manifest themselves as physical.

Unlike other animals, however, humans perceive not only those physical threats as stressors but also a whole host of other complex experiences that we can characterize as emotional/psychological: deadlines, car troubles, disputes with coworkers and bosses, finances, and family relationships, to name just a few. These nonphysical threats are just as potentially threatening to our survival as are physical ones. The difference is that the nonphysical threats we face are more complex and can't be as easily handled with the fight-or-flight response as the dangers most animals face. Come April 15th and tax day, the two options of fight or flight aren't going to do a whole lot to reduce the level of stress we're feeling about our finances, although, illogically, people often employ one of the two options to no real benefit.

Acute and Chronic Stress

The physical, chemical, and emotional/psychological stresses we humans face differ in another way. Animals nearly always face an *acute* form of stress, with a quick onset and resolution. If a dog is wandering in the woods and encounters a sow bear with her cubs, he has just an instant to make his choice about what to do. The matter is, relatively speaking, quickly resolved. In these acute stress situations, the animal's body becomes alarmed, and when the fighting or the fleeing is over, the body returns to homeostatic balance, usually within a matter of hours. The effects of acute stress like these are usually finished in a short amount of time. The body is able to return to a more relaxed state, standing down from the emergency alarm and going about the routine business of cellular restoration, repair, and reproduction. Most mammals have bodies superbly designed for short-term physical emergencies.

However, if we're presented with a situation such as when our boss confides in us that a coworker is going to be fired in a few weeks, and the coworker, unbeknownst to our boss, is a friend of ours, the onset may be acute, but resolution is likely to take a lot longer to come around. If we choose to run from paying our taxes, the consequences of that choice, and our worry over it, can last for years.

We humans tend to live in these *chronic* stress situations. On a daily basis, we are subjected to continuous stressors (physical, chemical, and emotional/psychological), moment by moment. Due to our elevated social mores, fighting or fleeing is not socially acceptable. Instead, we worry, anticipate, reason, suppress, rationalize, and compromise in different situations. With trillions of synaptic connections, we are so good in our ability to remember that we can turn on the stress response without the stressor being physically present. In other words, just thinking about the stressor creates the same stress response. This is what begins to create the more harmful result called chronic stress.

Emotional/Psychological Stress

Humans suffer the greatest damage from chronic emotional/psychological stress and suffer from it most commonly. Because of our sophisticated neocortex and our complex interaction with the environment—animals don't have to deal with deadlines, irrational requests, and complicated bureaucratic regulations—it makes sense that emotional/psychological stress is much more prevalent in the modern world.

What is also interesting to note is that, in humans, an emotional/psychological stress produces a physical stress. (For example, we may have an argument with our mother and end up with tightness in our shoulders or neck.) That physical stress now produces a chemical stress. (We're in pain, and the body sends out an alarm producing an adrenal response.) That chemical stress, in turn, produces an ongoing physical stress. (When we're in emergency mode, vital repair and healing resources are minimized, so our shoulder and neck problems become chronic.) The ongoing concern over this physical pain produces a psychological stress. We can probably see how this will continue to spiral in on itself like a snake devouring its tail.

EXERCISE AND STRESS

A Yale University study conducted over 20 years ago involved actors and exercise. The researchers used actors because of their ability to access emotional states. The actors were divided into two groups. The first group was asked to make themselves angry. They worked themselves up by imagining frustrating and disturbing situations. The second group was asked to remain as calm, peaceful, and stable as possible. Both groups were monitored for physiological functions, including heart rate, blood pressure, and respiration.

They were then asked to engage in various forms of light exercise, such as climbing a set of stairs. The so-called angry group maintained or showed less-healthy levels in each health function. For the placid group, however, the benefits we usually associate with exercise were truly evident. Only in this group, despite both of them doing the same exercise, did the exercise prove advantageous. Common wisdom held that exercise reduced stress, but our state of mind and state of being while exercising are just as important as the number of repetitions and sets we do to improve our health.[3]

Additionally, physical stress, like an injury, produces a chemical stress, and both lead to emotional/psychological stress. For example, at the site of most injuries, we develop swelling, which is the result of a chemical process. That injury and the resulting chemical stress means that the body is no longer in homeostasis and results in psychological stress. Am I going to be able to get to work? How will I be able to concentrate? Am I going to be able to get the sleep I need? In humans, all stress, regardless of its origin, seems to end up as emotional/psychological stress.

Recent estimates indicate that as many as 90 percent of the people seeking medical care are doing so because of a stress-related disorder.[4] More and more, researchers are establishing links between physical illnesses and extreme emotional conditions and reactions.

Not everyone responds the same way to stress, and not everyone suffers the consequences of it in the same way. For example, I knew two high school teachers. Twice a year, their supervisor would come into their classrooms to do a performance evaluation. In truth, the evaluations were perfunctory—it wasn't as if the teachers' raises were determined by the visits, and after they achieved tenure, it was nearly impossible for them to be fired except for the grossest of misconduct. However, Bob was a wreck in the weeks leading up to his evaluation. He fretted over what his lesson would be, he fantasized about bribing certain misbehaving students to be absent on that day, and slept little the night before. Beverly, in comparison, loved having her boss (or anyone else, for that matter) come into her classroom. She loved the additional feedback and attention, and she loved what she perceived as a challenge—to impress the person who hired her. She treated the evaluation days as nothing special, made no effort to choose a particular lesson that would show her in her best light, and definitely slept well the night before.

That every person has a distinctive response to stress in terms of its effects should come as no surprise, given that we are all uniquely hardwired by our genetic inheritance, our experiences, and our learning. Humans do tend to exhibit typical effects of stress on the body, however; among them are the surges of adrenaline that eventually exhaust the body and alter acid secretion in the digestive tract, limiting our ability to break down and thus absorb essential nutrients like proteins. As a chiropractor, I've seen how the musculoskeletal system is affected as the body contracts, as muscles tighten, as joints stiffen and ache, and as vital energy is sapped from our systems. I don't know whether you can relate to any of these conditions, but I know I can.

Another way to look at stress is that it is a result of perceiving that we are no longer in control of elements in our environment, because we can't predict the desired outcome. I can't tell you the number of times I've been sitting in traffic, stopped at what seems to be an interminable red light, and I can feel my stress level rising.

The Stress of the Anticipated

The example of the two teachers who had performance evaluations illustrates another crucial difference that separates humans from our four-footed friends: we can look ahead and anticipate stressful situations. In fact, we can experience stress even before the event we are stressing about takes place. Although animals are subject to the immediacy of stress, they don't have to deal with anticipatory stress. Because of the relatively small size of their neocortex, animals can store a memory of a stressor being present in their lives, but they don't worry about the same thing happening to them again soon. Humans, however, activate the stress response in anticipation of various complex psychological and social situations that never even enter into the consciousness of a dog. Perhaps that's one of the things that we admire about our pets. They seem to live completely in the moment, living totally free of anticipatory stress.

On the other hand, we humans can turn the stress response on by thinking about a past or future stressful situation, and that can be a physiological stress response as if we were confronting a real-life circumstance. It takes only one stray thought about the possibility of a stressor in our future to change the degree of acidity in our stomach's secretions. Without ever moving a muscle, we can cause our pancreas to make hormones, alter our adrenal gland's hormones, get our heart to pump faster, direct our blood flow to our legs, change our rate of respiration, and even make ourselves more prone to infection. Humans are powerful entities in this regard. We can simply entertain a thought about that stressor and become physiologically prepared for it, as if the event were actually taking place.

Is this good or bad? Well, how many times have we patted ourselves on the back for correctly identifying where and when a stressor would appear? When we're successfully able to predict that appearance and adequately prepare for it, we're generally thrilled by the outcome. None of us wants to be like Charlie Brown, hurtling ourselves toward Lucy, believing in our heart of hearts and networks of neurons that this is the time she won't pull the football away just as we're about to kick it. Yet how many times have we had our trust in someone prove misplaced?

In one sense, what gives humans a superior evolutionary advantage is our ability to predict what *might* happen. What diminishes that advantage is when we fail to properly predict the correct outcome. What then results is an increase in anxiety, depression, phobias, insomnia, neuroses, and a host of other ills that weren't necessary. We prepare ourselves for a stressor and alter our internal balance, but often we can't control the outcome, and we are either overprepared for what we consider an eventuality (that then doesn't materialize), or we are surprised by another stressor we didn't see coming at all.

Either way, being constantly vigilant, always directed outward toward the environment, can take its toll. Chronic stress, the repeated process of keeping the stress response activated all the time, is what really does the damage. Our bodies are not designed for long-term stress. When the stress response is constantly activated, we are headed for disease.

Additional Stress Effects

We're sitting in our office working away on a project, when our supervisor bursts in and says, "Listen, I need your help ASAP. The VP of production just sent me an e-mail telling me that we're having a budget meeting in an hour. He needs me to have his PowerPoint presentation up and running in 30 minutes so that he can review and correct it. Drop whatever you're doing and get me those spreadsheets I mentioned last week." So, what do we do? We stop working on the sales projections for the third quarter, and we do what our boss tells us to do. Instead of looking at ways that we can grow our business, we have to deal with immediate issues.

The same thing happens when our body engages in a stress response. We have to attend to an emergency in that moment. Delay is not possible. As a result, any long-term regenerative cellular repair that was going to go on is halted. The stress response is all about mobilizing energy for our muscles to use in the flight-or-fight response. Even digestion can wait: it's a slow process and takes up too much energy for us to spare, because we have to move and we have to move *now!*

And we know what happens at work when we have to drop one thing to do another. This creates a cascade effect of new deadline crunches and emergencies. The same is true of the body. If we are constantly using our energy resources and mobilizing them against threats, we never get ahead. We never are able to build up a surplus. It's like living from paycheck to paycheck and not quite making it. Eventually, we have to rob Peter to pay Paul. When our body gets to the point that its energy supply is so depleted that it can't perform vital tasks like fighting off invaders, we get sick. High cortisol levels break down the immune system. Once our immune system is compromised and we're ill, our already-weakened systems take a double dose of hits—both by the illness itself and the stress created by being ill. How many times have we said, "I really can't afford to be sick now!" Why is that exactly the time when we do get sick? Worried sick, perhaps? And what about the fact that illness produces a physical, chemical, and emotional/psychological stress in our body?

When we are involved in a stress reaction, the body systems responsible for repair and regeneration are compromised. If there is a tidal wave approaching our beach house, it's probably not a good idea to remodel the kitchen. Instead, we have to prepare for the emergency state of affairs and abandon long-term building projects. Remember that the flight-or-fight response is all about mobilizing energy for immediate action. In a sense, we become fixated on the short term. Why repair and regrow now, when we're faced with a more immediate set of needs? If we are repetitively under stress, it will take us much longer to heal, because that process isn't a high-priority item.

Most people who are under stress sleep less than they do when they are relaxed, because their circulating levels of adrenaline keep them prepared and vigilant. Sleep is the time when much of the restorative processes take place. The less time we have for sleep, the less time we have for repair. The less sleep we get, the more stressed we are. Just about anyone can relate to lying there in the middle of the night in self-absorption, worrying about everything from our health to our future. All those thoughts push us further away from homeostatic balance.

And it's not like we're spending time with our partner in acts of procreation, when we should be sleeping in bed. The reproductive process is also affected by stress. Ovulation, sperm production, and growing a fetus all take a backseat to fight-or-flight, whether we have a literal tiger or a figurative one (like an impending divorce) on our tail. Impotence, infertility, and miscarriages are all common side effects of chronic stress.

Among the other primary functions that can be affected by stress, one of the most crucial is our immune system. Once that system is compromised or shuts down completely, we're unable to fight invaders like bacteria and viruses, so we can be ravaged by infections and dogged by illness. In particular, we can suffer from immune-mediated diseases like allergies, infectious influenza, even rheumatoid arthritis. How well can our immune system detect early tumor cells and discard them, when we are fighting an emergency elsewhere requiring all our energy? Cancer cells can reproduce with impunity when the immune system is shut down in response to stress. Quite simply, the more stress in our life, the more frequently we get sick, and the effects of a compromised immune system show up in many forms. Suddenly, we have more pressing problems than the stressful situation that produced those problems.

People think, "I'll deal with that when this stressful situation subsides." Too often, that stressful situation doesn't subside, and we are caught in a vicious circle, compounding stress upon stress. In time, the stress response is doing more damage to us than any of the other conditions or ailments that initiated it or that it initiated. We always presume that it is the monkey chasing the weasel, but in the case of stress and our stress response, it becomes difficult to tell which is which. In humans, the stress response derived from our thoughts and feelings most often causes greater long-term damage than the stressor itself.

All we know is that we are running and running and not getting anywhere, except closer to the state of exhaustion. Exhaustion is the point at which our body can no longer fight off invaders—our hormones and immune systems are so compromised that we get sick. And that illness further taxes our body.[5]

Studies have shown that too much CRH, a chemical produced during the stress response, reduces the body's production and secretion of growth hormone. In chronically stressed children, their growth is slowed. For adults, this means that the production of muscle and bone is inhibited. In addition, excess CRH affects digestion, so irritable bowel syndrome can result. If the hypothalamus-pituitary-adrenal connection is hyperactive, cells in the body may stop taking up glucose in response to insulin, and diabetes results. And it's not just our bodies that can suffer. Recent indications are that excess CRH plays a role in mental disorders, and contributes to phobias and panic attacks.[6]

Russian researchers performed an experiment on rats that shows just how far the effects of stress can go. They performed a taste aversion experiment in which rats were given an immune-suppression drug flavored with the artificial sweetener saccharine. The immune-suppressing drug made the rats nauseated. After many instances of subjecting the rats to the drug/saccharine combination, they stopped giving them the nausea-inducing drug and gave them just the saccharine. The rats still got sick. They had been so conditioned by the taste of the saccharine that they associated it with the physical symptom. Many of the rats died. Even though they were no longer being subjected to the nausea-inducing drug, their anticipatory thoughts so weakened their immune system that they were defenseless against their environment. In a very real way, their thoughts killed them.[7]

The Heart of the Matter

Back when we lived at the mercy of stealthy predators, humans benefited greatly from having our cardiovascular systems respond when we first spotted that saber-toothed tiger heading our way. When blood pressure and heart rate rose to get vital energy stores to our legs and arms, that was a good thing. But when our heartbeat increases and our blood pressure rises as we drive our Impala and someone in a Jaguar cuts us off to make a left turn from the right lane, that's not such a good thing.

And let's face it, although that Jaguar turning in front of us may be an extreme example, every day we face all kinds of stresses. Our cardiovascular system, as remarkable as it is, was never designed for that kind of repeated emotional/psychological stress. As recent studies have shown, rather than getting us up and running, repeated and long-term stress can lead to heart disease.[8] If we continue to live in chronic stress, the adrenaline signals the heart to beat faster and the blood pressure to rise. But we don't do anything in response to the stressor—we don't fight or flee. As a result, we train our heart to stay at that accelerated rate. It's like turning up the thermostat and keeping the temperature at that level all the time. Our heart is racing continuously in a state of preparedness. What is the effect of setting the cardiac bar to this new height? Arrhythmia, tachycardia, and high blood pressure are all the result of stepping on the gas and the brake at the same time.

If acute stress causes our blood pressure to go up quickly for a short period, chronic stress will cause our blood pressure to go up and remain there chronically. The hypertension that results makes our blood flow in a more turbulent and pressurized manner throughout our vascular system. As the blood flows, it reaches thousands of bifurcated arteries that continuously split into smaller and smaller arterioles to supply tissues and, eventually, individual cells. No cell in the body is more than five cells away from a blood vessel. At each of the thousands of forks in the road, the hyper-pressurized blood is forced to make contact with the point where the two vessels split, and this is what damages their smooth inner surfaces. At every point that the circulatory system splits into smaller arteries, there is a whirlpool of this hyper-pressurized blood that leads to trauma to the vessel. Once damaged, other types of cells rush to the site of injury to stop the insult and inflammation. As a result, things tend to get clogged up inside the vessels. This is how plaque builds up. Additionally, increases in chronic stress mobilize fat stores into the bloodstream and cholesterol levels rise. Now things are getting more complicated for our vascular system, with more probabilities to clog or explode.

So maybe we're better off using our head when faced with the kinds of everyday stressors that can dominate our life if we let them. But when it comes to our head, the news isn't so good either. The stress response impairs our basic cognitive functions. When we are in chronic stress mode, most of the blood flow to the brain is diverted to the hindbrain and midbrain and away from the forebrain, which is our higher cognitive center. We unconsciously react instead of consciously planning our actions. We often say that some people lose their heads and others keep their heads in times of stress. Obviously, what we're really talking about is whether people can or can't think clearly under duress. Most people, under the influence of the stress response, don't think clearly.

Recent evidence suggests that cortisol, one of the chemicals produced during the stress response, is responsible for degenerating brain cells in the hippocampus. This organ is responsible for helping us form new memories and acquire new knowledge. If we damage the neurological machinery that craves new things, we end up craving routine instead of novelty. We cannot learn, make new memories, and explore new adventures, because the organ that makes new memories stick in the brain is breaking down.[9]

Novelty, Stress, and the Hippocampus

A number of years ago, scientists conducted an experiment with laboratory animals to test the effects of a damaged hippocampus. After having explored different areas of their surroundings, the animals got a dose of radiation directed at their hippocampus, which is directly involved in the encoding of information for storage in the brain, including the acquisition of memories.

Once the hippocampus had been rendered incapable of functioning through exposure to radiation, the animals were placed back into their surroundings. Instead of eagerly and enthusiastically exploring new regions of their environment as they had done before, they stayed in the same region of their surroundings in which they had been placed. Curiously, it was as if they were no longer curious. We know that the hippocampus is involved in making known the unknown and in processing novel experiences, and without one, these animals stopped craving new experiences entirely.[10]

What are the implications for humans? Chances are, our hippocampus won't be irradiated. But stress chemicals like glucocorticoids, which are released when we have an emotional reaction in response to our environment or during long-term stress, do break down the neurons in our hippocampus. Typical of our behavior as humans, when we are stressed, we resort to doing what is most familiar to us— we seek out routine, the ordinary, the everyday. Yet, for many of us, the routine and the ordinary means being stressed and responding emotionally. Behaving in that manner produces more chemicals of stress, which further damages the hippocampus, which makes us crave the routine experiences and avoid novel ones.

Recent studies have shown a correlation between chronic stress, the breakdown of neurons in the hippocampus, and clinical depression.[11] If you've ever been around a depressed person, you know that getting out and having new experiences is usually low on the daily agenda.

There is good news, however. Despite what we've been told, the brain can regenerate and produce new cells. So all those stories about the tequila we drank depleting our finite number of brain cells may be incorrect. In fact, *neurogenesis* (the production of new neurons) takes place very actively in the hippocampus.[12] Regeneration in the hippocampus implies that when we break out of living life in survival mode, we may get a second chance. It is entirely possible that if the machinery that is essential in making new memories repairs itself, our sense of adventure should return. The organ that is designed to make new memories should now spur our motivation for new experiences, instead of craving the familiar and the routine.

Antidepressants have been shown to be effective in spurring neurogenesis in laboratory animals. Interestingly, in a recent study, it typically took one month for the antidepressant medication Prozac to elevate mood in human beings, and that is about the same time neurogenesis takes.[13]

When We Can't Stomach Stress

Chronic stress has another harmful effect. It increases our blood sugar levels by altering the output of the pancreas, the liver, and the storage mechanism in fat cells. When we increase sugar levels repeatedly as the result of chronic stress, we lower our insulin levels. Adult onset diabetes, as well as obesity, can afflict us.

What about digestion? Why is our digestion compromised—whether by ulcers, acid reflux, constipation, or irritable bowel syndrome? The main reason is that when we are stressed, the body moves blood away from the digestive tract to the extremities. Even though we may be eating healthfully, we are in the wrong frame of mind. That, combined with the lack of proper blood supply in the organs of digestion and assimilation, means that we aren't breaking our food down properly. We're burning food improperly and inefficiently: the food is sitting there, but the body doesn't have the necessary energy and blood supply to digest it properly. We can eat all the organic foods we want, we can eat macrobiotically, we can ingest all the vitamins in the world, but if we can't metabolize our food properly, those efforts go for naught. We just might want to take a breath or two before our next meal, just to switch from the sympathetic to the parasympathetic nervous systems.

Stress Hurts

Lastly, chronic stress is responsible for many of the aches and pains we experience. Our muscle cells are bathed in adrenaline for a flight-or-fight response. Adrenaline in small amounts acts like liquid energy for the entire body, especially for the muscles. When it ends up not being used, it sits in the tissues. That causes the muscles to get tight, get hard, contract, and feel sore.

I can't tell you how many times someone has entered my office with a neck so stiff it looks like he has one of his ears sewn to his shoulder. Typically, I take a history, then ask, "Did you do anything to cause this condition?" Most of the time, I hear the same response. "No. I think that I just slept wrong." I then say, "Did you sleep in any different situations, like another bed that you weren't used to, or did you use a different pillow?" Their response is, "No." Then I say, "You have been sleeping in the same bed for how many years?" Their answer, "The last ten years I have slept in my same bed."

I then ask, "Tell me what has been happening in your life for the last three months." Most recite a list that goes something like this: "Well, I got fired from my job two months ago, my mother was diagnosed with cancer and she is dying, I filed for bankruptcy two weeks ago, my house is going through foreclosure, my wife and I are separated, and I am manually digging ditches eight hours a day for a living at fifty-four years old." I then ask, "Do you really think that you just slept wrong?" Most stress ends up as emotional/psychological stress, and that means it's the autosuggestions of our own thinking that affect the body so intensely.

Does this sounds like anyone you may know: Chronically fatigued, depressed, lacking in energy (from overtaxed adrenal glands), sleeps poorly, is often sick, has a low sex drive, cannot think or remember clearly, lives in a routine, reacts easily, experiences heart problems, and has digestive disturbances, sore muscles, muscle cramps, backaches, anxiety, obesity, high cholesterol levels, and/or blood sugar problems? No wonder 75 to 90 percent of Americans show up at a health care facility due to a stress-related disorder.

Frequency Matters

Stress is unavoidable. The key is to limit the kind of stress we experience to acute stress, which is much less harmful to the body than chronic stress. Acute stress happens, it ends, and we have time to recover from it. Chronic stress allows our body no recovery time. This is when our body starts to steal energy from other vital processes. If our external protection system is working overtime, as it always does when we are living in survival mode, the internal protection system can't function as well. They are both drawing power from the same energy source, and when we constantly shift to emergency power, we're ultimately going to tax the system. If we have an internal Mr. Scott (*Star Trek*'s Scotty), he's eventually going to shout, "I'm sorry, captain, I'm giving you all she's got!" Unlike Mr. Scott and the *Enterprise*, we may not be able to figure out some way to make our energy source compensate. Repeated stress responses act much like the repeated firing of neurons. The more times we activate the response, the more difficult it becomes to turn it off. Which leads to this question: Why would we want to turn it off?

One thing to keep in mind about homeostasis is that it doesn't deal in absolutes. In other words, over time, what is considered a normal level will change. If we continually raise the level of stress chemicals in our body, the homeostatic mechanism will recalibrate itself to a new normal level that is higher than it was previously. If we repeatedly turn on the stress response or if we cannot turn off the stress response during long periods of time, the body will recalibrate itself to a new internal level of homeostasis. This new internal balance now becomes the body living out of chemical balance. It's like setting our internal thermostat to a higher level. We then function from that higher level all the time.

Simply put, that ain't good. Obviously, it will take greater and greater levels of these stress response chemicals for us to get to the heightened state of awareness and energy necessary in a stress response. In time, our cells will grow accustomed to the adrenal hit they receive, and they will need more to get themselves to the appropriate level. Sounds a lot like addiction to me. In addition, the greater the quantity of those stress chemicals circulating in our body, the more frequently they aren't used up in a flight-or-fight response and are subsequently stored in our tissues, and the more damage they can do.

Each time we have a stress reaction from our environment, our brain starts to associate this change in chemistry, this internal change, with a cause in the external world. Therefore, we tend to associate people, places, things, times, and events with the adrenal hit, the chemical rush, the high, that makes us feel alive.[14]

This is the next stage of how we become addicted to our environment or stressful circumstances. Remember that when we experience the rush and can tie the external stimulus to a change in internal chemistry, that identification is an event in and of itself. We notice the person involved in the stressful situation, and we associate that rush and feeling of aliveness with him or her. Eventually, we start to associate nearly everything in our world with that rush or that high. We start to look for that rush in the external environment or in the people, places, things, times, and events that make up our entire life.

Our Biochemical Fix

Although some researchers—Robert Sapolsky, Ph.D., professor of biology at Stanford University, most prominent among them—claim that not all stressors produce the same degree of chemical reactions within the body,[15] nearly all agree that the process by which this reaction is produced is the same. For example, you are driving to work down a four-lane highway that has few traffic lights. The flow of traffic is steady and you are keeping pace with traffic, but then you see that a light ahead of you has turned yellow. Not wanting your momentum to be interrupted, you hit the gas, accelerate to nearly 20 miles over the speed limit, and get through the intersection just as the light turns red.

At first you breathe a sigh of relief, but a moment later, something flashes in your rearview mirror. You move out of the left lane and slow a bit, hoping that the police car is responding to some emergency and not to your mad dash through the intersection. You experience that pit of the stomach sensation, and you grip the wheel tighter, forcing yourself to stare straight ahead and not look in the mirror again. Your heart is thumping in your chest, and your breathing becomes ragged. You really don't need this, and especially not now.

From the instant your brain first perceived the stressor—the flashing lights in your rearview mirror—it initiated a chemical stress response. The chemicals and chemical reactions that you produced are one of three kinds: neurotransmitters, peptides, or those of the autonomic nervous system (ANS).

Neurotransmitters

As you have no doubt committed to semantic memory, *neurotransmitters* are chemical messengers that pass important information to other nerve cells and to other parts of the body in order to coordinate a specific function. Among the most important of them are glutamate, GABA, dopamine, serotonin, and melatonin. They are but a few of a whole family of neurotransmitters produced in the brain. Neurotransmitters are made primarily in neurons and are released in the synaptic space.

When your visual sensors picked up the flashing lights and you made the association with a police car, neurotransmitters were at work in the synaptic space, sending signals to other nerve cells and eventually to the brain. Here, all your associations with flashing lights and police cars, all the neural nets containing those memories and all your knowledge were fired, and those neurotransmitters were released in the synaptic space. Your neurotransmitters turned on a level of the mind and a specific set of neural networks. Neurotransmitters can do their work only across the synaptic space, because of the receptors that reside on the surface of every cell.

Receptors are rather large, vibrating molecules. Every cell has thousands of receptors, and nerve cells have millions of them that function as sensors. They are waiting for the right chemicals to come along. The classic analogy is that these protein-based receptors are like a keyhole, and the chemicals that come along are keys. Only a certain key will fit in a specific keyhole.

The chemicals that come along and act as the key are called *ligands*. The word *ligand* is derived from the Latin root *ligare,* which means "to bind." There are three types of ligands—neurotransmitters, peptides, and hormones. We've already talked about neurotransmitters as ligands. Now let's talk about peptides.

Peptides: The Chemical Signatures of Emotion

It was once thought that neurotransmitters were the biggest contributors in making chemicals that influence the body and the brain. We now know that peptides are by far the most common of the ligands, comprising 95 percent of their total number. Peptides play a crucial role in regulating various life processes. Together with receptors, they control much of our cellular destiny and, consequently, much of our life. These are the chemicals that most influence our mind/body connection. They are the second type of chemical communication we utilize, and they facilitate the sending of messages between the brain and the body.

Once any of the ligands insert themselves in the receptor site, they cause the molecule to reorganize itself so that the information/message can enter the cell. In her wonderful book *The Molecules of Emotion,* Candace Pert, Ph.D., describes the effects of this process on the cells by stating, "In short, the life of the cell, what it is up to at any moment, is determined by which receptors are occupied by ligands or not. On a more global scale, these minute physiological phenomenon at the cellular level can translate to large changes in behavior, physical activity, even mood."[16] Bottom line: biochemical processes, starting with ligands like peptides and their corresponding receptors, are responsible for how we act and feel on a daily basis. Whether we feel anxious or sexually aroused, depressed or delighted, the action of the peptides produced in the brain is responsible for how we feel at every given moment. When peptides signal the body, they turn on hormones and other secretions from organs that make the body respond in different ways to further alter its functions. For example, when you have a sexual fantasy, your brain immediately releases peptides that turn on hormones/secretions that make you ready for intercourse. Hormones also act as ligands to bind to other tissues to further stimulate systemic activity.

Perhaps a more appropriate analogy than a lock and key for how peptides and receptors work is that the cells have a kind of receiving department responsible for the incoming packages that the many shippers send to us. Just as in most companies, the receiving dock is located so that there is easy access to the outside of the building, the receptors are on the outside of the cell. This facilitates the receiving end of the process.

To continue our analogy, each receptor site has a specific "bar code" for which it is attempting to find a match. As these packaged messages come moving down the line, the receptor sites employ a type of scanning tool to try to identify a matching bar code. Once they do find a match, they exert a force that pulls that similarly bar coded message to them. They then immediately send that package to another site deep within the cell. There the package containing the message will be opened, the instructions will be read, and then tiny machines go to work carrying out the specified work. Each receptor is responsible only for one specific bar code. We refer to this as *receptor specificity*. Without that level of specificity in the receptors, the messages would not get to their intended destinations, and the instructions would not be carried out correctly. In some cases, the message and instructions indicate that the word should be spread to other sites, and the shipping function takes over.

Autonomic Nervous System

That's exactly what happens when the neurotransmitters in the synaptic space are released. As soon as the brain recognized that a police car was behind you, through a part of the brain called the amygdala, one of two nerve paths was fired. In this case, because it was a relatively high-stress situation, the message was sent via a nerve path directly to the more primitive centers of the brain—the midbrain and the brainstem. The midbrain controls the ANS or autonomic nervous system (we have no control over the automatic responses generated here), and is divided into the sympathetic (SNS) and parasympathetic (PNS) systems. The one (SNS) speeds us up; the other (PNS) relaxes us and slows us down by allowing us to coast.

In the case of you as a speeder, the SNS was engaged in the stress response. That's why you immediately experienced that sensation in your stomach, why your heart rate increased, why your breathing became rapid and ragged, and why your senses sharpened. The SNS turned on the adrenal glands and produced those responses. The SNS pathway is like the express lanes on an interstate. Information travels down the spinal cord and goes directly to the adrenal glands in milliseconds. Unlike most other organs that have two different nerves going to them, the adrenals have only one. As a result, the response can be direct and immediate. Signals reach the adrenals faster than they do any other tissue in the body. Because the body sensed that you needed to respond instantly to this threat, it initiated this pathway. It got you moving *now!* At this point, the body itself is turned on.

Once the body is turned on by adrenaline, we start producing chemicals that influence other functions. That's why you were able to get your foot off the gas and pull over to the right lane so quickly and without thinking. The adrenal hormones stimulated the body with immediate energy and you acted quickly. You were "instructed" to move your right foot off the gas pedal and your arms and hands turned the steering wheel to the right—all without conscious thought, thanks to the autonomic nervous system.

At the same time, the neurons and neurotransmitters passed the message of a potential problem on to the hypothalamus, which then cooked up the chemical peptide called CRH (see page 270), and shipped it off to the pituitary gland. As we can tell by its name, CRH is a chemical that tells the pituitary to release a hormone. The pituitary then instantaneously mixed up a batch of the peptide called ACTH (see page 270) to be released into the bloodstream.

THE ROLE OF THE PITUITARY

Most of the time, the pituitary acts as a kind of chemical bartender. It knows what most of the regulars want, and it mixes up their favorites. It's also an arrogant bartender—it knows, better than we do, what we want and need, and gives us just that. The pituitary is sometimes referred to as the master gland because of that skill. It reigns over all the other glandular systems. Because it works at the only bar in town, so to speak, the glands don't complain. They don't know anything different. That's one way to look at it.

The other is to say that the brain is really the master gland. It oversees all the systems of the body as well as all the glandular systems. When the stress reaction is initiated, the signals come from the brain; it regulates the production and flow of the chemicals. We now know that the hypothalamus contains a large array of releasing and inhibiting hormones that instruct the pituitary to start or stop producing other neurohormones. In some cases, a pituitary hormone is controlled by both the inhibiting and releasing hormone from the brain, something called *dual control*. So as much as our bartender pituitary thinks he's running the joint, he also has to take orders from his customers and from his boss.

The ACTH traveled immediately to the adrenal glands—where its cells' receptor sites do the scan-and-match thing again—and obeyed the signal to produce the stress hormone glucocorticoids, the most common of which is cortisol. By using the SNS and the hypothalamic-pituitary-adrenal gland axis, you got quicker results. Both hormones—adrenaline and cortisol—are responsible for most of the chemicals produced during the stress reaction. If the stress becomes chronic, the glucocorticoids influence the production of noradrenaline (a sister stress hormone of adrenaline) that communicates with the amygdala. The amygdala then produces more CRH, and the cycle starts again.

The Feedback Loop

During the fight or flight response, peptides produced in the brain turn on the body. Once that process is in motion, it establishes a kind of downhill momentum that is difficult to stop. Once the body has taken control of the process, we are in the middle of a feedback loop. Think of it this way. We perceive a threat or stressor. Our midbrain turns on the body to respond. The midbrain gets the body to produce the chemicals of the stress reaction. Because the body wants to maintain a homeostatic condition, it will, over time, come to demand more of the chemicals produced during the stress response. The hypothalamus signals the pituitary to produce the chemicals involved in the stress response. Those same chemicals have their effect, which results in the cells once again making their demands on the brain.

At the point where the stress chemicals are finally released in the body, it seems as if the body is now in control and doing the thinking, and it will continue to signal the brain to produce more chemicals. This is the cycle of chemistry that continues to produce the same chemical state in the body. As the brain and body are involved in this feedback loop, we are kept in a state of chemical continuity. For most people, unfortunately, that carnival ride is less of a benign Ferris wheel than it is a Tilt-O-Whirl of agitation and anxiety. Because attitudes are so influenced and determined by these chemicals, and the brain and body are locked in this two-step, it is difficult but not impossible to affect a change in attitude.

Now it starts to make sense how so many of us begin to break our bodies down by our own thoughts and reactions. People who experience spontaneous healings from disease (see chapter 2), may do so because they stop the process of repetitive thinking that had worn their body down to a weakened state. When we overcome the thoughts that initiate stress responses, the body just may have enough energy to begin healing. In the next chapter, we'll take a closer look at how that happens.

CHAPTER NINE

THE CHEMISTRY OF EMOTIONAL ADDICTION

The existence of "emotional control centers"
within our heads stirs up visions of a race of robots
created by "nature" to experience and act in certain ways.
To an extent, our conscious self—interested in career
advancements, personal happiness, or whatever—must
negotiate a compromise within the brain's neural circuits between
what we "know" and the ancient knowledge
"hard-wired" within our limbic system. Could this explain the
ambivalences and paradoxes that have confounded a "model"
or theory of the human mind? In a sense, conflicts are built into
the system; what we want for ourselves may not be the same thing
that would favor the development of the species.

—RICHARD RESTAK, M.D.
THE BRAIN: THE LAST FRONTIER

I n chapter 8, we took a look at how we respond both neurologically and chemically to stressors in the environment through the flight-or-fight response. In this chapter, we examine how people become addicted to the familiar host of chemicals that are produced any time we have a thought. When we understand the chemistry of this addiction to our own thoughts, we can free ourselves to evolve.

As we've seen, all memories have an emotional component associated with them. Consequently, almost all thoughts are emotionally based, and when we recall them, we are also associating the emotions stored with them. As we recollect our combined memories related to people, places, things, times, and events, each with its own emotional association, we are turning on the independent neural networks connected to each. Once activated, that frame of mind produces a plethora of chemicals, both in the synaptic space and from the midbrain's hypothalamus, to stimulate both the brain and body. Each thought has its own chemical signature. The result is that our thinking becomes feeling— actually, our every thought is a feeling. We do this constantly and unconsciously.

How does this relate to addiction? The easiest definition of an addiction is this: an addiction is something that we can't stop doing. Let's say that you are in a highly agitated state. Your significant other has just brought up something you did six months ago—you failed to communicate an important message— and you're really ticked off about what seems to you to be the 1,000th reminder of your mistake. Sure, the comment was couched not in accusation but in a subtle suggestion, "You're *sure* no one called while I was out?" You can read the underlying subtext, so you respond, "Yes, I'm sure. I'm not an idiot. I know when the phone rings. I know how to ask, May I take a message." And your partner responds by pouring gas on the fire, "I never said you didn't know how to take a message. I'm just not sure you know how to pass it on to the appropriate person."

From that point on, the two of you go at it, dredging up every sin, major or minor, since the two of you met. What if I were to step in at that point and say to either of you, "I know that you're really angry right now. I can see it in your face, and I can hear it in your voice. I'm asking you to stop. Right now. Just stop being angry."

Your response is likely to be, "Stop? Are you insane? Did you hear what he just said? He's talking about something that happened six months ago, when I was at home working on balancing our checkbook, which he can't seem to do himself. It was nine o'clock at night and he was out with his buddy Phil at the sports bar watching a stupid Red Sox game, while I was here busting my butt with a calculator that had a number five key that kept sticking every time I hit it. And then his moron of a brother called about their damn fishing trip. So I forgot to pass along the message. But I didn't forget how to seal the potato chip bags so they won't go stale!"

Stopping that rush of emotions and those recollections of all the wrongs that you associate with them isn't easy at all. As much as your system is gearing you up to fight or to flee, you can't do either of those two things in this situation. Social conventions, laws, and your good sense tell you that you shouldn't engage in a physical confrontation, and it's often too much fun to walk out on a good verbal battle. So, you've got this overabundance of chemicals that have produced all that energy to mobilize you, and you're stuck. You suppress. You rationalize. You deflect. You get into silly arguments. You drag up everything from your past. You can't change the channel even if someone steps in and suggests it. Why?

Before I answer that, let's go back to an example from chapter 8. Remember when I brought up an imaginary scenario about you speeding through an intersection to avoid having to stop at a light? You then spotted the patrol car's flashing lights in your rearview mirror, and that stimulus initiated the fight-or-flight response. Well, of course you wouldn't flee or fight in that situation.

But why not? More to the point, why *do* some people choose to run from the police? Most often, I suppose, they have other legal troubles and they don't want to go back to jail. But what if you *chose* to flee and engage in a high-speed chase? I have to admit that I've fantasized about it on occasion. Someone might do that because they are already in jail—that jail of their own making: the routine, ordinary, commonplace, everyday life that lacks excitement and novelty. I'm certainly not advocating that you break the law as a means to get out of a rut, but I've often wondered what prompts some people to suddenly do something that is completely out of character for them. Can we ever say that an action we take, a decision we make, or a path we follow is out of character for us? After all, we chose to do it; it's a product of one particular neural network, so where has that action been lurking all these years?

In the case of the arguing couple (who, by the way, share similar neural nets), the reason they both got so embroiled in this argument is relatively simple: it felt good. Good not in the sense that we typically think of it, but in terms of it feeling *familiar*. And if you're wondering why two people stay together who clearly have some issues with each other, hang in there, this chapter answers that question as well.

Settling In and Settling For

You've surely heard of the midlife crisis, and you have probably seen its effects as well. The number of marriages ended and sports cars bought are probably directly proportional to the number of people turning 50 each year. Why is midlife so fraught with people wanting to make a change in their life? We know that emotions and feelings are the chemical markers of prior experiences. As we grow older and embrace new experiences in life, there is a period in our late twenties and early thirties in which we think that we have experienced most of what life has to offer. Perhaps we have pretty much stopped having new experiences and are repeating the same experiences, which produce in us the same feelings. Because we've had diverse experiences in our earlier life, we can say that we know what most of our unique experiences feel like—and so, we can predict them. In a midlife crisis, it is as if we are trying to feel the way we did the first time we experienced the emotions associated with novel experiences.

From childhood through young adulthood, we are learning and growing from our environment. Then we reach a point in midlife—whether midlife is a genetic, natural phenomenon or a learned, environmental effect—in which we certainly have experienced a lot of what life's experiences and emotions have to offer. By this time, for the most part, we understand sexuality and sexual identity because we have experienced it. We have embraced pain, suffering, victimization, and pity. We know what it is like to feel sad, disappointed, betrayed, unmotivated, insecure, and weak. We have reacted without thinking. We have been afraid. We have sunk into guilt. We have been embarrassed, shamed, and rejected. We have blamed, complained, made excuses, and been confused. We know success and failure. We have been envious and jealous. We know tyranny, control, importance, competition, pride, and anger. We have had moments of total power and recognition. We have demonstrated personal conviction, self-discipline, dedication to something or someone, and self-empowerment. We have been selfish and controlling. We know how to hate and judge another, and more important, we know how to judge ourselves.

All these feelings and emotions are there for two reasons. One reason we are familiar with those feelings is that our life experiences activated preexisting neural networks that we inherited from our parents and forefathers, and we turned these memories into attitudes and behaviors. We also know what those emotions are like because we have created certain situations and experiences in our life, and our environment has prompted our neurons to make new connections from those experiences. When we remember the feelings that partner with those memories, we have come to believe that those thoughts are who we are.

Since feelings help us to remember an experience, and because by this time we have become quite experienced, we have gained scores of memories through countless different feelings. Because we have experienced so many of life's emotions by our late twenties and early thirties, we are able to predict the outcome of most situations.[1] It becomes easy to determine how they will feel, because we have experienced what similar prior circumstances felt like.

In this way, feelings become the barometer to determine our motivation in life. We then begin to make choices based on how they will make us feel. If the personality self knows that a potential experience is familiar and predictable, we feel good in choosing that option. This is true because we feel confident, and that feeling tells us that we have already experienced the event before, so we can forecast the outcome.

However, if we cannot predict the feeling of a situation, more than likely we will not be interested in engaging that experience. In fact, if we can predict that a potential experience is likely to have an unpleasant or uncomfortable feeling associated with it, we will tend to avoid that situation.

By the time we are thirty-five, then, we are thinking almost exclusively based on feelings. Feelings become the means of thinking. The two are nearly inseparable. Most of us cannot think greater than how we feel. The feedback loop of thoughts and feelings that are intrinsically connected to the body becomes complete right around this point in our life, because we spend more time feeling than learning. Feelings are the past memories of experiences; learning is making new memories that have new feelings. At this life stage, we are forced to stop focusing primarily on growing and learning, and start surviving. Jobs, homes, cars, mortgages, finances, investments, kids, colleges, extracurricular activities, and maintaining a relationship or marriage are just the right ingredients to begin living in survival instead of expansion.

And so, given the opportunity for a new experience at this stage of our life, we typically try to predict the outcome based on how it might feel. This is when we say things like, "What will it feel like? How long will it take? Will it hurt? Do I need to bring something to eat? Do I have to walk a lot? Will it be raining? Will it be cold? Who will be there? Will we be able to take breaks? Who are these people?" All these concerns reflect our anxieties about the body, the environment, and time. This is a sign that youth is slipping away and we are beginning to age.

To continue this line of reasoning, now we become further trapped within the limits of our box. We hesitate to step outside the familiar to experience anything unknown or new to us because we will not be able to identify a feeling to go along with that potential experience. The box of our limited thinking creates the same "frame" of mind.

The explanation is simple. A new experience evokes a new feeling. An unknown experience might expose us to an unknown feeling, so it initiates the survival mechanisms of the personality. Because we have not experienced this novel event, the "self" runs through its databases of prior experiences, looking for familiar patterns and associations to forecast what feelings that situation might bring. The neural nets of inherited memories are also activated in an attempt to evaluate the future. When we run out of options, we will simply steer clear of the unfamiliar experience. The chance to experience a novel opportunity is now overridden by the firing of our old neural hardware. In other words, it is outside the limits of our comfort zone. And so, we resist the unknown.

The Chemical Dimension of Addiction

For many years, the accepted model of the brain and its function was that it sent electrical impulses along its complicated nexus of wires (that, if strung together, would cover thousands of miles) to regulate various functions and allow us to operate in the world. Now we are discovering that, in addition to this electrical model based on neurons, axons, dendrites, and neurotransmitters, the brain functions on another level as well.

Candace Pert refers to this *chemical brain* as a *second nervous system*, and points out our collective reluctance to accept this model: "Especially difficult to accept was that this chemically based system was one indisputably more ancient and far more basic to the organism. There were peptides such as endorphins, for instance, being made inside cells long before there were dendrites, axons, or even neurons—in fact, before there were brains."[2] This may be a startling revelation for you, or it may be a restatement of what you already know.

Let's take a closer look at what she's saying, to help us fully understand how the "self" develops, and how we can become habitually addicted to who we are neurologically (and, consequently, addicted to our emotions). First, we'll explore the chemistry of thought and emotions. We will build an understanding of how those chemicals work in concert with, and are produced by, the neurological structures we've discussed. Just as we are neurologically hardwired to our environment and we react based on the most hardwired neural networks in the brain, we are equally addicted to the rush of chemicals and emotions that our brain and body produce in response to inputs from the environment, the body, and our own private thoughts. To understand this chemical component of emotions and behavior, we're going to look at two aspects of this chemical dimension.

• What processes take place in the brain to initiate chemical responses
  and cause them to be released in the body?

• How does this release of chemicals affect the body?

First of all, it is important to understand that we are chemical beings. We
are a product of our biochemistry, from the cellular level—where millions
upon millions of chemical reactions and transactions take place as we respire,
digest, fight off invaders, move, think, and feel—to our moods, actions, beliefs,
sensory perceptions, emotions, and even to what we experience and learn.
Whereas psychologists, behavioral scientists, and others once debated whether
heredity or environment was primarily responsible for our behaviors, new
investigations and findings have shifted the focus of much research to the
chemical basis of emotion.

The Bottom Line on Chemistry

The most basic, baseline information we need to remember is this: every
time we fire a thought in our brain, we make chemicals, which produce feelings
and other reactions in the body. Our body grows accustomed to the level of
chemicals coursing through our bloodstream, surrounding our cells, and
bathing our brain. Any interruption in the regular, consistent, and comfortable
level of our body's chemical makeup will result in discomfort. We will do nearly
everything we can, both consciously and subconsciously, based on how we feel,
to restore our familiar chemical balance.

Just as we did when we initiated the acute flight-or-fight response, we do a
similar thing every time we fire a thought—we respond by producing various
chemicals. The three means by which we communicate chemically are neurotransmitters, peptides, and hormones.

Thus, whenever we have a thought, neurotransmitters are at work in the
synaptic space, firing the neural nets connected to that particular concept or
memory.

Any memory has an emotional component attached to it, which the peptides reproduce chemically. As we have learned, the part of the midbrain called the hypothalamus manufactures a host of different peptides. It has a laboratory of recipes that take each thought we fire in our brain and each emotion we experience and use peptides to produce a corresponding chemical signature. This is why so many references to the limbic brain or the midbrain describe it as the emotional brain. It makes our sexual juices flow, our creative juices turn on, and our competitive juices motivate us. This emotional brain is responsible for making the chemicals that initiate our emotional reactions and thoughts.

When a chemical "thought" is in the bloodstream, it turns on the body, much like ACTH does with adrenal glands and the production of glucocorticoids (cortisol). Once the body is turned on, it communicates through a *negative feedback loop* to manage the appropriate levels of chemicals in the brain and in the cells of the body.

Let's illustrate how this negative feedback loop operates. Because the hypothalamus is the most vascular part of the brain (it has the richest blood supply), it monitors circulating amounts of each peptide with every chemical response in the body. To use our example, when there are high levels of ACTH there will be low levels of cortisol, and when the hypothalamus detects high levels of cortisol, it responds by decreasing the levels of ACTH. Specific chemical levels are based on each person's individual internal chemistry. Every man or woman has their own unique homeostatic balance that is, as we have said, directly affected by their genetic program, their response to environmental circumstances, and by their very own subvocalized thoughts.

Figure 9.1 shows how the brain and the body work together to regulate chemical communication. High levels of circulating peptides signal different glands and organs of the body to release hormones and secretions. When the brain registers high levels of hormones or secretions and low levels of circulating peptides, it functions like a thermostat and stops making hormones. As the circulating hormone levels fall in the body, the brain, through the hypothalamus, senses these lower levels and begins to manufacture more peptides, out of which more hormones can be made.

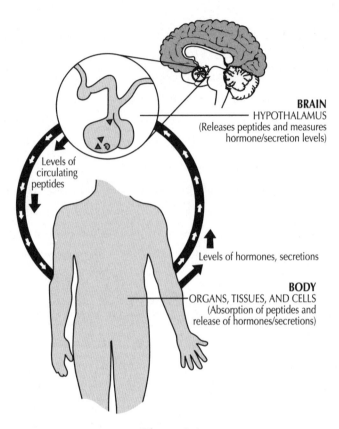

Figure 9.1
The negative feedback loop between the brain and the body.

Emotions, Chemistry, and You

Scientists used to think that we demonstrate four basic primitive emotions, based on how we are wired in a particular part of the midbrain called the amygdala. In initial testing, researchers electrically stimulated the amygdala and observed the feelings or actions of different species. The basic reactions were always anger, sadness, fear, and joy. In a more primitive sense they are aggression; submission; fright or surprise; and acceptance, bonding, or happiness. Presently, due to much work in neuroscience, the model has evolved to add three more to the original four: surprise, contempt, and disgust. It is pretty easy to see that surprise is related to the reaction of fear, and that contempt or disgust can be easily connected to anger and aggression.[3]

Many sources say that the subjective experiences that are unique to humans involve some combination or blend of each of these primary emotions. Secondary emotions or social emotions are then created from the primary ones, comparable to mixing paints. These secondary emotions include embarrassment, jealousy, guilt, envy, pride, trust, shame, and many others.

I think of how we create feelings like this: The neocortex reacts, feels, or thinks. The midbrain then supplies neurochemical factors to the brain and body, which then endorse or activate various compartments and neural nets to specifically create both our unique and our commonly shared feelings.

Our feelings, you'll recall, are the result of comparable experiences we have all had, due to similar environmental or social conditions (how we become wired from learning and experiencing; that is, nurture); short-term genetic traits we inherited from our parents (their hardwired emotional experiences; that is, nature), and our overall, long-term genetic traits (human brains are structured the same; therefore, we have the same universal propensities; also nature).

This software and hardware then make all within our species perceive and behave with relatively the same emotions. Incidentally, I do not want to split hairs between emotions, feelings, drives, and sensory reactions; let's simply agree that they are chemically driven states of mind, and that emotions are just the end product of both our common and unique experiences.

Let's return to the fighting couple from the beginning of this chapter to illustrate how this works. Partner A comes home and asks whether there were any messages. Partner B's neural nets fire off the complex pattern and sequences that are involved in this concept of taking messages. Among the bits of information stored there is the associative memory of the failure to deliver a key message six months ago. The neurotransmitters in her brain fire in the synaptic space, sending a signal from the neocortex to the midbrain. This signal contains both information about phone messages, as well as the past emotion that Partner B has associated with the memory—shame. Essentially, Partner B is now producing the mind of shame based on how her brain is turning on neural patterns. Her midbrain passes the message on to the body to produce the chemicals associated with the feeling of shame.

The point is, shame isn't the only feeling that Partner B has. Shame actually produces another emotion—in this case, anger. If we like, we can think of the emotion that Partner B is feeling as "shanger." I'm not calling it this to be funny; instead, I want to illustrate the point that our emotional states are often a combination of feelings. The peptides that produce the chemical equivalents of these blended emotions are like spices that, once combined, produce a rich and multi-layered flavor. The chemical recipe—the ingredients and the proportion of their use—is designed to reproduce the original emotion associated with the experience stored in the neural net.

In other people, this memory of a failure might produce sadness or feelings of helplessness or regret. Regardless of the emotion, once that signal is sent to the pituitary gland, the body comes alive, just as it did in the flight-or-fight response. Instead of fear or survival, the motivating emotion that is a product of the memory stored in Partner B's brain is shame/anger.

At this point, the pituitary gland puts its spin on the message, and now the pituitary gland, along with the hypothalamus, cook up a batch of peptides corresponding to shame and anger. Those peptides are released in the bloodstream and make their way to various places in Partner B's body. The receptor sites in the body's cells and glandular systems are scanning for a match for this emotion, and they attract those chemicals of shame and anger to them. Partner B has manufactured these emotions for years, so the cells may have developed an astounding number of receptor sites for shame and anger. The more we experience a particular emotion, one probable scenario is that we will develop more receptor sites for that emotion on our cells. Figure 9.2 depicts how thoughts/feelings of anger and shame become chemical signals to activate bodily reactions on a cellular level.

Originally, Partner B was not angry in that moment when she was asked, six months later, whether there were any messages. She became angry because she

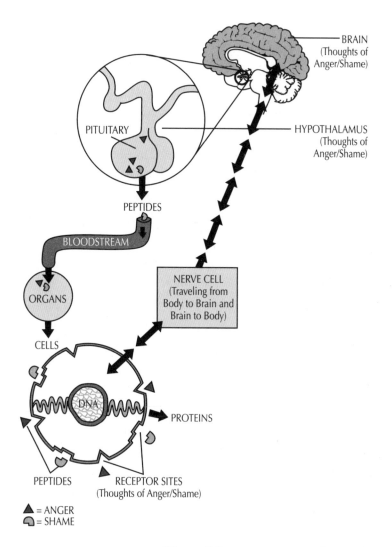

Figure 9.2

The biochemical expression of anger/shame and the chemical/neurological self-monitoring system between the brain and the body.

has been living in and responding to something from the past. In her case, it's likely that she has a highly developed neural net and hardwired pathway for shame. She may have inherited that from one of her parents or through experience; in any case, she has developed an incredible sensitivity. She hates to be wrong. And she hates to be reminded of wrong things she has done. Maybe her parents were particularly hard on her and had high expectations for her. She may, in turn, have developed and refined these expectations to such a high degree of perfectionism and standard-setting that she has hardwired a hair-trigger anger response, which activates whenever her competence or abilities are questioned. The shame she feels that so easily gets converted to anger is most likely anger at herself for having failed. If she has spent her lifetime feeling shame and inner-directed anger, with those memories of all her failures imprinted in her neural nets, she has also lived a life with those chemicals of shame and anger coursing through her system. As a result, her cells have developed thousands of receptor sites to which the chemicals of shame and anger can dock.

Our body reproduces different kinds of cells on a regular basis. Some cells are reproduced in hours, others in a day, others in a week, some within months, and some cells even take years to reproduce. If high peptide levels of shame and anger are maintained on a daily basis for years on end, then when each cell divides to make daughter cells, it will respond to this high demand and alter the receptors on the cell membrane. This is a natural regulation process that takes place in all cells.

Imagine you are at an international airport, and everyone is waiting in line at immigration or customs. There are four gates open out of a possible 20 gates, and 400 people are waiting. As you stand there, you know that this airport would be more efficient if it just opened more gates to meet the overflow. That's the wisdom in how our cells work. If we are sensitizing the cell with enormous amounts of peptides, then when the cell divides, its natural intelligence upgrades the next generation to meet the demands coming from the brain. In this case, the cell "up-regulates" by making more receptors.

Over time, if enough of this *up regulation* occurs, the body will start to do the thinking for us, and it will become the mind. It will crave the same message it has been receiving, to keep the cells turned on. The body as a huge cellular organism will need a constant fix at the cellular level to keep things in chemical continuity. Does this start to sound like addiction?

In some cells, which are too overly sensitized, the receptors become indifferent to the peptides and just shut down. In this case, they regulate in the other direction. The cells make fewer receptor sites because the overabundance is too much to handle. Some cells may even malfunction because they cannot process the crowd of chemicals that are assaulting the cell. Remember, a peptide's job is to turn on the inner workings of each cell so that it can make proteins or change the cell's energy. When overly high amounts of peptides repeatedly bombard the outside of a cell, it receives too many instructions for one cell to process. The cell cannot handle all the orders at the same time, so it closes down the doors. The movie theater is full and there are no more seats.

Figure 9.3 illustrates up and down regulation. In up regulation, the cells respond to the demands of the brain and create additional receptor sites. In

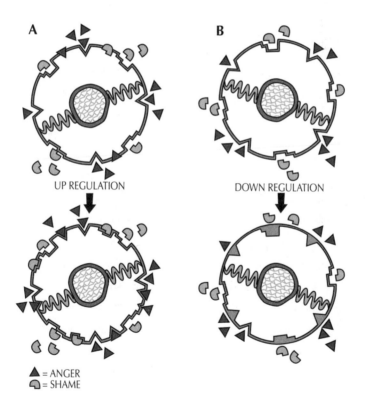

Figure 9.3
The regulation of receptor sites due to high levels of peptides traveling to cells.

down regulation, certain receptor sites shut off from overstimulation and become less active.

In the case of down regulation, imagine being in a relationship with someone who always nags you and makes you out to be the bad person. Over time, you become less responsive and you just stop reacting to his or her accusations. Cells, especially nerve cells, usually become chemically desensitized (they become more resistant to the stimulus) and therefore, over time, they need more chemicals to reach the threshold of action on a cellular level. In other words, we have to react more, worry more, fret more, or feel more aggravated. It takes more of the same feelings to turn on the brain, because the receptors have been overstimulated and desensitized.

This is the basis of addiction to a drug like cocaine. When someone takes cocaine, it causes an enormous release of dopamine, which gives the person that incredible sense of pleasure. However, the next time, he or she has to take larger quantities to produce the same response. And the cycle goes on in much the same way with our emotional states.

Here is another way to look at this phenomenon. Receptor sites are made of proteins, and the number of receptors in a target cell usually will not remain constant day to day, or even minute to minute.[4] They are as plastic as neurons. Each time the peptide docks at the receptor site, it alters the shape of the protein. When the protein's shape is changed, its function changes and it becomes more active. As the cell repeatedly performs the same function at the same receptor site, the protein receptors become worn out, and the peptide is no longer recognized. The binding of peptides to protein receptor sites causes the number of receptors to decrease, either because of the inactivation of some receptor molecules, or because the cell cannot produce enough protein molecules to make receptors in time. As a result, the protein receptor will no longer function properly. The key essentially will no longer fit into the lock. When the overtaxed cell divides and reproduces to make a carbon copy of itself, to pass on its wisdom, it makes fewer receptor sites, to maintain a balance in the body. When this type of desensitizing occurs, it seems the body just can never get enough peptides to maintain the chemical state to which it is accustomed. We are never satisfied.

When the body has taken control of the mind and we feel the way we are thinking (because of the chemical cocktail that our pituitary mixed to match the original emotion), we will now think the way we are feeling. This is because our cells, which are all connected by nervous tissue, will communicate to the brain via the spinal cord when they notice that there are no signals from the brain.

Our cells also communicate with the body through the brain's chemical feedback loop (its internal thermostat). As the chemicals that were produced are used up, the body does what it normally does. It wants to preserve that chemical state we are used to. The body enjoys this rush of anger/shame chemicals, because it makes us feel more alive, and in a heightened state of awareness and energy. And because the feelings are so familiar, we can recreate the affirmation of ourselves as a person who feels a certain way. If we've been experiencing shame and anger for most of our life, those chemicals have been present in our body for most of our life. Because one of the primary biological functions is the maintenance of balance through homeostasis, we will do nearly anything possible to maintain that chemical continuity, based on the needs of the cells on the most simple biological level. The body now houses the mind.

Issues in the Tissues

We know that *peptides* are small proteins that are chemical messengers made in the hypothalamus and released by the pituitary. When they are released into the bloodstream, they find their way to different organs and tissues of the body. When they arrive at the surface of a cell, they interact with the *receptor sites,* large proteins that float on the surface of every cell so that the cell can selectively choose what can enter its internal environment and influence its inner workings. Once a peptide fits into a receptor site, it changes the structure of the receptor and sends a signal to the cell's DNA.

All cells are protein-producing machines. Muscle cells make muscle proteins called actin and myosin. Skin cells make skin proteins called elastin and collagen. Stomach cells make stomach proteins, enzymes, and so on. The DNA of every cell is what produces a cell's proteins. Proteins are made from the

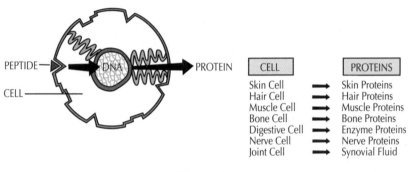

Figure 9.4
A demonstration of various cells being signaled to make different proteins.

building blocks of smaller molecules called amino acids. Once a peptide docks to a receptor site, it carries a message to unzip the cell's DNA to begin to make various related proteins. Figure 9.4 simply displays how cells make proteins.

We *express* about 1.5 percent of our DNA (our genes), and the remaining 98.5 percent has been called *junk DNA*. When a cell makes different proteins, it expresses those genes. (An example is the gene expression for proteins that make eye color.) Our DNA is like a library of potentials that the cell uses for its protein expression. If that 98.5 percent of our DNA isn't really junk, it may be latent, waiting to be activated by the right type of chemical signals. Scientists are now discovering that the storehouse of excess DNA has important functions. We just might have a lot of latent genes to express for future evolution.

Out of the 1.5 percent of the DNA that we express by making proteins, we share over 96 percent of the same DNA as chimpanzees. The totality of our genetic expression is what we physically look like, how we biologically function, and how we are wired neurologically: dad's short temper, mom's self-pity; dad's broad shoulders, mom's small nose; dad's poor eyesight, mom's diabetes. Our body produces different proteins through the expression of our genes, and this makes us who we are.

As the peptides "instruct" a cell, they activate the DNA to make proteins equal to the orders from our neural networks. If the orders are the same frightful attitudes or similar aggressive states of anger that we have been sending as signals to the cell over and over again for days or years, over time, the cell's DNA begins to malfunction. In other words, we have had no new experiences with a new chemical signature (in the form of different peptides) that can signal the cell to activate new genes in order to make new proteins. If the cells are getting the same chemical orders from the same emotional states, our genes will start to wear out—just like driving a car in the same gear.[5] If the DNA begins to become overused, the cells begin to make "cheaper" proteins from their DNA.

If we think about it, all aging is the result of improper protein production. What happens when we age? Our skin sags. Skin is made of proteins. What happens to our hair? It thins. Hair is protein. What happens to our joints? They get stiff. Synovial fluid is made of proteins. What happen to our digestion? It gets compromised. Enzymes are proteins. What happens to our bones? They get brittle. Bone is made of proteins. When we make cheaper proteins, the body begins to express itself in a weakened state.

The expression of life is the expression of proteins. If we continuously give the cells the same orders from the same repetitive attitudes based on the same feelings, we make the same chemical peptides. As a result, we do not send any new signals to the cell to activate any new gene expression. We are repeating the same thoughts that are either genetically wired or connected to some familiar emotional attitude from experiences gone by. If we are living by the same feelings every day, rest assured that those chemicals will overuse the cell's DNA and begin to make altered proteins. The cell's DNA will begin to malfunction.

So, when we become angry, frustrated, or saddened by anyone or anything, whom is it really affecting? All our emotional attitudes—ones we may believe are caused by something outside of us—are not only the result of how we perceive reality based on how we are wired, but also of how much we are addicted to how we want to feel. Studies at the University of Pennsylvania have shown that people who are depressed see the world equal to how they think and feel. If we show two different pictures rapid-fire to depressed people and to a control group of normal people—one a scene of people feasting at a table and one a funeral scene—and ask them which they remember, the depressives will remember the coffin scene at percentages greater than chance. They seem to perceive their environment in a way that continuously reinforces how they feel.[6]

In addition, the chemical continuity of any emotional state that we maintain over years of feeling the same feelings on a daily basis yields destructive thoughts turned on ourselves. What we think and how we react ultimately affects us. Now we understand the deeper meaning of the saying, When we judge another, we are really judging ourselves.

As adults, if we no longer learn anything new or have any new experiences that will change the brain and mind, we will be using the same neural machinery as our parents did, thus activating the same physical and mental genetic conditions. When we can activate only the genetics equal to what we have inherited, invariably we will manifest the same inherent physical and psychological conditions of disease and cellular breakdown. When we express degraded proteins, we are now manifesting a different expression of life.

The expression of proteins is the expression of life and therefore, the expression of health. Who, then, gives the orders to make the chemicals that determine our health? We do. It is our attitude, either conscious or unconscious, that fires our neural nets, which initiate the chemicals in our hypothalamus to send a signal to the cell in the form of a peptide, which turns on the DNA to express our genes in order to make the same or different proteins. To change the proteins that we express on a cellular level and that affect our health, we must change our attitude, so that a new signal can arrive at the cell.[7]

Since the expression of proteins is equal to the health of the body, our attitude and how we manage our thoughts are directly related to our health. Figure 9.5 demonstrates how our thoughts and attitudes correlate to the health of the body.[8]

When we rise out of survival, fire new thoughts (which make new chemicals), change our mind (which alters the chemical message to our body), and modify our behavior (to create a whole new experience, thus bringing new chemistry that affects our cells), now we are on the path of evolution.

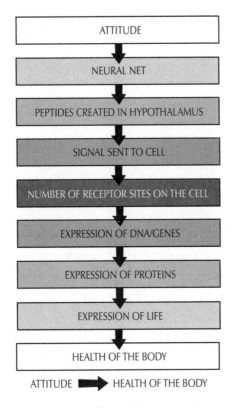

Figure 9.5
The effects of thoughts on the physical body.

The Role of Memory in the Chemical Mix

When we leave a situation in our life that has caused emotions such as shame and anger, or we leave behind the people, places, things, time, and events associated with those feelings, we stop thinking and feeling with the same mind. Now that we are out of the circumstances that initiated those thoughts and reactions that defined us, why do we still feel the same way? We have stopped getting the constant stimulation that was producing the chemicals our cells have come to crave. When our cells are no longer getting their daily chemical "bath," the cells utilize the potential of our memory. Remember, we can make thought more real than anything else.

Our cells send a signal back up to the brain, notifying it that they need those chemicals. In order to get the body to produce the desired chemicals, the brain turns on its associated circuits—those neural nets that contain the past memory of an experience that produced anger/shame. In our example, then, Partner B's angry response to Partner A's question has more to do with Partner B's chemical needs than the question Partner A asked, or how it was stated.

Later on, long after this particular argument has ended, Partner B can now use this more recent argument, or the original one six months ago, to produce the chemistry of anger she needs to maintain her state of being.

Another way to think of the memories and experiences we can recall is that they are the "voice" we hear in our head all the time. RSE teaches its students that the voice we hear in our mind is just memories of the past, and that when we are in the midst of change, this voice is the loudest. Few people ever say aloud all the things they think or feel. But the voice we hear in our head is how the body tells the brain to think the way it is feeling.

We also carry on an inner monologue that more accurately reflects how we are feeling than what we say aloud. For example, let's go back to our battling couple. After they've calmed down a bit, they sit in the same room watching television. Here's what transpires.

Partner A: "Do you mind if I watch the game?"

Partner B: "Doesn't matter." *(Do I mind? What the hell kind of question is that? Him and his stupid baseball games. Sitting there like this is some kind of life-and-death matter. Why the hell do I bother? He's never going to change. Picks on every little thing I do wrong. But do I ever say anything about him? Do I ever go off when he screws something up? Just like my dad. Exactly like him. Sit on your butt and criticize. He does the same thing with the players. If he is so damn good at the game, why isn't he out there playing instead of sitting here watching?)*

Imagine the chemicals the brain is making to feed this body its dependent emotions.

Partner A: "Thanks." *(Doesn't matter? Yeah, right. What, do you think I'm stupid? Roll your eyes. Okay. You say it doesn't matter, so I'm just going to sit here and enjoy this. See if I care.)* Now he is in the chemical loop, too, with his fix in motion.

Although this isn't the most mature exchange, it is typical, and it illustrates briefly how our internal chatter serves to keep our chemicals at their usual levels. If you notice, Partner B reconnected with her father and her memories of his behavior. We commonly choose a mate who will reproduce the wounds of the past, and therefore, allow us to maintain the chemical state of being we've "enjoyed" and become conditioned to for the previous 20 or 30 years.

Even if the two of them were to split up, Partner B would still have memories of these experiences to give her the chemical hit she craves. The entire process of splitting up would reinforce her feelings of inadequacy and shame for falling short of an internal standard. The voice in her head would tell her, "*You can't do anything right. You can't even find somebody and stick with him. How hard can that be? What am I going to tell my parents? How am I going to be able to look my father in the eye? Damn it. Damn it. Damn it.*" And she will take another spin on the shame and anger loop.

The real questions for this couple, if they are interested in change, are, "Are you aware that the two of you are addicts partying together? Can you stop your automatic thoughts, actions, and reactions in midstream? Can you become self-aware, take conscious control of your thoughts, and modify your behaviors without making anyone else responsible for how you are presently being? Is love holding this relationship together, or is it an emotional cocktail of chemicals so overpowering that you are unconsciously living in past memories and their emotional monologues? Can you become aware that you are using each other for your own selfish chemical needs?" If the answers are all no, this couple will continue its pattern for a long time.

Chemistry and Behavior

Chemicals and chemical reactions on the smallest level are fundamentally important in shaping how we act, think, and feel. Flight or fight is most illustrative of the way in which we can become addicted to our emotions. And emotional addiction is one of the most profound and revelatory concepts to which we can be exposed.

Now we can see that the brain is both neurologically hardwired to, and chemically dependent upon, our emotions. When our current life circumstances don't produce in us the particular chemicals we need to maintain our customary state of being, we will do whatever we must to ensure that those chemicals are present in our body. If we aren't faced with any kind of external threat or stressor, we will seek one out. If we can't find one, we will create one—physically or mentally. I'm sure that you know a drama king or queen, someone who turns the most innocuous of situations into a stressful, emotion-laden scene. I'm certain also that at one point or another, you've probably said of someone (perhaps even of yourself) that, "She loves to suffer."

Because of the biological imperatives that drive the body—the urgent mission that it undertakes to maintain the status quo, restore equilibrium, seek comfort, avoid pain, and respond to stressors both perceived and real—we become addicted to the chemistry of our own emotional entropy. Given this biological imperative, doesn't it make sense to say that we can't *help* but become addicted in this way?

It's true. We can't help but become addicted, but we can also do an enormous amount to break that addictive pattern or cycle. Before we examine that process, however, we need to explore the ways in which our biochemical propensities play out in our life.

Breaking Up Is Hard to Do

Here's an example of addiction: people return to the same relationship after they know intellectually that they do not work well together. Why is breaking up (for good) so hard to do? Throughout a relationship, even a bad one, both people synaptically fire neural nets that make chemical neurotransmitters and peptides, causing their experiences to feel a certain way, and those feelings reaffirm each party's personality. They become so habituated to the relationship that although they decide to leave it, they cannot break the neurological wiring and the chemical bonds tying them to it. After the breakup, each person's memories of their experiences remind their body that it's being deprived of its accustomed chemical stimulation. He or she (or better said, his or her body) feels a sense of loss. The heartache of relationship breakups may be due to the disruption of a neuro-chemical habit. Considering the chemistry of emotional addiction, is it surprising that so many couples break up, then come back together, then repeat this cycle?

It is interesting to point out that when all the aspects of our life stay pretty much the same, they come to define how we are wired. Accordingly, most people pick relationships based on what they have in common with someone else—by how they are both wired synaptically. In the "dating game," we're talking about neural net matching. But when the circumstances of a relationship change, most people, having done little to change from the inside, look for the same neural order in the next person, thus repeating the same types of relationships over and over. We may break up with a person, but we remained chemically addicted to the feelings that relationship engendered. In the vacuum created by the absence of the former mate, we usher in another candidate whom we know (on an unconscious level) will produce that rush of chemistry we crave and have grown accustomed to.

Even if we break the neural order that is reflected in our life's situations, the change will produce the recognition of a loss of familiar feelings. The loss of those feelings may be interpreted as discomfort, independent of the polarity of "good" or "bad." Our life change is causing us to rethink and react, rather than allowing us to be proactive—to think and act in a way that creates a new reality for ourselves. Rethinking and reacting is no more than firing old neural circuits that we can recognize as familiar. This whole process creates the same neural nets, which fire over and over again, resulting in the same thoughts and reactions that we experience daily, independent of whether we see our situation as positive or negative, successful or a failure, happy or sad.

All these feelings associated with our external world define our "self" as a "somebody" who feels a certain way, and those feelings then give rise to the way we demonstrate actions, behaviors, opinions, prejudices, beliefs, and even perceptions. Our feelings drive our thoughts.

Anxiety and the Feedback Loop

For years, we've been hearing and reading about the prevalence of clinical depression in America. We've also heard the debate about the efficacy and potential dangers of many antidepressants. Recently, however, a new disorder has entered the scene: five associated conditions that we can simply group under the name of *anxiety disorders*. According to a 2006 report by the National Institute of Mental Health, the five anxiety disorders—generalized anxiety disorder (GAD), panic disorder, obsessive-compulsive disorder (OCD), posttraumatic stress disorder (PTSD), and phobias (social anxiety disorder, agoraphobia, and the like)—afflict approximately 40 million Americans age 18 and older.[9] This comprises 18.1 percent of the population. Depression, still the number-one cause of disability among Americans, affects over 14.8 million American adults. Anxiety disorders are more prevalent than depression, but no single form of anxiety disorders approaches the numbers of depressed patients. The NIMH also reports that many people who suffer from one of the anxiety disorders also suffer from others, and that the concurrence of depression and anxiety disorders is also high.

What is going on? Are we simply better at labeling and categorizing these conditions? In the past, would we have dismissed people who claimed to be anxious as suffering from a "touch of the nerves" and left it at that? No matter the numbers, anxiety and its relationship to stress, and the chemical addictions of the body, need to be examined.

In many ways, anxiety is a healthy response to external stimuli. We should be in a heightened state when we have to deliver a speech, give a presentation or performance, or encounter a potential threat. But when our anxiety spills over into our everyday life and becomes chronic, it becomes very problematic.

An anxiety disorder forms when, for no apparent reason, a person begins to feel his or her heart race and experiences difficulty breathing, immense fear and emotion, loss of control, chest pain, excessive sweating, and difficulty in thinking clearly. Given what we are learning, we can begin to see that when panic attacks occur, the sympathetic branch of the autonomic nervous system is now in control.

Anxiety attacks are created when someone has thoroughly trained their body to become vigilant and prepared in anticipation of the next stressful experience. Panic attacks that occur automatically and repeatedly in some people are the result of either their rigorous mental practice of worry and anxiety or overexposure to the same stressful environmental conditions.

It is my experience that if we could trace anxiety back to the beginning, for most people it starts off with some major difficulty that caused intense emotional pressure. After the event, the memory of that experience causes the person to think about that episode, over and over, in anticipation of a similar event occurring again. As they mentally review their past, the brain starts to make the appropriate chemistry, and those thoughts signal the sympathetic (SNS) impulses to begin. They become anxious and afraid about their future moments and what potentially might happen. Their attitude (cluster of thoughts) now is making the chemicals for anxiety and worry. Their thoughts about a particular stressor, not the stressor itself, are creating the stress response.

If we worry every day about what may happen in the following moment, we will fire a series of thoughts that will create a mindset of uneasiness. In the recesses of the neocortex, a series of particular hardwired neural networks will fire, supporting continuous thought processes related to various worrisome memories. When these thoughts activate specific patterns of synaptic connections, the body will then create those chemicals related to those unsettling thoughts. Now that those chemicals of vigilance are loose in the body, the body feels unsettled. Once the neocortex assesses how the body is feeling, we will probably say, "I feel worried." When we feel apprehensive, we are aware of our body's internal state. If a panic attack then ensues, we will feel a genuine loss of control, a very fright-inducing situation. Now we have more to worry about, because we certainly do not want to have another one of those. That worry and anticipation will neurochemically draw the next experience nearer.

Once the self is aware that the body is experiencing anxiety, the neural network associated with anxiety is now activated. We feel exactly the way we are thinking, and we think exactly the way we are feeling. In order for the brain to recognize the feelings of worry, it will use the existing neural network of worry to evaluate what it is sensing. As a result, we will then think the thoughts related to our concerns, because that neural net is turned on. We will then make more brain chemicals to reinforce how our body is feeling, because our immediate assessment of the body causes us to feel how we were thinking. Whew!

Now our initial thoughts have become real. If we can feel it, it is genuine, right? We are on the way to training the body to have another panic attack. Our fearfulness then breeds more worry, which then makes us more anxious, which then causes us to feel more worried. The reason for this is simple. Once our state of anxiety was created, our state of being created a continuous feedback loop from the body back to the brain, to activate the same neural network of worry, which then made the body more anxious, and on and on it goes.

We now know that when we respond to the feelings of the body by thinking the way the body feels, the brain will manufacture more of the same chemicals, feeding the body the same chemical signals for it to experience. This is how we maintain a "state of being." Any repetitive feeling, whatever that feeling is, creates a state of being—be it happy, sad, confused, lonely, unworthy, insecure, joyful, or even depressed. A *state of being* means that the feedback loop between the brain and the body is complete. When the feedback loop is cycling over and over again by chemically endorsing the brain and the body, we are in a completely fulfilled chemical state of being.

Over time, we will maintain this neurochemical state, based on how we continuously activate the same patterns of neural synaptic firing from our prior memories. This chemical continuity of the body, based on how we fire our own unique patterns of neural feelings from our individual personal identity, is different for every person. But the mechanics of the loop are the same. Anxiety feeds anxiety. Imagine what might happen if we felt joy, gratitude, or calm instead? Is it possible that the same feedback loop could serve us instead of enslaving us?

Why Change Is Difficult

Every person, place, thing, time, or event that is consistent in our life will define us more lastingly as a personality by its repetitive exposure. We associate every one of these elements, and the effect is that they become part of our neural processes and reaffirm who we are. For every known element in our life, we have an existing neural representation in the form of people, things, times, places, and events, and each neural representation connects every person, place, thing, time and event to a specific feeling. We can begin to see why change is so difficult. Changing a person, place, thing, time, or event in our life means that we are breaking the neurochemical circuit that we have kept intact by continuous stimulation.[10]

If I ask you to start using a new order of action while brushing your teeth or drying yourself off after your shower, you may not be able to do it, you may do it but feel a great deal of discomfort, or you may do it but quickly abandon the effort. You will most certainly tend to return to the easier, more familiar way. That tendency is the habit you need to break if you want to change your mind and no longer remain stuck in the familiar.

Imagine, then, what kind of effort it would take if I were to ask you to end a relationship with someone who repeatedly deals blows to your self-esteem and has done so for the last 15 years. If we have grown accustomed to feeling unworthy, we want to continue to feel that way because we are in the neurochemical habit of being unworthy. It is the routine, familiar, natural, easy way that we have been thinking and feeling about ourselves. Those thoughts are based on memories that we have of our interaction with that person. Those memories have feelings associated with them, and those feelings are neurochemically based.

More important, if we decide to alter the dynamics of our relationship with a particular person in our life who has been close to us, the change that is represented by heartache and suffering is likely just the chemical feeling that we are missing from ceasing to fire the same synaptic neural networks.[11] The lack of stimuli from the environment (not seeing, touching, smelling, feeling, and hearing that person) will no longer fire the neural nets associated with that person. That stoppage prevents the release of specific chemicals from the brain that feed the body to make a feeling. Regardless of whether a feeling is positive or negative, it results from the release of certain chemicals. Love (or what we think is love), then, may indeed be all about chemistry.

Addicts and Withdrawal

So what happens when we decide that we've had enough and want to stop thinking a certain way? What happens when we finally make the choice to stop thinking and feeling shame, anger, or hatred for a single day? This decision is really no different than what happens when we decide to go on a diet, to cut out a particular food, or try to stop a habit like smoking or drinking. Deciding to stop feeling shame takes as much intention and will as it does to stop doing any of these other actions. Once our will is engaged in overcoming our thoughts, it's as if we wake the body from its slumber and it hasn't had its morning cup of coffee—in this case, its fix of shame, for instance. As a result, the body starts to voice its displeasure to the brain. "What do you mean, you aren't getting your shame chemicals? Whose smart idea was this?"

What starts out as subtle urges and cravings from the body in the form of an impulsive thought usually—when not carried out—turns into a louder and louder internal monologue that pleads for an immediate action. The body goes into chaos, as a result of this chemical deprivation and its inability to return to its homeostatic state. It does not want to recalibrate itself, because it has grown accustomed to the over change of receptor sites dedicated to shame. The body has been calling the shots for quite a while, and now it feels out of control. At this point, we will be bombarded with all kinds of urges. The chatter in our head will be clamoring to be heard, to make us feel shame.

We know that "voice" that we unconsciously respond to every day. We listen to it and act as if it is the gospel of our own inner guidance. Many times, it can talk us out of anything, even our greatness. When we are in the midst of change, it nags and whines the loudest. It says things like, *"You can start tomorrow!"* *"Go ahead, this is a great reason to break your promise with yourself."* *"Any other time but this one!"* And my favorite, *"This just doesn't feel right!"* Then we say, "I have to trust my feelings because I'm so in tune with them," and of course, we rationalize ourselves back to the starting point. The voice that we are listening to is our body telling us to restore internal order and stop the suffering and discomfort it was feeling.

We can surely identify with this, because most of us have tried to break a habit or to fast from a particular type of food like chocolate, for example. We start our resolutions with good intentions, but in a matter of hours, we begin to remember all our past experiences when we ate chocolate. We begin to think about mom's famous double-dark, devil's food cake. Out of nowhere, we recall the time we ate chocolate-covered strawberries on our honeymoon and how delicious they were. In a moment, we are remembering the time we were laid over in the airport in Brussels for four hours and we had three desserts, all made of Belgian chocolate.

While we are thus being coerced into this kind of mindset by what appears to be some demon, what if, in the next second, life presents us with the opportunity for a bit of mother's chocolate cake? The second we set our eyes on the cake, our body responds immediately (maybe even salivates). Next, we begin to hear those subvocalizations that I just mentioned, egging us on to forget about what we intellectually decided earlier in the day, and to consume the whole cake. We're not consciously thinking those thoughts; they come from our body telling us what to think and do. As soon as our body becomes chemically stimulated by the sight of the dessert, it causes us to think about what it wants.

When we are willfully changing an emotional state, we will react the same way to loud and adamant messages from our body. Perhaps one day you intellectually decide to no longer be a victim. You start your day with great intentions, but by the middle of the day, while driving to do an errand for your job, you begin to think about how your husband hurt your feelings the day before. You think of all the other times, in the last 30 years, he hurt you by his unconscious actions. You are now starting to feel bad. You catch yourself, but an inner voice starts telling you to forget about what you originally committed to, because, *"You'll never change, you're just not strong enough, and besides, your mother was abusive to you as a child, so that's why you are the way you are. You can't stop, those scars are just too deep."*

What are you going to do? If you respond to these thoughts, you are headed for a release of a lot of chemicals that will reinforce who you have always been. If you stop your automatic thoughts, you will feel very uncomfortable with not being your normal, habitually thinking self. To top it off, what if this day, all the reasons to be a victim start falling from the heavens? You fall off your porch in the morning. Someone at work decides to claim the week that you wanted for your vacation time. When you walk out of the supermarket, someone has hit your car door and dented it. Now you have even more reasons to feel like a victim. The body is egging you on to take the first step, so you can reaffirm your neurochemical self. If you decide to respond to the internal chatter and act on it, you will restore yourself to a state that seems more comfortable. There is a greater level of familiar comfort in being a victim than the discomfort of being a victim . . . and the discomfort of not being one as well.

Running the Loop

When all this is cascading through our brain and our body, here is what is happening. Once the homeostatic continuity of our body is altered because we no longer think the same way or react to the same set of circumstances, the cells of the body get together and gang up. They send a message to that particular neural net to fire a certain level of mind, so that we can make the right kind of chemicals to keep the body in balance, controlled, and moderated. If the receptor sites are not getting the regular peptides of familiar emotions and those cells sense a change in normal balance, they will send a message through the peripheral nerves to the spinal cord to the brain. They will be calling to say, "Hey, what's going on up there? It's been a little too long for you to not feel like a victim. Can you start firing those thoughts that will make the chemicals so that everything returns to normal?" Equally, the self-monitoring feedback loop between the limbic brain and the body, which is filtering volumes of blood through the hypothalamus, notices that levels are dropping and tries to readjust the body's internal chemistry back to our normal victimized self by making the right type of peptides. All of this occurs in a matter of a few unconscious moments, and the next thing we know, we're thinking the way we're feeling. You can review Figure 9.2 to see how the cells signal the brain both neurologically and chemically.

And if we are feeling really bad (which, due to its dependency, may actually be interpreted as really good by the body), it seems that as we fall prey to those urges, voices, or cravings, we can't stop the process of emoting. It is as though we can't just eat one bite of the chocolate cake, we eat the *whole* cake. Have you ever noticed that when you were in an emotional storm and you felt frustrated, you felt angry? And when you were angry, you hated. When you hated, you were judgmental, and when you were judgmental, you were jealous. When you were jealous, you became envious, and when you were envious, you became insecure. As you felt insecure, you became unworthy, and when you were unworthy, you felt badly. When you felt badly, you felt guilty.

That's eating the whole cake, because like an addict, you could not stop until you totally stimulated the body to a chemically higher level for a greater rush. As the chemical brain turned on all its emotional peptides and altered your internal chemistry, you activated those related neural networks that house associated memories. You created all the levels of mind that matched each chemical thought with a feeling. The body became an unbridled horse running out of control.

This is where our will and self-discipline have to kick in. We need to achieve mastery over ourselves, but can we? Do we cave in and let in the flood of long-term memories that define us and reaffirm our old self? Or do we stand fast in our commitment to avoid thoughts and feelings of victimization? Do we settle for immediate relief, or can we willfully hold onto a greater vision of the self in spite of what we are feeling? In any case, the conscious mind is now trying to establish its authority over the body. The tables just may be turning.

As another example, by seeing a certain movie character that reminds us of a person we used to know, the show is activating an associated neural network that is tied to former experiences, and that network has a certain feeling in the form of chemicals. When the chemicals are released from the appropriate neural net, we become aware that we are missing that person in our reality, and we now feel worse. In essence, the whole neural network fires, which makes us think about what we do not have in our reality. As a result, all that thinking is just creating more of the feeling and awareness of what we do not have. That hurts.

Consider also the person who has the problem of always, somehow, attracting the wrong type of men into her life. She has the hardest time figuring out how she manages to fall for guys who wind up being as wrong for her as the previous ones. Whether they turn out to be married, on the rebound, emotionally unavailable, too needy, domineering, passive-aggressive, or whatever other ills they suffer from, she manages to find them. No matter that the haystacks have thousands of good choices, she always manages to find the one guy who is the needle to prick her bubble of happiness.

Significantly, she can't ever blame anyone else for her feelings, because if one of those men leaves her, she will still remain wired the same way. In other words, she will attract the same type of person because like attracts like. She will continuously make the same choices because of how she is wired. She can't even blame her last lover for it ending so poorly. If she were really self-reflective and honest, she would have to agree that regardless of what her last boyfriend did, she remains the same person with the same neural net and the same memorized feelings that will draw the same people to her.

The solution is simple: she has to change who she is fundamentally, because she is hardwired and neurochemically dependent on having a person in her life who will help produce the state of being a victim. Other persons didn't make her feel sad, rejected, misunderstood, or unappreciated. She already felt that way. That is her state of mind. She simply brought those other people into her life, so they could behave in ways that would produce the chemical response of victimization to which she was already addicted, and for which she had a comfortable, routine, familiar set of hardwired neural nets to determine her actions and choices.

The end result of this phenomenon is that, in time, we crave the familiar, the routine, and the predictable because we are wired to the familiar through our environment. Continuous exposure to our routine reality only wires us to be more habitual and predictable. We begin to live in the habit of past memories. We have caged ourselves in a box of our own repetitive thinking, rethinking, acting, and reacting. Our limited thinking is literally our limited frame of mind. We become the product of our own environmental responses, which make us become more rigid in our own "neuro-habitual" ways, and less free. Unless we can break the habit of "self," we are destined to endlessly repeat these cycles. Our uniquely different personality becomes predictable because we have consistently memorized the state of our "self."

POSTTRAUMATIC STRESS DISORDER

For some 1.9 million Americans suffering from posttraumatic stress disorder (PTSD), recalling an emotionally scarring situation from our past, such as rape, devastating events in war, or severe accidents, can elicit the same panic responses as the event itself. With PTSD, these past instances produce strong and lasting effects in our nervous system. It seems the greater the trauma, the more readily a memory of the event chemically triggers the victim to think, act, speak, and behave within the frame of mind of that past incident.[12]

How does PTSD develop? When we experience a trauma or highly stressful scenario, the event triggers the hypothalamus along with the amygdala to release stress hormones, which enhance memory formation in the brain. The chemicals released by this primitive nervous system serve a crucial function, helping us survive life-threatening situations by heightening sensory perception. Our sharpened state of mind brands the event as a memory in our brain, so that it will be easy for us to remember anything remotely associated with the sights, smells, and sounds related to the distressing experience. Because those chemicals also drive memory formation, we can learn from the experience.

Memories of the trauma are first stored in the hippocampus. The chemicals manufactured by the hypothalamus and the amygdala activate the hippocampus to turn on different synapses to store the memory. This chemical reaction then encodes the memories into a distribution of neural networks in the cerebral cortex, cementing long-term memory storage as a particular level of mind.

When a person recollects a trauma or a highly charged emotional experience, the memory transfers back to the hippocampus, where it can trigger the release of more stress hormones in the hypothalamus and amygdala. Once this occurs, recall of the ordeal produces the same blend of chemical signals, causing the body to reexperience the past event as if it were happening at that moment. As a result, the fight-or-flight nervous system initiates a host of physiological responses. Many times, the body changes abruptly in response to an impulsive thought about a past trauma, because the body is disrupted from homeostatic balance. As a result, blood pressure increases, breathing patterns alter, and the body may shake uncontrollably. Without warning and for no apparent reason, a state of panic is created or the body becomes depressed.

With this understanding of PTSD, it becomes obvious that the body can be turned on automatically by a mere thought. In essence, we condition (in the Pavlovian sense) the neocortex to turn on the autonomic nervous system by repeatedly thinking about a stressful memory and then experiencing the associated familiar feelings that turn on the body. In this process, we chemically link the mind to the body. As the person with PTSD continuously relives the past event, the chemicals created by that recall ultimately produce in the body a state of homeostatic imbalance. That imbalance can now be more readily tipped by just a few lone thoughts.

Is it possible that we do the same when we remember past events that are linked to any emotion? If so, think of what our body receives as daily messages from our mind. How do we want to train our body to feel?

Change Is Uncomfortable

In all my studies, travels, and lectures on change, my personal experiences, as well as the study of spontaneous remissions, the most common insight I have noticed in people who are in the midst of change is that it does not feel good and it is uncomfortable. If you remember one thing about change, remember that it causes the "self" and the body to go into complete chaos, because the self no longer has any feelings to relate to in order to define itself. If we stop having the same thoughts, feelings, or reactions, we stop making the same chemicals, which sends the body into a state of homeostatic imbalance.

Biologically, the internal chemical values of homeostasis are initially regulated and controlled by what we genetically inherited to be "normal" for us. Our thoughts and reactions further keep our chemistry in check, so that we essentially stay the same person, both physically and cognitively. Therefore, when internal order is altered by our change in thinking, we do not "feel" like the same person.

As a result, our identity wants to return to the feelings of the familiar, and our body is trying to influence our brain to return to a recognizable state of being, so that the body can recalibrate itself with past feelings. Our body wants to identify with known associations. Once the "mind" of the body talks a person into making that choice to return to the known, we will inevitably return to the situation as it was before we tried to change, and we will feel relieved. We will say of the circumstances we tried to change, "It just did not feel right." In other words, our identity, which had been comfortable with the feedback loop between the brain and the body, got chemically distressed and, for a few moments, we became really uncomfortable. We did not like the way that felt; we like the way we usually feel, so we returned to the familiar set of conditions in our life, and now it all feels better and right.

Imagine that you live in a valley at the base of a tall mountain. You've lived there your entire life, and you've never climbed above the treeline, which sits 2,000 feet below the peak. You live every day of your life in the valley, surrounded by the same few people. You've gotten to the point where you can predict with considerable accuracy what everyone will be doing each day—from the exact time your nearest neighbor will walk out into the pasture with his dogs to when you will see a curl of smoke rising from the chimney of the man who lives at the head of the road. Nothing new ever seems to happen.

Late one afternoon, you see someone traversing his way down from the woods behind your house. He is using a walking stick and carrying a knapsack. As he gets closer, you notice that he is heavily bearded, but that beard belies his age. You step out of your house and greet him. It's obvious that he has been traveling for a while. You invite him in, and over dinner, he tells you all about his journey. You learn that the peak right behind your house offers an expansive view of the territory around you—yet you've never set foot outside the walls of the valley. From the top of the mountain, he says, not only can you see great distances, but you can also gain easy access to other towns and villages, and meet people who speak other languages and embrace customs that sound exotic and inviting.

The next morning, when your new friend leaves, you vow that you will climb your backyard mountain. You prepare for a few days before you set off. You're determined to experience new things, and you see this as your one great chance in life to climb out of the shadows and into the light. As you make your way across the field of grass that borders your home, you look back at the familiar surroundings—the decaying barn that seems to be bending in prayer, and the meandering fence you and your father have mended your whole life, whose every post stands sentinel as a reminder of the passage of time.

When you experience change, it is like leaving your familiar surroundings and memories. Once you leave that grassy field that borders your home and begin the climb up, you face a number of obstacles—an overgrown path, dense thickets of trees, falling temperatures, predators, and as you climb higher, snow-slick stones. You understand on an intellectual level that you are making progress toward a new set of experiences. You started out firmly convinced that this is what you want.

Halfway into the climb, though, you're not sure you made the wisest choice. You recognize the dangers, feel cold and wet, and understand that you are now very much alone. Where you came from was secure, familiar, and comfortable.

At this moment, most people turn around and rush back to their comfort zones. They settle for that feeling they can remember and bring up at any moment. They compare the memory of the past with their present feeling of discomfort. When the feelings of the past are in constant competition with our idea of a new future, the past has a stronger grip on us because we cannot compare the future to any feeling from the past.

The future has no feelings because we haven't yet experienced it. Remember that all our episodic memories are stored ultimately as emotions. The past has that emotional component, but the future does not. The future has only the sense of adventure we initially started with, but that easily gets lost in the feelings of our body and the memories of the past. The neuro-synaptic self gets homesick, and when this happens, it wants what it can predict and depend on in the next moment. Dreams of a different future usually get smothered by the feelings connected to the feedback loop of the body. When our identity (which is made of past memories) and the feedback loop of the body reign, we can easily rationalize returning to the known. We think that we're making the right choice only because it "feels" like the right choice to make in the moment. This is how we resist change.

All the associations that are connected to change have now insulted the chemical continuity of how our personal identity feels, and the "somebody" who is connected to past memories is absolutely challenged. The old identity that has defined "the self" just wants to return to familiar, routine circumstances, the normal feelings that define it. If we give in to these urges, we are making choices only with our body, never with our mind, and we will never change. Our life is a mirror of how we feel and how we are wired neurologically. In order to create any new experiences, we must leave behind the thoughts, memories, and associations of the emotional past.

Recovery: Life After Addiction

I want to be clear that there is nothing wrong with choosing from feelings. What we need to assess is a matter of what type of feelings we customarily have and how often we repeat the same emotions. I also want to state that emotions are not bad. They are the end product of all experiences, good and bad, known and unknown. But if we are having the same feelings every day, this means we're not having any new experiences. There must be experiences we have yet to embrace that could produce new emotions.

How often, if ever, have you had emotions based not in the familiar feelings of survival, but rather, those somewhat elusive feelings, such as inspiration and the joy of creation. Those heightened moments of gratitude, self-love, bliss, freedom, and awe are within us. They are just too short-lived. And if we can create a cascade of chemicals that cause us to spiral downward into more contagious emotional states and influence the next series of thoughts and feelings, we can also willfully spiral upward, and allow other chemicals to drive other emotional states that provoke thoughts related to those feelings.

In fact, did you ever notice that when you were truly joyful you were in love? And when you were in love you were inspired, and that inspiration led you to be allowing and unconditional with everyone? When you felt truly unconditional, you loved yourself. When you loved yourself, you gained a rich sense of gratitude and a freedom of self-expression without self-judgment. This flood of thoughts and feelings created a wave of more virtuous thoughts and actions, and it seemed so enriching that you did not want it to end.

The physiology of emotions can work both ways. Surely, our limbic system and the alchemical laboratory of our hypothalamus have produced those upward spiraling chemical emotions for us at rarefied moments in our lives. I am also sure we can whip up a few new recipes for a few new emotions that will sit as potentials in our human evolutionary destiny. Is it possible that we could live the majority of our lives in a more evolved state when we retire from survival?

To change our brain, then, is to change the future. Theoretically, the different peptides from more evolved thoughts and experiences should be able to find their way to the cells of the body and send a new signal to the library of genetic potentials in our DNA, so it can trigger a few new genes to make a new expression of self. There seems to be quite a bit of latent machinery resting in our genetic code for future evolution.

If we have been expressing only a short list of predictable thoughts and emotions and habitual chemical states on a daily basis, we only influence our cells to turn on the same genes that our parents and grandparents have already expressed. When we stop learning, growing, changing our habitual behavior, and dreaming of greater outcomes, we are left with the same fabric of synaptic connections we inherited, and we can only feed our body the same chemical information. We are now headed for the same biological destiny. Without learning and experiencing, we never upgrade our neural architecture.

Being in survival is not evolving our brain. It is only activating a more primitive neurological/chemical part of our gray matter that then drives our conscious neocortex to a state of unconscious behaviors, mapped within the brain, so that we react with the body in mind . . . and the mind in the body.

In the chapters that follow, we will take a closer look at how we can break out of the cycle of repetitive feeling. Take heart: by learning all of this new information, we are taking the first step toward emerging from a life of the routine, and the familiar. We have in our possession, ready at our disposal, an island of calm in a sea of turbulence. It is evolution's greatest gift to us.

CHAPTER TEN

TAKING CONTROL: THE FRONTAL LOBE IN THOUGHT AND IN ACTION

*What this power is I cannot say:
all I know is that it exists and it becomes
available only when a man is in that state of mind
in which he knows exactly what he wants and is
fully determined not to quit until he finds it.*

—ALEXANDER GRAHAM BELL

he frontal lobe is a doorway we must enter if we choose to break the cycle of repetitive thinking and feeling, feeling and thinking. If we want freedom from the chemically based emotional addiction that has a grip on our life, we must learn to utilize this marvel of our evolutionary development called the frontal lobe.

In 1848 Phineas Gage, a young railroad foreman, headed a demolition team whose job was to blast the mountainsides of the continental United States, making it easier to lay railroad tracks through those areas. A near-fatal accident caused damage to his frontal lobe that gave scientists valuable data about this part of the neocortex.[1] Since Gage's time and from studies of his and many other patients' damaged and altered frontal lobes, we have come to understand that this part of the brain is the navigator of our life, the executive in charge of all the other parts of the brain.

Because it is sometimes easier to study malfunction than normalcy when learning about an organ's function, we can start with the simplest of questions: what happens when the frontal lobe ceases to function normally? Because the frontal lobe has connections to all the other parts of the brain, when this command center becomes injured or damaged, we become like a missile without its guidance system, or more accurately, like an army without a general. Other areas of the brain that are coordinated through the prefrontal cortex (another name for the frontal lobe) consequently become dysfunctional, and the whole person is affected. This type of damage to the frontal lobe is known as *executive dysfunction*. Medical science has progressed far in its understanding of prefrontal cortex damage compared to 1848, when Phineas Gage was injured.

Phineas, who worked for the Rutland and Burlington Railroad in Vermont, had many great physical skills and admirable personality traits. At 26, he led a team of men who respected his leadership qualities and his skill for handling dangerous explosives. Gage had a unique combination of sensible intelligence and athletic ability that made him perfect for this job, which required constant focus. As officially noted, he was the most efficient and capable man in the railroad company's employ.

But even someone as capable as Gage can have a bad moment when he's distracted. One day as Phineas was "packing a hole" by tamping gunpowder with an iron rod, a random spark caused the dynamite to explode prematurely. An iron bar a little over three feet long penetrated Gage's head below his left cheekbone and exited through the top of his head, landing some 300 feet away.

To everyone's surprise, Gage survived the terrible blow. Witnesses reported that he was thrown to the ground and experienced a few convulsions, but shortly after the incident, he was alert and rational. He was taken quickly to a nearby hotel, where Dr. Edward Williams first examined him. Dr. Williams then consulted with Dr. John Harlow. Gage was still completely conscious and aware at the time of the examination, answering several questions about the accident.

At this point, the doctors did not believe he would survive. Yet Gage's great health and youth allowed him to heal without complications. Amazingly, Gage showed no loss of motor skills, nor was his speech affected. He had full memory, and his physical strength gradually returned. Dr. Harlow even thought that Gage was lucky because his injury involved an area of the brain that was considered unimportant, the frontal lobe.

As Gage regained his health, however, his personality made a 180-degree turn. Everyone who knew him said the same thing, Gage was no longer Gage. Dr. Harlow said that Gage had lost the balance between his intellectual faculty and animal propensities.

Once sincere and well mannered, Gage was now out of control and malicious. He demonstrated selfish behavior and frequently used terrible profanity. He became unreliable and unpredictable. He became socially inept. He made decisions and choices against his best interests. He had difficulties following through on his plans. He stopped thinking before he acted. On many occasions, Dr. Harlow tried to reason with Gage to get him to understand that he was going to lose his job unless he changed his behavior. Gage wouldn't heed this advice, and lost his job with the railroad contractors, not because of any physical disability, but because of his changed personality. It took years for Dr. Harlow to admit that although his most famous patient survived, he never really recovered.

By 1868, two decades after the accident, Dr. Harlow was ready to accept the surprising message inherent in Gage's altered personality, that the frontal lobe is linked with the personality. The incident and its aftermath began the search for a "self" in the brain that has to do with how we personally regulate our behavior, control our impulses, make complicated choices, and plan our future. All these attributes go well beyond the basic functions of memory, motor and speech processing, and animal reflexes.

Incidentally, today scientists better understand what happened to Gage's brain. Almost 160 years after Gage's accident, some researchers finally isolated the brain regions responsible for his strange personality change. Hanna Damasio, distinguished Professor of Neurology, University of Iowa, and director of the Laboratory of Human Neuroanatomy and Neuroimaging at the University of Iowa College of Medicine, has reconstructed Gage's injury and subsequent brain changes, proving that he had damaged the inner part of both prefrontal cortices (Damasio released a video of her research in 1994).[2]

The History of Frontal Lobe Research

In the years following Gage's accident, many other physicians began documenting patients who had experienced frontal lobe injuries and undergone radical personality changes like those seen in Gage. A pattern began to develop. Most victims had difficulty holding a job. They also exhibited detachment from the feelings of the people around them. They had no concern for social ethics. They sometimes made grandiose plans but they never carried them out. Their behavior and their choices went against their best interests. Immediate gratification and impulsive action always reigned over long-term plans. Autopsies of these case histories revealed severe damage to the prefrontal cortices.

Unfortunately, nearly 70 years passed after Gage's accident before any real advances in frontal lobe research were made. For example, more evidence linking personality changes to prefrontal lobe damage came from a Yale study conducted in the early 1930s on chimpanzees.[3] The researchers were observing two apes who were especially aggressive and uncooperative. They were frustrated easily and tended to lash out in retaliation at other chimps in the social structure. Scientists then performed a novel type of surgery on these apes that severely affected their frontal lobes. After the surgery, both chimpanzees were easily controllable and more cooperative. These findings were released at a medical conference in 1935.

Researchers speculated that this kind of surgery could produce similar changes in humans. This hypothesis led to an infamous kind of psychiatric surgery known as the *frontal lobotomy*. Countless patients with different kinds of psychoses voluntarily and involuntarily underwent this type of surgery, intended to purposely damage their frontal lobes in an effort to experiment with, take control of, and "cure" their conditions.

The Rise of the Lobotomy "Cure"

In the late 1930s, many people with psychiatric conditions were treated with medications in an attempt to reverse their antisocial personality disorders. However, medications were quite expensive at that time; the United States was in the final stages of the Great Depression. Thus some physicians attempted to help these patients using a gruesome, nonmedical solution.[4] In certain medical facilities, doctors would wait until selected patients went to sleep, and then anesthetize them. They would take a scalpel, slip it in under the upper eyelid between the eyeball and the skull, and puncture the skull in that spot. That particular area, right behind the upper part of the orbit of the eyes, is the softest part of the skull. Then the scalpel would be moved like a windshield wiper across the area of the prefrontal cortices.

Patients who underwent these "treatments" exhibited many common traits. Because the aftereffects of the frontal lobotomy suggest just how momentous a role the healthy, functional frontal lobe plays in our lives, I will describe the outcome of these lobotomies in some detail.

The first thing their doctors noticed was that each patient became markedly placid, lazy, and lethargic, and showed no interest in their surroundings. There was also a distinct loss of initiative, and these patients became uninspired. As well, they displayed a significant desire for sameness. Most subjects became deeply attached to routine behavior. In fact, they became predictable, after having been so unpredictable that they had required hospitalization. For example, they loved to listen to the same radio station, they always wore the same clothes, and they liked to eat the same type of food at the same time every day. If any of these familiar routines were interfered with or disrupted, these patients would fall apart emotionally.

Moreover, these poor souls also lost their ability to modify their actions and behavior. They performed the same actions repeatedly, every day, to create the same results. They were so rooted in their habitual routines that they could not change any of their actions to produce a different outcome. Although many people crave routine, these patients would make the same mistakes over and over, at any cost, without any conscious effort to do things differently. For example, if a lobotomized patient who liked milk experienced the ill effects of drinking sour milk, he could not learn from the experience and make a different choice. When it was "time" for him to drink milk again, he would drink from the same container of sour milk. These patients were so addicted to following their structured behaviors, that the rigidity of their actions was more important than any ill effects of their routines. In other words, they could not stop putting the square peg in the round hole.

Almost every lobotomized frontal lobe patient demonstrated an inability to focus on single-minded tasks. They would start an activity or initiate a speech pattern, and then become completely distracted and never finish what they started. Many would become sidetracked from an activity by any trivial event in their surroundings.

These patients also failed to gain meaning out of situations, which signified that they could not learn or memorize any new information. They could not comprehend intricate actions or ideas. All their complex behavior patterns were replaced by simpler, more predictable ones. Projecting into the future was also beyond their ability. They had no future goals—not even short-term ones—since they were unable to make plans and carry them out. Certainly, these people were unable to adapt to new situations. If a patient broke a shoelace, it would not occur to her to ask for a new one; she would continue to tie the shoe with a broken lace.

Many lobotomized patients also became child-like and immature. They lacked social constraints and any sense of responsibility. They lacked control over their immediate impulses. Several patients would break out in fits of bad temper over insignificant situations. Childish tantrums and pouting were extremely common. They often repeated the same phrases of speech. Their communication skills declined more and more, over time, until they were able to emit only grunts and noises.

Eventually, lobotomized patients lost their ability to take care of themselves, use language, and recognize objects, and they could not exhibit any signs of critical judgment. They experienced a consistent cognitive decline until their faculties of "self" collapsed. Finally, they became lost in a narrow, primitive world of almost animal-like behavior.

Today, we no longer allow this kind of radical, unauthorized experimental procedure to be routinely performed on patients. Although frontal lobotomies represent a very dark era in mental health care, those experiments did shed a great deal of light on the functioning of the frontal lobe. We can all agree that it would have been better if this knowledge came from another source, but we now possess much better tools for observing the functional capabilities of most parts of the brain. By conducting animal research, studying patients with brain damage, and using the recently available functional scanning technologies, scientists now have a far greater understanding of the frontal lobe. Since the time of Phineas Gage, we now know that there are degrees of damage and degrees of dysfunction to this most sacred area.

Before we leave the subject of lobotomies, I would like to point out that in many ways and to varying degrees, those of us who are emotionally addicted (and that probably means most of us) suffer from some degree of enervation, crave our own routine existence, shy away from many new or unfamiliar experiences, and live our life in a nearly catatonic state.

Let's think about this. Damage to the frontal lobe causes human beings to have one or more of the following symptoms.

- We tend to become lazy, lethargic, and uninspired.
- We desire sameness or routine.
- We have difficulty focusing on single-minded tasks; we start projects or endeavors such as diet or exercise routines, and never follow through.
- We fail to gain meaning out of situations. In other words, we hardly ever learn anything new from situations, so that we can modify our actions to produce a different outcome.
- We seem to have emotional outbursts when our routine world is disrupted.
- We do not project into the future by making any plans.

Does this sound like anyone we may know?

Damage to the frontal lobe never seems to inhibit or alter the basic functions of sensory, motor, memory, or emotional systems that are carried throughout the rest of the brain. Instead, when the frontal lobe is injured, it seems to lose its ability to lead, synthesize, and coordinate all other brain regions that affect so much of who we are.

The biggest reason most people cannot utilize the frontal lobe is because we are addicted to our emotions and feelings from the body. In a very real sense, we have self-lobomotized our own brains by relying solely on the hardwired, oft-repeated, and oft-fired neural networks that require little or no thought to initialize. When Henry David Thoreau spoke of people living "lives of quiet desperation," he very well could have been speaking of our inactive and under-utilized frontal lobe. Recent studies in brain scan technology have shown that the less activity in the frontal lobe, the greater the tendency toward impulsively overemotional behavior.[5] In fact, in recent research done by Richard Davidson, Ph.D., at the University of Wisconsin, subjects who demonstrated heightened frontal lobe activity on functional brain scans had lower levels of the stress hormone cortisol.[6] So, the greater the brain activity in the frontal lobe, the more ability we have to willfully control our reactions and impulsive behaviors.

The frontal lobe, when fully activated, gives us the capability to be much more in control of who we want to become than we probably realize. To break free of our emotional addictions, we must put the king back on the throne. To be controlled by the impulses of the body is to live with the body as the mind. When we live in survival mode, those powerful age-old chemicals influence the rest of our thinking brain to put all our awareness on our environment, our body, and time. In a sense, then, we must move our mind out of our body and put it back in the brain. To do so, we first have to gain an understanding of what the frontal lobe does for us, and how our evolution has blessed us with this marvel of supervision, control, and high-level thinking.

Our Greatest Gift

Through evolution, we have been given a remarkable gift: the frontal lobe that sits at the front and center of our brain. This most recent development in human brain anatomy is our crowning achievement, the most highly evolved area of the human nervous system. From its position just behind the forehead, this largest of the four lobes of the neocortex serves as our control center, filtering out interference, focusing our attention, and quieting the storm that our centers of perception produce in keeping us connected to our outer and inner worlds.

Many images of the human brain, as well as the language we use to describe how our synapses function, lead us to believe that the brain is a very unquiet place. We talk about the firing of millions of neurons, and the brain is often pictured as functioning like a Midwestern summer storm, full of thunder and lightning. We tend to believe that the brain is in a constant state of tumult, and that image may best capture what we often feel like.

Consider for a second, though, what you are doing as you read the words on this page. I hope that you are so drawn in by the concepts I'm discussing that your mind is quiet: that you are not aware of the chair in which you sit, that the nagging pain in your shoulders and neck has eased, that the environment beyond the edges of the pages you hold has somehow receded into nothingness, that the sounds of traffic and other noises coming from outside your window have all faded, and that all you hear is the sound of your own inner voice sounding out the words on this page. Your frontal lobe centers your attention.

The frontal lobe is also responsible for the choices you just made—to shift in your seat, to take one hand from the edge of the book to scratch your scalp, to look at the clock across the room, or any one of a thousand different actions you may take in an hour's time.

More than anything else, the frontal lobe is responsible for the conscious, willful, purposeful, intentional choices and actions that we undertake countless times each day. It is the home of the "true self." Think of the frontal lobe as a conductor in front of an immense orchestra. It has direct connections to all other parts of the brain and, therefore, controls how the rest of the brain operates.

Only the frontal lobe is capable of the kind of high-level functioning necessary to perform those high-level tasks. If we are ever going to be able to overcome our habitual states of mind and our predisposition to feel rather than think, we are going to need to become intimately familiar with the frontal lobe and how it functions.

It is only when we purposely impose our will through the use of our frontal lobe that we can achieve the kind of quiet and control necessary to break out of the cycle of neurological and chemical responses that dominate and dictate most of our personality, the choices we make, and the reactions we set in motion. If we do not, we will be at the mercy of factors in our environment, the needs or reactions of our body, and memories of our past. If we cannot think beyond how we emotionally feel, then we are living according to what the environment dictates to our body. Rather than truly thinking, innovating, and creating, we merely fire the synaptic memories in other areas of our brain from our genetic or personal past; we instigate the same repetitive chemical reactions that have us living in survival mode.

In short, we are at the mercy of the effect instead of being the initiator of the cause. The frontal lobe is the area of the brain that changes all these so-called "normal human traits." To think greater than how we feel requires a will that is manifest only in the frontal lobe. That will and the frontal lobe's ability to help us focus our concentrated attention is what primarily separates us from other species.

Human Uniqueness Identified

For centuries, scientists and philosophers have speculated on the unusual differences that set our species apart from all other life forms. What makes human beings unique in comparison to other creatures on this planet is not that we have opposable thumbs, that we stand upright and walk on two legs, or that we have two eyes that point forward. It is not that we have very little body hair, that we speak a sophisticated language, or even that we have large brains. Certainly, other animals have bigger brains than those of humans. An elephant's brain, for example, is far larger than that of an adult human being.

What distinguishes us from all other species of animals is the size of the frontal lobe relative to the rest of the neocortex. In cats, the frontal lobe makes up 3.5 percent of their higher brain's anatomy. The frontal lobe of a dog comprises seven percent of the total new brain. In chimpanzees, and in other smaller primates like the gibbon and the macaque, the proportion of the frontal lobe to the rest of the cortex is about 11 to 17 percent. In humans, however, the frontal lobe makes up 30 to 40 percent of the total volume of the neocortex.[7]

Until recently, scientists knew little about the frontal lobe. They once considered it "the silent area," because when they tried to measure activity in the frontal lobe using the tried-and-true EEG machine, they picked up no signs of activity that resembled what they found in measuring other parts of the brain. As we know, the routine thinking areas and the regions that process all our sensory stimuli in the rest of the cortex are always busy; EEG machines detect brain-wave activity by sensing changes in electromagnetic fields. However, this old type of instrumentation provided very little data regarding what was taking place in the frontal lobe.

As is true of most brain research, with advancements in technology, we gained valuable new insights and were able to toss aside old assumptions. We now know that the frontal lobe oversees almost all the brain's activities. It is our seat of inspiration, what mystics have called the *crown*.

Although they could not have known as much about the frontal lobe as we do today, ancient cultures, when crowning a great king, presented him with gold and jewels over this part of the brain, symbolizing that he had the mind to lead a nation. A peacemaker in times past would be crowned with a laurel wreath, placed over the frontal lobe to acknowledge his ability to resolve differences and to see through chaos. Similarly, when an athlete was celebrated with a laurel wreath over his forehead, this signified his mastery over his body and the environment. Great initiates and advanced civilizations in ancient times knew that the jewel worn in the middle of one's forehead was there not to accentuate the face, but to acknowledge the power of the brain, specifically the frontal lobe. For centuries, the frontal lobe has been recognized as the most elevated area of the human brain.[8] Yet the frontal lobe was also considered fit for experimentation, as we've seen in the lobotomizing of thousands of patients.

Throne of the True Self

From a scientific standpoint, the frontal lobe (also called the prefrontal cortex) can be considered the seat of power in human beings. The frontal lobe is capable of an amazing array of tasks, because it is the part of the brain most densely inter-connected to all other distinct functional areas of the brain.[9] It has direct connections to the cerebellum, all the other parts of the neocortex, the midbrain, the basal ganglia, the thalamus, the hypothalamus, the hippocampus, the amygdala, and even the brain stem nuclei. (See chapter 4 for more on these other sections of the brain.) Moreover, the frontal lobe houses the brain's most sophisticated patterns of neurological networks, which equip it to manage, coordinate, and integrate the activity of all other brain regions. If we recall our discussion of the homunculus, or "little body" imbedded in the brain's tissue (also discussed in chapter 4), the frontal lobe has a similar kind of map. Within its own structure resides a map of all the other neural connections comprising the entire neocortex. If the neocortex is the motherboard of our brain, the frontal lobes are the central processing units.

When the frontal lobe is in action, we exhibit our highest, most elevated level of consciousness, our self-awareness, and our ability to observe reality. It is the seat of our conscience. Because this area of the brain is where all our neural connections converge, it stands to reason that we can understand and observe our own thoughts about ourselves. The concept of "self," which is the highest form of understanding that the conscious mind can possess, is in the frontal lobe, the area of our greatest expression as a human being. In other words, if we can use the frontal lobe and control it, we can know and control ourselves and our future. To what greater achievement can we aspire?

The Two Hemispheres and Frontal Lobe Specialization

There is a very strong correlation between learning new things and blood flow to the frontal lobe. Scientists performing functional scans in controlled experiments have noticed that both frontal lobes were most active when the task was novel or new.[10] Scientists asked subjects to say the appropriate verb that represented a picture of a noun. The blood flow to the frontal lobe was measured when the task was first introduced. As might be expected, the blood flow to the frontal lobe was the highest when the task was novel or new. However, as the subjects continued with the experiment and the process became more familiar, the blood flow to the frontal lobes almost completely stopped. In other words, the more familiar the activity, the less the frontal lobe was required. When a new task was introduced that was similar to the first but was not exactly the same, the blood flow to the frontal lobe increased but not to the same level as the initial level. This means that the more a task is "relatively" familiar by association, the less the blood flow that is needed at the frontal lobe. In essence, familiar tasks or routine information are easier for the frontal lobe to process because they require less concentration and focus. Because there is an element of familiarity, the brain can associate with the preexisting task based on how we have already wired the experience neurologically.

Therefore, blood flow to the frontal lobe is highest when any task is novel, and it is lowest when the task becomes familiar. As any task becomes more routine, blood flow to the executive area decreases, and the rest of the neocortex takes over. This suggests that learning and wiring new information requires the frontal lobe to initially handle the novel data. As it begins to map that information, it can lower the incoming signals from the rest of the brain so that we are not distracted by extraneous stimuli. Once the frontal lobe has learned the new task and it has become routine, other lobes of the cerebral cortex log it and encode the information as familiar or learned throughout the cortex.

Let's continue by saying that the right frontal lobe is larger than the left frontal lobe. No one can say for sure why that is, but scientists agree that where there is a more developed structure, it stands to reason that we will have a more highly evolved function. Stated another way, the organ that has greater development has a greater capacity to perform. Think of the difference between how our hands and our feet have developed—our fingers are capable of performing much finer motor skills than our toes, and fingers even appear more highly refined.

Numerous experiments have proven that the two sides of the frontal lobes have different, independent functions. In one experiment, researchers found that this hemisphere specialization of the frontal lobe and the two halves of the brain are both correlated to novelty and routine. While using PET (positron emission tomography) scans to measure cerebral blood flow, they introduced a new task to the subjects. Researchers noticed that the right frontal lobe became more active than the left during unknown or novel task experiences. When the subjects practiced and became familiar with the tasks, the left frontal lobe became more enlivened and required more blood than the right. Therefore, when we are learning unknown information in an attempt to make it known, the right prefrontal cortex is mainly activated. As the task begins to become routinely familiar by mental rehearsal and practice, activation moves to the left prefrontal cortex. Blood flow ultimately moves toward the posterior (back) of the brain as we begin to wire the task and mold the experience in the brain's very fabric.[11]

Researchers have also determined that the right frontal lobe, along with part of the right hemisphere, is responsible for sustaining our attention for extended periods of time. We know this to be true because people who have strokes in this area have difficulty maintaining continued attention. The right frontal lobe holds the new concept in place so that it can familiarize itself with the unknown idea and imprint that concept in our neurological tissue. As the task becomes more familiar, the left side of the frontal lobe takes over so that it can be catalogued as known, before we file it away in our remaining gray matter. For example, if we were to learn how to cook Mandarin cuisine, our right frontal lobe would maintain our attention on this novel information and new experience. We would have to sustain our focus in a methodical fashion to begin to memorize the information, until it became routine and was stored as memory.

In many ways, the frontal lobe is a lot like what we think of as our personality self. It loves to learn new things and keeps us focused on what's novel and exciting. When a skill is new and essentially "fun," the frontal lobe is all over that activity. After a few repetitions, when all the surprise and newness is gone, the frontal lobe passes the work off to another area of the brain. That's the privilege of being the boss: let the grunts do the boring, routine work. I don't know whether you've ever worked for a boss like this, but because the frontal lobe is like an executive in charge, this concept shouldn't come as a surprise.

As long as we are inspired by a new activity or idea, we know that this sustained focus center works extremely well. Don't be fooled by the boss passing on some of the workload to others; it's not as though the frontal lobe is incapable of focusing sustained attention, passes off the routine task, and then goes to sleep. No, the frontal lobe, at that stage, is still actively multitasking, and one of the things it's monitoring is what the rest of the "employees" are up to.

In fact, the frontal lobe will often act as a whistle-blower. It notices when we become bored and start letting our mind wander to extraneous activities instead of paying attention to the matter at hand. For example, you've surely listened to a boring lecture. Even though you were disinterested and unstimulated, you knew that you had to pay attention to learn the subject matter, because you might be tested on it at a later date. It was mostly the frontal lobe (especially your right frontal lobe) that kept you paying attention to processing this new information, even if your other systems were clamoring for you to walk out. If not for the frontal lobe, we'd probably never learn much of anything.

The frontal lobe also has the ability to turn up activity in particular synapses, when we are intentionally using it to repetitively fire a series of synaptic connections so that we can wire them together as a community. This is how we make new memories. In addition, because the symphony leader in the frontal lobe can make the rest of the brain operate in any sequence, combination, or pattern, it can therefore make new levels of mind by combining diverse neural networks together. Given that our definition of *mind* is the brain in action, and given that there are billions of neurons with almost infinite possible connections, when the symphony leader conducts the orchestra to play a new song or a variation of the same song, the new musical score is the same new level of mind.

The frontal lobe can also "turn down" neural nets that have already been wired, so that it can selectively use dissociative memories as building blocks to understand novel ideas. It can pick up a variety of information in a nonlinear way, so that new ideas are examined, analyzed, invented, and even created, while it "cools off" other neural nets so that we will not be distracted by irrelevant data. It will inhibit them from firing so that our attention can remain on whatever we have on our mind. And we have a great deal on our mind, all the time.

Our Busy Mind

According to some of the latest research, scientists have demonstrated that the brain processes about 400 billion bits of information every second. Usually, however, we are conscious of only about 2,000 of those bits of data.[12] Out of those 2,000 bits, the inputs the brain is processing pertain only to our awareness of the body, our awareness of the environment, and our awareness of time. In other words, our daily thoughts and concerns are about taking care of our body, about how we "feel." We also monitor the environment and time in terms of how they affect our body.

For example, does this sound familiar? We're supposed to be focusing on a task at work or at school, but we find ourselves thinking: Does my back hurt? Am I tired? Am I hungry? Is it too cold or too warm? Do I like the way my business associate smells? How long will it take me to finish reading this page? Isn't it time for lunch yet? Is it time to leave work? Essentially, in the survival mode in which most people live each day, it is our limbic system that chemically powers the neocortex to function with such awareness on these important cues.

Without the direct involvement of the frontal lobe, our daily thoughts primarily concern the survival of the body. We spend most of our waking day anticipating and responding to external stimuli that our senses receive from the environment and, a result, all other lobes of the brain are busy thinking. This preoccupation ultima causes the brain to stay busy trying to predict the next moment. Put another without the frontal lobe's involvement, we spend a great deal of our time foc on future events based on our memories. Most people, most of the time, d direct their frontal lobes to be in control.

Perhaps we should ask s more often, who's in charge here? The frontal lobe can act as a kind of eper, letting in certain types of information and presenting it front and attend to them later, or not at all. r, it can shunt other inputs aside and

Our conscious awareness is dictated by what we choose to tune in to and whatever we can learn as new knowledge. However, a huge difference exists between the brain simply processing information and our awareness of that information. Although the brain processes 400 billion bits of data every second, the frontal lobe enables us to actively select what data we choose to put our awareness on.

As we sit here and read this page, our brain is taking in information from all of our senses, but we aren't aware of them all because our frontal lobe is filtering them out. Similarly, we can get into our car on any one of a hundred different days, turn the key, shift into drive, and pull away. On 99 of those 100 days, we won't even hear the sound of the engine. Then, one day, we hear the squeal of a fan belt or some other noise coming from under the hood. This time we hear the motor, because the frontal lobe monitored the incoming message from the sensory cortex, noted the novelty of the noise, and put us on high alert to focus on the engine's sound.

We can learn only when we selectively place our conscious awareness on the inputs and information we choose, based on our free will. As human beings, we have the privilege to choose where to put our attention, and for how long. Consider this idea, then: reality may exist wherever our mind is. For example, we can unfold a painful memory from a dark closet deep within our mind, and within moments, it will come to life. We can even relive the experience emotionally. When we do, whether we like it or not, our brain creates an onslaught of chemical signals to the body, and it produces almost the same chemical effects as the original experience. That is how mobile our attention is—we can cast it into the future or we can anchor it to the past. Our freewilled attention can be our greatest gift or our biggest curse.

Consequently, if we can use the frontal lobe to help us to achieve focused concentration, our thoughts can be made more real than the external world. How is that possible? We are talking about controlling the elements of our reality on which we choose to focus.

Again, consider all that is going on around you and within you as you read this book. Think of all the hundreds of thousands of cells reproducing within you, the enormous activity that is taking place in the world just outside your window, and your spouse in the next room watching a television program that you started off hearing but that has since receded into nothingness. Did all those activities stop when you became engrossed in your reading? Of course not, but to you, they were no longer a part of your reality.

Can reality be what we choose to focus on? Can reality pose multiple options to us that we simply aren't attuned to? Can we sharpen our ability to use this sophisticated region of the brain so that we can selectively choose where and on what to put our attention? This initiates the question, how might this have an effect on our life?

We should also keep in mind the experiment we mentioned in chapter 2 involving Buddhist monks. If you will recall, these highly trained and expert masters of meditation were able to achieve results that were off the charts in terms of measurement of frontal lobe activity. The monks were able to single-mindedly focus on one thought—compassion—and hold that thought by virtue of their frontal lobes. What might happen if we were able to employ those same skills of focus and concentration? Clearly, the monks had mastered the skill of quieting the other centers of the brain in service of holding this single thought in their minds. If they did have figuratively bulging muscles of concentration, how did they get them?

Just as we might go to a gym and work out with a great deal of purpose and commitment, that's what they had to do—practice and exercise those powers of concentration. That's really no different from what we do when we learn to play tennis. Have you ever seen the forearm of a professional tennis player? The arm with which they play dwarfs the size of the nondominant arm. That happened not because of some genetic abnormality, but through the near-constant use of one arm in favor of the other. We can do the same thing with our mind: we can practice the skill of attentiveness over and over to develop our frontal lobe, so that it functions at a higher level. We can make our own brain work better. After all, that's the point of those muscles developing in a tennis player—not for looks, but for function. The larger muscles give the players more power and more control over their strokes. In the brain of someone who has a greater attention span,

frontal lobe endows human beings with the virtue of conscious choice and free will. Without it, much of what we believe makes us human would be absent.

Who we are as individuals, what we want, who we want to be in the future, and what kind of world we want to live in, are all determined by how we use our frontal lobe. Let's take a look at this enormous gift in more detail.

Intent Defines Our Heroes

The frontal lobe makes choices that support our desire for a particular outcome. When we use this part of our brain to its capacity, our behavior matches our purpose, and our actions match our intent—our mind and body are one. How many times have our behavior and purpose matched completely? How frequently do we find ourselves at odds with our own intentions and actions? "I intend to get back into shape and run two miles every day. I intend to stop drinking soda and other sugary beverages. I intend to be more patient with my children, spouse, and coworkers. I intend to devote myself to a charitable cause like being a Big Brother or Big Sister."

There's an expression that goes something like: our ego sometimes writes checks that our body can't cash. Well, the ego is merely following orders from the brain, so let's put the failure for follow-through squarely where it belongs: on our will to act. We often don't follow through because we just "don't feel like it." When we let our feelings get in the way, the frontal lobe goes back to sleep, and we are running on automatic programs, responding each day to the constant chatter in our head. The frontal lobe can silence the internal dialogues and suggestions that talk us out of our own aspirations and greatness. Used properly and to its capacity, the frontal lobe will marshal the forces needed to cash those checks for us.

Properly employed, the frontal lobe affords us the ability to look at situations objectively, organize our thoughts, make a plan of action, follow through on that plan, and evaluate our actions as successful or unsuccessful, based on our intention. We might think of our prefrontal cortex as the brain's disciplinarian, a built-in internal manager. Thomas Gualtieri, M.D., Medical Director of the North Carolina Neuropsychiatry Clinics in Chapel Hill and Charlotte, North Carolina, provides an excellent description of the frontal lobe as having "the capacity to for-mulate goals, to make plans for their execution, to carry them out in an effective way, to change course and improvise in the face of obstacles and failure, and to do so successfully, in the absence of external direction or structure."[14]

These traits are inherent in the frontal lobe, and are possible because of its direct connections to all other distinct regions of the brain. No other species that we know of has this ability. Has our dog ever stopped, in the midst of wolf-ing down food it stole off a kitchen counter, to consider the ramifications of its actions? How often do we regulate and reflect on our own behaviors? How often, instead, are we running those neural networks while on autopilot, living in survival mode and thoughtlessly enjoying the chemical high of our emo-tional addictions?

Another demonstration of the power of the frontal lobe involves certainty and clarity of choice. When we make up our mind about something, independent of present circumstances, the frontal lobe experiences its greatest moment. When we firmly resolve to be, do, or even have something—regardless of how long it will take, or what is happening in our environment, or how our body feels at that par-ticular moment—we spark this structure of the brain into action. At such a moment, we no longer care about the external world or how our body might feel; we align with an internal representation or concept of our intention. When we make up our mind, without considerations or concerns as to how our choice to do or be something might happen, the frontal lobe is now fully activated.

What is so amazing about our brain and the frontal lobe is that we have the ability to make a thought become the only thing that is real to us. Because of the size of the frontal lobe, human beings have the privilege of making thought more important and more real than anything else. We are all naturally wired to be this way. When we make our thoughts all that is real and we pay attention to them as if they were, we unite the frontal lobe's primary functions into a force as powerful as anything in the universe.

I hope that you've had this experience in your life when your intention, your focus, and your will have all come into alignment. I've had friends who run marathons tell me that we don't run a marathon with our legs, but with our mind. My experience as a triathlete bears this out. In spite of all evidence to the contrary as we enter the last few miles of the running portion of a triathlon—the reports coming in from our legs begging for more fuel, our feet informing us of the impending loss of our toenails, our pancreas informing us that it is not able to produce enough fuel for our starving muscles—our brain still wills our body across the finish line.

This power of intention is what we most admire about our heroes. Through them, we see the frontal lobe at work, inhibiting the need for immediate gratification by allowing the brain to maintain long-term goals. William Wallace, Martin Luther King, Saint Francis of Assisi, Mahatma Gandhi, and Queen Elizabeth I were all masters of the frontal lobe. They kept total focus on an intended outcome—a principle of freedom, honor, or love—and never wavered long from that ideal, no matter how difficult or chaotic the circumstances they faced. They had the ability to intentionally make an ideal so real that through their constant attention on a particular concept, it became more important than the needs of their body, the conditions in their environment, and even the concept of time. In other words, it didn't matter if their body was in danger, how difficult the obstacles were in their immediate life, or how long it would take to overcome almost unanimously opposed circumstances. Only the ideal mattered. Nothing tempted them from their purpose. Their intent was clear, and it mattered more to them than any other considerations. Throughout history, our heroes have demonstrated total focus of thought and intention coupled with consistent behavior and action. In effect, they molded reality to match the internal image they constructed. That is true power, and the frontal lobe is the structure that gives us that ability. This is what we secretly admire about greatness. It speaks to our own potential.

Think back, then, to chapter 2 and the people who were able to heal themselves. When we consider what they were able to do in light of the various capabilities of the brain, faith in a certain outcome might take on a new meaning. Maybe faith operates when we hold a particular intention in our mind for an outcome, and we trust and believe in that outcome more than we believe in what the external world is telling us. If so, *faith* can be defined as believing that the only real thing is thought—independent of the circumstances. When we pray to a higher power for change in our life, aren't we just believing in and making thought more powerful than our present reality? The frontal lobe makes that happen.

That's why Dean, the man in chapter 2 who was afflicted with leukemia, wasn't really "afflicted" at all. Although his disease went untreated, he had already far outlived the expectations of his doctors. He had simply made up his mind that he was going to live independent of the feedback from his body (what he looked like in the mirror), regardless of feedback from his environment (what his doctors told him), and without the restriction of time (the diagnosis of six months to live).

People use the expression "made up my mind" all the time, but I hope we're beginning to understand those words in a different way. We are literally capable of making a new mind for ourselves, just as Dean did. We can make up a mind that operates independent of the usual constraints of time and environment. We can conceive of and bring into existence a reality that is far different from the one we presently inhabit. And the first step in this process is using the frontal lobe to take command again. Why is it that so few people are able to achieve at the level of their heroes? Are those heroes endowed with brain structures that are different from those of other people? The answer, of course, is no. Those heroes simply learned to "live" within their frontal lobes more frequently than everyone else does.

Focus and Impulse Control

In college, I knew someone I refer to as "the Magpie." Magpies are seemingly intelligent and intensely curious birds. They are also renowned as thieves. If any bright and shiny object comes into their field of vision, they have to investigate. Their nests are often a veritable junkyard of pilfered items that their curious natures drove them to take. This classmate of mine wasn't a thief as far as I knew, but he had the same kind of easily distracted nature that characterizes his avian counterparts. We were in a study group together, and it was nearly impossible to get him to focus on the work in front of us. Whether we met in a dorm room, a library conference room, an off-campus apartment, or coffee shop didn't matter. Any movement or any object seemed to hold his attention more closely than the matter at hand. His eyes would dart about the room at an unusual pace. Worse still, it seemed that no thought that ran through his head got filtered out as unfit for vocalizing. His stream of consciousness patter was a series of non sequiturs. I knew something about Attention Deficient Hyperactivity Disorder back then, and I don't think he suffered from it in its purest form, but even at that, his inability to sit still and concentrate made it seem as though he responded to every impulse that his body and hyperactive mind transmitted. Clearly, he had a frontal lobe, but it seemed constantly to succumb to an onslaught of calls to action from his body.

When we are clear about what we want, the frontal lobe forbids anything from distracting us from our purpose and intent. How often are we aligned to this function of the frontal lobe? Imagine how you might respond in the following scenario. One Saturday morning at 10 a.m., you set out to mail your mother a birthday present. She lives 600 miles away, and her birthday is in five days. The post office will be closed Monday for a holiday, so today is your only opportunity to mail her gift so that it will arrive on time. After you complete this task, you are to meet your husband for lunch at noon. Your frontal lobe has a clear picture of what you need to accomplish in the near future.

On your way to the post office, you see that your favorite store has a sale on all the spring items that you adore. The store's huge sale banner is an external stimulus that triggers an impulse. Which of these actions would you take?

Action A: You become so excited that you forget your initial intention, and your feelings override your initial purpose. Immediately, you pull into the parking lot of the store to shop. When you finally look at your watch, it is 2 p.m. The post office is closed, and you missed your lunch date.

If you chose this option, this is what happened: When you discovered the sale at your favorite store, this external stimulus proved to be such a distraction that the brain's disciplinarian stopped restraining your mind from wandering to other stimuli. Impulse control was lost, as was your focus on your original plan. Your priorities changed, and shopping became your frontal lobe's new intentional action. As a result, your behavior no longer matched your initial goals. Your immediate feelings of short-term gratification and need overrode the lack of feelings related to your long-term intention. You did not make a new decision to reschedule the lunch date with your husband, you never analyzed the future consequences in reference to your mother's gift, and above all, other people were affected by your absentminded behavior.

Action B: Feeling an urge to check out the sale, you engage your frontal lobe and look at the landscape of possibilities. It brings up a mental picture of the time-sensitive nature of your errands. You weigh your priorities, and decide to follow your original plan of action. However, your frontal lobe presents you with an option that will resolve your conflict and adds new intentions to your list—after lunching with your spouse, you will spend the afternoon at the sale.

This is what happened if you chose Action B: your prefrontal cortex allowed you to hold on to your internally pictured goals so that your actions matched those intentions.

In this way, the frontal lobe restrains the brain from paying attention to external stimuli that don't pertain to our goals. In addition, the frontal lobe gives us the internal strength not to respond to stimuli that create feelings of immediate gratification. Instead, our frontal lobe gives us the ability to hold on to long-term dreams, ideals, purposes, and goals instead of what might feel better in that moment. It restrains us from our quick, knee-jerk reactions.

Action A is typical of someone who is easily distracted by external stimuli. This is how we may go through our days if we don't engage the frontal lobe. We can become easily distracted by familiar opportunities or circumstances in our external world that do not match our original internal intention. We do this because we want the feeling of immediate pleasure, instead of having the ability to choose beyond the familiar feelings of the body triggered by something in the environment.

Some part of the brain has to be able to filter out the enormous amounts of stimuli that we receive on a daily basis, and keep our attention on the most important stimuli based on our free will, our choice, and our most important goals. In other words, some part of our brain has to act as a sorting house, enabling us to process all this information. For example, right now there are sounds around you that you are not paying attention to. If you stop and listen, you will hear something that was not in your focus seconds before. Your brain has been processing that information because your brain has been hearing it, but it's not until you shift your conscious awareness to that sound that you are actually able to hear that auditory stimuli. The frontal lobe gives us the ability to choose what stimuli we want to pay attention to, by monitoring diverse signals from the external world.

The Frontal Lobe and Focus

So, what happens to our ability to focus when we activate the frontal lobe? When we are concentrating, paying attention, or learning with great intent and complete focus, the frontal lobe prevents our brain from wandering off any chosen path of activity. To keep our mind from being distracted, the frontal lobe disregards signals from the body related to feeling emotions and sensing the environment. Just as important, our frontal lobe "lowers the volume," restraining those regions of the brain that handle sensory as well as motor information. It also quiets down the motor cortex so that when we are paying attention or focusing, we tend to get very still. That's because the motor functions to that part of the brain get slowed down or turned off; we actually move into a state of trance, and the body follows. There is no longer any mind in the body's movement centers of the motor cortex. When the sensory circuits cool off, it is as if we are no longer sensing or feeling the environment or the body, because there is no mind being processed in the feeling area of the cortex.

If we also are no longer turning on the circuits of the visual cortex, we will stop seeing the external world, and our thoughts will take front and center stage in our mind. If we are no longer activating neural nets in the auditory cortex, we will no longer be aware of sounds, like cars passing by our home. Even the emotional centers are cooled off in the limbic brain. As a result, what we are thinking about or focusing on will become more real to us than the external world. As those neural networks are shut off by the frontal lobe, we no longer process any level of mind or awareness in that part of the brain and we, therefore, are no longer conscious of the body, the environment, and even time.

Our frontal lobe also puts the reins on other parts of the brain, to inhibit the mind from wandering to memories and associations, other thoughts, or external stimuli not related to the subject at hand. For example, it curbs the associative role of the temporal lobe from drifting to images and their relative emotions that are unrelated to the topic of focus.

Let's say we decide to concentrate on changing our thoughts and actions related to our sister's constant suffering and complaining. Our frontal lobe is the area of the brain that keeps our thoughts in alignment with our initial goal, and it will cause us not to stray from that path. The frontal lobe begins to gather data and initiates us to think about how we will want to behave, based on our past experiences and our philosophical knowledge base. Our intention is now coming to life, if we are focused.

But what if, as we begin to think of new ways to be around her, we begin to make some past associations in our mind that are related to our sister but are unrelated to our intent? In a matter of moments, our mind goes from how we are going to think and behave around her to all the times she blamed us for everything that went wrong with her in our shared childhood—from the bicycle the two of us shared and fought over as we grew up, to wondering whether the bicycle was red or pink, to the time we fell off the bicycle when we were 12, to the memory of the event of our hospital stay, to eating ice cream that our Uncle Frank gave us, to thinking where that uncle is today . . . you get the idea. Your original thought was to change your actions related to your sister, and the next thing you know, you're eating ice cream with your Uncle Frank.

It is the frontal lobe that keeps our mind from moving to associative circuits and memories that lead far from our initial thought processes. If we have the strong intent to hold a picture in our mind, the "boss" will prevent the picture from fading away. It does this by turning down the signals to the brain in a matter of seconds. Scientists call this *lowering the signal-to-noise ratio*. For our purposes, we'll call it *lowering the volume to the external stimuli*.

In the case of a person who is having an explosive emotional response to a minor upset, the signals his body is sending to him are so loud and so persistent that the frontal lobe can't hold a greater ideal firmly in focus; chemicals are rampaging through the body and the brain, and the autonomic nervous system has seized control in order to meet the body's demands.

As discussed, however, the frontal lobe can make a conscious thought so important that, in effect, nothing else exists. This internal picture takes up so much of our conscious attention that it seems as if the external world disappears. If we were able to summon the skills of our frontal lobe, we'd be able to tune out the distractions and misbehaviors of our family and get everything done that we need to accomplish. All those other thoughts about our family and recent events would, in one sense, cease to exist.

RELIGION AND THE BRAIN

For a long time, the spiritual world and, more specifically, the transcendent experiences that many people have in a state of spiritual ecstasy were considered to fall outside the realm of the biological, the natural, or anything "real." A new field of study, called *neurotheology*, has experienced a boom over the last few years. Researchers, most prominent among them Andrew Newberg, M.D., at the University of Pennsylvania, have sought to quantify spiritual experiences and to learn what happens in the brains of Tibetan Buddhists while meditating and Franciscan nuns while praying, for example. Employing sophisticated techniques, including SPECT scans that use a radioactive tracer, in the brains of test subjects who are having a so-called mystical experience, Newberg and others have identified the regions of the brain that are active during these experiences. Working with subjects deep in a meditative state or in prayer, they've determined that the bundle of neurons in the superior parietal lobe—the *orientation association area*—go quiet during these periods of intense focus and concentration. As we may expect, the frontal lobe lights up with activity.

The orientation association center is involved in locating us in time and space—establishing how our body is physically oriented in space, and delineating for us where our body begins and ends. With activity quieted in that area, it's no wonder people experience a sense of "oneness" with the universe. The brain's symphony leader, while being involved in active focused concentration, quiets the center that defines the body's boundaries, akin to silencing the horn section of the orchestra. The frontal lobe has also suspended our sense of being located in a particular time and space. So there we are, lacking a boundary between ourselves and others and the environment, with no sense of time or space, no sense of self, and as Dr. Newberg puts it, we begin to "perceive the self as endless and intimately interwoven with everyone and everything."[15]

Having worked with people capable of great concentration and focus, skilled in observation, and possessing a highly developed sense of self-awareness, these researchers have proven that there is a direct correlation between spiritual contemplation and altered brain activity. While in a state of intense contemplation, experiences of the mind are as real to these meditators as the view outside our window. Linking the spiritual experience to a neurological function doesn't necessarily mean that the experiences exist *merely* in the mind or that the neurological changes cause the experience. The brain may be perceiving a spiritual reality.

Remember, whenever we experience anything and store it in the brain as memory, through association, we can reexperience those feelings and associations when the right environmental trigger occurs. If we walked into our mother's house and smelled her fried chicken cooking, went to the kitchen and saw the chicken cooling on a platter, and then dug in and tasted a piece, all our associative cortices would be firing, and fried chickens of the past could appear in our mind like Jacob Marley's ghost. Certain neurological changes would be taking place, and if a scientist were to inject us with a radioisotope in that moment of gustatory reverie and put our brain through a PET scan, he or she could produce a picture of our brain under the influence of fried chicken. That doesn't mean the chicken didn't exist in reality. Why should a religious experience and a particular spiritual neurological response be any different?

The Disappearing World

When we are driving down the road and thinking about something that has importance and significance to us, we can drive 30 or 40 miles with absolutely no memory of the external world. That's because our frontal lobe quiets down all the other brain areas, and our internal picture of what we are thinking about becomes more real than the external world. When this happens, the brain literally becomes unaware of time (because we lose track of time), we lose awareness of the environment (we don't see anything because our visual cortex shuts off), and we don't have any concept of our body. In fact, we won't feel like we are in our body anymore—all we see is that important thought in our mind. This process is called *disassociation*. It happens when we naturally disassociate from the constant sensations of the body in the external world in linear time. We are no longer associating our sense of self with our environment. What is so amazing is that we disassociate all of the time in our normal lives. When that happens, the "operator" (the frontal lobe) is disconnecting all the phone lines so that we can pay attention to the most important thoughts without being distracted.

When the frontal lobe takes the lead, we abandon many of our neurological circuits and neural nets; we are disconnecting from the synaptic self—the personal identity mapped in the rest of the brain. We actually move out of the landscape of self, along with all its sensory associations and its associations to the events and memories of people and things, at a particular time and place. We abandon our associations to the totality of what makes up our individual identity.[16] Therefore, not only do we disassociate from our body, the external world, and our sense of time, we leave the domain of how we are wired as a person with a history. We lose our association to the "self," and we move from being a "somebody," with all of its identifications, to being "nobody." We disappear. We forget our "self" and what we remember our "self" to be. Instead, we literally become the thought we're thinking about. That natural ability that we have when our identity disappears while we're driving our car is the same deliberate action we use to rewire our brain.

I recently had trouble with my car's engine and took it to a neighborhood mechanic who's famous throughout the area as a garage guru. From the outside, one wouldn't expect that anything or anyone special was present in the building, but as I spoke with him, I was impressed by the intensity of his gaze. After I described the symptoms for a moment, though, that intensity waned and was replaced by a kind of blank stare. I got the distinct impression that he and I were no longer inhabiting the same time and space.

When he told me to start the car, I stood alongside him as he listened with his head cocked to one side, looking very much like the dog on the old RCA records logo. I asked him if he heard the pinging sound I did, but he didn't respond, and that blank look came over him again. I could tell that he was analyzing the data, speculating on possible causes of the noise, and doing a thorough inventory of possibilities and solutions. My mechanic was comparing this sound with other similar sounds he'd heard in the 30-something years he'd been in business. All those experiences had continued to fire those nerve cells and as we know, nerve cells that fire together, wire together. Even though my car's problems weren't electrical in nature, my mechanic had a bundle of wired neural circuits that were processing a stream of consciousness, ready to diagnose any problem my car might have had.

I thought of my experiences at the dealership where I had taken my car in the past, where the first thing the technicians did was hook the car up to a diagnostic machine. Here, a more highly sophisticated diagnostic machine with a greater memory capacity was at work! Each "machine" shared a similar quality:

to reduce the field of inputs to those that would allow it to solve the problem at hand. My local mechanic did exactly that, and the engine has been trouble-free ever since.

MUSIC TO MY EARS

My dog Skakus and I were sitting by the fire one midwinter evening. James Taylor was singing "Sweet Baby James" in the background, and I was, once again, amazed at how great my Italian sauce had turned out. As I looked over at Skakus, I wondered if he even heard Taylor "sayin' like it is" or if he could appreciate the rhythm of "Carolina in My Mind." What I mean is, I know that he can hear, but is he at all capable of comprehending and assimilating these sounds from his environment into meaning? Can he distinguish music from nonmusic? Does he even hear the music at all?

We know that through evolution, all species respond to their environment, and then develop specialized anatomy and physiology over generations to adapt to environmental stimuli for survival. In other words, the slow process of evolution over hundreds of thousands of years has made Skakus, or any dog for that matter, better able to hear sounds than humans can. That's evolution, isn't it? However, even though his ability to hear a broad range of sounds is superior to mine (he certainly has bigger ears than I do), he still may not be "hearing" the music at all. Skakus has never had, and may never have, a need for rock'n'roll. He needs only an acuity for fine sounds, and that is a genetic requirement for guarding, hunting, and assessing his environment to detect predators. It's a dog's life. So the question remains, Does he hear the music? Maybe his brain is just not wired for James Taylor. Music might just be too harmonious for him to hear.

Skakus's brain is conditioned for disruptions or changes in his external world. He hears the music being shut off and, by the same means, he might hear it when it is initially turned on. If I change the volume of the music, that might get his attention too. His brain, though, probably tunes out the music that I am listening to because it is not important for him to attend to it. It's not a sound that his brain, or the brain of any dog, needs to hear consciously.

On the other hand, just as we humans probably never pay attention to or hear the phone ringing at our coworker's desk while we are working at our computer, we can hear our own phone when it rings. Our phone is important enough to get our attention, and this phenomenon suggests that something is happening—the sound of our own phone triggers our attention, awareness, or focus.

Skakus's ears pick up many types of sounds (being able to swivel them like an antenna is a neat trick), and that information is relayed to the brain. However, his brain tunes my music out because his awareness is not present with those stimuli. He does not hear the music because his frontal lobe is not developed enough to integrate these relatively new sounds into meaning. His canine brain is wired for reaction, not integration. For Skakus, the music doesn't exist.

Maybe the same is true for human beings. Maybe as human evolution continued for eons, we tuned out billions of data bits because we did not think the information was important to attend to. If so, we might be missing out on great opportunities far beyond what we think we know. What if all those bits of information already exist for our brain to process, and doing that is as simple as deciding where to put our awareness? Genius may already be at hand.

In the Zone

We've heard athletes describe the phenomenon of *being in the zone*. A baseball player in the middle of a hot streak talks about a pitch coming in that looks as big as a grapefruit. Michael Jordan talked about feeling that his shots simply couldn't miss, as though the basket were as big as a garbage can. In both cases, the crowd noise, the other players on the field or on the court, even the very playing venue itself seemed to disappear. Nothing existed but ball and bat or ball and basket.

Most of us have experienced a similar occurrence, when what we've been working on becomes the only thing in our field of vision, and all other sights and sounds disappear. We move into *the zone*. We're there only intermittently, but if we can learn to harness the reins of our attention and ability to be present, we can extend the length and frequency of our stays in the zone.

When we are so focused that we become unaware of all extraneous stimuli except the few we consider the most vital, we will begin to notice that our sense of time slows down and our perception of objects in space seems to warp. When nothing else exists for the brain except a single action or intention, it seems that there is no future or past, no success or failure, no right or wrong—there is only this moment, right now. We lose track of the boundaries between self and nonself.

When a person's focus is so single-minded and mobile that they can transfer all of their attention from their identity onto a thought, action, or object, their frontal lobe will filter out all of the random sensory stimuli in the environment. One hundred percent of their brain's attention becomes centered on the relationship between thought and deed. Essentially, the person's identity is no longer the self with a history; instead, their new identity becomes the thought or the intention they are holding. Their mind becomes one with (unified with) whatever they are focusing on. The brain and mind are no longer firing the neural networks that comprise one's baseline identity; they are not repeating the past at all. Mind is now in the best position to intentionally learn, create, and perform a skill. The frontal lobe is that part of the brain that allows us to be completely in the present moment.

New Hope in Attention Deficit Disorder

An old joke states that, "When I was a kid, I was so poor I couldn't even pay attention." But the inability to pay attention is no laughing matter. A frontal lobe condition that has become recognized as a clinical problem is called *attention deficit disorder* (ADD).[17] According to Daniel G. Amen, M.D.'s substantial research into the six types of ADD, ADD occurs when the prefrontal cortex does not function properly when a person is trying to concentrate and focus. Most studies have shown that the causes of ADD are primarily genetic. Other cases are the result of head injuries involving direct impact to the skull. Some people who suffer from ADD are ex-drug and alcohol abusers, while others are the children of alcoholics. In addition to the medical component, some experts also state that ADD is caused from a lack of the proper social structuring during childhood development.

ADD is a real clinical problem. The latest brain imaging techniques show how sufferers struggle severely when they initiate concentration. Instead of frontal lobe activity increasing with concentration on something new, ADD has just the opposite effects. Clinical tests conducted on people with ADD show that, when they concentrate, there is a decreased amount of cerebral blood flow to the frontal lobes. Brain imaging studies have clearly shown that the harder ADD sufferers try to focus, the worse the blood flow to the prefrontal cortex gets, until it ultimately shuts off.

Many of the symptoms of ADD are almost the same as in individuals with frontal lobe damage from surgery or injury: short attention span, difficulty learning from experiences, poor organizational skills, a tendency to be easily distracted, low level of planning skills, an inability to focus on tasks and finish them, lack of control over actions, and a tendency to be so fixed in their opinions and actions that they will not compromise their behaviors, even if they know that those behaviors do not serve them.

People with ADD appear normal because they can function within routine tasks that are already wired in the rest of the cortex. When it comes to matching their internal representations with their behavior, focusing on novel tasks, or organizing their lives, it is apparent that ADD sufferers experience serious problems. For example, almost half of hyperactive boys with untreated ADD will be arrested for a felony criminal offense. Half of all prison inmates have ADD. A little over a third of ADD individuals never finish high school. A little more than half abuse alcohol and drugs And parents of ADD children get divorced at a rate three times greater than seen in non-ADD families.

Through the latest functional brain scan technology, dedicated researchers and a few committed doctors have found that when the frontal lobe malfunctions, several different types of ADD can manifest. If the brain's conductor is compromised, it can't orchestrate the entire brain in harmony. As a result, the different centers in the brain become over- or underactive. Remember, the frontal lobe has connections to all other parts of the brain. So if the frontal lobe isn't working properly, researchers can see how other areas are influenced. This creates different types of ADD, and according to Dr. Amen, clinical neuroscientist and acclaimed author of several books on ADD, anxiety, depression, and brain imaging, ADD symptoms are now being correlated with different brain imaging patterns.

For example, a specific type of ADD called *attention deficit hyperactivity disorder* (ADHD) affects thousands of people in the United States. Its most common traits include the inability to control their actions and to maintain proper behavior in social settings. ADHD sufferers tend to act out of control in classroom situations, defy rules at home, and even take certain liberties without asking for permission. Given our present understanding of the frontal lobe, it is quite easy to see that children or adults with ADHD cannot restrain themselves from taking action in response to their impulsive thoughts. They are frequently in trouble, and the emotional high they receive from stressful circumstances is enough to increase their awareness with a nice cocktail of adrenalin. The rush of adrenalin is exactly what heightens their awareness, and thus wakes their brains up for few moments. Once they receive a fix and it wears off, they will invariably be in trouble because they need a greater stimulus, giving them a bigger rush and a bigger high. The blessing is that the treatments being administered using different medications are now being matched to these individual brain patterns. There is hope. In recent years, we've seen amazing advances in the diagnosis and treatment of ADD.

The Frontal Lobe and Free Will

One of the human attributes that most separates us from other species is our free will—our ability to determine a course of action free of the constraints imposed on animals by their biologically driven impulses. The debate surrounding just how truly free we are is beyond the scope of this chapter, but the relationship between the frontal lobe and our freewilled choices is an intimate one. The frontal lobe allows us to make conscious choices, not based on memory but based on the ability to choose what we want to choose.

If we make choices based on memory, we aren't employing the frontal lobe to a great degree. But when we have to think and make choices that are outside of our memory (the "box" of what we know), the frontal lobe is in its heightened state. Researchers have conducted experiments showing that the frontal lobe is most active during a freewilled kind of decision-making. The choices these subjects made do not involve clear right or wrong answers, but rather, ambiguous situations in which the choice is made based on what the subjects would enjoy the most.[18]

Elkhonon Goldberg, Ph.D., a professor at the New York School of Medicine, has shown in some of his experiments that the frontal lobes are critical in freewilled decision-making. He took a group of subjects and showed them a geometric symbol, then he asked them to choose one of two options in the form of additional pictorial designs. The subjects were clearly told that no answer was either right or wrong. Their choices and their responses were just a matter of personal preference. They were encouraged to pick and choose as they pleased. They were also informed that they would go through numerous trials, and that no two trials would be exactly the same.

Here is where it got interesting. Goldberg used two types of people in the experiments. One group consisted of healthy individuals with no neurological history of disease, and the second group consisted of patients with various types of brain damage. What he found was that people who had damage to the frontal lobes experienced dramatic difficulty in formulating their responses, while people with damage to other areas of the brain experienced little or no impairment of their freewilled decisions. In other words, the people who were frontal lobe impaired had difficulty in freely choosing whatever they liked. The patients with other injured brain areas, as well as the normal subjects, had no difficulty in completing the exercise.

Dr. Goldberg then further advanced the test. He told the patients with the frontal lobe lesions to make the choice "most similar to the target," and then he told them to make a choice "most different from the target." He did the same with those with healthy brains and used them as the control group. This was a simple test in familiarity (knowns). Under these test conditions, with no ambiguous choices to make, the patients with frontal lobe lesions performed the tasks as well as the control group.

This experiment yielded two distinct conclusions. The frontal lobes are eminent in freewilled decision-making situations, especially when it is up to the individual to decide how to interpret situations in which there is more than one definitive outcome. Second, the frontal lobes are no longer critical when situations are reduced to the simple act of a correct response or an incorrect response. Perhaps making the "right" decision, then, may not require thinking as highly evolved as making a freewilled decision.

The study also revealed that when we make decisions based on what we already know and have wired in the neocortex (those familiar neural networks), not only do we no longer activate the frontal lobe, but we also demonstrate no free will. In other words, when we do not have the frontal lobe turned on, we think we are choosing freely, but in fact, we are choosing based on limited choices of familiar data. Instead, we rely on the memory-based existing machinery to become activated, based on our ability to choose what we already know instead of what new information we can potentially learn from the frontal lobe. It takes very little brain activity in the frontal lobe to choose a familiar, routine, common, known situation. So although we think that we are making a choice based on free will, maybe we are just choosing what we already know, and that is not really a freewilled choice at all. Instead, it is just pattern recognition. It is a response and a reaction, not free will.

How often do we do that in our daily reality? Are the right or wrong, good or bad, Republican or Democrat, success or failure choices we make forcing us to behave as though we have a frontal lobe lesion? For example, when we recognize familiar situations in our life, do those known situations turn on the existing associated neural networks, which then cause us to think and behave in ways equal to how we are wired? And does that mean we haven't freely made a choice? Have we instead initiated a response that is connected to an automatic program, which begins to process information in our brain in an unconscious, automatic manner?

If so, perhaps advertising is just a way of repetitively encoding the memory of a product into our brain so permanently that when a situation arises in which we need to take action, we remember the most immediate neurological pattern that meets our need. In that case, no free will is involved. Instead, we're simply responding to a stimulus from a limited assortment of preprogrammed patterns. It takes effort to think and to contemplate new possibilities that exist beyond right and wrong and beyond known choices, and that means we have to interrupt the programs that are hardwired in our brain.

When the frontal lobe is not activated, we can respond only to what we know and what is already stored in our brain, and we will always choose what we know. We think we are choosing, but actually, we are just using automatic response mechanisms designed for immediate relief and gratification. In that case, then, our emotional responses—the ones that are so repetitive, routine, and predictable; the ones we can say we are addicted to—are a product of the numbing inaction of the frontal lobe. If the frontal lobe is asleep, so are we.

The Frontal Lobe and Learning

We should think twice about the current means of testing in contemporary educational systems. So many times, students memorize material so that they can give the right answer, and when they take a test, all they have to do is regurgitate that information. Students had to use the frontal lobe to study and memorize the material originally. But choosing the correct answer on a test requires very little use of the frontal lobe.

Other types of learning evaluations, like essay questions, require a lot more of the frontal lobe (and, therefore, of the student). When students are asked open-ended questions, they have to formulate answers based on what they learned. This approach requires taking all that information originally learned, thinking about possibilities and potentials, and reformulating the material into a greater understanding. At this point, students are using the frontal lobe to its greatest degree. Utilizing the Socratic method and its reliance on questions takes us outside the known and challenges our assumptions—an excellent way to avoid the rote recitation that characterizes too much of our educational system and is sorely underutilizing the frontal lobe.

The Frontal Lobe and Evolution

Imagine we are working at a new job, and we are carrying items into a basement storage area. The first time we go down the stairs, we hit our head on a low beam. We experience immediate pain. As we exit the basement, we look up at the beam in frustration and notice how low it really is. Upstairs, we pick up more objects to carry into the basement. As we begin our descent, we start talking to a coworker about last night's football game. Forgetting about the low threshold, we smack our head a second time. We feel even more pain in the same place as our previous injury. This time, we stop, make a mental note about that beam, listen to our internal dialogue telling us to pay attention the next time, and direct our frontal lobe to become more present and aware of what we are doing. The third time we descend the stairs, our brain's CEO will remind us to duck.

By giving us the ability to learn from our mistakes, the frontal lobe has been crucial to our survival and evolution as a species. When activated, it frees us from repetitive or routine results, granting us heightened awareness so that we may experience a different outcome.

If a species is subject to repetitive external environmental stimuli over the course of several generations, in time that species will adapt to those stimuli. The genetics of that species will change to support a new internal state, one that will help the species survive that external stimuli for generations to come. This is called *survival of the species*. It is a linear, slow process for most species.

The human frontal lobe allows us to transcend the slow, linear process of evolution and advance beyond the natural progression of adaptation used by most species. It affords us the ability to learn and adapt in such a nonlinear pattern that we can make immediate changes by our thoughts and actions. Our memories thus serve as a foundation so that we can do a better job in similar circumstances. This nonlinear evolution allows us to modify our behavior and create a completely new range of experiences in just one lifetime.

The Frontal Lobe: On or Off?

The following is a simplified list of what we can do or be when our frontal lobe is activated.

- Intentional awareness and long attention span
- Contemplation of possibilities, acting on them
- Decisiveness
- Clarity

- Joy

- Usable skills

- Adaptability

- Ability to learn from mistakes and do things differently the next time

- Ability to plan a future and stick to projected plan

- Focus

- Daily review of options

- Strengthened sense of self

- Ability to take action toward goals

- Disciplined behavior

- Ability to build greater options from prior experiences

- Ability to hold an ideal independent of external circumstances

- Ability to make dreams, goals, and intents more real than external world and feedback of body

- Concentration to the exclusion of everything else

- Ability to stay present with the self and internal thoughts

- Proactiveness

- Individuality

Now, here's a list of what we can do or be when our frontal lobe is *not* functioning fully.

- Listless and lazy

- Uninspired and unmotivated, with no initiative

- Desirous of sameness, routine, and predictability

- Unwilling to learn

- Able to be easily distracted

- Unable to make future plans

- Behaving in ways that never match desires
- Unable to complete actions and tasks
- Reactive
- Mentally rigid, disliking change
- Fixated on the same negative thoughts
- Unable to listen well
- Disorganized
- Impulsive
- Overly emotional
- Forgetful
- Unable to see options
- Follower

At various times, we almost certainly possess attributes from both lists. However, we have probably labored too long under the assumption that the negative traits listed are beyond our control. Too often, if we have the power of self-reflection to recognize ourselves at all, we say, "I am disorganized," or "I am impulsive," or "I am lazy." The choice to use a form of the verb "to be" says a lot about what we believe regarding our ability to change. To say, "I am" is a shorthand way of saying, "My state of being is, was, and will always be." We now know that we do have control of our mind and how it works.

For too long, we have labored under the assumption that we have made freewilled decisions about our identity and our future. Now, I hope I have made my case that, most of the time, we aren't exercising our free will at all. We have simply been selecting from a prescripted menu of choices based on our past. We haven't yet begun to utilize our free will, and we haven't taken full advantage of the gift that is our frontal lobe.

Let's look next at how it is possible to begin to utilize, to a greater degree than anyone ever thought possible, the full capability of our mind to create the life we choose.

CHAPTER ELEVEN

THE ART AND SCIENCE OF MENTAL REHEARSAL

There is only one admirable form
of the imagination: the imagination that is
so intense that it creates a new reality,
that it makes things happen.

—SEAN O'FAOLAIN

A friend of mine recently called me from the road. He was on his way back to the Pacific Northwest after a trip to upstate New York, where he went to visit his family. John is single, the youngest of six children, and is a professor of philosophy at a nearby state university. To put it simply, he lives a life of the mind. He doesn't own a television, listens only to National Public Radio, and spends most of his time reading or hiking with friends. Visiting his home is like going to a retreat center; his nearest neighbor is more than a quarter of a mile away. He has kept it sparsely but comfortably furnished, and while I sometimes find it disconcerting that he has no clocks in the house, in time I get used to the rhythms of the day.

When John called, I could hear agitation in his voice, a change from his usually placid tone. Just before leaving on this planned trip, he had heard from a professional journal that had accepted one of his articles for publication. He only had ten days to do the required revisions. He couldn't change his travel plans so late in the game, so he had decided to do the revision work while visiting family, and send the manuscript to me for my opinion before sending it back to the publisher. An ambitious plan, but John is one of those people whose intentions usually match his actions. Now he was calling to tell me that he wasn't going to have the article to me on the date he'd specified. At first he was vague about how "other things had intruded" on his time.

I could guess at what those intrusions might be. From previous conversations, I know that John is about as different from the rest of the family as is possible. Each of his five siblings is as hyperkinetic as he is contemplative, and is as prone to emotional outbursts and dramatics as he is stable and even (and they all have children). On the phone, he described trying to organize any outing— even one as simple as getting everyone together for a meal—as being "as difficult as herding cats." Trying to coordinate all the kids' schedules (this was at the height of soccer and T-ball season), and dietary preferences (from vegan to voraciously and insistently carnivorous) was difficult enough. Trying to deal with the varied emotional states of 26 other humans (including his parents) had proved to be nearly impossible—but not entirely so.

After four days of a scheduled six-day visit, however, he was heading to the airport for a flight home. He had had enough of the incessant noise, the conversations that required a pickaxe to wedge a word in, and the constant attention the children demanded. He told me that he once considered himself capable of being the calm at the center of any storm, but, wind-whipped and sodden, he had retreated below decks on this trip. Originally, one of his sisters had volunteered to drive him the two hours to the airport, but he declined her offer. Driving the freshly secured rental car would be just the buffer he needed to decompress; otherwise, he was certain I would have seen him on the local news being led off his flight for threatening to jump out one of the cabin doors.

We both laughed, knowing that he really wasn't capable of such a thing. I also smiled when he told me that what he'd been working on for the last two months, with my help, had made it possible for him to survive the visit with his family, at least briefly.

John had been intrigued about my background. He'd never been much of an athlete himself, but he was fascinated by the mental discipline of judo, karate, and the rest. He joked that he wanted to become not a ninja warrior, but a ninja writer. So I had told him about the approach I'd taken years earlier, when I was about to go for my black belt. I was going to have to spar with other members of my class—sometimes two or even three at a time.

While I was able to work in some actual training sessions with those classmates, I had also spent as much time as possible sitting on my couch, sparring with them in my head. I had worked with all of these people before, and knew their tendencies and their strengths and weaknesses, so I knew a good bit about what to expect from them. To prepare for the black belt examination, I mentally went over and over my own approach to sparring with each of them—I could see my blocks and kicks, and the sequences and combinations that I, and they, would use. In my mind, I also practiced all my forms and techniques, making sure that my fundamentals were precise and flawless. As these mind sessions progressed, I would lose track of time and space, and it was as if I were at the gym actually working out, and not at home. When I came out of the sessions, I felt prepared and also noticed, with some curiosity, that although I felt I had just sat down, more than an hour had passed.

John had been eager to learn how to achieve a similar state of mind with his writing, and had practiced this skill during the two months prior to his trip. He took his work with him as planned, and he told me that for an hour or two every day, he managed to get some revisions done. At first, the cacophony and chaos his siblings and their children created swirled around him in a cloud of commotion. I visualized him sitting in a chair as each of his nieces and nephews vied for his attention. His failed attempts to organize and structure the day lay scattered about, trampled beneath their overenthusiastic disorderliness. However, in a few early morning sessions, and even for a short time after the youngest children and their bleary-eyed parents rolled out of bed to pour cold cereal in their progeny's bowls, John carved out the time to get some work done.

His parents still live in the same house where he grew up. An enormous, sprawling Victorian, its most prominent feature was a wraparound porch that was screened to make it a three-season structure. He said he felt as he had as a child when, to find a quiet moment, he would climb a cottonwood tree on the far edge of their property. There he would read for hours, or stare up through the lake of leaves as the cloud formations drifted past. He'd stay there until dinnertime when, his absence finally detected, his parents would send out a search party to find him.

Prompted by childhood memories, John went out onto the porch shortly before dawn every morning, before anyone else got up. Instead of sitting in the main portion of the porch, he chose an area farthest from the kitchen, a kind of cubby space where he pulled a wicker chair and sat.

During those early morning work sessions, his family and all their distractions were as silent and invisible to him as he was to them. He told me how surprised he was that by the time he was discovered and reeled back into the madness, three hours had passed. After the early-morning riot of bird calls emanating from the nearby woods had subsided, John hadn't heard the sound of pancake batter being beaten, Elmo laughing, and Thomas the Tank Engine huffing and puffing. All the sights and sounds of the busy household faded away, and all that existed for him was the bluish glow of his laptop's screen.

John told me that those moments felt like gifts or grace, but he wasn't able, during the remainder of each day, to sustain them or the feeling of calm they engendered. I told John that I was impressed that he managed to get those hours in at all. He said that the house they all grew up in had seemed to cast a spell, so that his siblings had reverted to their adolescent selves. When he felt himself drawn into the bickering and pettiness, and his morning hours of solace had dwindled, he knew it was time to leave.

I see in John's experiences another metaphor for how our brain and body work together—and sometimes how they also seem very much at odds with one another. As we've learned, when it comes to emotional addictions (see chapter 9), the body communicates with the brain in ways that are sometimes unhealthy. At times, so many parts of our body are clamoring for our attention that it's a wonder we are able to function at all. We receive so much input from our environment and from our internal state that we are awash in a sea of inputs and stimuli, all competing for our attention, and with very little cooperation going on.

Fortunately for us, as we now know, we can also find a state of grace amidst the tumult of our environment. What John experienced in those moments on the porch, and how he interrupted the chaos, is a lesson in how we can quell the emotional turmoil that we all too frequently experience. If John were to examine more closely what he did, in finding a calming haven where he could work and in losing track of both time and space, he would discover that the keys to breaking emotional addictions and the habitual routines of our daily lives are based on memories of the past. He would better understand how we all possess the ability to alter ourselves, change our behaviors, undo the effects of certain traits, and break the links that chain us to our inherited propensities.

The amazing thing is that, like John, we all possess the skill to tune out our environment. How many times have we sat and watched television while someone was talking to us, and we weren't even aware of his or her presence, let alone their running commentary or questions? How about when our spouse is pointedly lecturing us about some moral issue regarding our behavior? Do we not sometimes lower the volume to the lecture and tune out everything on which our spouse is pontificating?

When we want to be, we are masters of selective hearing and selective action-taking. What if we put those skills to better use? And if we already have an unrefined and untapped ability to focus and concentrate, what would happen if we really tried to master those skills? More important to our understanding at this point, how is it that, as unpracticed and unskilled as we are now, we can even perform this "blocking out" at all?

Perhaps John's experiences prior to the trip can provide some answers. He had already taken additional steps beyond using his frontal lobe to turn down the volume on the other centers of the brain. When he is writing, John has learned to quiet his sensory cortex, still his motor cortex, calm the brain's emotional centers, and move into a trance-like state. Since I also write, I'm interested in the process other writers go through to get themselves into the zone of concentration necessary to do their work.

For example, I knew that John had what he called his "mystical moments" when he sat down to create. The first thing he did was to turn on some music. Not just any music—he found that if the music included lyrics, he had a harder time concentrating. For that reason, he always chose instrumental music— everything from classical to movie scores to New Age. Jazz he found to be too "busy." When he was working on first drafts and didn't need to consult notes, he would use candles for softer illumination. The combination of music and atmosphere helped him to find a calm center—and he always did his initial drafting late at night when, as he put it, "The rest of the brain was pretty tired and easier to put to bed."

John arrived at this strategy without knowing about the frontal lobe and its effects and powers. He had intuited the benefits of focused concentration and devised his own way of getting to that calmed state. In the last few months, he and I had talked more explicitly about the frontal lobe and its role in concentration and focus. John had a very specific purpose in mind for using this information: he wanted to write better and more easily get into the writing mode. He'd suffered from writer's block after completing his thesis, and he was determined never to go through that experience again. He began to pay attention to his environment and state of mind on good days, when the creative process seemed as easy as sailing downwind on a sunny day, as well as what was going on during those days when he felt like he was sailing into a strong headwind with waves breaking over the bow. Eventually, he arrived at some conclusions about what worked and what didn't work. Over time, he refined the process and repeated it so many times that even without the music and the lighting and late-night time of day, he was able to get into the flow of his work, seemingly on command.

In his phone call to me, John lamented that he wasn't able to reproduce these results outside the "lab" of his home. When he went to his parents' house, it seemed to him that everything had fallen apart. I reassured him that his process was a good one, and that he should think about the times that it had worked during the trip, and consider those a major success—something to be learned from. When he got back home and was freer from distractions, he could look more objectively at those good days and bad days (in terms of his writing), and come to some solid conclusions about what made them more or less productive. The key thing was to begin at the beginning—with the skill of observation.

Mastering the Skills of Observation

Although it has become a cliché, it remains true that the first step in healing ourselves is recognizing that we have a problem. So how do we know when we have a problem? Recognition depends on our ability to observe ourselves—that is, to become self-aware. What I had asked John to do was to become self-aware about a very particular part of his behavior and personality, and decipher what had affected his ability to be creative under different circumstances.

Most people lack John's highly developed self-awareness, and also lack the patience necessary to slow ourselves down and really examine or analyze our life and personality. However, just because those qualities aren't fully present in our life doesn't mean we don't possess the skills and can't refine them. We simply need to turn down the volume of noise that interferes with our ability to focus our concentration. We can observe ourselves in general to consider any specific skill or attribute, or we can look at ourselves more globally. What proves that we have the ability to observe our own behavior critically is how often we use these skills in looking at other people and their behavior.

I'm sure we've all been in countless situations when we've wondered about someone else's inability to see themselves clearly. We've speculated whether a person knows what she looks like in a particular outfit; we've witnessed a volcano of an emotional reaction to a seemingly trivial incident. At these times, we've likely asked ourselves, Can this person see what he or she is like? The answer is that many people cannot. They lack the skill to not only observe the larger world around them, but also assess themselves clearly. They haven't taken the time to self-reflect, or they have failed to develop an awareness of how they behave in certain situations. They haven't even considered the more important questions: Why is it that I keep producing the same self-destructive feelings? Why is that I keep expecting that my behavior and comments will elicit one response, yet in return,

I get the complete opposite of what I expect? If we don't ask ourselves these cru-cial questions about our very nature, we can't see who we truly are.

If we activate our frontal lobe, however, we'll be able to see ourselves with astounding clarity. Because we're so focused on the externals, all we have to do, like a motion picture camera panning a scene, is to be more selective about what we want to have in the frame. To overcome the propensity to be outwardly focused and run by our environment, and/or to be a slave to our body and its emotional responses, we need to become a better observer of ourselves. Often, that simply means disengaging from the environment, as John does, and aban-doning all the programs that keep us emotionally addicted to it.

I hope I haven't given the impression that my friend John is some kind of freak. He is far from a hermit. He has an active social life and sits on committees both at work and in the community. Yes, he doesn't own a television, but only because he has had one in the past and he spent too much time getting sucked into programs. He knew that he was weak, and the only way to avoid having tele-vision be such a "time suck" was to go cold turkey and keep it out of his house entirely. He is, however, predisposed to be contemplative, and that probably sets him apart from many people these days. He fills the hours that he used to spend staring vacantly at the television and numbing himself to the world, by immers-ing himself in the natural world and in interesting books. He has sharpened his skills of observation while hiking, by observing wildlife and cataloging many of the wild flowers and plants that grow in his area. And he has applied those same skills of observation to himself.

In John's desire to improve his efficiency as a writer, he employed some of the techniques a scientist might use in an application of the scientific method. He would alter one part of his writing routine at a time, checking to see whether that variable made a difference in his performance and productivity. He also had to be aware of how his own mind was working. After going through several months of mini-experiments with much trial and error, he figured out what he could do to be a more productive writer. Of course, he was motivated to get better because writing is one of the things that will determine his future career as a professor. It is this notion of desire that we'll turn to next.

Making the Commitment to Change

Because most people are poor observers and don't often see the obvious links between behavior, health, and overall mood, it often takes a major, life-altering event to get our attention focused on ourselves, our predilections, and our propensities. The good news is, the fact that you're reading this book indicates that you have a desire to change. As much as anything else, possessing the proper motivation goes a long way toward enabling us to make changes in our life and in ourselves.

In an ideal world, we would recognize that we are addicted to our emotions long before we had evidence of the harm they are doing to us. As we talked about in chapters 9 and 10, the main way that people become aware of their emotional addiction is through a physical manifestation of the stress reaction on the body. Those backaches that flare up every time we have an important deadline, or the cold we get after burning the midnight oil for weeks on end to complete a project, are a result of stress. When we find ourselves short-tempered and exploding at the slightest provocation, that's also a function of increased stress and decreased frontal lobe activity. And so are many other more serious and consequential disorders and diseases.

Please take another look at the list in chapter 10 of attributes that healthy frontal lobe activity promotes.

We can see how important the frontal lobe is in initiating and governing change. And, although the frontal lobe helps us focus on an intention, we still need to activate our will in order to let the frontal lobe do its thing—that is, unite intent with action. Commitment to change is always a tricky thing. Those regular, routine, hardwired neural networks that we've created allow us to live a life that is easy, natural, and comfortable. We seek comfort, but change equals discomfort. We make a vow to begin a diet, start an exercise routine, cut down on the amount of television we watch, spend more time and lavish more attention on our kids, only to have all of the circumstances in our life trample that intention.

To change takes a great deal of effort, will, and commitment. I can remember when I first started to do triathlons. Running and cycling were fairly easy, natural, and routine—I'd done them for so long that I never had to think about what I was doing. I had also learned to swim as a child and had been doing that for years, and I didn't need to think too much about what I was doing in the water. I just did it. After the first triathlon I competed in, I realized that I could swim, but I couldn't really *swim!* I got my butt kicked in the swimming leg.

So I searched around and found a coach who taught swimming—not in the sense of learning to not drown, but someone who could break down my stroke, and build me back up with improved technique. I was stunned in the first class to learn that I had not been taught to swim the most efficient way, or in a way that would allow me to go the fastest. I'd been taught the most expedient method that would keep me afloat and help me survive. Sound familiar? Most of us have learned to survive—in fact, that's what we do most of the time in our life. We get by.

Because I was a competitive person, however, I wanted to do more than just get by. I wanted to go faster. So I sought out someone with greater knowledge and experience than mine who could teach me. It was an enlightening experience on many levels. I had to unlearn the stroke technique I'd been using for many years and learn a completely different way to use my arms and legs. I grew frustrated when I felt like I was going slower—because I now had to think so much about what I was doing—but over time, the new method began to feel more natural. When I was timed in a 100-meter swim and saw the improvement in my performance, I was even more willing to put up with the discomfort.

I didn't need to nearly drown to motivate me to improve. I found a reason to make a change. I wasn't satisfied with the status quo; I wasn't satisfied with finishing in the pack; I wasn't satisfied with just getting by. In addition, only when I gained some new knowledge and had to wire a new neural network labeled "swimming" was I able to be a better observer of my technique. I was eventually able to self-correct.

We'll return to these ideas in chapter 12, but for now, keep in mind the importance of finding motivation. Once we do, we will be amazed at how our powers of observation will also improve—we'll no longer be satisfied with getting along in any part of our life. We'll find that discomfort no longer acts as a deterrent—it will motivate us to move out of that mode and into a new and improved comfort zone.

The question remains, what can we do to put the frontal lobe to best use? There is an old joke that goes something like this: A man is walking along a crowded New York City street. He asks a passerby, "Excuse me, can you tell me the best way to get to Carnegie Hall?" Without bothering to turn around, the man questioned responds, "Practice!"

Mental Rehearsal: Magical Thinking and Getting Wired

I use the term *mental rehearsal* to describe how we can best employ our frontal lobe and take advantage of its advanced faculties to make significant changes in our life. When we rehearse, we have a more focused and purposeful intent. We don't simply run through a routine set of exercises; we perform as if the occasion were a concert. That's the key difference in the mind. A rehearsal is supposed to replicate the experience of the actual doing of the thing. In this case, mentally rehearsing and the actual doing are *one and the same*. Each time we initiate some action, engage in a behavior, perform a skill, express an emotion, or make a change in our attitude, we should get better. That's why we rehearse— so that we can get better and so that the next time we perform that experience, it becomes easier for us to do it.

Simply put, I define mental rehearsal in this way: remembering what we want to demonstrate, and then cognitively experiencing what it is like to physically do the action step by step. It is mentally seeing our "self" physically demonstrating or practicing an action or skill. In terms of personal change, mental rehearsal is conceiving ourselves in a situation and behaving differently (or simply being a different person) from how we acted (or who we were) previously. Instead of living in survival and being angry, depressed, a victim, a victimizer, in ill health, or any of those limited things that we allow our emotional addictions to impose on us, we can rehearse, from a purely cognitive standpoint, being healthy, calm, compassionate, or any of the other more positive things we've wanted to be.

One of the many interesting things about the process of mental rehearsal is that we don't have to involve the body at all, or to a far lesser degree than we'd imagine, and still reap the benefits. If you'll recall the piano-playing experiment in chapter 2, we learned that people who physically touched the keys to produce the sounds of the musical scale developed their proficiency (that is, they had the same amount of neural circuits as measured by a brain scan) only to the *same* degree as those who simply practiced the skill mentally. Remember, the one group had a piano keyboard in front of them and spent two hours a day for five days practicing scales. The other group watched and memorized the practice technique and then devoted the same amount of time, only those in that group didn't have the keyboard in front of them—they just had it in their mind. They changed the physical composition of their brain just by activating their frontal lobe, to make that mental rehearsal so real that the brain actually perceived it as a three-dimensional reality. The brain didn't care whether the keys were physically there or not; it wired those circuits regardless. The thoughts of the people in the mental rehearsal group became that real. With mental rehearsal, if we can stay focused, the brain does not know the difference between physically doing the activity and remembering the activity.

The idea that we can change our brain just by thinking has enormous implications for affecting any kind of change in our life. Mental rehearsal gives us the ability to create a new level of mind without doing anything physical other than thinking.

Interestingly, as noted in chapter 10, we are already fairly skilled at tuning out the other signals in our environment. When we want to, we can use our selective hearing to hear only what we want to hear. (All we have to do to find out how proficient we are at this skill is ask our spouse, a family member, or our significant other.) We literally disassociate by moving our attention away from our external world. Clearly, what those mental piano players were able to do is direct a great deal of attention on the project at hand and block out the extraneous thoughts that characterize much of our mental activity.

That initial quieting of the other centers of the brain and focusing on a skill at hand are the first steps to ending our pattern of thinking via familiar feelings and a reliance on emotional states. The frontal lobe is quite proficient at that task when we direct it to do so.

The next steps are equally easy: We have to create an ideal in our head of what we want to rehearse. We have to ask the right kind of self-reflective questions. Who do I want to be? What do I have to change about myself to get there? Whom do I know or what resources can I find to help me develop this working model in my mind?

What is also interesting is what happens when the conductor steps to the podium and directs all the instruments to fall silent. When the frontal lobe asks for quiet, it not only gets those centers quiet, it is as if our consciousness completely vacates those other circuits. To extend this metaphor, the horn section, the woodwinds, and whatever other instruments the frontal lobe requires stay on the stage, and all the others retreat to the wings. Powerful changes take place in brain activity and in our perceptions when we lock in our focused concentration. We lose track of time and space. Most significantly, our body grows quiet, and we enter a trance-like state. During those moments when we are truly quiet, we can learn and change how the brain regularly works, and therefore change our mind.

Before we get to the learning process, let's talk a bit more about how we can use mental rehearsal to our fullest advantage.

A Matter of Choosing

When we are not using the frontal lobe at its functional capacity, and especially when we are not using it at all, survival-oriented questions inundate us. When am I going to eat? How soon before I can go to bed? Why are my lips so dry? When did I last drink something? What do I look like and am I accepted by this person?

To answer those kinds of questions, as well as to pose them, requires very little of the frontal lobe. However, one of the great things about the frontal lobe is that it can act like a mental bouncer. Like a bouncer in a bar, the frontal lobe can clear the room for us, so that even if we were once at a noisy, smoky mental lounge, we can focus on more of the "what if," open-ended, speculative type of questions that are a function of our higher processing powers. These are the kinds of questions that we are able to ask ourselves when the other brain centers have fallen silent. These higher-order questions have to do with our future or potential self. How can I become better? How can I modify my behavior? How can I reinvent myself? What would my life be like if I (fill in the blank)? What do I have to change about myself to achieve this particular outcome? How can I be different from how I am now? What is the highest ideal of myself I can imagine? What do I really want?

The frontal lobe is where our imagination and ability to invent are located. It allows us to take what we already have experienced and know, and employ all those old circuits of memory as building blocks to speculate about new outcomes. The frontal lobe is also able to silence that inner critic that is intent on reminding us of our past failures—it can tune out what hasn't worked in the past and give us the blank slate we need to produce a new level of mind. And if we can repeat this process of blocking out the old and focusing on the new, and do that time and time again—like the mentally rehearsing piano players did a couple of hours a day—we will get so good at it that we will be able to produce that new level of mind whenever we want to. Remember, when we are mentally rehearsing, those circuits are being fired, and as the Law of Repetition and Hebbian learning tell us, nerve cells that fire together, wire together. Once they are wired together as a new set of circuits and are activated, we are producing mind. We know that, given the immense amount of synaptic connections we can fabricate, we have infinite levels of mind that the brain can produce on command.

A friend of mine who played college baseball shared this story with me. He was a pitcher, and his pitching coach in college had played in the minor leagues. This coach told him the story of how a particular team had "owned" him. Every time the coach pitched against that team, the players lit him up—home runs, doubles, singles, solid line drives, and mammoth fly balls over the fence. Against every other team, he didn't struggle like that. He pitched the same way against his nemesis as he did the others, so why such drastically different results? After three or four starts against this team, he was fed up and figured he had to do something different.

Like most pitchers, he kept a log of what the opposing hitters did against him—what pitch and in what location got hit and what the result was. The night before he next started against this team, the future pitching coach sat down in his hotel room, took out that book, and crafted a plan of attack that he would use on all the hitters. He knew their weaknesses, strengths, and tendencies. He sat with his notebook and wrote down, pitch by pitch, how he was going to approach that next game. He wasn't going to vary from that list of pitches no matter what happened. He sat there for hours memorizing the sequence of pitches he was going to throw. Then, he closed his eyes and mentally pitched that game. Slider on the inside corner and low. Fastball up and away. Change up down and away. Fastball on the hands resulting in a weak ground ball to the first baseman. He did that for all 27 outs. Then he ran through it again and again. As he sat in his hotel room that night, mentally pitching the game, time and space faded away.

The next day, he stuck to his game plan. Of course, he couldn't produce the exact results that he had in his mentally rehearsed game, but he did pitch a four-hit shutout—the best results he ever had against that team. He started to use that approach against every other team, and he started to win more and more. He had to be an astute observer of the other players' tendencies, and that certainly helped him, but more than that, it was his ability to focus that made such a big difference. Once he was in a game, he also found it easier to concentrate; after all, he'd already been through this game and had succeeded in his head; now all he had to do was reproduce the same results. In fact, his brain and mind were now ahead of the actual experience. By mentally rehearsing all his future actions, he was essentially warming up the associated neural circuits before every game, and as a result, he was already in a winning frame of mind. Now imagine what kind of difference we could make in our life if we practiced joy instead of pitching.

A Brief Interruption . . . For Now

One of the added benefits of employing the frontal lobe to quiet the other centers in the brain and focus on mental rehearsing is that we interrupt the programs that are routinely running all the time. We shut them down cold. When meditators are fully focused on an idea, the other parts of the brain receive no blood flow; no blood flow means no activity in that area. No activity on a neuro-logical level means the mind that is usually produced is now turned off. Just as when we lean on our hand in the grass for too long and the blood flow gets inter-rupted briefly and our hand goes numb, the same thing happens in the brain.

If we were to cut off the blood supply to an area of the body for a prolonged period of time, that body part would die. That doesn't literally happen in the brain. Instead, when we repeatedly interrupt the blood flow—when the electri-cal activity in that portion of the brain, or more specifically in that neural net-work, ceases—the neurons no longer fire. To examine Hebb's law again, it is also true that when *neurons no longer fire together, they no longer wire together*. That means if we slow ourselves down, get our mind focused on specifics of who and how we want to be, and start to put a mental image of that new person in the sights of the frontal lobe (or mentally practice a new act of any nature), by our cognitive effort, we get a double bonus. Not only are we able to wire new circuits, but also prune the previously hardwired connections.

Do you recall the Braille readers we mentioned whose functional brain scans revealed a remarkable adaptability? These people had lost their sight and learned to read through touch. What is important to remember is that the cen-ters normally used for seeing in a sighted person are converted to touch circuits in the nonsighted person. Eventually, many of those old circuits the person once employed to see became severed. The neural growth factor that bound them together was then used to cement the bonds of the newly developed circuits. This demonstrates an important corollary to the fire-together, wire-together mantra. When we interrupt certain thought processes repeatedly, nerve cells that no longer fire together will no longer wire together.

The good news is that those nerve cells don't want to remain inactive. Instead, they seek out new connections and they use recycled neural growth fac-tor to attach themselves to new neurons. It's a shuffle. Neural growth factor is exchanged from one set of old circuits to a set of new circuits. We can take those old patterns and the sequences we routinely fired and reuse the neural growth factor in forming new and improved patterns and sequences, bonding the synaptic connections to cement the new connections we are forming.

For example, let's imagine we've decided to mentally rehearse patience with our children. After we ask the big questions—the "what if" types—our mind will begin to formulate a model of who we want to become. Through mental rehearsal, attention, and repetition, and by firing new neural networks in new patterns, we cause communities of neurons to wire together in new combinations to create a new level of mind called patience. As the nerve cells gang up and wire together, those old circuits, which formerly wired us to lash out verbally at the slightest provocation, stop firing together and will unwire over time because we won't be using those circuits any longer. Our brain uses the same materials, through repetition, association, and mentally rehearsing our new responses to familiar situations, to wire new circuits of patience in place of the old circuits of petulance. We lose our old mind of impatience and make a new one of patience. One neural network is replaced by a new one. The astounding fact is that the brain will accommodate our free will by erasing the old synaptic footprints and making new ones. This is the true biology of change.

Here's how that works. For three weeks, for an hour a day, we seek out a quiet place each morning after the kids have gone off to school. Once we settle into a chair, after turning off the ringer on the phone, we mentally rehearse what this new, patient person will be like. We take some of the articles we've read in *Parenting* magazine about a modified count-to-ten mentality (our semantic memories), recall our mother's unflappable demeanor and how she responded to our acting out (our episodic memories), add other examples and bits of information, both old and new, and create a new model of patience.

Essentially, we combine our philosophical semantic knowledge with experiences that are already wired in our brain, and merge them in a new way to create a new possibility. We intentionally run scenarios through our head, with the help of our frontal lobe, learning to block out the critic (who wants to show us reruns of our most impatient moments) and developing a highly refined and focused portrait of our new, patient self. As we mentally rehearse who we want to become, we are really just remembering the most evolved way to be, based on our learning and our memories. When we assemble new neural nets to fire in different sequences, combinations, and patterns, we make a new level of mind. Remember, the mind is produced when the brain is at work. Our brain is working differently than it had been prior to our rehearsal.

Then by the repetitive firing and wiring of new neural networks in new combinations, we make stronger, more long-lasting synaptic connections that, when fired at will, create the new mind called patience. In fact, we decide that we are not going to get up from each mental workout until we completely attain this state of being. And the mind of patience becomes more natural the more we practice it. A new mind creates a new brain.

We figure out that the previous circuits we employed, in the manic, environmentally driven, chemically addicted state that created our parental flare-ups, were a part of our drama queen persona. They had been fed a steady diet of upset and anger, followed by a dessert of remorse, topped with self-flagellation. After a few weeks of mental rehearsal, these previous circuits have sat idle. They don't like being ignored and they're eager to go to work. They see activity going on in another part of the brain, and they decide to get out of this dead town and move to where things are happening—over on Patience Street. So they disconnect from the other nerve cells in the neural network and join the newly formed neural network of patience. Not wanting to be viewed as party crashers, they come bearing a house-warming gift of neural growth factor. Check out Figure 11.1 to see the shuffle of neural growth factor when a new neural net forms and another is pruned.

We have now been mentally rehearsing over on Patience Street for about three weeks. One day our seven-year-old and six-year-old come home from school. It's raining, and the landscaping work is not complete, and the backyard is a quagmire. We see our two boys in their brand-new sneakers making a bee-line for the swing set, which sits right in the middle of the muddy bog. Instead of dashing out and haranguing them like a mad woman, we gather up the kids' old boots, stick our head out the door, and ask them to meet us in the garage for a quick shoe-change pit stop. The look on their faces tells us that they are either frightened that someone has kidnapped their mother and replaced her with a Stepford wife, or that our mental rehearsal has paid its first dividend.

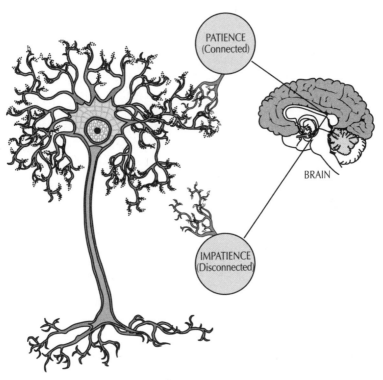

Figure 11.1

The shuffle: neural growth factor is used to bind the new mind of patience as the old mind of impatience is pruned away.

Incidentally, let's fine-tune one part of this process. We've talked about the piano players who mentally rehearsed in chapter 2. There were, however, actually four groups in the experiment. Two of the four groups physically played or mentally rehearsed by receiving specific instructions to play the exact same exercises. But one set of piano players did not receive any instructions; they played randomly for two hours a day for those five days. Because they did not receive any instruction and information, they could not repeat the same mind by firing the same set of circuits every day. Because they could not remember what they did the day before, they were unable to activate the same neural networks. Therefore, we must be precise and consistent in making our brain review the new self we're going to become.

As the neural architecture of our brain changes into more refined, more evolved neural circuits and old patterns are pruned away, we are sending a new signal to the cells of our body. Because all our cells are touched by nervous tissue, as we develop new circuits and break old synaptic connections tied to the old self, the body becomes modified and changed on a cellular level. Therefore, if our cells are spying on our thoughts, then as the gray matter of our cortex changes by even a few circuits from some unwanted emotional neural net, our cells will receive a different neurological signal, and they will begin to modify themselves.

For example, if the neural network of guilt is starting to be pruned away by our replacing an old ideal of self with a new ideal of self, we will be modifying the neurological signal to the cells of our body about being guilty. As we become less mapped for guilt, we are now less likely to wire that signal to the body. The breaking away of those circuits in the brain will then cause the cells to begin to alter their receptor sites for guilt. In other words, if the neural net is gone, the cells will no longer need those receptor sites, and they will regulate into other, more profitable receivers. Equally, as we no longer fire guilt, because the structure of the neural net is falling apart, we will not produce the same peptides that initiate the chemical flux on a cellular level to the body. This is how our body heals from disease when we finally overcome our emotional addictions. We retire unwanted emotions by creating new memories and moving beyond the familiar territory of the mind.

Figure 11.2 illustrates the process of change. As we build new neural networks (patience) and eliminate old ones (impatience), theoretically we send new chemical and neurological information to the cells of the body, which then change their old receptor sites.

Let's take a closer look at how we can combine our powers of concentration and our frontal lobe's love of a mental challenge into a powerful force for change.

Mental Rehearsal and the Art of Contemplation

You may be wondering who has the time to mentally rehearse. Do I really have an hour a day that I can devote to doing nothing but thinking of being someone else? Can I reasonably be expected to sit still that long?

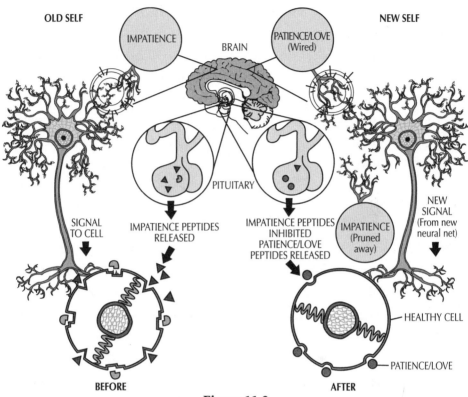

Figure 11.2

The process of change: as we build new neural networks and prune away old ones, we begin to send new neural chemical signals to the cell.

What we may not realize is that, if we mentally rehearse properly, our memory of time and space will be absent, and that hour will seem like five minutes. We can't see where those hours can come from until we are motivated to find them. Frontal lobe activity is all about making decisions and employing our free will to make choices, plan our actions, and develop a sense of our future.

We are asking ourselves to ignore certain feelings of the body and override those inputs and the emotions they produce. Those old hardwired circuits and states of being will always try to talk us out of change—from the lowest level (*Go ahead and eat that bag of chips, we can start the diet tomorrow*) to the highest (*Sure, that person is making ignorant, racist comments, but it's really not my place to say anything about it).* Both of these examples require us to be a bit more courageous, and to move farther out of our comfort zone than we may have been prepared to be in the past. If we like our comfort, we like familiarity. Success may frighten us.

Sitting silently with ourselves may be overwhelming, but is a necessity. I marvel at the number of people who tell me how overtaxed and overstimulated they are, who long for a few moments of peace and quiet. Yet, that peace and quiet they yearn for often ends up being some kind of mindless diversion. What I'm suggesting is that a *mindful conversion* is more what they need—and mental rehearsal is exactly that.

I think most people have in their bag of tools something called a *contemplator*. We may not take it out and use it very often, so it may have grown a bit cloudy from disuse. But it can be cleaned up. The contemplator is much like a magnifying glass. Remember when we were kids and we wanted a magnifying glass, microscope, or telescope? We just had to have some kind of scientific instrument that was going to help us penetrate the mysteries of the universe— or at least set a piece of paper on fire. Kids are naturally curious, and curiosity and contemplation go hand in hand.

If we really want to know about something, we think about it a lot. I don't want to hammer too hard on this point, but something about our education system results in children having their curiosity squelched. I saw this happen to a degree with my own kids. As a parent, it was sometimes frustrating to have to deal with all the "whys," "how comes," "what ifs," and "I wonders" that young-sters naturally come up with. But those questions are crucial to the process. As adults, we are probably too quick to answer these questions. Whether we make up an answer or give them the "true facts," we encourage a "Let's get this over with and move on" mentality. Teachers, I'm sure, face even more questions of this type and are under even greater pressure to move on—after all, there is a certain amount of curriculum to be covered on any given day. But oddly enough, what I remember most about the classes I took in junior high and high school and later in college are what might be labeled "digressions" from the content. I loved it when a teacher took a tangent, and instead of memorizing each of the amendments in the Bill of Rights, I heard a story about Thomas Jefferson's life, or something else that wasn't strictly germane to the topic at hand.

Similarly, in my mind, contemplation is more discursive; it wanders farther afield than what we traditionally think of as an act of intense focus on a precise thought, idea, or concept. When we start the mental rehearsal process, we may have a precise idea in mind, but when we contemplate it, we also start to ask ourselves those "what if" and "what would it be like" kinds of questions. "What if I decided that from now on, I was going to be a more evolved person?" "What would my life look like if I could be more enthusiastic?" "What do I already know or what have I just learned that I can apply in the next moment so I can do it better next time?" When we contemplate those questions, we start out in speculation—and that's a good thing, because it begins the process.

The reason it is so good is that speculation means we are posing possibilities and not looking for absolute, right-or-wrong, black-or-white, yes-or-no, dualistic kinds of answers. The great thing about the frontal lobe is that it loves to be engaged in that kind of speculative contemplation. We have tons of dualistic answers stored in our brain. We have recitations of facts and recountals of experience filed away all over the place in the brain. We can sort through these kinds of data to answer questions in an instant and with little effort and involvement of the frontal lobe. However, when we ask speculative questions, when we begin to consider alternatives and possibilities, the frontal lobe gets excited. The reason is that the answer isn't stored in any one place—it's going to take some digging to get there, and the frontal lobe loves to get its hands dirty.

At my local library, we have great reference librarians. These women and men spend most of the day answering questions about where the water fountain and the restrooms are. On a good day, they'll get a question about where a patron can find the U.S. population statistics. The reference librarians are invariably friendly and polite to everyone, but when I go in there and ask them how I might find information about the frontal lobe and its possible relationship to foot size among aboriginal peoples in the American Southwest, or the correlation between rainfall and the Anasazis' rise and fall, their eyes light up. They're chomping at the bit to explore this kind of question. So does our frontal lobe. It loves to build new models of thought based on looking for new possibilities.

Most questions asked of the librarians require them to go to one source for the answer. When we ask a more far-ranging speculative question, our frontal lobe "librarian" has to go to multiple sources to pull facts and inferences in order to put together a model that will answer our question. If we ask ourselves what our life would be like if we were to be more unlimited, the frontal lobe, by virtue of its many connections to all the other parts of the brain, will spring into action like a group of fighter pilots scrambling to their planes. It will naturally dig up memories of the past when we were freer, and will sort through our list of family, friends, classmates, acquaintances, and so on to find others who've exemplified the trait. In addition, the frontal lobe will stop all the other programs that are running in order to complete this task. We don't have a program for "future life if lived as a free-thinking genius" that it can go to as a single source. It has to put that together from an assortment of pieces—and it wants to put this jigsaw puzzle together.

The difference between our putting a jigsaw puzzle together and this kind of speculative contemplation is that the frontal lobe doesn't have an image on a cardboard box that it can consult. That box-cover image corresponds to our past and present personality. When we ask—and then answer—the kind of speculative, contemplative questions that I've used as examples, we've stopped the typical patterns, sequences, and combinations of circuits that normally fire within our definition of our self. We stopped the programs of our affirmed identity, and we have stepped outside the framework of the established personality. We've also asked our brain for a new synthesis of information that it doesn't presently have stored in a habitual hardwired pattern. We are actually interrupting some of our hardwired patterns, and creating a more plastic, flexible brain. Our frontal lobe is in love with this task, and we should be also—we are about to reinvent ourselves. We are about to fire and wire new circuits in our brain—that is the task to which we will turn our attention next.

From Attention to Wiring:
Mapping Change and Changing Maps

The moment all our awareness converges on an internal representation, and that picture becomes more real to us than the external environment, we begin to rewire new connections in our brain. The prefrontal cortex creates new wiring outside the familiar territory of our personality, so the brain can store, and then experience, new data. In this way, the frontal lobe can leave a map of our conscious awareness in the brain, stored as a new memory. This storage and mapping process provides physical evidence that the mind has experienced thought; thought is then tangibly represented as tracks in the human brain. Through new scanning technologies and microscopic cameras, we can now literally watch the mind experience thought as neurons actively reach out to form neural nets, their branches waving in their watery bath.

How does the way we use our attention affect how we rewire our brain? Suppose we are studying directions on how to use the remote that came with our new home theater system. The instructions contain so many unfamiliar words that understanding the process requires all our concentration. While we are trying to piece everything together, our dog is licking our face to elicit some affection. Also, the phone is ringing, we have a headache, and in ten minutes, we have to pick our daughter up from school.

Certainly, having so much of our attention displaced to various stimuli lowers our focus on the immediate task. Our greatest obstacle, though, is that various persistent neural nets are being activated by our dog (a thing), the phone (a sound), a headache (our body), and an appointment (time). These neural nets are literally becoming electrically activated in the sensory and motor areas as well as the associative areas of our neocortex. However, we cannot make our brain focus on anything new while all these familiar neural networks are firing. Our brain is already attending to so many known stimuli that it cannot wire in new information. We are out of sync.

Let's take this concept a little further. When our attention shifts to preexisting neural nets—our dog, for example—our consciousness returns to familiar past experiences and knowledge, with all their associations to our identity of self. Our awareness once more occupies the previously wired neural nets containing all our past associations that define us. We find that we just can't learn the skills needed to operate our home theater system—our attention has strayed to an already-wired section of the brain connected to our identity.

This is why we can't succeed at learning differential calculus while simultaneously thinking about who is coming for dinner and what we should wear. Similarly, being online and trying to make decisions about our vacation flight arrangements is not the wisest move when those thoughts are competing for attention with the shopping list for dinner or the ill health of our cat.

To wire new, long-term networks in our brain, we have to selectively choose from among our neural nets to build the model that we can associate with what we're learning. The frontal lobe allows us to decide which neural nets to fire, and to inhibit the activity of other neural nets so that we can pay attention to what we're learning. The problem isn't that we're entering virgin territory, it's that we can't mix novel thoughts or original ideas with old territories that have absolutely nothing to do with the new connections we're making.

When we place our mind solely on a single thought, our frontal lobe can lower the firing frequency of the synaptic connections in the existing neural nets in other areas of our brain. Remember, the frontal lobe has numerous connections to all other parts of the brain, and it controls how the rest of the brain functions, based on what we are attending to. Consequently, our complete attention and focus allows the frontal lobe to mentally hold whatever images we choose, without the interruption of any other associative neural nets. That's why mental rehearsal requires us to separate ourselves from distractions, and should be done when we are prepared and able to devote our full attention to the concepts we have chosen to make real in our life.

Let's return to our mission of learning how to use the remote. If we have developed the skill of concentration or focus, and have learned to use our frontal lobe to a greater degree than the average person, we can so greatly increase our attention on what we are doing that we lose track of our headache. The dog licking our face or lying on our foot will no longer exist, the sound of the phone ringing won't register with us, and all our attention can actually be on what we are learning, free of distraction.

Without that level of concentration, however, we will never rewire those old circuits with new ones. This is why, when we are first learning how to focus, it is more effective to just find a quiet place, sit down without distractions, and mentally rehearse what we want to learn. And why, in the case of learning to operate that entertainment system, our best bet would be to tackle that job when we can be by ourselves, with the phone off the hook and with no other distractions or demands on our time and attention. We want results, and focused attention and concentration will achieve them. There is no other way.

Why Lift a Finger?

So when it comes to all this mental rehearsal stuff, what's in it for us? We may believe that we can change our brain by thinking, but what effects, if any, will this have on our body? Through the simple process of mentally rehearsing an activity, we can derive great benefits without lifting a finger. Here's an example of how that literally happened. As described in an article published in the 1992 *Journal of Neurophysiology*, subjects were divided into three groups.[1] The first group was asked to do exercises during which they contracted and relaxed one finger on their left hand, for five training sessions per week for four weeks. The second group rehearsed the same exercises in their minds, on the same timetable, without physically activating any muscles in the finger. People in a control group neither exercised the finger nor their mind.

At the end of the study, the scientists compared their findings. The first set of participants had their finger strength tested against the control group. A nobrainer, right? Of course, the group that did the actual exercises exhibited 30 percent greater finger strength than those in the control group. We all know that if we put a load on a muscle and do so repeatedly, we are going to increase the strength of that muscle. What we probably wouldn't anticipate is that the group who mentally rehearsed the exercises demonstrated a 22 percent increase in muscle strength, simply by doing the exercises with their minds. The mind, then, produced a quantifiable physical effect on the body. In other words, the body changed without the actual physical experience.

If we can do that with our fingers, why can't we apply the same principle to other areas, such as healing ourselves of disease or from an injury? For instance, let's say that we have sprained our right ankle. It would normally take four to six weeks for that to heal, during which time the repeated applications of ice, compression, and elevation would be beneficial. But what if, instead, we mentally rehearse walking, jumping, and running on that ankle and imagine flexing and extending it beyond the range typical of an injured joint? What signal will our brain be sending to our ankle, what effect will it have on our healing process, and could our mental imagery strengthen that joint to prevent a recurrence of the injury?

The process would be no different from the finger-strengthening exercises. Our mental conception of normal activity levels of the right ankle will fire the corresponding motor circuits and neural networks already mapped in the motor cortex. The repetitive rehearsal of this mental act will begin to shape, embroider, and remold more advanced circuits of the brain's neurological network assigned to the right ankle. Repetitively firing those circuits will enhance their wiring. If we are able to marry our intent with concentrated effort to send a message to the tissues, the ankle should heal and become stronger. The signal from the autonomic nervous system (remember, that's the system responsible for repair and maintenance work) will contain a specific signature and message to promote the healing processes in those tissues.

Consciously activating the brain produces a level of mind with intentional energy or frequency that carries a message to the body. It produces measurable effects in the tissues, and it also creates new, more intricate neural nets in the brain—and we don't have to lift a finger to create them.

A Brief Interlude on Love

Before we go any further in this discussion of mental rehearsal and the process of making change in our life, I want to say a few words about love. You may be thinking that a few pages from another book got inserted into mine, but this is the real deal here. When I was talking about motivation earlier, I tiptoed around the subject of love. Now I think it's time to just come right out and say that I want us to fall in love. And not just in like, but deeply and completely in love—with some idea of ourselves or our world that we want to see come to fruition. The reason is simple. Love is a powerful motivator. The brain chemistry of love is completely different from the chemistry that we produce in survival mode. The love potion released in the midbrain creates bonding in all mammals. By falling in love with our ideal, we are chemically bonding with a new version of ourselves.

Remember what it is like when we are first in love with someone (or at least think we might be), and we will leap over tall buildings to get to see him or her again? No scheduling conflict is so great, no prior commitments too important that they can't be changed to accommodate this new love in our life. That's how the process of mentally rehearsing this new vision of ourselves should be. We must fall in love with this vision, never tiring of, or becoming bored by, this concept of ourselves. We are all a work in progress. We should always feel that we want to be with our new concept and visit with it. We must bond with a pattern of thinking that repeatedly inspires, enlivens, and heals us. After all, making new synaptic connections is a creative, joyful process. All animals in the wild are at their most playful and joyful during early development, when they are forming new synaptic connections on a large scale.

And just like when we are first in love, when the object of our affection seems to us to be an idealized incarnation of all that is pure and true, that's the vision we want to create for our new self. After all, what would be the point of not striving for perfection? How are we going to be motivated to spend the hours necessary to sit and reflect and contemplate on anything less than an ideal? Why set a goal for ourselves that falls short of winning? As clichéd as it sounds, I do believe that anything worth doing is worth doing well.

Be assured that this isn't some pie-in-the-sky, Pollyannaish, traditional self-help, feel-good message. I really believe that if we are going to spend the time rehearsing a new ideal in our frontal lobe so that idea can become more real to us than our environment, the image we hold ought to be nothing short of the most highly evolved version of what we are or can ever remember being—whether we are exhibiting a more evolved concept of patience, decisiveness, health, or gratitude.

For example, changing yourself by overcoming an illness activates a level of mind that changes the entire body. Creating a new neural network that severs a streak of bad, dysfunctional relationships and brings a healthy, meaningful, loving union into our life has its roots in being wired to worthiness. Having more energy and losing 40 pounds first starts in the mind. Being more organized creates windows of opportunity. Rehearsing a new state of confidence can open doors in our job and throughout our life. If mind and the body are aligned, we have the force of the universe behind us. This is the level of mind in which our intent and our actions produce our desired results, time and time again.

Einstein said that no problem can be solved with the same level of consciousness that created it. In terms of those people who experienced a healing from physical ailments, the same is true. They created a new level of mind, in which their body received new neurochemical signals, different from the mind that had created their conditions. They understood that if they engaged in cognitive workouts while sitting there immersed in those same emotions of desperation, self-doubt, or fear, their efforts to change would not succeed. Their former self, they realized, was not only riddled in self-defining emotions, but encompassed the very states of mind that had turned on the cellular genetics that had made their condition status quo for their life. Instead, they moved to a joyful state of being. Essentially, when we rehearse, we become someone else to the point that when we finish, we are a new person with new thoughts and mannerisms.

Imagine if the folks I talked about in chapter 2, who healed themselves of serious illness, had envisioned for themselves a tumor that merely shrank by a half inch to stop pressing on a nerve, or a life with something other than a complete cure of their condition? They simply practiced being well and happy instead of depressed and sick. Certainly, they could have derived some benefit from thinking short of the finish line. But because they set the bar high, their motivation was greater, and the rewards matched their efforts of focused concentration.

There's another reason to aim high: it's important that we get our frontal lobe involved in a *novel* task. We've talked about novelty a great deal and how it functions in terms of hardwiring new circuits. As we envision a new self, we aren't simply going to form new circuits. Instead, we will put together a three-dimensional, holographic image or ideal of ourselves through the act of mental rehearsal. The frontal lobe loves to solve complex puzzles. It thrives in meeting challenges that require it to combine newly learned information with bits and pieces of prior knowledge and past experiences from a wide variety of sources, and then to work those into new patterns and combinations. The frontal lobe is so skillful that the only limitation on its ability to construct these models is our own skill at envisioning the ideal of ourselves.

Let's take this further. To fall in love with a concept of "self" that we haven't experienced yet means that we have no prior emotional component associated with it (remember that all memories have an emotion attached to them). Therefore, the only emotion we can attach to this new vision of self is the love we bring. Let me state this again: If we love the concept of our new self from the start, love is the only emotion we can associate it with, because we have yet to experience that new self. Those experiences are yet to come, and they are an important part of evolving our brain to the highest degree possible. The side effect of this creative process is joy.[2]

Mental Fitness and Mindful Results: Creating Our New Self

The purpose of this book is to show us how to evolve our brain. What we are talking about is taking advantage of the brain's biology—in particular, the frontal lobe's enormous capacities—to build new circuits; consciously abandon old, outdated, and no-longer-needed circuits; and literally build a new mind. We've heard this before and it bears repeating: we can make up our mind to change, and we can literally make up a new mind. A new mind makes a new brain, and a new brain facilitates a new mind.

We have already talked about the first step in this process of evolving the brain—mental rehearsal. Now let's go a lot deeper into just how to use this process to evolve our brain and change our life.

Setting the Stage

Manipulation of our environment comes first. My friend John had discovered aspects of this process in trying to maximize his creativity as a writer. If you remember, one of the first things he did before writing sessions, whether at home or when he visited his family, was to prepare his surroundings. For example, he would set the stage at home by sitting with candles glowing and instrumental music playing. By doing those two things repeatedly, he began to associate them with good writing days. Our brain is always active in making associations. Those positive associations with the candles and music were beneficial, but eventually, John was able to get into writing mode without them.

John's manipulation of his environment demonstrates that it is essential, in order to use mental rehearsal effectively, that we get away from the usual people, places, things, times, and events that make up so much of our daily routine and thoughts. One random interaction with any one of these distractions can initiate automatic associative thinking. That is one reason why travel often enables us to think more clearly about situations that have developed in our life, to plot our future more clearly, to arrive at decisions more easily, and to plan our next steps more fluidly. We are out of our usual element and all the associations we have with it. When we abandon our typical, predictable world, the environment will no longer trigger us to activate the circuits of our automatic, routine, reactive responses. Mental rehearsal can be like taking a trip, if we alter our environment in some way so that we have no previous associations with it or with the mental state we bring into the new environment.

Of course, once we prepare our surroundings, our next step is to decide which area in our life we are going to change or improve. Along with that, we will need to learn new knowledge to reconceptualize ourselves and to put that new self into action.

Learning New Knowledge

When we're learning new material from our external world, the frontal lobe refires its existing hardwired, mapped patterns and neural nets in different *com-*

binations, patterns, and sequences. Billions of neurons with trillions of connections can create an infinite combination of possibilities in our mind.

Mental rehearsal (and the evolution of our mind that comes after) relies on the acquisition of new knowledge and the application of that information, so as to modify our behavior and embrace new experiences. Thus far, we've concentrated our discussion of mental rehearsal and change by focusing on using the raw materials, knowledge, and associations that we presently have. We've only casually mentioned how research—exposure to new concepts, reading books, watching informational television shows, and countless other ways in which we learn new knowledge or have new experiences—is critical to the process.

If we want to be a new person or exhibit new behaviors, we shouldn't limit ourselves to what we have previously stored in our brain. If we want to explore new possibilities, it is imperative that we gain new knowledge and apply that knowledge so that we can create experiences that involve new emotions. In chapter 12, I discuss this idea further.

Now that we have incorporated new knowledge into our toolkit, we are ready to build our new ideal of self. For example, if we choose to become more compassionate, we utilize all the circuits that we presently have in place related to that concept. We may think of an aunt who did a great deal of charitable work and served as a foster parent to developmentally disabled children. We recall how large her heart seemed to be to encompass so many children and their needs at the expense of her own gratification; we realize that we never heard her complain and never saw her turn anyone away who needed help or was less fortunate than she was. We may also think of our own mother and her compassion toward us when a relationship failed and we were down. We've experienced compassion in our life and we've seen it in action from a distance. We have read about Mother Teresa and her work, and seen movies in which dedicated people get much of themselves out of the way in the service of others.

We already have those building blocks of associative memory in our brain. The next step is to take those raw materials and use them to build a new ideal. Again, we take what we already know and put those pieces together differently. As the orchestra's conductor, we can access all the associative memory centers in the brain, get certain instruments to play, and get others to join in to produce a new level of mind related to that concept of compassion. We can take our aunt's open-hearted generosity of spirit, our mother's empathetic understanding of our emotional needs, what we've read about Mother Teresa's work in Calcutta, and what we've learned from Buddhist texts about letting go of illusions, and combine them all into a new model of how we want to be as a compassionate person.

Through mental rehearsal, for instance, we can place an image in our frontal lobe of how we will respond with compassion the next time our sister, who has complained about her ne'er-do-well husband for the last 15 years, comes to us with the same laundry list of complaints. In creating a vision of that new response, we will not be activating those routine circuits that have us angry and stonewalling her with silence. By adding new knowledge about what happens to women who feel trapped in a relationship they know is not working, we will begin the process of building a new model of compassion, one that can be hard-wired in the brain using those raw materials of previous experience, prior knowledge, and newly acquired learning. This new response will become more wired with the neural growth factor that once held our emotionally addicted response in place. We now have the machinery to behave differently, because the circuits we created by mental rehearsal have prepared the brain ahead of reality.

The only thing it takes to become a more compassionate person—or to create any new attribute we desire—is focused concentration, will, knowledge, and understanding. Then we must rehearse being our new self as if we were one of those piano-playing subjects devoting those two hours a day to form new circuits—regardless of whether that keyboard is in front of us or in our frontal lobe. Again, that is how the people in chapter 2 were able to bring about healing from their physical afflictions. That is how Malcolm X reformed himself from being a criminal to becoming a revered civil rights leader. We are capable of consciously reinventing ourselves as a new individual by using some of the same tools we used to unconsciously form our "old" self. These tools include understanding the Laws of Association and Repetition, firing new sequences and patterns based on knowledge and experience, learning to quiet the internal chattering that results from a nearly obsessive focus on the external environment, and attending to the resultant emotional state we've become addicted to; they all put to use our greatest gift—the frontal lobe.

Starting Early

To truly reinvent, revise, and reconceptualize ourselves, we have to use the process of mental rehearsal to fire those new circuits on a daily basis and at every opportunity. If we rehearse every day, especially first thing in the morning, we walk out of the house with those circuits already warmed up. Since we've already been that new person in our mind—we are already in that mindset—it's a lot easier to be that person when we encounter a situation that challenges that new concept.

For example, we wake up at 5 a.m. and we're determined to work on being a less angry person. We spend an hour holding that ideal in our frontal lobe (built from memory, experience, and new knowledge) of our more understanding and peaceful self. Then, when we climb in the shower, our significant other chooses that moment to start the washing machine, and our warm shower turns cold. Having been through our mental rehearsal, we will simply smile at the reminder of how fragile our resolve can sometimes be, and how often it can be tested. How would the same situation unfold if, instead, we woke up, hit the snooze button, scrambled out of bed knowing that we would have to rush to avoid being late, and then the same cold shower scenario took place? We would likely run those old circuits, stomp out of the shower, stick our head out the door, and yell like a person possessed, accusing our significant other of insensitivity, stupidity, and crimes against hygiene. If letting go of anger is our vision, which way would we rather start the day?

The Road Ahead

By firm intention and by quieting the rest of the brain, we can become more astute at observing ourselves. We can better identify our tendencies and weaknesses. Once we've become more adept at self-observation, we can start to ask the larger questions. We can employ this executive in our head to deal with larger-scale, longer-term problems, instead of focusing solely on satisfying the immediate needs of our body and our emotional addictions. We can use mental rehearsal to prepare ourselves for the tougher tasks ahead. Although, like an architect, we can build a model of the dream house we envision as our new self, the true test comes when we actually bring that ideal to fruition and expose it to the elements of the real world. The brain will always follow the lead of the mind's design by building new struts and footings. I will talk about this more advanced stage of mind in chapter 12. For now, we simply need to realize that our work isn't done when we've begun to use mental rehearsal.

Choosing to break free of the routine of living in survival mode and creating a new self are not easy tasks. It is so much easier to live in a reactive, rather than proactive, manner. We are so adept and practiced at using those hardwired routines that are a combination of our inheritance and our experiences. For so long, we've actively avoided new experiences and gained little new knowledge. When the foundation of our life is rocked by something calamitous, or if we manage to step out of the fog of our own repetitive nature and our own desire for routine, we can set out to discover new things about ourselves, examining who we are, who we want to be, where we are, and where we want to be.

To change is to break the habit of being yourself. You are being asked to commit to finding a quiet spot where you can spend, at minimum, an hour a day maintaining that idealized vision of yourself in your mind. You are being asked to sever the umbilical cord that connects you to your environment and to the rush of chemicals to which we all have become so addicted. You are being asked to sit still and release yourself from the overactive, overstimulated, highly stressed, and ultimately soul-killing and body-destroying life that you may have allowed to take control over you. Mental rehearsal asks of you to make clear your intention to the universe by mentally practicing what your new and improved self will be like.

When you bring into reality that idealized vision you've created, what you receive in return will far exceed the sacrifices you have to make. The clarity of that vision and the depth of your commitment will ultimately pay off in ways that you have just begun to imagine. You can move from a state of survival to the state of creation, just by changing your thinking.

In chapter 12, we will finalize our study when we explore what neuroscience has to say about thinking, doing, and being. When we learn to enter a state of being, our mind and body are one, and all the gears are set in motion to have change be a permanent state of mind and body. That is evolution.

CHAPTER TWELVE

EVOLVING
YOUR BEING

We are what we repeatedly do.
Excellence, then, is not an action, but a habit.

—ARISTOTLE

I n chapter 11, I talked about the success my friend's coach experienced when he mentally rehearsed a game, inning by inning, hitter by hitter, and then went out and pitched that game, exactly as he had thought it through the night before. He enjoyed great success against a team that had previously plagued him. Just imagine how powerful a tool mental rehearsal can be when we use it to improve our being, and not merely our baseball skills. For now, though, let's stick with baseball for a bit longer.

In this chapter, we'll outline the most important element of mental rehearsal. None of the mental preparation my friend's coach went through would have mattered if he hadn't gotten himself to the ball field, warmed up in the bullpen, and then faced live hitters in a real game. Just as he'd envisioned, he had to go out there and demonstrate his skill, show command of his pitches, display his ability to locate the ball in and out of the strike zone. He went from using just the mind, to using the body *and* the mind.

Demonstration is the crucial final step from mental rehearsal to personal evolution. My baseball-playing friend, a pitcher himself, learned a term that he applied to certain players: "He's a six o'clock hitter." That hour was the time when players took batting practice before the actual game. These guys could put on prodigious displays of hitting—sharp line drives to the gaps and mammoth tape-measure home runs. The problem was, when the actual game started, they couldn't hit their body weight in batting average, nor could they generate the kind of power they did in practice.

Thus, it is vital that we move beyond mental rehearsal to actually put into practice the evolved ideal of our imagination. Imagine a concert pianist who does his or her best work in practice sessions, but struggles during a concert; a professor who executes faultless presentations in his mind the night before a class, but succumbs to nervousness in the lecture hall; or a spouse who is the model of understanding on the drive home from work, but devolves into an impatient pouter as soon as he or she comes through the door. Without the playing field of life and the opportunity to live what we have mentally rehearsed, we will never embrace the true experience and all of its sensory memories that the body as well as the mind can enjoy.

How can we take this evolutionary step from thinking to doing, and then to a state of being? To get there, I'll add just a few more concepts to our knowledge base. We're already beginning to appreciate that *being it*—exhibiting whatever behavior we want to embrace—means to have our evolved understanding and our experiences so hardwired and mapped into our brain that it's no longer necessary for us to even think about how to put our new skills into practice. Nike has reminded us to "just do it." My goal is to take that decree out of the level of clichéd sloganeering and demonstrate how we can integrate all our skills and knowledge to make that truism a reality. Putting into practice what we have learned, we can evolve our brain and break the habit of being the old neurochemical self. When we form a new mind and a more evolved identity, we will "just be it."

Let's start by refining our understanding of how we form and use memories. In previous chapters, we described memory as thoughts that stay in the brain. Primarily we register conscious thoughts in the brain by recalling, recognizing, and declaring what we have learned. Conscious thoughts can include short-term and long-term memories, or semantic and episodic memories. Knowledge, short-term memories, or semantic knowledge (for our purposes, these have similar meanings) are filed away in the brain by the intellectual mind. On the other hand, experiences, long-term memories, or episodic memories (also synonymous) are formatted in the brain by the body and the senses, in order to reinforce the mind and the body to remember even better. The latter types of thoughts tend to stay in the brain longer, because the body participates in sending important electrochemical signals to the brain to create feelings.

Explicit Memory Versus Implicit Memory

Most memories fall into the category of *explicit* or *declarative memories,* those we can consciously retrieve at will. Here's a helpful way to think of what makes these kinds of memories distinct: we can declare that we *know* that we know them. Declarative memories are statements like the following: I like garlic mashed potatoes, my birthday is in March, my mother's name is Fran, I am an American, the heart pumps blood, and I pay taxes each April 15th. Also, I know many things about spinal biomechanics, I know my address and phone number, and I know how to plant a winter garden.

Explicit, declarative memories mainly involve our conscious mind. I can consciously declare all of those above thoughts. I learned about these things either via knowledge (semantically) or experientially (episodically) in order to consciously remember them. Accordingly, there are two ways we form declarative memories: through knowledge and through experience.

The neocortex is the site of our conscious awareness and, therefore, our explicit memory storage. Various types of explicit memories are processed and stored differently in the brain. Take, for example, the different ways our neocortex handles short-term versus long-term memory.

Short-term memory is held in our frontal lobe for the most part, so that we can make our way in the most functionally efficient manner. When we memorize a phone number, we repeat it in our mind as we walk from the phone book to the telephone, and hope for the best. It is our frontal lobe that maintains those numbers in our head while we scramble to take immediate action. This feat involves not only laying down new memories, but also being able to retrieve them.

Long-term memory is also stored in the neocortex, but the means by which we store new information long-term is a little more complex. When our sensory organs take in data from a novel experience, the hippocampus (as you'll recall, a part of the midbrain that is most active when we are making known the unknown) functions as a kind of relay system: it takes that information from the sensory organs and passes it on to the neocortex through the temporal lobe and its association centers. Once that learned information makes it to the neocortex, it is distributed throughout the cortex in an array of neural networks. Long-term memories, therefore, involve both the neocortex and the midbrain.

To recall a long-term memory, when we fire the thought associated with that memory, we essentially turn on the neural patterns in a specific sequence that will then create a particular stream of consciousness and bring it to our awareness. If the neocortex is like a computer hard drive, then the hippocampus is the save button: as we make different memories appear on the screen of our mind, they are stored when we hit the key to save the file. In effect, we can also perform "file open" to retrieve those memories stored in the neocortex.

WORKING MEMORY: DOING IT IN OUR HEAD

As a side note, we possess another kind of short-term memory that helps us learn. In the 1960s, scientists coined the term "working memory." Though some think of this as a synonym for short-term memory, the two have slightly different meanings, since working memory emphasizes the active, task-based nature of the storage. We use *working memory* particularly in carrying out complex cognitive tasks. The classic example is mental arithmetic, in which a person must hold the results of previous calculations in working memory while they work on the next stage in the calculation. For example, if someone asked us to multiply 6 times 4, and then subtract 10 and add 3, at each stage when we calculated an answer, that preliminary number would be stored in our working memory. In the case above, when we did the first multiplication and got 24 as the answer, we held that number in working memory and then subtracted 10 from it to get 14, which we also held in working memory until we could add 3 to it. In both short-term and working memory, our frontal lobe is the area of the neocortex that is instrumental in making our thoughts stay there long enough for us to function with any degree of certainty.

There is a second type of memory system called *implicit* or *procedural memories*. Implicit memories are associated with habits, skills, emotional reactions, reflexes, conditioning, stimulus-response mechanisms, associatively learned memories, and hardwired behaviors that we can demonstrate easily, without much conscious awareness. These are also termed *nondeclarative memories*, because they are abilities that we do not necessarily need to declare, but that we repeatedly demonstrate without much conscious effort or will. Implicit memories are intimately connected to the abilities that reside at a subconscious level. We've done these things so many times, we don't have to think about them anymore. We use implicit memories all the time, but we do so without being consciously aware of them. Implicit memories are thoughts that not only stay in the brain, but thoughts that stay in the body as well as the brain. In other words, the body has become the mind. Figure 12.1 shows the two different memory systems—explicit and implicit memories—and how they are stored in different regions of the brain.

To better understand implicit memories, think of them as intrinsically linked to our ability to train the body to automatically demonstrate what the mind has

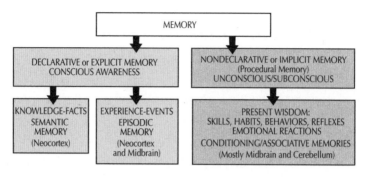

Figure 12.1
The memory systems of the brain.

learned. Through the mind's ability to repeat or reproduce an experience at will, the mind has thought about, rehearsed, and planned so well that when the mind instructs the body to perform a task, the body now has an implicit memory of how to do it, and no longer needs the conscious mind. If the body keeps experiencing the same event as a result of the instruction of the mind, the body will become "mindful" enough to be able to naturally produce the action or skill. With implicit memories, the body remembers as well as the mind.

Athletics abounds with examples of this seemingly automatic functioning. How does a diver go off a ten-meter platform, turn two and one-half somersaults, spring out of that tucked position to complete a series of twists, and then orient the body so that they can enter the water head-first at a close-to-perpendicular position? How much conscious thought can go into a highly sophisticated and technical physical performance that lasts mere seconds? Athletes tell us that they get their minds out of the way and let the body do the work. Similarly, when we learn how to drive a car with a stick shift, after we consciously master the skill, we demonstrate that ability without having to think about each step in the process.

Implicit memories abound in our brain; they are the automatic neural nets that we have developed merely through physical repetition. Brushing our teeth, shaving, riding a bike, tying our shoes, typing, playing a musical instrument, and salsa dancing are all examples of implicit or procedural memories. All these habitual actions take place without too much of our conscious direction.

Remember, these memories did not start out being automatic or implicit. Initially, we had to consciously and repeatedly practice these skills; it took attention and a willful, focused effort to hardwire them. When the mind has repeatedly instructed the body to perform an action, the body will begin to remember the action better than the thinking brain. The mind and the body, both neurologically and chemically, will naturally move into a familiar state of being. Eventually, we can reproduce the same neurological level of mind and internal chemical state of that associated event just by thought alone. Implicit memories ultimately become our subconscious programs.

Once an implicit memory is complete, the body has neurologically memorized the intention of the brain. In addition, the repeated experiences register in the body, and the neurological and chemical signal to the cells is automatically and completely connected to that same level of mind. Intellectual philosophy never makes it to this level in the body because it is devoid of any experience.

As we have learned, consistently repeated experiences write the genetic history of any species. Implicit memories, therefore, are the strongest signals that are genetically passed on, and most certainly, they become the starting point for new generations to follow. When the mind repeatedly unifies with the body, the body encodes what it has learned from the environment.

We learned with episodic memories that knowledge is the forerunner to experience. When we apply knowledge or personalize information, we have to modify our behavior in order to create a new experience. This requires us to consciously apply what we learn not just intellectually (through simple recall) but we must also involve our body in the act of doing. Furthermore, when we use knowledge to initiate a new experience, it is not enough to have the experience only once. We have to be able to repeat that new experience, over and over.

We change explicit memories to implicit memories all the time, and this is the same as making conscious thoughts, subconscious thoughts. When we can do any action without conscious effort, we have formed an implicit memory. Once a memory becomes implicit, any thought to act, or desire to demonstrate what we are thinking, automatically turns the body on to carry out the task, without the conscious mind.

Mastering a language is an example of how we make the transition from explicit to implicit memory. When we are learning a new language, we have to memorize nouns, verbs, adjectives, and prepositions, storing them by association. For instance, we memorize that the Spanish word *hombre* means man. When we can consciously declare the word *hombre* every time someone asks us the word for man, the semantic memory of *hombre* is now stored in the database of our neocortex as an explicit memory. As we learn more words, we store the meaning of each item in the personalized folds of our neocortex.

Next, we listen to our Spanish instructor sing a song about an *hombre,* and the sensory (auditory) nature of this experience, as well as the Law of Repetition, further wires the meaning of *hombre* into a long-term memory in our brain. If we progress in our study, we will probably learn most of the Spanish words that are related to various objects, actions, and meanings in our world.

However, this will do us no good unless we put it all together and apply that knowledge by actually speaking the language. As we speak and listen to Spanish in different situations, with diverse people, at different times, and in various places, that system will begin to become implicit. Once we can speak the language fluently, it is wired implicitly. We merely have to think of what we want to say, and the next thing we know, we automatically activate our tongue, teeth, and facial muscles to move in a certain way to produce the right sounds. When we no longer have to consciously think about what language we are speaking, it has become a subconscious, hardwired system.

When people can do something well and we ask them, "How do you do that skill and make it look so easy?" almost all will typically respond, "I don't know (I cannot declare how I consciously know how I do it); I've just practiced so many times that I no longer think about how to do it anymore." This is the non-declarative, implicit state—the person has done the action so many times that he or she can do it "un-consciously." The ability has become so automatic that the body (which is the unconscious mind) takes over.

In contrast to all forms of explicit memories, implicit memories are handled by the cerebellum. If we recall from chapter 4, the cerebellum regulates our body movements, coordinates our actions, and controls many of our subconscious mechanisms.

The cerebellum has no conscious centers; it does, however, have memory storage. Its essential purpose is to demonstrate what the brain is thinking: to memorize the plan the neocortex has formulated and put that plan into action without actively involving too much of the neocortex in the operation itself. When we can take knowledge and practice it, coordinate it, memorize it, and integrate it into our body until we can automatically remember it, the cerebellum now has taken on the memory. At this point, the neocortex serves as a kind of messenger, signaling the cerebellum by a thought to start the activity that the cerebellum already knows and remembers.

Ever had the experience of picking up the phone to dial, and you just cannot make the phone number come to your conscious mind? You find yourself staring blankly at the keypad. But then, you think of the person you want to call, and like magic, your fingers push the correct numbers. It was your subconscious mind that stored that information in the form of a procedural memory, and your body knew how to automatically dial the number better than your conscious mind did. When you thought of the person you intended to call, it activated the neural network in your neocortex, which then signaled the cerebellum, and the procedural subconscious memory of the body took over to dial the phone. We can see a similar phenomenon when we ask some people to spell a word for us—often, they can't do it unless they skywrite it with a finger or actually take pencil to paper. The body remembers better than the mind; the body *becomes* the mind.

Remember back to your high school locker, and being so proficient at spinning the dial on your combination lock that your hand automatically performed the left-right-left number sequence without the brain's intervention? Your neocortex was involved in the original memorization of the combination, but in time your body took over, thanks to the coordination of the cerebellum. Since the primitive cerebellum houses no conscious awareness, if someone had asked you how to open your lock, you would have had to stop and call up the instructions from your neocortex. This unity of thinking and doing into a state of being is the hallmark of the cerebellum's activity.

In fact, studies of archers have shown that when they line up the sight with the center of the bull's-eye, activity in the neocortex ceases, and there is no thinking; the cerebellum has taken over at that point.[1]

We enter a trance-like state when the cerebellum has the space and time to remember what it has been conditioned to do, without interference from the neocortex. That's how we master any action. We rely on the rich dendrite connections of cerebellar memory. Because the cerebellum is responsible for body movements, it is this part of the brain that takes over and runs the show. It is the subconscious mind that now is performing the action, and the seat of the subconscious mind rests in the cerebellum.[2]

Once an implicit memory is demonstrated and the actions have been easy, routine, natural, and second nature, the neocortex will start the process with a conscious thought, and it is then left to the cerebellum to continue the action. Think of the conscious mind in the neocortex as the system that initiates the subconscious mechanisms driven by the memories and learned abilities in the cerebellum. The conscious mind is the key that starts the engine running. So as the skater turns in preparation to do a triple toe loop, the conscious mind is in charge and is the one that says, "Go!" After that, the conscious mind checks out and lets the body take over. Now the cerebellum gets busy doing its thing, keeping the athlete moving, balanced, and oriented in space during all those jumps, twists, and spins. After years of practice, those systems are now hardwired in the brain and the body.

In truth, when we have used the word *hardwired* to this point in the book, we were actually talking about the automatic neural nets that are hardwired to the subconscious mind in the cerebellum. The cerebellum functions as the keeper of what the body learns from the mind, while the neocortex stores the mind's memories.

There are innumerable examples of patients that have amnesia, Alzheimer's disease, or damage to the hippocampus, who cannot consciously remember their family and friends, and specific things that happen to them on a daily basis. Yet, they still know how to play the piano or knit a scarf. Their ability to retrieve old explicit memories and make new ones has been compromised, but their disease has much less effect on their implicit memories. Their body still knows what their conscious mind in the neocortex has forgotten or cannot learn. It is the brain system below the conscious mind that is executing these tasks.

Thinking, Doing, and Being

I know that these additional terms and concepts regarding memory add a greater burden to your understanding. I'd like to simplify some of this for you, and Figure 12.2 should serve as a handy guide as we go along.

First, think of learning knowledge in the form of semantic memory as a way to declare consciously that we have learned that information. When our conscious awareness activates those newly formed circuits in the neocortex, we are reminded of what we learned; we can declare that we know this information, because we have embraced it in the form of a memory. Knowledge involves our "thinking" or our intellect.

We also said that knowledge paves the way for a new experience. To apply knowledge, we have to modify our habitual behavior to create a new experience. Experience, then, is our second type of declarative memory. If learning knowledge is thinking, then having the experience is "doing."

To firmly establish a long-term memory, whatever we want to remember must have a high emotional quotient, or involve repeated conscious experiences or recitation of an idea. For the most part, though, experiences that we have never embraced before provide just the right newness of cumulative sensory information to create a new flush of chemistry and newly activated circuitry. An increase in the threshold of freshly combined stimuli from seeing, smelling, tasting, hearing, and feeling is almost always a sufficient cue to form long-term memories, because now the body is involved. Doing is what puts the experience into long-term memory.

The first time we have the novel experience of staying up on a surfboard, we can call that "doing it," and that experience will likely stay with us as a long-term memory. If we can repeat this experience over again at will, now we are "being" a surfer. To make a memory non-declarative, we have to repeatedly reproduce or recreate the same experience over and over until it makes the transition to an implicit system.

In a sense, when we become an expert in any particular area—when we possess a great deal of knowledge about a subject, have received significant

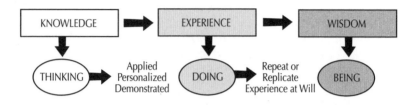

Figure 12.2

Learning knowledge is thinking; applying knowledge is doing and experiencing. Being able to mindfully repeat the experience is the wisdom of being.

instruction in that area, and have had plenty of experiences to provide us with feedback—we move from thinking to doing to being. When we possess sufficient knowledge and experience, when we can recall our short-term and long-term memories to a significant degree and with unconscious ease, then we have progressed to the point of being. This is when we can say "I am"— whether that means, "I am an art historian," "I am a very patient person," "I am wealthy," or "I am a surfer."

When we can make what we have intellectually learned so hardwired that we can easily demonstrate or physically do what we have diligently practiced, we are now procedurally demonstrating what we know. As we possess a memory in implicit form, we are on our way to being a master of that knowledge. In other words, we can demonstrate our knowledge by automatically "being" exactly what we have learned. To learn from our mistakes (or our victories) takes a level of conscious awareness that allows us to willfully make a mental note on what we did to produce that result, and then to become mindful of how we might do it differently or better the next time. Applying what we just learned, we will inevitably manifest a new experience for ourselves. By changing our behavior, we will create a new experience with new emotions, and now we are evolving. Not only do we evolve when we pursue this endeavor, but so does our brain. We will then be using philosophy not only to experience the truth of what we can declare, but to become the living example of that philosophy. Now it is permanently wired in the recesses of our subconscious mind, and it takes no effort at all.

Thinking is what we do when we are using the neocortex to learn. Doing is the act of applying or demonstrating a skill or action, so that we can have a novel experience. Both are part of our explicit declarative memories. Being, on the other hand, means that we have practiced and experienced something so many times now, that it has become a skill, habit, or condition that requires no conscious will to activate. This is the state we strive to achieve with all our actions.

The final stage of learning is produced when we make a conscious effort to unconsciously *be* exactly what we have learned by the natural effects of repeated experience. If we "have" the knowledge, we can "do" the actions, so that we can "be" whatever it is we are learning. "Being" exists when a skill has become easy, simple, effortless, and natural enough that we can consistently demonstrate what we've learned.

Cognitive Workouts

As we begin the mindful mental practice of rehearsal, we are declaring who it is we would like to become, and we are attempting to consciously remember that concept of our new personal identity. Mental rehearsal trains the mind to stay conscious of self, and not run rampant to the unconscious programs we have practiced so well. Initially, we have to live in the explicit realm. As we begin to fabricate new circuits and repeatedly create a new level of mind, we are executing will through the frontal lobe.

Mental workouts are a necessity. They are the way we stop the unconscious self from wandering off ("going unconscious") and becoming distracted by familiar things in our environment, with associations that could cause us to think in terms of the past. In a sense, rehearsal lays down tracks so that the mind has a path for the body to follow. Rehearsal has to be done so well that we can call up this new mind at will. Repetition has to continue, then, so that we repeatedly remember and use that new mind to modify our actions and demonstrate new behaviors and attitudes. Even one experience of applied information will begin cementing knowledge into a deeper meaning.

When we can activate the same level of mind to recreate the desired experience again and again, we are in the final stages of change. By doing, doing, and doing again, we eventually get the body to become the new mind, and the body can take over. Initiating—just by a single thought—the action of who or what we are demonstrating, and letting the body act as the mind's servant, is how we move to a new self.

The Role of Nondeclarative Memory in Change

Our implicit memories are the consistent demonstration of our explicit memories. In this state of being, we know that we know without thinking. With implicit memories, things become routine, familiar, habitual, and easy. Simply put, we know how—we know what we are doing. At some point we've all experienced this sensation of knowingness. It is marked more by an absence of thought than anything else. In a way, it is declaring that we have a nondeclarative system in place. We have trained our body to be one with our mind, and we can call up that memory at will.

To have our actions consistently match our intent is always what separates us from the average in anything we do. Those actions must be implicit in us before we can call ourselves a master of anything. Once we've been able to construct an implicit system, we can repeat an automatic action at will and can further refine it at a later time. Keep in mind that in evolving our brain, we are always in the process of moving from explicit into implicit systems, over and over again. We are constantly moving back and forth from conscious awareness to unconscious.

If we were to consciously self-reflect about some unwanted attitude, we would be observing the nondeclarative habits and behaviors that we unconsciously demonstrate on a daily basis. This process takes what is nondeclarative and makes it declarative. We now can see and know who we were being. We can say, "I am a victim. I am a complainer. I am an angry person. I am addicted to unworthiness." Once we consciously know this (we declared it), we can now reshape a new way of being, by asking ourselves those important questions we discussed earlier, on who we want to be.

As we build a new model of self by remembering who we consciously want to become, we can use mental rehearsal to build the circuits to facilitate a new level of mind. Our mental practice is declaring whom we are consciously choosing to become, by remembering how we want to be. This prepares us to consciously act equal to our intention. As we begin to alter our behavior, we demonstrate a new way of being that will produce a new conscious experience. When we are able to repeatedly demonstrate that experience at will, it becomes a hardwired, nondeclarative memory. After we have arrived at this subconscious state of being, nothing in our environment should cause us to fall prey to our past attitudes. We are truly changed.

I am certainly not saying that change will be easy. Consider that when we have implicitly memorized being a hateful, angry, jealous, or judgmental individual, mentally rehearsing it on a daily basis and physically demonstrating it at will, moment by moment, making it look natural, automatic, and effortless, we are physically and mentally coherent to that attitude. We have trained the body and the mind to work together. So when we want to change to a new state of being, we may consciously like to think that we are sincere and willful. But in the moments of true challenge, it is the body that is directing the affairs of the mind, and most of the time, it wins. This is why we cannot change so readily—the conscious mind and the body are at odds.

Then again, if we have mentally rehearsed and physically demonstrated joy on a daily basis, the same science holds true. In difficult circumstances in our life, if we are wired to be joyful, the environment cannot change how we are.

We should always be evolving ourselves and our actions. When we self-reflect, self-observe, and ask ourselves how we can do something better to refine our skills, actions, and attitudes, we are affirming that we are a work in progress. To self-correct on a regular basis is to observe our automatic thoughts, unconscious actions, and routine habits. Once we declare them as a part of us, we can begin to add a new way of being into the equation of our internal model, during rehearsal. Our ability to change is no different from the people who were able to achieve a spontaneous remission from disease. Everyone has the same frontal lobe capability. We can all ask the what-if questions, formulate an idealized model of ourselves, and prove to ourselves that we can achieve what we set our mind on.

Changing Implicit Habits
May Be Harder Than We Think

Why, then, is it so hard to change? Because the body has remembered a repeated action so well that it is in charge, rather than the mind. Remember, implicit memories are hardwired programs that require little or no conscious effort. The body holds the reins on the mind, determining most of our unconscious, hardwired actions. Everyone has had a conscious intention to change a habit, and then, so quickly, a sort of mental amnesia sets in and we "go unconscious," finding ourselves in the realm of the familiar. We fall back into our mental wheelchairs and behave just as we swore we never would. Imagine what it takes to break the habit of being ourselves, by monitoring our thinking processes that result in depression, anxiety, judgment, frustration, or unworthiness. We start out with good intentions and clear resolutions, but our unconscious mind begins to override our conscious thoughts, and in moments, we are asleep at the wheel of our old self once again.

The familiar is so seductive. Whether we are drawn back into unconscious programs by some thought sent from our body due to its chemical needs, by some random stimulation from something or someone in our environment, or by a hardwired action in anticipation of a future moment based on a memory of the past, we can fall prey to the mental chatter that talks us into the convenience of our identity and its cumulative programs.

Try a simple experiment. Lie or sit with your legs crossed, left over right. With your left foot, draw the infinity sign: ∞. As you are doing that, with your right hand, draw the number 6.

Having trouble? As you can see, even though you had clear intentions and the conscious thought to do these two actions, you probably could not break these two neurological habits. To change any behavior and modify our hardwired actions requires conscious will and consistent mental and physical practice, as well as the ability to interrupt routine actions to override the memory of the body and reform a new set of behaviors. Most people will make one or two attempts in actually trying to accomplish the above feat. The ones who persist and continue with effort and practice will master the act, and like anything we do with consistent frequency, intensity, and duration, we can change the brain neurologically. Once it has been changed, this little trick will look as simple as riding a bike.

Knowledge, Instruction, and Feedback: Change Takes Three Steps

As I mentioned above, it is crucial that we not stop at the mental rehearsal stage. We have to move from thinking it, to doing it, to being it. Conveniently, those three stages also have three corresponding steps that are necessary in order to move through that process.

My friend's coach, the baseball pitcher, who mentally rehearsed against the opposing team's lineup, learned something each time he went out and actually pitched. He didn't mindlessly repeat the same sequence of pitches against every hitter, or against every team each time he faced them. In fact, the next time he pitched the team that was his nemesis, he used what he had learned in the previous winning outing against them to formulate a new plan of attack. Knowledge that we pay attention to, we learn.

He also solicited instruction and feedback from his catcher, his own pitching coach, and another pitcher on the team. This process of self-observation and self-awareness falls under the domain of the frontal lobe. By quieting all of the other centers of the brain, the frontal lobe helps to sharpen skills of observation. By self-correcting and learning from our mistakes, we will naturally perform better the next time. This is how we evolve our thoughts, actions, and skills. What is wonderful about going out and demonstrating our skill, or a newly minted aspect of our personality, is that we will receive immediate feedback. If we're really fortunate, we'll also receive additional instruction. Receiving feedback and instruction are crucial to the process of evolving ourselves.

Whenever we decide to make a change in our life, learn a new skill, adopt a new attitude, enrich our beliefs, or alter a behavior, we make a conscious choice. Whether this choice completely reflects our innate and altruistic desire to be the best person we can possibly be, or is forced on us by negative circumstances, doesn't really matter. What matters is that we know that we desire something greater for ourselves.

Most important is the idealized self that we construct. The building blocks of that model consist of information that we gather from a variety of sources, regarding who we want to become, or what we want to change about ourselves. Consider that nothing we've learned has come without knowledge as a forerunner and as a fundamental part of that learning. On the simplest level, our personal development has relied on our ability to learn and to gain knowledge. Think of the spectrum of skills and information that we use just to navigate our way through any one day, and then think of that knowledge acquisition from a more long-term perspective, as we've developed from an infant into an adult.

No matter whether we are learning how to line dance, shed pounds, become a more cheerful person, overcome insecurity, or cut seconds off a 5K race time, we use a three-step process as the opening moves in our attempt to meet our goals:

1. Knowledge

2. Instruction

3. Feedback

THE INTERPLAY OF KNOWLEDGE AND EXPERIENCE

To illustrate how knowledge can personalize and alter an experience, let's say I showed you a painting of water lilies by Monet. After studying the canvas, you might comment, "This painting is beautiful." You would have one experience of Monet's work. What if I then took the painting down and told you the following things about Monet's life, career, and technique: He liked to capture

different types of light with pastel colors. He was particularly interested in morning and evening light and how they looked in nature.
Monet hoped to inspire people who experienced his work to look at
nature and the world in a new way. He worked diligently at seeing
things differently than the common man. Throughout his life, Monet
looked to see how all things were connected. He was known to make
statements such as, "The wisteria and the bridge are one and the
same." I could also say that as Monet got older, he developed
cataracts, which began to diffuse and blur his vision. Since he only
painted what he was seeing, those characteristic pixels or impres-
sionistic dots that typified his work were really just the way he was
processing sensory information.

Now, imagine that I showed you the same Monet painting a second time. You might see it differently, based on the knowledge you just
learned about him. Nothing in your environment would have changed;
you'd simply acquired new semantic knowledge, and that knowledge
had altered your experience of his painting. You made a few important
synaptic connections that modified your personal perception. Because
of the interplay between knowledge and experience, it's likely that you
would remember both the semantic knowledge and the episodic
memory, and store them in your long-term memory.

This simple example demonstrates how important is our perception of reality. When we are exposed to new information, we accumu-
late new experiences. They upgrade the neural nets of our brain, and
we begin to see/perceive/experience reality differently, because we
have made a new level of mind in our brain's existing hardware.

There's another point to consider about perception and the role
it plays in evolving our brain: perhaps we are missing out on what
really exists. Do you remember our earlier description of the wine
connoisseur? The same fabulous bottle of wine may be shared by an

expert and by a novice. The connoisseur's more evolved mind with its more enriched circuitry will enable him to enjoy a greater level of reality. We, too, can upgrade our brain, and when we do, we upgrade our experiences, and thus we upgrade our perceptions of our life and reality. Knowledge and its application change us from the inside, and change our world from the outside in.

Gathering Self-Knowledge

What we are primarily concerned about now is acquiring new knowledge with a purposeful intent—as a means of evolving our brain and, by extension, our life. We discussed this at length in chapter 11, so we know how important it is to secure a baseline of knowledge that we can expand on. To become a more patient person, for example, we need to think about people who exhibit this quality, read books on the art of acceptance and tolerance, read accounts of people who've demonstrated a remarkable ability to endure hardships, and so on. We also have to gather some self-knowledge and observe how we respond in various situations, so that we can compare ourselves to the model we're creating.

Let's make this even more concrete. One of the most frequently cited desires for change is to gain self-control in the form of losing weight. The first stage of many weight-loss programs is to have those enrolled gain knowledge about proper nutrition, the caloric values of foods, body mass index, the hypoglycemic index of various foods, portion control, the do's and don'ts of when and how to eat, and hundreds of other concepts. Many diet programs also recommend that we keep a food diary, noting everything we eat in a day to show ourselves exactly how much we consume. This eye-opening exercise is designed to help us gain self-knowledge. Knowledge allows us to look at who we are being, what we are doing, and how we are thinking, and to compare and make the distinction between that and who we want to become.

Seeking Out Instruction

After learning different concepts, the next step is that we receive a great deal of instruction from the experts. This can be in meal preparation, balancing our intake of various food groups, exercise routines, and so on. Without this key component of instruction, most diets—or self-improvement plans—will fail. We can seek out knowledge and information on our own. But at some point, our progress slows, and we need assistance from someone with more expertise than we have, to get us to the next level. Instruction, usually from someone who has experienced what we are endeavoring to learn, teaches us how to apply knowledge. Instruction teaches us how to do what we intellectually learned.

For example, I know someone (I'll call her Melissa) who learned to play the guitar. She was self-taught, and her grasp of strumming, picking, and basic chords was impressive for someone who never took a lesson. Although her initial progress was rapid, the learning curve flattened out. She grew frustrated and a little bored, so she sought out a teacher who could help her to progress at a faster rate than she could have on her own. One of the key ingredients of instruction is that we are given guidelines as to how to reach an intended result, by someone who has mastered a skill to some degree. Instruction is the how-to stage.

How Am I Doing?
The Role of Feedback in Evolving the Brain

As we attain knowledge and receive instruction, getting feedback allows us to know how we are doing. Melissa knew that she was doing some things incorrectly, but it took expert eyes and ears to help her pinpoint her weaknesses and assist her in finding ways to overcome them.

Feedback, in its strictest sense, is a response to an input. Generally, it can be either positive or negative. It answers our "How am I doing?" questions. Sometimes we seek out feedback explicitly by asking that question of others and ourselves, and sometimes, agents in the environment provide feedback without our asking for it. For example, if we are driving erratically, either other drivers will beep their horns at us, or the lights of the police cruiser pulling us over will let us know how we're performing that task.

Ideally, we have the ability to self-monitor, but that isn't always the case. As is true of all aspects of human behavior, how we react to feedback varies from person to person. Some people respond more favorably to negative than to positive feedback. I've worked with several people who, during informal performance reviews, have stated, "That's nice of you to compliment me, but I really learn more from criticism than praise. Tell me where I need to improve. I already know what I'm doing well." Conversely, I've worked with individuals who crumbled in the face of criticism and needed to have their negative assessments couched in very soft language. How people respond to the timing of feedback also varies. Some people appreciate receiving immediate feedback; others prefer that it be delayed, so that they are no longer in the heat of the moment. Immediate feedback is often the most beneficial, because the cause-and-effect nature of the input is clearer.

Feedback in any form and from any aspect of our immediate environment should never be taken personally. It simply helps us make the distinction between when we are doing (applying knowledge) something correctly, and when we are not.

One of the chief reasons many diets don't work is that most people like to receive *immediate feedback*. In talking about the baseball pitcher, we saw that he received immediate feedback in terms of his performance. For a pitcher, a ball whizzing past his head on a line drive toward center field delivers a pretty clear message: don't throw that particular pitch, in that particular spot, to that particular hitter, at that particular count again.

For dieters, on the other hand, the feedback mechanism is not as immediate. Many programs include weigh-ins and the measurement of body parts to monitor progress. Perhaps even more important to dieters is recognition from family, friends, and peers: "You look great!" and "Have you been exercising?" or even "Something's different about you." That can and often does have an even greater effect than tipping the scales a few pounds less than the previous week.

For any committed person who wants change, feedback can also come in the form of the efforts he or she makes. For example, a person who is altering his lifestyle over time can chart what he should eat daily in proper amounts, along with the exercise he wants to do. By looking at that chart over time, he will see the fruits of his disciplined efforts. The visual feedback of seeing his chart fill up with the records of daily wins will serve as important self-recognition. He is on target by matching his intent with his actions.

Often, we also receive self-feedback from our body, based on our own emotional or physical responses to changes we are making. If we are working to lose weight, and we notice that our respiration rate doesn't skyrocket when we walk up the two flights of stairs to our office, that internal feedback and sense of "I feel pretty good" serves as a strong motivator.

Feedback Can Overcome Paralysis

In an experiment performed at the Department of Neurology at Bellevue Hospital in New York City, researchers created a testing and feedback environment to make the paralyzed limbs of stroke victims work again.[3] How is this possible, based on our model of what we know about the brain's ability to learn and change?

The subjects first learned some important knowledge about what might be possible for stroke patients, and then received specialized instruction. After rehearsing a new plan in their mind, patients were ready for a new experience. Using the frontal lobe, they wired new information in their brain, beginning to cause their neural circuits to organize into corresponding patterns.

Now it was time to practice, to turn their knowledge into experience. The patients began to pay attention to immediate feedback they were receiving, on a monitor that showed their brain-wave activity. In the initial part of the experiment, each subject was asked to focus on moving his or her healthy limb, while observing on the screen a specific pattern of his or her brain activity. After repeating this pattern at will through repetitive practice, in a short amount of time patients could easily reproduce the same mind patterns on the screen by their thoughts alone. Each patient became aware of the automatic, unconscious level of mind that it took to move their healthy limb.

As the experiment progressed, the subjects then concentrated on that healthy pattern—thinking about that pattern and making an intentional decision to move the healthy limb (without actually moving that limb). They eventually learned to transfer the healthy brain pattern to the paralyzed limb. The result was dramatic: the paralyzed limb was able to move again.

Through feedback, patients learned to repeatedly create the same level of mind by causing their brain to fire in the right combination of neural nets in the same sequence and order. And by doing so over and over, that new level of mind became a familiar, routine activity. Each time they recreated the brain pattern on the screen, it became easier, because the feedback they were receiving showed them when they were doing the task or action correctly.

Feedback helps us distinguish between when we are reproducing the right level of mind and when we are not, so that we can navigate our way to a particular end. When, through repeated feedback, these subjects were able to create the "level of mind" of normal, healthy movements, they began at will to transfer that mind, to make their paralyzed limb move just as the healthy one did. It took the same frame of mind for these stroke patients to move their paralyzed limb that it took to move the healthy one, and the body will always follow the mind.

This was one of the first experiments to validate that the mind can influence the body through the proper feedback and instruction.

Need an Attitude Adjustment?

When we get out in the world and put into practice our new skill, belief, or attitude, we're taking a necessary step in evolving ourselves. What's important to note is that when we demonstrate our skills and receive feedback, that feedback supplies more knowledge and instruction that we can use, to refine ourselves and our approach to the goal we've set. If we receive great knowledge and expert instruction, and we can properly apply that information to produce action, we should expect to accomplish exactly what we set our mind to do. Until we can repeatedly accomplish that end at will, we need feedback to hone or enhance our actions. To finally achieve our intent is the ultimate feedback that makes the experience complete.

Suppose you've decided to reduce your level of anger. You've long exhibited a hair-trigger response, and you want to become a more understanding person who doesn't blow up so easily. So you create a new internal representation of serenity, and undertake a process of mental rehearsal. Each day, you do your mental rehearsal exercise, firing together and wiring together new circuits in your gray matter by remembering and reaffirming whom it is you want to become. You feel you've been able to get the frontal lobe to quiet all those other areas of the brain, so that you can plan and focus on your goal. The brain then combines and coordinates different neural nets of philosophy and experience to invent a new model of being. When each mental review session is over, you are in the desired frame of mind.

After a month of following this regimen, you feel it's time to take this new attitude out for a test drive. So you visit Mom. You and your mother have been at odds in the last few months. She's had to struggle with some minor health issues, but based on how much she talks about them, you'd think she has only one month to live and is in excruciating pain. Every conversation turns into a recitation about her woes and anxieties. You have tried to be sympathetic, but there's a limit.

After not seeing Mom for a month, you go to her house for a visit, and it's a repetition of the same old situation. She doesn't ask about you, your recent promotion, or anything to do with your family, your siblings, or the rest of the world. In the past, you would call her on her behavior, but this time, you simply sit and listen, nod when appropriate, empathize with her, and then leave after an hour, still on good terms with her. You feel like you've done a good job of producing a different result. But on the drive home, you notice that your teeth are clenched and you're strangling the steering wheel, and when you get home, a splitting headache drives you to bed. How did you really do?

When we set out to demonstrate our new skill or ability, we inevitably rely on the environment to provide clues to how we're doing. Whether we want it to or not, the feedback from our environment is going to give us a status report. This is fairly simple when it comes to improving a physical skill. I knew, based on the number of times I fell, felt out of control, or didn't cut a turn as sharply as I wanted to, how I was doing when I first learned snowboarding. If the number of words we type per minute increases, we know we're moving toward a higher level of proficiency. But what if we're trying to be less prone to displays of anger?

When our goal is to change an unwanted neural habit, replace it with a new level of mind, and then demonstrate our new attitude automatically and naturally, if our demonstration (external feedback) does not match the internal state of our body, we are still not there yet.

In our example, even though you demonstrated patience and control in being with your mother, you still left the scene in a suppressed state of rage and frustration. In your mental rehearsal you had practiced being not angry, but compassionate. By visiting Mom, you received some good feedback that you can work with, because you controlled your impulses; however, you did not complete your intended desire. Your internal state did not match your external demonstration and, therefore, you were not "being" compassionate. When the demonstration of our modified actions produces the desired external feedback, *and* our internal state matches that intent, we are controlling the mind and the body, both neurologically and chemically.

How can we accurately assess our new level of mind? We must self-reflect to examine whether what we are doing is congruent with how we are feeling. If it is not, then we must insert a new plan in our mental rehearsal so that the next time, we improve both our actions and our feelings.

Priming, Behavior, and Implicit Memory

When we make anything implicit—driving a stick shift, knitting, buttoning our shirt, playing the martyr—we do these things without the intervention of the conscious mind. We have wired those circuits to the cerebellum, and both the brain and the body have these tasks memorized almost like blinking, breathing, repairing cells, and secreting digestive enzymes.

Once we have a conscious thought in our neocortex, an unconscious thought/associative memory/implicit memory fires in response to our environment, and causes us to think equal to this stimulus. This process is often referred to as *priming:* we have an unconscious response to an external source that makes us think and act in a certain way, without even being conscious of why we are doing it. Priming finds its origins in the nondeclarative memory system.

Have you ever noticed that if you think about flowers and recall the image of a rose, the other flowers you have stored in your brain are likely to fire as well? That's an example of priming. Psychologists use the term priming because of its relation to the priming of a pump. To get a pump system to function properly, a liquid must already be present in the system in order to get the pump to draw more liquids out.

In neurological terms, priming involves the activation of clusters of neural nets that are surrounded by, and connected to, other clusters of nets holding similar concepts. When one cluster is activated, those other nets connected to it will be more likely to come into consciousness. Priming can also refer to a phenomenon that we've all experienced: once we buy a new car, say a Nissan Sentra, we begin to notice many more Sentras on the road than we did before. Because of our exposure to one event or experience, we're more acutely aware of other, related stimuli.

With priming, a brief, imperceptible stimulus provides enough activation for a *schema* (a mental structure of some aspect of the world) to be rolled out. Schemas enable us to function in the world without necessitating purposeful thought. For example, we have a schema for a door, so that no matter what kind of door we encounter, we negotiate it.

Unfortunately, we also have schemas that are stereotypes, scripts, or even worldviews to help us understand the world. That is why we may have unconscious, reflexive responses to happenings in our environment. Many African-American males, for example, report that when they enter an elevator with Caucasians, they notice that the women will clutch their purses more tightly, and men and women will both edge farther away.[4] If we were to ask Caucasians why they exhibit these behaviors, they are either unlikely to recall having done so, or claim that it meant nothing—it was simply a habit. Priming is an implicit reaction that happens beyond our conscious awareness.

Along with this kind of response to stereotypes, we exhibit a host of other behaviors that are implicit, hardwired body memories, which have either been conditioned as a part of our genetic inheritance, or that we have taught the body to do automatically through repetition. For example, our environment constantly triggers implicit responses. Why is it that we can be having a pleasant day, and then, inexplicably, one irritant (a neighbor's son drives by with a thudding sound system in his car) sets off a cascade effect of mood-dampening responses? We immediately recall the slight irritation we felt when the same neighbor invited nearly everyone else on the block over for a holiday get-together, but didn't invite us. Then, anger swells as the vision of our mailbox dangling from its post, the clear victim of a baseball bat attack, rises before our eyes. Suddenly, we're running all the programs in our head that tell us how much people disrespect us. That nice day turns dark, and we can't explain why, because so much of this has been an unconscious, reflexive response.

These functions that produce what we commonly refer to as our *mood* are part of our limbic system, which acts as a kind of subconscious thermostat. Because these are also subconscious systems, the body will follow the command of the brain, because that is what we have trained it to do so well. It doesn't ask questions like, *Are you sure, boss?* It just takes orders and follows through on the commands of the mind. The more unconscious our thoughts are, the more we are allowing the body to be in command. This is why it takes conscious awareness to stop the process.

How much of our day is about allowing the environment to cause us to think? This is exactly what priming is. When we allow the environment to rule our thoughts, it turns on all the implicit, associative memories we have hardwired, and we are then running programs—unconscious streams of consciousness—with no conscious awareness. This means we are unconscious most of our waking day. We are "being" our familiar memories that we have wired from so many unconscious habits. If we are not getting the chemicals we have become accustomed to, a voice from our past begins to fire in our brain. Once we have that thought (which is a result of our chemically addicted body screaming back to the brain that it needs a fix), the corresponding neural network will fire. The next thing we know, we are unconscious and acting without thinking, creating states of anger, depression, hate, and insecurity.

In what may be an example of priming, several studies suggest a link between acts of homicide in school settings and continuous exposure to violent video games. Although this is difficult to prove, such games, along with many other factors, may contribute to priming certain at-risk youths to commit violent actions, in what could well be unconscious demonstrations of aggression.[5]

Advertising is a key priming mechanism. Sometimes an unconscious thought triggers a circuit that fires as a result of the numerous, repetitive television commercials we see. We tune into mental programs that highlight sickness, or feelings of being deprived, or a separation from self. As a result of the "mental rehearsal" of seeing so much advertising, and having practiced these feelings mentally and instructed our body on how to demonstrate them so well, the next thing we know, we think we need a new prescription drug for a syndrome we're now sure we have, or we feel that our old car is now inadequate, and we have to replace it. All this happens without much conscious thought. We all unconsciously respond to cues in our world, matching our own social and personal limitations. Are we really freewilled?

What's so remarkable is that we allow this process of creating unconscious conditioning to produce the current (and perhaps, sad) state of our existence. When we are living from our past unconscious memories, we are priming what is familiar in us. In truth, the more routine we are, the more controlled we are by the environment, our associative memories, and our unconscious social beliefs. To be primed is to be unconsciously controlled by the external world, and we behave accordingly.

Turning the Tables on Priming

A break in our routine—whether a two-week trip or another alteration of our daily life—can sometimes prompt this type of perspective shift. Most people who go on vacation will vouch that by being out of their environment, they can get a greater sense of perspective. Mental rehearsal is another type of escape from the enslavement of environmental priming. Going within to rehearse provides us with the type of perspective alteration that is a necessary precursor of truly evolving our brain and behavior. When we rehearse long enough, we will produce a deeper change that occurs at a deeper level of consciousness.

Just as priming allows us to notice more cars like the one we recently purchased, if we focus on becoming a more grateful person in our mental rehearsal, we will not only realize more things that we have to be grateful for, but we will also witness more acts of gratitude that we can assimilate into our ideal. When we change our implicit perception from a negative one (the world is inherently unfair) to a better one (I deserve good things and I have them all around me), we go from seeing things unconsciously, based on past memories and experiences, to seeing things consciously. When we consciously choose to focus our attention on exploring more evolved virtues, we have gone from an implicit, unconscious view of the world to an explicit perception. As we practice this new attitude consistently, we will change this new state of mind into an implicit memory.

We can use this concept of an unconscious cue triggering our implicit system to our advantage. Mental rehearsal serves as a self-priming mechanism. If, for instance, we work on creating a model of ourselves as a restrained and patient person, then as we sit in solitude, that concept of ourselves becomes more real than anything in our environment. Thus time and space recede, and our past identity and experiences as an angry, impatient person also recede. If that thought of the new version of our self becomes real to us, then we have primed ourselves for another, more positive kind of cascade effect. We have primed ourselves to be tolerant, instead of the environment causing us to think and act with unconscious neural habits. Because priming activates circuits that cause us to behave in certain ways, we can prime our brain to function equal to a focused ideal. Instead of spiraling downward, we can rise upward. In this way, we demonstrate that it is possible to change, that we can disconnect ourselves from the environment and the collective influences that have shaped us. When we mentally rehearse, we are priming the brain to help us be at cause in the environment, instead of feeling the effects of it. Self-priming allows us to be greater than the environment. And being greater than the environment is what evolution is all about.

Let's go back to the example of the booming car stereo triggering our internal war with the neighbors. Our perception of the events themselves could be altered, if we had been doing the kind of mental rehearsal we've discussed, and had trained our frontal lobe to still the emotional centers that (in our example) run riot in our brain. Instead of thinking, "That damn kid drives up and down the street just to piss me off," we would either ignore the sensory input entirely or think, "Mark must be on his way to work." Instead of thinking, "They took out my mailbox. Everyone's out to get me," we would think instead, "Random acts of stupidity and violence are everywhere. I should be grateful it wasn't worse." That shift in perception will start out as explicit and ultimately become implicit.

In reality, we have been mentally rehearsing those negative states of being and demonstrating them our entire life. Our unconscious thoughts and behaviors dictate what we believe and how we behave. Why is it that we can focus on one little irritant of a stimulus to the point that we create an entire web of unhappiness, frustration, and anxiety? We can be in the grocery store, and just as we are approaching the shortest line, the clerk says that the person just in front of us will be the last one he will check out. Every other line is jammed with people. We have only 15 items, and we're in the express lane. It's clear that the person in front of us is well over the limit. There's that conspiracy again— those who play by the rules get screwed in the end. And now, because of the jerk in front of us, and the miserable clerk who probably can't count to 15, we're going to have to get into one of those other lines and wait. The litany could go on, and it does, in our head. As the old adage goes, reality is eleven-tenths perception . . . and somehow the mind seems to be a factor in influencing it.

What we may fail to understand is that the brain doesn't discriminate among thoughts on the neurological level. It takes no more effort to form a positive thought than it does a negative one. Attitudes are simply accumulations of related neural nets, and positive attitudes are as easy to construct as negative ones. (I use the terms *positive* and *negative* to demonstrate actions, behaviors, attitudes, and thoughts that serve us and don't serve us.) Yet, few people construct those positive ones. Few people arrive at the conclusion that just as we can develop the habit of being depressed, angry, sullen, suffering, or hateful, we can be happy, content, joyful, and fulfilled. We take the negative states of mind that we've inherited from our parents and other ancestors, and we reproduce them. We then reinforce those states of mind, based on our own prior experiences.

Scientific evidence shows that the brain is as changeable as the words we write in our word processing program. The irony of this is that the way out of the mess we've created requires us to use the same tools we used to get ourselves into it. We don't need a simple twist of fate to write a happy ending to our own life story; considering things from a slightly different perspective may be all that's required.

All we can ever know is based on what we perceive. What we perceive is based on what we experience, along with the tools of interpretation we inherited and employ, time and time again. Do we perceive the world as a place filled with negativity, because we have trained ourselves to look for it and ultimately be its reflection? Colin Blakemore and Grant Cooper at the Cambridge Psychology Laboratory conducted an experiment on cats that sheds some light on this question of how and what we perceive.[6] The researchers placed kittens in two groups. The first group was raised in a chamber lined with horizontal stripes. The second group was raised in a chamber lined with vertical stripes. Because the kittens were placed in their environment at a critical time in the development of their sensory apparatus, and because they were exposed to only one type of line, their visual receptors were limited. The so-called "horizontal cats" were unable to perceive vertical objects. When a chair was placed in their environment, the cats walked right into the legs as though they weren't even there. The so-called "vertical cats" could not perceive horizontal objects, so when they were placed in an environment with a tabletop, they would either avoid going on it, or they simply walked off its edge. All the objects in the cats' reality already existed, but they could not see them. The lesson here is that we are able to perceive only what our brain is organized to tell us.

Could it be, for example, that our brain is organized to perceive injustices directed against us? Might this have happened because we inherited from our parents, and then heard while growing up, constant reinforcement of the idea of persecution and incessant replays of life's unfair events? If so, then we aren't able to perceive the opposite situation. We lack the receptors for fairness, and no matter what we do, we won't perceive a situation as anything but unfair. Clearly, how we perceive and respond to the environment is intrinsically linked to our habits of being and our state of mind on a most nondeclarative level.

Remission Revisited

Not everyone gives in to self-imposed or inner-directed perceptual biases. We saw this illustrated clearly in chapter 2 with people who experienced healing from disease. As we recall, the prognosis for most of them was not good. They could have retreated and run all the programs that were hardwired in their brain, but instead, they chose to believe a different set of truths than most people would in their situation. For example, they believed that an innate intelligence inhabited their body, giving them life and possessing the power to heal them. Along with that conviction, they held firm to the notion that our thoughts are real and can have a direct effect on our body. They also held that we all have the power to reinvent ourselves. In the process of inward attention, they experienced the ability to focus so intently that time and space seemed to disappear. As a result, they were able to employ their mind in doing work very similar to what I've described as mental rehearsal. They used knowledge, instruction, and feedback to affect cures on a wide variety of conditions and diseases. They constructed a paradigm of themselves as healthy, and they held that idealized image in their frontal lobes with an intensity of concentration that literally cured them.

We spoke extensively about change in the previous chapter, and this model should help you to understand how change is possible. To change is to have a new mind in spite of the body and the environment, and to train the body to follow in that new direction. When the body has become trained by our repetitive actions and experiences to be the mind, it will take all of our conscious will to stop the body's conditioned mind from controlling us. To change is to break the physical and mental conditioning of being ourselves—that is, what we repeatedly think and do. If we can modify our regular, normal, unconscious daily actions enough times by using our conscious mind, we will redirect the body toward a new experience of ourselves and our reality. When we learn something new and want to apply it, we must take control of the habitual actions of the body's mind, and use the conscious mind as a compass. With the proper knowledge, instruction, and feedback, we can replace those old patterns of thinking, doing, and being with new ones, and evolve our brain through new synaptic connections and rewired neural networks. Then the same subconscious mind that is keeping our heart beating will navigate us to a new future.

From Unskilled to Skilled

When we are learning anything new and taking it to a level of skill and mastery, we follow four basic steps.

1. First, we start out *unconsciously unskilled.* We do not even know that we don't even know.

2. As we learn and become aware of what we want, we become *consciously unskilled.*

3. As we begin to initiate the process of demonstration (the "doing"), if we keep applying what we learn, we eventually become *consciously skilled.* In other words, we can perform an action with a certain amount of conscious effort.

4. If we go further, continuously putting our conscious awareness on what we are demonstrating, and we are successful in performing the action repeatedly, we become *unconsciously skilled.* When we begin the process of change, this is where we want to end. Take a look at Figure 12.3 to examine the flow chart of skill development.

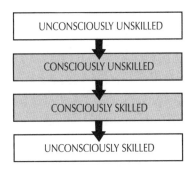

Figure 12.3
Skill development.

I briefly mentioned snowboarding earlier when I was describing learning a new skill. A few years ago, I decided to learn to snowboard. I was *unconsciously unskilled*. Once I decided that I wanted to learn how to do this new thing, I crossed into the territory of being *consciously unskilled*. I knew that I didn't know how to snowboard. Through the process of instruction, in which I gained knowledge about the how-to's of snowboarding, and put that knowledge to use when I practiced the activity, I made the transition to being *consciously skilled*. I was able to perform the skill with conscious awareness—in other words, I had to think about what I was doing nearly every second in order to remain upright, pointed downhill, and in control. I had to be consciously present every second with my intent, and when I lost my concentration, the result was pretty painful. With any skill we learn, this formula applies—whether it is a sport, an attitude, a virtue, or a supernatural feat. To master anything is to make it an implicit memory and make it look easy.

In time, with more practice, and fewer falls, I could make it down the hill without having to remind myself of every bit of instruction I'd learned about how to snowboard. Then my body had to relax enough to make snowboarding second nature without too much exertion. I began to think less, and let my body remember what to do. Once I got to the point when I didn't have to think about what I was doing and was able to just do it, I was now at the stage of being *unconsciously skilled*.

From Thinking to Doing to Being

As I was researching this book, one of the people I interviewed told me that he had suffered from debilitating depressive episodes from his adolescence through his late twenties. This surprised me, because upbeat, compassionate, and spontaneous Larry seemed like the last person in the world who would have a history of depression.

Like many functionally depressed people, he was a good actor: most of his colleagues at the design firm where he worked would have never guessed Larry harbored a secret. He often stayed late on the pretext of having to work, but in reality, he feared going home to an empty apartment.

During weekends, Larry purposefully avoided most human contact, because routine social exchanges were a reminder that he lacked meaningful and emotionally intimate relationships. Thus, he had become a member of what he called the Dawn Patrol. On Sunday morning, he'd arise before 6 a.m. to do his weekly marketing. He'd developed the habit because, following the painful dissolution of the one long-term relationship he'd had, he'd be in tears as he walked the grocery aisles, plagued by memories of the two of them shopping together. After a failed marriage, he went into a tailspin, ultimately not showing up for work and lying in bed, his apartment strewn with garbage. After that, a psychiatrist diagnosed his problem and suggested antidepressants. Larry declined.

Just a few months after his diagnosis, he was feeling as good as he ever had in his whole life. He told me that when he discovered that what was causing his oddly morose behavior was biochemical in nature and not some parental curse (his parents were undiagnosed depressive recluses who remained emotionally distant from Larry and his siblings), he felt enormous relief. Once he could apply a label to the disorder in his life, he could formulate a plan to overcome it.

Larry applied some mental discipline to his personal transformation. He read up on depression and its causes and cures. He even dabbled in some self-help reading. But instead of imagining how he could regulate the action of his serotonin uptake inhibitors, he started thinking about who he wanted to be. He created a mental catalogue of the circumstances and events from his past and from his observation that he could label as "happy." Larry then created an ideal of what he wanted his life and his personality to be like.

It was easy to find inspiration for this "creature" he was "Frankensteining" together. He'd spent the better part of his life admiring the ease with which other people seemed to move through their days and engage in social activities. From one person, he "stole" a sense of humor; from another, a social adroitness that manifested in always being able to say the right thing; and from another, a self-confidence that never veered into cockiness. When he'd assembled parts from donors real and imagined (he did a lot of "homework" watching television and movies, imagining how the newly configured Larry would behave), he speculated about how that conglomeration of parts would make up his new personality.

Larry inserted himself mentally into situations, real and imagined, to practice the behaviors that he would have to change. He already had a strong set of skills; his professional life was a good platform from which to build. That Larry hadn't been able to transfer those skills to his social life was one of the major symptoms of his particular form of depression. He saw that there were two different Larrys. For a long time he had to ask himself in social situations, "WWWLD?" (What Would Work Larry Do?)

After he'd assembled all that knowledge, much of it semantic, he set out to demonstrate what he'd learned and mentally rehearsed. Intuitively, Larry understood that he had to change some of his habitual actions. One of the first things Larry did in his quest for change was to force himself to go shopping after work or in the middle of the day on Saturday. Larry also practiced being "happy" on the weekends. In time, he was able to leave his apartment anytime he wanted, or whenever he felt himself sliding too comfortably into his old routine. Eventually, when he went to the grocery store or for a run or a bike ride around the neighborhood, he noticed that people would smile at him, and he could smile back.

In addition to taking up karate, Larry challenged himself by taking classes at a local improv theater. He had no intention of ever performing—although the last class project was to participate in a show—but he wanted to be able to think more quickly on his feet. At first, he responded more in his head than aloud during classes and exercises, but his confidence blossomed, and he emerged from his shell in surprising ways. Larry understood the implications of his on-stage transformations.

Over time, Larry was able to stop asking himself, "WWWLD?" When he applied some of those social skills to his personal life, people responded to him. Once those new circuits were more firmly wired, once he was out in the world practicing being more open and exposing himself to new experiences, he eventually got to the point where Work Larry and Home Larry were just Larry. Being this new, modified, version of himself was becoming easy.

Eventually, Larry even started to date Rebecca, a brown belt in his karate class and an intensely vivacious woman any man would be attracted to. Her presence provided a whole new set of emotional experiences that he loved and enjoyed.

There were still occasional bumps in the road. Sometimes Larry felt like he was slipping into his old routines again, but he eventually learned not to compare himself to others. He knew he still had a ways to go but, as he said, the very fact that he could tell me all of these things about himself was a pretty good indication of the level of comfort he felt.

He had grown so accustomed to being this new Larry, that the other Larry seemed to be a character in some dimly remembered movie he'd rented. In a final, shrewd observation, Larry told me that he didn't want to forget about the other Larry entirely. "It's like when I learned that I was clinically depressed: the fact that I could identify the source of my unhappiness was a great comfort. I need to keep in mind who I was and how I was, before. I don't think about that often, but every now and then, I take those pictures out and look at them as a reminder. The thing is, I can look at them, but I don't go back there." Larry had certainly produced a different outcome in his life, and the fact that he could revisit that past self and didn't have to bury it completely seemed a remarkably healthy thing.

You see, Larry intellectually understood from his doctor's diagnosis that he had a hardware problem in his brain. His neurotransmitters, circuits, and brain chemistry were out of balance and had resulted in depression. He also realized that a software problem had contributed to his depression: the stressful events of his divorce and their ensuing memories had changed his behavior. He needed the knowledge that he had both a hardware and software problem, but that intellectual understanding didn't change how he felt. Medications and therapy might have helped him to some degree, but relying on pharmaceuticals meant to him that the moment he stopped the medications, his depression would return. For those reasons, he took it upon himself to intentionally change both the hardware and software in his brain, by using a progression of thinking, doing, then being.

Let's look at Larry's healing from a more neurological perspective. When he decided to change his life, one of the first things he did was create a new model of himself, based on semantic knowledge and episodic memories. Drawing on his past and his workday behaviors, he assembled new circuits based on previously stored and wired concepts. He added new information that he could try out and ultimately become. Larry used mental rehearsal to develop that new self-image in his frontal lobe. He spent a lot of time planning that new ideal, to the point that those novel combinations, patterns, and sequences of freshly acquired and stored information could be hardwired in his brain as a new level of mind.

But Larry still had to modify his behavior, not just his thinking. Altering some of his old habitual behaviors in the process, he attempted to apply what he knew. Although he had speculated about the possible approaches he could take in his encounters with other people, and posited what his life would be like if he did x, y, and z, the possibilities that his frontal lobe created weren't yet personalized. He had to apply what he had been rehearsing to create new experiences for himself. Once he had his first pleasurable experience, repeating these experiences began the process of forming implicit memories.

All of what Larry wanted went against the chemical continuity of depression. He really didn't feel like doing any of this—what was more familiar and comfortable for him were all those feelings that reminded him of his depressed self. What had always felt right before was to be unhappy, unworthy, and miserable, and it took much will to want to feel anything else. The moment he tried to do anything contrary to how he was used to feeling, he felt out of balance.

As a result, Larry initially felt uncomfortable, because he was no longer thinking the same thoughts, feeling the same feelings, making the same brain chemicals, and being the same person he was previously. In the beginning, he felt like his personality was under assault and his chemical addiction to depression was being attacked. The mental chatter and subvocalization that screams and makes deals with us arrives in the brain when we have made the body the ruler.

Larry had experienced all of this. Before he decided to change, he could intellectualize that his habit of being depressed was not healthy for him, but it was difficult to see a future beyond how he was feeling. His mother called every day, and he complained to her about his failed marriage. His sister brought him dinner once each week. His house cleaner listened to his lamentations and heard all about his insomnia. All of this was whom he had become, so what would happen if he changed? No dinners, no maternal offerings of comfort, nothing to talk to his housekeeper about. His whole identity had been wrapped up in being depressed.

It took applying that insight and seeing what effect his efforts had created, to both personalize that knowledge and produce a new experience. Larry learned from his mistakes, and rehearsed how he would behave differently at the next opportunity. He reviewed his actions every evening with self-awareness and self-observation. He consciously changed his behavior and produced different outcomes as a result. Every day, he repeated this process and evolved his thoughts, actions, and attitudes.

In time, his actions were consistent with his thoughts. He stored new memories as a part of his evolving neural network of a more social and more happy Larry. The best way for us to be rid of old memories and painful past associations is to make new memories. We can steal the neural growth factor that once cemented those painful old memories, and redistribute it to create new bonds.

What is crucial to understand is that Larry was able to summon these new patterns at will. He wasn't just firing off stored patterns at random: he was consciously picking and choosing from a menu of behaviors that he hoped would fit each social situation in which he found himself. In time, the level of consciousness necessary to fire those newly formed and still-evolving patterns decreased.

The new, more socially balanced Larry had become an automatic, unconscious process. He broke the old habit of self and formed a new habit of being.

The cerebellum played an important role in this conversion from highly conscious to unconscious storage. When Larry first repatterned his past knowledge and experiences, and incorporated his new knowledge and experiences into his revised neural network, it was stored in the neocortex. As Larry's familiarity with these circuits and subroutines grew, the information wired itself to the cerebellum, the site that governs the body's coordinated memory functions. When we hardwire some trait or action to be implicit, the cerebellum, like a microprocessor, sends power to the neural net that contains those functions, attitudes, and beliefs. It takes just a small amount of brain activity to turn it on, and the cerebellum has a direct conduit to the neural nets stored in the neocortex.

Like Larry, at this stage, we don't have to consciously activate the system responsible for our new happiness, our snowboarding, our patience, our gratitude, or whatever retuning of skills, attitudes, beliefs, and behaviors we've made a conscious effort to change. Just as we develop implicit memories, we can also train our brain to have implicit systems of behavior that are as subconscious as all the other systems that sustain our life. Our ultimate goal in evolving our brain is to move not only to a higher level of mind and consciousness, but also to move through the evolutionary process to the point at which we don't have to keep our attention fully focused on this new ideal.

Nurturing Nature and Natural Nurture

We can evolve our brain only by first becoming conscious. When we awaken our consciousness and become aware, we can make a new mind. That new mind then creates a new brain system, by leaving the efforts of our conscious mind in the neural patterns in the brain it has helped evolve. If we take this process to the next level, the brain will continue to upgrade its systems through experience. As we hardwire these new neural networks to the body and we chemically signal the cells to activate new genes through new experiences, these new systems will be a part of the genetic legacy now stored and expressed in the body. Once the physical body has been trained to know what the mind knows, that vital information is passed on to the next generation. By neurochemically encoding repeated events through the mastery of learning and experience, we will genetically become what we have mastered. We inherently encode what becomes "natural," and it manifests itself in nature. Once we can perform anything naturally, it is now our very nature. Then we can pass on what we learned and experienced exactly as it is, contribute it to nature, and leave our mark for future generations to nurture. It is our job to nurture our very nature until what we nurtured becomes natural. That is evolution.

Of course, one experience is not enough to produce this cascade of permanent effects. We have to be able to adapt to life's circumstances, and then repeat an experience many times in order to be able to pass it on. Think of any species that has overcome its environment by consistently being able to endure harsh conditions. An organism must master its external environment by altering its internal chemical state until the change is incorporated as a natural way of being. To unfailingly reproduce a new level of mind and body in a changing environment, and not revert back to old habits, initiates true evolution. Therefore, whatever specific adaptation that allows a species to survive tough conditions will be passed on, not just once, but repeatedly over generations, until it becomes a characteristic of that species. In the case of domesticated animals and selective breeding practices, we choose which specific traits we want to propagate and which we want to extinguish. Through careful selection and monitoring of breeding pairs, we are able to produce animals with the most desirable traits. While we may not want to control mating choices as a part of our human evolution, we should consider the traits that we want to pass on to future generations. Evolving our brain can have a more long-term effect than simply improving our own life.

Biofeedback and Scientific Objectivity

A question remains: how do we know when we know, and when we can move beyond conscious thought to our ultimate goal, an implicit hardwired system we have evolved of our own will?

Communication theorists refer to anything that prevents a message from being accurately conveyed as *interference*. This interference can be one of two types.

- *External interference* refers to anything that has the potential to disrupt communication and that arises from outside the two communicators—a radio playing loudly that prevents them from hearing one another, for example.

- *Internal interference* refers to anything that prevents a message from being communicated that arises from within one of the two communicators—one of the pair being distracted by a problem, for example.

Just as a large part of our success in conversational communication depends on feedback (someone folding her arms and rolling her eyes tells us a lot about how successful we're being in persuading her), the same applies to our attempts to evolve. Internal or external interference can occur in any feedback situation when we are attempting to demonstrate the neural nets we evolved during our mental rehearsal. To eliminate some of the interference, we can use tried-and-true technologies to reduce some of the human unreliability factor.

Technology allows us to measure various elements of brain function, to provide us with ever more accurate pictures of what our brain is doing. In the 1940s, the concept of feedback gave rise to a new field of study called *cybernetics*. This was an attempt to link mankind and human minds to machines. According to the cybernetic model, humans are like machines, in that inputs and outputs can be measurable, changeable, and valuable. The theory held that we could be programmed like a machine to operate more efficiently.

Later on, biologists applied their own spin to the theory to create a field of study called *biocybernetics*. These scientists were primarily interested in how the brain manages to regulate the many functions of the body. For example, our blood's acid level has to stay within a very small range, and that range can be difficult to sustain, given how widely diet and other environmental factors can influence it. Eventually, the question arose that, because all these regulatory functions occur at an unconscious level, can we do anything willfully and purposefully to influence some of those body functions?

Some of the early experiments in what is now called *biofeedback* involved subjects who were taught to modify their blood pressure. They also were able to change their heart rate. Finally, they were instructed on how to change the heart rate and blood pressure together, but in opposite directions—to raise their heart rate and lower the blood pressure, and vice versa.

Of interest here is that most subjects didn't note a difference in how they felt, and they didn't think they'd had much impact on how they responded. The brain couldn't monitor itself to know what it was accomplishing, but the results were there—the subjects were able to do what was requested of them. One way to understand this brain "numbness" is to consider that if someone were to stimulate the region of the brain that involves our being able to move our toes, we could feel the toes moving, but not the stimulation that influenced that movement. How, then, can we transform information from the interior of the body into some form of external signal the brain can use to increase its powers of self-regulation?

Because all the brain's activity is electrochemical, scientists had to devise a way to make biofeedback speak the same language as the brain. In time, they devised machines that could take those measurements of activity and translate them into visuals they could use with their test subjects. What they arrived at was based on some early studies of color visualization. Barbra Brown, Ph.D., UCLA Medical Center, developed a device that would illuminate a blue light whenever the test subjects' brain waves indicated they were in a relaxed state (as measured by an EEG that detected between 8 and 13 Alpha waves per second), and researchers watched the light go on and off as subjects moved into and out of that relaxed state.[7] Normally, we can't readily measure our own brain-wave activity. We may think we are relaxed and believe we are relaxed, but this notion of a visual representation showing us whether or not we are truly in a relaxed state was definitive feedback of a kind the brain is not capable of producing.

Based on this notion of biofeedback, researchers hoped that we could somehow learn to do what only Eastern mystics and yogis had been capable of doing—voluntarily slowing, or in some cases even stopping, their own heart. They termed this type of training *visceral learning* and thought of it in counterpoint to more classical types of conditioning. Visceral learning is voluntary, while conditioning (think of Pavlov's dogs) generally occurs whether or not we are conscious of it taking place.

To Consciously Access the Subconscious

How are yogis able to reduce their heart rate and blood pressure? These functions are regulated on an unconscious level; they are subcortical functions. Accessing the subconscious is not a capability we ordinarily consider possible. In truth, however, we can access our subconscious and consciously control those functions.

As you know, I studied and practiced hypnosis, and that is essentially what hypnosis allows us to do—to consciously enter the subconscious realm, to reformat the implicit systems there. We are able to do this because we regularly move through four states of brain activity every day. To offer hypnosis instruction is beyond the scope of this book, but as we will see, we have already learned a tool that we can use by ourselves, to produce similar results.

When the neocortex is functioning and circuits are firing, and our level of awareness of the environment is active, that electrical activity is referred to as the *Beta state*. It produces the highest frequency of waves while we are, quite obviously, fully conscious. The Beta brain-wave state is our thinking state, when we have our awareness on our body, the environment, and time.

When we relax, take a few deep breaths, and close our eyes, we shut out some of the sensory stimuli that are being measured as electrical activity. As a result of that diminished input from the environment, the neocortex slows and, consequently, so does the electrical activity in our brain. We enter what is called the *Alpha state*. This is a light meditative state, but just as when we are in Beta state, we are conscious (but less conscious of the external world).

The third state we can enter is called the *Theta state*. We've been in this state when we are halfway between a wakeful condition and asleep. The door between Alpha and Theta is like a half-awake, somewhat conscious state, but the body is relaxed and catatonic. We can also get to this state when we employ our frontal lobe to quiet the other centers in the brain and still the neocortex. As the frontal lobe signals circuits to calm down and cool off in the remaining neocortex, brain-wave activity decreases there because mind is no longer being processed in that part of the brain. Thinking decreases and we begin to slip into deeper subcortical brain regions, away from the neocortex.

Last is a subconscious level called *Delta state*. When we are experiencing deep restorative sleep, our brains are producing Delta waves. For the most part, in this state, we are completely unconscious and catatonic, and there is very little activity in the neocortex.

This ability to move among these four states is important because if we can remain conscious and slow the brain's rate so that we are producing Theta waves, we can be conscious in the subconscious realm. Because most of our associative memories, habits, behaviors, attitudes, beliefs, and conditionings are implicit systems and are, by definition, subconscious, as we move into deeper levels of brain-wave activity, we are moving closer to the root of where these elements are held in place. Unfortunately, our will works only in the conscious realm. If we want to change those habits, associations, and conditionings that are responsible for our unhappiness, we have to access them somehow. Using our conscious mind and the Beta brain-wave level of consciousness will produce little result.

Therefore, if we could train ourselves, just when we fall asleep, to let the body begin to relax further (the body, which has become mind, is no longer in control), we could gain dominion over somewhat subconscious mechanisms. We would be entering into the area of the brain where nondeclarative memories or subconscious memories are held in place.

This is where mental rehearsal enters the picture again. When the frontal lobe cools off all the other centers in the brain, and we are able to focus and hold in our mind a single thought, we move from a Beta state to an Alpha state to a Theta state. The reason is the same: conscious mind has been vacated from the rest of the neocortex, because the frontal lobe silences those centers so that our thought can be the only object of our attention. Our mind is no longer preoccupied with the environment and needs of the body. It is now in a creative state, and it has no tendency to react to the outside environment. When this happens, thinking slows down, we change the frequency of brain-wave patterns, and now, if we can stay pseudo-conscious of where our attention is, we will be able to change unwanted patterns, because we are now in the realm where they are housed. Finally, if we continue to focus and make our thoughts more real than anything in our environment, we can unify our conscious and unconscious minds.

In this state of mind, by rehearsing a new way to be, we are able to change our behaviors because we have gained access to the subconscious realm, bypassing our analytical faculties. We gain access to the implicit systems. The new image we hold in our mind replaces our old image and repatterns it in the brain as a new, implicit system. By being able to enter the subconscious realm through entering deeper brain states, we arrive at a state of mind where our habits and behaviors are first formed, and where they are eventually held deeply in place. Now we are in the realm where true change happens.

Biofeedback Revisited

As the study of biofeedback continued, most applications of its principles involved the subject receiving either visual or auditory cues that represented some function of the body. For example, subjects in blood pressure experiments learned to associate a particular color or sound with a lower blood pressure measurement. Through association and repetition, the brain learned that a visual or auditory input corresponded to the regulatory process by which the blood pressure could be lowered. While researchers still don't understand how the brain and the body are able to do this, we do know that the process produces results—we can voluntarily lower blood pressure through biofeedback training. In a sense, this is much like learning how to control our bladder. We gain conscious control over somewhat subconscious mechanisms.

This has enormous implications for us in terms of evolving our brain, and it may provide another clue as to how the people who were able to affect spontaneous remission were able to heal themselves. The simplest definition of an illness is that it has deregulated the normal functioning of the cells in an organ or a system. The brain is responsible for regulation; consequently, it is responsible for maintaining our health.

Similarly, our mental and emotional health is also a function of regulation, and what is called *disregulation.* For example, if we have frequent and debilitating acid indigestion, it is because our body can't properly regulate the amount of acid our stomach is producing. If we have generalized anxiety disorder, that's a malfunction related to our brain's inability to regulate the stress chemicals we produce. The hope is that the brain can be taught to take measures to terminate this disregulation in the body and once again seize control. We used a metaphor very early on to describe some regulatory functions of the brain as operating like a thermostat. When we move into deeper brain states—slowing down thinking in the neocortex—we enter deeper levels of the subconscious mind, where we can better influence our autonomic nervous system. That is the hope and promise of biofeedback: that our brain can be taught to regulate its own functioning to enable us to control both our health and our emotions.

It Takes Time

The Law of Repetition is crucially important in the creation of wired neural nets. "Once and done" won't get us where we need to be; it is physically impossible to wire circuits that way. As much as I wish I could say otherwise, the truth is that it takes time and effort to make the kinds of neurological and behavioral changes that we desire. We have to think and use our brain in new ways, rather than relying on entertainment, media, or the environment to cause us to think in certain predictable ways. Thinking in predictable ways takes neither will nor effort, just rote reactions that allow us to be lazy. We must begin to assemble new thoughts with information that we have not experienced previously. We have to make a conscious effort to plan our future actions and behaviors, and rehearse those actions in our mind so that our body will be trained to follow. Once we can begin to change how our brain is working on a daily basis, we have forced our brain to work differently and, therefore, to produce a new mindset. Once we can self-reflect and become more acutely aware of how we are doing each day, we can reinsert more data on how we can be the next day, so that we add to the ideal of who we are becoming.

Any new state of being will initially take a lot of conscious effort to achieve. We are replacing the neural habits of our old self with an ideal of our new self, so that we can become someone else. The next stage in our evolution—wisdom—involves becoming subconsciously great, noble, happy, and loving, and that will feel as easy and normal as brushing our teeth.

So, aligning our intentions with our actions, or matching our thoughts with our behaviors, leads to personal evolution. To evolve, we must progress from explicit memories to implicit memories; from knowledge to experience to wisdom, or from mind to body to soul. Mental rehearsal prepares the mind. Physical rehearsal trains the body. The union of mental and physical rehearsal is the union of mind and body to a new state of being. When the mind and the

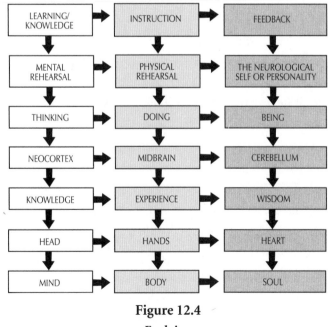

Figure 12.4
Evolving

body are one with anything, we have now reached true wisdom. And wisdom is always recorded in the soul.

This methodology can take you from being unconsciously unskilled, to consciously unskilled, to consciously skilled, to unconsciously skilled, so that you can move to the point at which you have implicit systems fully wired and in place. Then you will have evolved your brain to such an extent that your responses, behaviors, and attitudes are as natural and effortless as the original circuits you chose to modify. At the end of this process, you will be able to summon these new behaviors at will.

After all, our thoughts are created from our memories. Our sequential thoughts are linked together to produce our attitudes. The totality of our attitudes creates our beliefs. Our beliefs, when synthesized, make up our perceptions of the world and determine the choices we make, the relationships we have, the creations we manifest, the behaviors we demonstrate, and ultimately the life we live.

From willing ourselves to change, to changing ourselves at will, the process of evolving our brain is limited only by our imagination.

EPILOGUE: A QUANTUM CHANGE

*Then there is the further question of
what is the relationship of thinking to reality.
As careful attention shows, thought itself is in
an actual process of movement.*

—DAVID BOHM

Until now, we've talked about how changing our mind on a permanent basis has an impact on our physical and mental states of being. But does our "being" a new person or our creating a new attitude have any consequences in our life? If we believe that our thoughts have anything to do with our future and we evolve our brain to think differently, shouldn't that alter our life in some way? Put simply, if we modify our thoughts, does our reality change?

While pioneers on the frontiers of brain science are providing exciting new evidence that such is the case, another area of science is engaged in exploring the very foundation of our query: do our thoughts influence our reality, and if so, how is this possible? In terms of human evolution, we have barely begun to consider that everything in our environment is just a single manifestation of an infinite variety of possibilities, so to answer this question, let's start by examining what scientific theory—specifically in the field of quantum physics—has to say about mind and the nature of reality. Then we'll go on to some final thoughts on how we as individuals can live from an expanded state of mind.

For hundreds of years, the scientific explanation for the order and nature of the universe consisted primarily of a mechanistic view of reality, i.e., that everything in nature was predictable and could be readily explained. In the late 1700s, the scientist/philosopher/mathematician Rene Descartes developed a rational justification for a universal, mathematical/quantitative understanding of nature. To arrive at his understanding that the universe operated as a kind of automaton whose principles were knowable, he had to create an important intellectual division—between matter and mind.

As Descartes considered relatively large objects in space to follow repeatable principles, he decided that all matter was controlled by objective laws and, therefore, fell under the category of science. Concerning the human mind, on the other hand, there were just too many variables to deal with; the mind was too personal and subjective to measure and calculate. Because the mind has such freedom to choose, Descartes relegated the concept of mind to the auspices of religion. He thought that God must have a part in what is personal, what is inside us; and science has its part in what is neutral, what is outside of us. Essentially, Descartes stated that mind and matter are entirely different aspects of reality. Religion and philosophy should deal with mind, and science could deal with matter—the two were not to be mixed. This concept of mind and matter being separate (Cartesian dualism) was the pervasive mind-set that ruled Europe for centuries.

One hundred years later, along came Isaac Newton, with his mathematical laws that codified the mechanistic underpinnings of Descartes' dualism by providing equations and scientific constants that made classical physics a repeatable science. Now, the laws of matter were knowable and consistent and predictable. Nature was really just a machine, and man could offer rational explanations for how it functioned. Newtonian physics ruled the day until the century passed, and Einstein and his theories rocked the world.

Einstein's theory about the nature of matter and energy stands as one of the great intellectual achievements in human history, because his new concepts provided an explanation as to how energy contributed to the formation of matter. Unifying matter and energy was a giant leap forward in understanding the nature of reality. Einstein's work also opened the door to other new areas of inquiry. He postulated, for example, that if we take large bodies and accelerate them, the fastest they can move is the speed of light.

Relativity, based on Einstein's model, made it clear that the laws of physics are essentially the same for all matter (objects and particles) and energy (light and waves) that are traveling at the same speed. For example, if I am driving my car at 55 mph, and you are traveling in a train alongside of me at the same speed, it appears to the two of us that we are not moving, because our relative speed creates relative time for both of us. Therefore, space, time, and even mass are all relative to how fast we are traveling, where we are in space, and whether each of us is moving closer to or farther away from any destination.

Eventually physicists ran into an intellectual conundrum when they considered the nature of one of the fundamental elements of life on Earth—light. Although scientists initially thought that light was a wave and behaved wave-like in all instances, they later observed that light sometimes behaved like a wave, and at other times, like a particle. For instance, how do we explain light's ability to bend around a corner? Through a series of experiments by Maxwell Planck, Niels Bohr, and others, the physics community came up with the idea that light is both a wave *and* a particle. We had arrived at an understanding in scientific thinking called quantum physics, which told us that light behaved in certain ways because of the influence of the person observing the phenomenon.

Thus the tidy world of classical physics with its precise laws began to break down in the early 1900s, when innovative quantum physicists noted that when they measured and observed the very small world of subatomic particles, these did not behave like larger objects in nature. For example, scientists discovered that electrons appeared and disappeared when releasing energy. When energy acted on an electron, causing it to move toward the nucleus, instead of it behaving in a smooth and continuous fashion (like that apple falling from the tree, as demonstrated in classical Newtonian physics), electrons behaved more like a ball rolling down a set of stairs, gaining and losing energy.

The laws of classical physics and quantum physics diverged even further when physicists realized that the tiny particles that make up atoms responded to an observer's mind. For example, waves changed into particles when they were measured and observed. Moreover, whether an observer was present or not changed the outcome of quantum experiments. Subjective mind therefore influenced the behavior of energy and matter. All of a sudden, the objective world of matter and the subjective world of mind were no longer separate. Mind and matter were now related, and in the quantum world of subatomic particles, mind showed a direct effect on matter. This is a powerful and influential idea that I've greatly simplified for our purposes, but the essence of this radical shift in our understanding of how the universe operates is what's important to understand.

Make no mistake, most quantum physicists will tell us that the observer has an influence on the infinitesimally tiny world of subatomic particles. They will also tell us that when it comes to the very large world of objects and matter, classical physics still reigns. The observer has no influence on large objects and the objective world of matter, they will politely inform us. And the notion of using our mind to control an outcome in our life, according to their experiments, is simply impossible.

I have had such conversations with quantum physicists, and I always counter their arguments the same way: If basic particles on the subatomic level are capable of changing into energy and back again, and are subject to the effect of the observer, then we humans have enormous potential power to affect the nature of reality. When they tell me that our subjective mind and our observation affects the very tiny, but not the very large world of "solid" things, I assert that maybe we are just *poor observers*. Perhaps we can train the brain and the mind to work better, so we can become more mindful participants in observing reality. By evolving our brain and mind, we can possibly exert a greater influence on the objective world.

The theory is simple: Mind and the observer are paramount in the understanding of the nature of reality. There is an infinite field of energy that exists beyond our present concept of space and time, which unites all of us. Reality is not one continuous and consistent stream, but is instead, a field of infinite possibilities over which we can exert enormous influence—that is, if we tune into the proper levels of mind. The more powerful the subjective mind, the more influence it has on the objective world.

We learned in this book that we have the ability to change the mind and the brain. We saw how Buddhist monks, through the use of the frontal lobe, produce a more coordinated mind by practicing inner focus. We know that learning knowledge alone will wire the brain to see things in new and unusual ways. Remember the example of the Monet painting in chapter 12—just a few bits of information helped us to view the same picture of reality with new insight. We also now understand that experience further shapes the brain. Think of the wine connoisseur who, with repeated moments of being present with taste and aroma, perceives what others never know exists. Maybe the same applies on a larger scale to how we perceive our life. When we truly change our mind, we change our life.

It appears that we keep seeing the same things the same way in our life because we have been *conditioned* to keep looking for the same. Does the brain see or do the eyes see? If the brain sees, then we can only perceive reality based on what we have wired into our brain. In a simple experiment several years back, subjects were given goggles with colored lenses to wear for two weeks.[1] Each lens was divided in half. One half was yellow and the other side was blue, so that when subjects looked to the left, the world appeared blue; when they looked to the right, things looked yellow. As they wore the glasses daily, while performing their routine activities, over time the subjects no longer saw the colors of the world any differently than they had before they started wearing the special lenses. The study demonstrated that it is the brain that sees, and not the eyes, suggesting that the subjects were filling in reality based on their memory, and that behavior is determined by what is perceived. On a daily basis, do we perceive reality based on our memory? Do we, too, habitually see from our prior experiences instead of our future possibilities?

As we get better at paying attention and applying willful intention, our thoughts can affect our life. Throughout human history, great people who aligned their intention and actions moved mountains and transformed the future with the same brain apparatus that you and I possess. Studies using random event generators have proven that mind does change the objective, typical 50-50 upshot of a coin toss.[2] Many more studies are underway to explore the barely charted territory of the interaction between mind and matter.

As I said in chapter 1: Thoughts matter and they become matter. We can't separate them like Descartes did. Our thoughts influence physical phenomena; they interact with all the matter in the universe. In truth, our personal reality is just a reflection of our personality.

The implications for evolving our brain are extraordinary: if we think in new and different ways, we are altering our future. If we can go from thinking to doing to *being* by implementing the processes I've described in the last two chapters—focusing our attention, using mental rehearsal, and employing the tools of knowledge, instruction, and feedback—and if we can demonstrate our intent and act upon it, we are no longer riding upon the backs of giants. We *are* the giant.

We need not wait for science to give us permission to do the uncommon or go beyond what we have been told is possible. If we do, we make science another form of religion. We should be mavericks; we should practice doing the extraordinary. When we become consistent in our abilities, we are literally creating a new science. When our subjective mind has control of the objective world, we therefore are ahead of the present scientific laws and theorems. And when we repeat, over and over, the process of intentional observation by *being* a more evolved ideal of self, we become wired to be greater than our environment.

Knowing that our thoughts are controlling the environment, instead of having the environment repeatedly create our thinking, finally puts us at cause instead of effect. We will no longer live in stress, because there is no loss of control and no anxiety about what might happen in a future moment based on our memory of a past experience. There is nothing to be stressed about when we know the end result of our thoughts—when we know our future. When we can trust ourselves, our mind, and the quantum field of infinite potentials, we are freed from our primitive "survival" state of mind. There will be no fear of the unknown or the unpredictable, because our mind has already created the outcome in our environment. And the environment is now a product or reflection of our mind, which has already experienced and recorded the events to come.

We have learned that during mental rehearsal, the brain does not know the difference between what it is thinking (internal) and what it experiences (external). Applying these principles will cause the brain to be ahead of the environment. In other words, through mental rehearsal, we change our brain before the external experience happens, and the brain is no longer a record of the past, but of the future.

We have also learned that feelings and emotions are only the end products of past experiences. If we believe that our thoughts have anything to do with our future, then to live by familiar feelings and past emotions is to live by past memories. Past memories are processed in the brain as feelings. When past memories are filtered down to feelings that the body lives by, we are unconsciously producing thoughts that are connected only to the past. Thus to feel is to think in the past. This might explain why so many of us recreate the same difficult relationships, jobs with the same dynamics, and other recurring circumstances in our life. When we unconsciously feel the same feelings every single day, we create more of the familiar.

To rise above the familiar and routine and to become inspired is the true energy of creation. To think beyond how we feel is a great endeavor for any human being. If we cannot execute a level of mind greater than how we emotionally feel, we will never relate to anything unknown and unpredictable. Mind lives in the body when we live by feelings. To lift mind out of the body and put it back where it belongs—into the brain—is a true act of human will. When we finally overcome thinking as a body instead of a mind, we are on the adventure of new and unlimited experiences.

One of the factors that influence our ability to imagine and to create an ideal for ourselves is our limited perception of the order and the nature of the universe. Whether we're a skeptic or a believer doesn't really matter. What we need to understand is that the universe offers more possibilities than we have been trained and conditioned to accept.

We must remind ourselves that we are more than the sum total of our biological processes. We are the self-aware, immaterial essence called consciousness that animates a physical body. At the same time, we are also unified to a greater consciousness that gives life and form to all matter. Both levels of consciousness are inseparable, they are within us, and, indeed, they are who we really are. Ultimately, at a deeper level of consciousness (the dimension before matter has any substance), we are connected to everything in the universe. The energy that holds the universe and all of its components together can be influenced by our conscious interactions in life, because we are made from the same energy. Therefore, we cannot change what we think, how we act, and who we are being, without altering the infinite web of energy. When we truly change, the field of potentials in our personal life should change as well. The outcome of such efforts brings us new and different life circumstances equal to who we have become.

If there are innumerable events in the infinite possible universes of quantum physics, we can surely look forward to new experiences on our own horizon. We cannot even fathom what novel occurrences await us. With a new experience, comes a new emotion. New emotions, which we can create and recreate until they become our very nature, evolve us beyond our primitive animal programs. All we need is a new paradigm of knowledge that we can apply, so that we can embark on an improved experience of reality.

Some may say that this is too difficult to imagine, let alone to be true. Yet, why is it that we have a natural propensity to pray to some higher power or intelligence when conditions become too difficult for us to handle? To pray is to hold a single thought or idea of an outcome in the mind, and make it more real than our present circumstances. It is intentional thought, which affords us the opportunity to make contact with a greater mind. When we can call upon that innate intelligence living inside of us by making our desire the only real intention, it will answer the call. When our will matches the will of this mind, when our mind matches the consciousness of this mind, and when our love for an ideal matches its love for us, it invariably steps in. It is a willful and uncompromising mind that initiates an idea bigger than what we intellectually know. When we can make our thoughts more real to us than the external environment, and when we lose track of the sensory perception of our body, the environment, and time, we literally enter into this unlimited field of possibilities. Our brain is already wired to be this way, through our enlarged frontal lobe.

Can we develop a relationship with this innate order and mind? I say we can. How can this higher mind know all that it knows, and coexist with our conscious mind, but not be intelligent enough to respond to our intention? However, we do need to exercise our subjective free will and make the effort to contact our greater mind. When we take the time to interact with it, we should be bold enough to look for an answer in the form of feedback in our world. Now we are acting as the scientist of our own life. When we can see and measure how our thoughts and intentions unfold from our own inner efforts, we are now keeping track of our own personal experiment called life. It is my experience that as the mind of the unseen begins to respond, our creations come to us not on our familiar terms, but on terms that are new, exciting, unpredictable, and surprising. The emotions of joy and awe will then inspire us to initiate the process, again and again. Now we are developing a neural network to know that a greater power truly exists within us, and we can accept its gifts.

We must inspire ourselves to give this personal experiment in creation a try. Otherwise we stay locked in the intellectual thinking stage of declarative memories, never experiencing the wonder and joy that change can offer. We have to transform ourselves from being an intellectual thinker to becoming a passionate doer, until we can "be" what we set our mind to become. And when we can be anything, we can observe reality from an expanded state of mind, instead of the desperate states of mind that plague humanity. Aligning our thoughts, actions, and intentions brings this field of possibilities to us. When we live in a future that we have not yet experienced with our senses but have lived in our mind, we live by what may be the ultimate demonstration of quantum law.

It is not enough to put little time and effort into changing the mind. We must *become* that mind until it is natural and easy to express the new self. This is when doors open to novel and unexplainable possibilities.

In order to evolve our brain, we have to transform thoughts and memories from explicit to implicit, so that all systems are now influenced by mind. By being one with any concept, we know how to create that particular state of mind. And according to our understanding of implicit memories, perhaps enlightenment simply is knowing that we know.

Even if we cannot accept this new paradigm, we must admit that by changing our mind and our state of being, we will make a host of different choices that we would never have made when living as the old self. When we demonstrate a new expression of the self, we will think and act in new ways. By being a more evolved aspect of self, as one choice then leads to another, over time we will find ourselves in a new life with new circumstances. That is a new reality. It is human evolution in its truest sense.

NOTES

Chapter 1
1. *Ramtha: The White Book.* (1999) JZK Publishing Inc. ISBN 1578730171.

Chapter 2

1. Schiefelbein S (1986) The powerful river. In R Poole (Ed) *The Incredible Machine* (99–156) Washington DC: The National Geographic Society ISBN 0870446207.

   Childre D, Martin H (1999) *The HeartMath Solution: The Institute of HeartMath's revolutionary program for engaging the power of the heart's intelligence.* HarperCollins ISBN 006251605.

2. Popp F (1998 Fall) Biophotons and their regulatory role in cells. *Frontier Perspectives* Philadelphia: The Center for Frontier Sciences at Temple University 7(2):13–22.

3. Medina J (2000) *The Genetic Inferno: Inside the seven deadly sins.* Cambridge University Press ISBN 0521640644.

4. A concept taught at Ramtha's School of Enlightenment. For a comprehensive list of readings and other informational materials visit JZK Publishing, a division of JZK, Inc., the publishing house for Ramtha's School of Enlightenment, at http://jzkpublishing.com/ or http://www.ramtha.com.

5. RSE (see reference 4, Chapter 2).

6. Pascual-Leone D, et al (1995) Modulation of muscle responses evoked by transcranial magnetic stimulation during the acquisition of new fine motor skills. *Journal of Neurophysiology* 74(3):1037–1045.

7. Hebb DO (1949) *The Organization of Behavior: A neuropsychological theory.* Wiley ISBN 0805843000.

8. Robertson I (2000) *Mind Sculpture: Unlocking your brain's untapped potential.* Bantam Press ISBN 0880642211.

   Begley S (2001 May 7) God and the brain: How we're wired for spirituality. *Newsweek* Pp 51–57.

   Newburg A, D'Aquilla E, Rause V (2001) *Why God Won't Go Away: Brain science and the biology of belief.* Ballantine Books ISBN 034544034X.

9. LeDoux J (2001) *The Synaptic Self: How our brains become who we are.* Penguin Books ISBN 0670030287.

10. Yue G, Cole K J (1992) Strength increases from the motor program-comparison of training with maximal voluntary and imagined muscle contractions. *Journal of Neurophysiology* 67(5):1114–1123.

11. Elbert T, et al (1995) Increased cortical representation of the fingers of the left hand string players. *Science* 270(5234):305–307.

12. Ericsson PS, et al (1998) Neurogenesis in the adult hippocampus. *Nature Medicine* 4(11):1313–1317.

13. Draganski B, et al (2004 22 Jan) Changes in grey matter induced by training. *Nature* (London) 427(6872):311–12.

14. Lazar SW, et al (2005 November 28) Meditation experience is associated with increased cortical thickness. *Neuroreport* 16(17):1893–1897.

15. van Praag H, Kempermann G, Gage FH (1999) Running increases cell proliferation and neurogenesis in the adult mouse dentate gyrus. *Nature Neuroscience* 2(3):266–270.

   Kempermann G, Gage FH (1999 May) New nerve cells for the adult brain. *Scientific American* 280(5):48–53.

16. Restak RM (1979) *The Brain: The last frontier.* Warner Books ISBN 0446355402.

   Basmajian JV, Regenes EM, Baker MP (1977 Jul) Rehabilitating stroke patients with biofeedback. *Geriatrics* 32(7):85–8.

   Olson RP (1988 Dec) A long-term single-group follow-up study of biofeedback therapy with chronic medical and psychiatric patients. *Biofeedback and Self-Regulation* 13(4):331–346.

Wolf SL, Baker MP, Kelly JL (1979) EMG biofeedback in stroke: Effect of patient characteristics. *Archives of Physical Medicine and Rehabilitation* 60:96–102.

17. Huxley J (1959) Introduction in *The Phenomenon of Man* by Pierre Teilhard de Chardin. Translation by Bernard Wall NY: Harper.

18. Lutz A, et al (2004 16 Nov) Long-term meditators self-induce high-amplitude gamma synchrony during mental practice. *Proceedings of the National Academy of Science* 101(46):16369–73.

19. Kaufman M (2005 03 Jan) Meditation gives brain a charge study finds. *Washington Post* (A05) http://www.washingtonpost.com/wp-dyn/articles/A43006-2005Jan2.html Accessed 08/09/06.

20. Ramtha (2005 Sept) *A Beginner's Guide to Creating Reality.* Yelm, WA: JZK Publishing ISBN 1578730279.

21. Stevenson R (1948) *Chiropractic Text Book.* Davenport Iowa: The Palmer School of Chiropractic.

22. Ramtha (2005 Sept) *A Beginner's Guide to Creating Reality.* Yelm, WA: JZK Publishing ISBN 1578730279.

Chapter 3

Guyton A (1991) *Textbook of Medical Physiology 8th.* London: WB Saunders and Co ISBN 0721630871.

Snell RS (1992) *Clinical Neuroanatomy for Medical Students.* Little Brown ISBN 0316802241.

Ornstein R, Thompson R (1984) *The Amazing Brain.* Houghton Mifflin ISBN 0395354862.

Chapter 4

1. Restak R (1979) *The Brain: The last frontier.* Warner Books ISBN 0446355402.

2. MacLean PD (1990) *The Triune Brain in Evolution: Role in paleocerebral functions.* NY: Plenum Press ISBN 0306431688.

3. Glover S (2004) Separate visual representations in the planning and control of action. *Behavioral and Brain Sciences* 27:3–24.

Grafman J, et al (1992) Cognitive planning deficit in patients with cerebellar atrophy. Neurology 42(8):1493–1496.

Leiner HC, Leiner AL, Dow RS (1989) Reappraising the cerebellum: What does the hindbrain contribute to the forebrain? *Behavioral Neuroscience* 103(5) 998–1008.

4. Heath R (1997 Nov) Modulation of emotion with a brain pacemaker: Treatment for intractable psychiatric illness. *Journal of Nervous and Mental Disease* 165(5):300–17.

Prescott JW (1969 Sep) Early somatosensory deprivation as an ontogenetic process in abnormal development of the brain and behavior. In IE Goldsmith & J Moor-Jankowski (Eds) *Medical Primatology 1970: Selected papers 2nd conference on experimental medicine and surgery in primates New York NY* (357–375) Karger.

5. Amen D (2003 Dec) *Healing Anxiety, Depression and ADD: The latest information on subtyping these disorders to optimize diagnosis and treatment.* Continuing Education Seminar, Seattle, WA.

6. Tulving E (1972) Episodic and semantic memory. In E Tulving & W Donaldson (Eds) *Organization of Memory* (381–403) NY: Academic Press ISBN 0127036504.

RSE (see reference 4, Chapter 2).

7. Vinogradova OS (2001) Hippocampus as comparator: Role of the two input and two output systems of the hippocampus in selection and registration of information. *Hippocampus* 11:578–598.

8. Pegna AJ, et al (2005 Jan) Discriminating emotional faces without primary visual cortices involves the right amygdala. *Nature Neuroscience* 8(1):24–25.

9. BBC News: UK Version: Wales (2004 12 Dec) *Blind man 'sees' emotions.* http://news.bbc.com/uk/1/hi/wales/4090155.stm accessed 08/09/2005.

10. Amen DG (2000) *Change Your Brain Change Your Life: The breakthrough program for conquering anxiety depression obsessiveness anger and impulsiveness.* NY: Three Rivers Press ISBN 0812929985.

11. Allen JS, Bruss J, Damasio H (2004 May-June) The structure of the human brain: Precise studies of the size and shape of the brain have yielded fresh insights into neural development differences between the sexes and human evolution. *American Scientist* 92(3):246–254.

Peters M, et al (1998) Unsolved problems in comparing brain sizes in Homo sapiens. *Brain and Cognition* 37(2):254–285.

12. Fields, RD (2004 Apr) The Other Half of the Brain. *Scientific American* 290(4):54–61.

13. Penfield W, Jasper H. (1954) *Epilepsy and the Functional Anatomy of the Human Brain.* Boston: Little Brown.

14. Schwartz JM, Begley S (2002) *The Mind & the Brain: Neuroplasticity and power of mental force.* Regan Books ISBN 0060393556.

15. Weiskrantz L (1986) Blindsight: A case study and its implications. Oxford Psychology Series ISBN 0198521928.

Chapter 5

1. Lipton BH (2005) *The Biology of Belief: Unleashing the power of consciousness matter and miracles.* Santa Rosa CA: Mountain of Love/Elite Books ISBN 0975881477.

   Davis EP, Sandman CA (2006 Jul-Sep) Prenatal exposure to stress and stress hormones influences child development. *Infants & Young Children: An Interdisciplinary Journal of Special Care Practices* 19(3):246–259.

   Carsten O, et al (2003) Stressful life events in pregnancy and head circumference at birth. *Developmental Medicine & Child Neurology* 45(12):802–806.

2. Endelman GM (1987) *Neural Darwinism: The theory of neuronal group selection.* NY: Basic Books ISBN 0192850895.

3. Winggert P, Brant M (2005 15 Aug) Reading your baby's mind. *Newsweek* CXLVI(7):32–39.

4. Shreve J (2005 Mar) The mind is what the brain does. *National Geographic* 207(3):2–31.

5. Shreve J (2005 Mar) The mind is what the brain does. *National Geographic* 207(3):2–31.

6. RSE (see reference 4, Chapter 2).

7. Agnes S, Chan Y, Mei-Chun C (1998 12 Nov) Music training improves verbal memory. *Nature* (London) 396(6707):128.

8. LeDoux J (2002) *The Synaptic Self: How our brains become who we are.* Penguin Books ISBN 0670030287.

9. Sadato N, et al (1996) Activation by the primary visual cortex by Braille reading in blind subjects. *Nature* 380:526–528.

10. Pascual-Leone A, Hamilton R (2001) The metamodal organization of the brain. Chapter 27 in C Casanova & M Ptito (Eds) *Vision: From Neurons to Cognition: Progress in Brain Research 134.* San Diego CA: Elsevier Science ISBN 0444505865.

11. Pascual-Leone A, Hamilton R (2001) The metamodal organization of the brain. Chapter 27 in C Casanova & M Ptito (Eds) *Vision: From Neurons to Cognition: Progress in Brain Research 134.* San Diego CA: Elsevier Science ISBN 0444505865.

12. Pascual-Leone A, Torres F. (1993) Plasticity of the sensorimotor cortex representations of the reading finger in Braille readers. *Brain* 116:39–52.

13. Sterr A, et al (1998 08 Jan) Changed perceptions in Braille readers. *Nature* 391(6663):134–135.

14. Schiebel AB, et al (1990) A quantitative study of dendrite complexity in selected areas of the human cerebral cortex. *Brain and Cognition* 12(116):85–101.

15. Jacobs B, Scheibel AB (1993 Jan) A quantitative dendritic analysis of Wernicke's area in humans. I. Lifespan changes. *Journal of Comparative Neurology* 327(1):83–96.

16. Mogilmer A, et al (1993 April) Somatosensory cortical plasticity in adult humans revealed by magnetoencephalography. *Proceedings of the National Academy of Sciences* 90:3593–3597.

Chapter 6

1. Krebs C, Huttman K, Steinhauser C (2005 26 Jan) The forgotten brain emerges. *Scientific American* 14(5):40–43.

2. Ullian EM, et al (2001 Jan) Control of synapse number by glia. *Science* 291(5504):657–661.

3. Abrams M (2003 June) Can you see with your tongue? *Discover* 24(6):52–56.

4. Tulving E (1972) Episodic and semantic memory. In E Tulving & W Donaldson (Eds) *Organization of Memory* (381–403) NY: Academic Press ISBN 0127036504.

5. Goleman D (1994 11 Oct) Peak performance: Why records fall. *New York Times* (Late Edition) (East Coast) C1 NY.

   Chase WG, Ericsson KA (1981) Skilled memory. In J R Anderson (Ed) *Cognitive Skills and Their Acquisition: Symposium on cognition (16) 1980 Carnegie-Mellon University* Hillsdale NJ: Erlbaum.

6. Merzenich MM, Syka J (2005) *Plasticity and Signal Representation in the Auditory System.* Springer. ISBN 0387231544.

   Robertson 1 (2000) *Mind Sculpture: Unlocking Your Brain's Untapped Potential.* ISBN 0880642211.

   Steinmetz PN, Roy A, Fitzgerald PJ, Hsiao SS, Johnson KO, Niebur E (2002 9 Mar) Attention modulates synchronized neuronal firing in primate somatosensory cortex. *Nature* (London) 404(6774):187–90.

7. Richards JM, Gross JJ (2000 Sept) Emotion regulation and memory: The cognitive costs of keeping one's cool. *Journal of Personality and Social Psychology* 79(3):410–424.

8. Rosenzweig MR, Bennett EL (1996 Jun) Psychobiology of plasticity: effects of training and experience on brain and behavior. *Behavioural Brain Research* 78(1):57–65.

   Bennett EL, Diamond MC, Krech D, Rosenzweig MR (1964) Chemical and anatomical plasticity of brain. *Science* 146:610–619.

9. Goldberg E (2001) *The Executive Brain: Frontal lobes and the civilized mind.* NY: Oxford University Press ISBN 0195156307.

   Goldberg E, Costa LD (1981) Hemisphere differences in the acquisition and use of descriptive systems. *Brain Language* 14(1):144–173.

10. Martin A, Wiggs CL, Weisberg J (1997) Modulation of human medial temporal lobe activity by form meaning and experience. *Hippocampus* 7(6):587–593.

11. Shadmehr R, Holcomb HH (1997) Neural correlates of motor memory consolidation. *Science* 227(5327):821–825.

    Haier RJ, et al (1992) Regional glucose metabolic changes after learning a complex visuospatial/motor task: a positron emission tomographic study. *Brain Research* 570(1–2):134–143.

12. Bever TG, Chiarello RJ (1974) Cerebral dominance in musicians and non-musicians. *Science* 185(4150):537–539.

Chapter 7

1. Lomo T (2003 3 Mar) The discovery of long-term potentiation. *Philosophical Transactions of the Royal Society London* 358:617–620.

   Bliss TVP, Lomo T (1973) Long-lasting potentiation of synaptic transmission in the dentate area of the anesthetized rabbit following stimulation of the perforant path. *Journal of Physiology* 232:331–356.

2. LeDoux J (2001) *The Synaptic Self: How our brains become who we are.* Penguin Books ISBN 0670030287.

3. LeDoux J (2001) *The Synaptic Self: How our brains become who we are.* Penguin Books ISBN 0670030287.

4. RSE (see reference 4, Chapter 2).

Chapter 8

1. RSE (see reference 4, chapter 2).

2. Ramtha (2005 Sept) *Beginners Guide to Creating Reality.* Yelm, WA: JZK Publishing ISBN 1578730279.

3. Schwartz GE, Weinberger DA, Singer JA (1981 Aug) Cardiovascular differentiation of happiness sadness anger and fear following imagery and exercise. *Psychosomatic Medicine* 43(4):343–364.

4. Rosch P (1992 May) Job stress: America's leading adult health problem. *USA Today* Pp 42–44.

   American Institute of Stress. *America's #1 health problem.* http://www stress org/problem htm Accessed 11/03/06.

5. Cohen S, Herbert T (1996) Health psychology: Psychological factors and physical disease from the perspective of human psychoneuroimmunology. *Annual Review of Psychology* 47:113–42.

6. Thakore JH, Dian TG (1994) Growth hormone secretion: The role of glucocorticoids. *Life Sciences* 55(14):1083–1099.

Murison R (2000) Gastrointestinal effects. In G Fink (Ed) *Encyclopedia of Stress* 2:191 San Diego: Academic Press ISBN 0122267389.

Flier JS (1983 Feb) Insulin receptors and insulin resistance. *Annual Review of Medicine* 34:145–160.

Ohman A (2001) Anxiety. In G Fink (Ed) *Encyclopedia of Stress* 1:226 San Diego: Academic Press ISBN 0122267362.

7. Ader R, Cohen N (1975 July-Aug) Behaviorally conditioned immunosuppression. *Psychosomatic Medicine* 37(4):333–340.

8. American Heart Association: *Risk Factors and Coronary Heart Disease.* http://www.americanheart.org/presenter.jhtml?identifier=500 Accessed 11/10/06.

9. Arnsten, A.F.T. (2000) "The Biology of Being Frazzled," *Science* 280: 1711–1712.

Wooley C, Gould E, McEwen B (1990 29 Oct) Exposure to excess glucocorticoids alters dendritic morphology of adult hippocampal pyramidal neurons. *Brain Research* 531(1–2):225–231.

10. Restak R (1979) *The Brain: The last frontier.* Warner Books ISBN 0446355402.

Lupien SJ, et al (1998 01 May) Cortisol levels during human aging predict hippocampal atrophy and memory deficits. *Nature Neuroscience* 1:69–73.

11. Sheline Y, et al (1996 30 April) Atrophy in recurrent major depression. *Proceedings of the National Academy of Sciences: Medical Sciences* 93(9):3908–3913.

12. Eriksson PS, et al (1998 Nov) Neurogenesis in the adult hippocampus. *Nature Medicine* 4(11):1313–1317.

13. Santarelli L, et al (2003 8 Aug) Requirement of hippocampal neurogenesis for the behavioral effects of antidepressants. *Science* 301(5634):805–809.

14. RSE (see reference 4, chapter 2).

15. Sapolsky RM (2004) *Why Zebras Don't Get Ulcers: The acclaimed guide to stress, stress-related diseases and coping.* Henry Holt and Company LLC ISBN 0-8050-7369-8.

16. Pert C (1997) *Molecules of Emotion: Why you feel the way you feel.* NY: Scribner ISBN 0684831872.

Chapter 9

1. RSE (see reference 4, Chapter 2).

2. Pert C (1997) *Molecules of Emotion: Why you feel the way you feel.* NY: Scribner ISBN 0684831872.

3. Plutchik R (2002) *Emotions and Life: Perspectives from psychology, biology, and evolution.* American Psychological Association ISBN 1557989494.

4. Guyton A (1991) *Textbook of Medical Physiology 8th.* London: WB Saunders and Co ISBN 0721630871.

5. RSE (see reference 4, Chapter 2).

6. Beck A (1976) *Cognitive Therapy and Emotional Disorders.* NY: International Universities Press ISBN 0823610055.

7. Dispenza J (2000) *The Brain: Where science and spirit meet: A scientific lecture.* (Video). Yelm, WA: Ramtha's School of Enlightenment.

   RSE (see reference 4, Chapter 2).

8. Dispenza J (2000) *The Brain: Where science and spirit meet: A scientific lecture.* (Video). Yelm, WA: Ramtha's School of Enlightenment.

   RSE (see reference 4, Chapter 2).

9. National Institute of Mental Health (2006) *The Numbers Count: Mental disorders in America: A fact sheet describing the prevalence of mental disorders in America.* NIH Publication No. 06-4584. http://www.nimh.nih.gov/publicat/numbers.cfm#readNow Accessed 11/01/06.

   Kessler RC, Chiu WT, Demler O, Walters EE (2005 Jun) Prevalence, severity, and comorbidity of twelve-month DSM-IV disorders in the National Comorbidity Survey Replication (NCS-R). *Archives of General Psychiatry* 62(6):617–27.

10. RSE (see reference 4, Chapter 2).

11. Ibid.

12. Rosenwald M (2006 May) The spotless mind. *Popular Science* 268(5):36–7.

Chapter 10

1. Macmillan M (2002) *An Odd Kind of Fame: Stories of Phineas Gage.* MIT Press ISBN 0262632594.

2. Damasio H, et al (1994 20 May) The return of Phineas Gage: The skull of a famous patient reveals clues about the human brain. *Science* 264(5162):1102–4.

3. Fulton JF, Jacobsen CF (1935) The functions of the frontal lobes, a comparative study in monkeys, chimpanzees and man. *Advances in Modern Biology (Moscow)* 4:113–123.

4. Tierney AJ (2000) Egas Moniz and the origins of psychosurgery: A review commemorating the 50th anniversary of Moniz's Nobel Prize. *Journal of the History of the Neurosciences* 9(1):22–36.

   Kucharski A (1984 June) History of frontal lobotomy in the United States, 1935–1955. *Neurosurgery* 14(6):765–72.

5. Amen DG (2001) *Healing ADD: The breakthrough program that allows you to see and heal the 6 types of ADD.* Berkley Books ISBN 039914644X.

6. Lemonick M (2005 17 Jan) The biology of joy: Scientists know plenty about depression, now they are starting to understand the roots of positive emotions. *Time* (US Edition):12–A25.

7. Fuster J (1997) *The Prefrontal Cortex: Anatomy physiology and neuropsychology of the frontal lobe.* Philadelphia: Lippincott-Raven ISBN 0397518498.

8. RSE (see reference 4, Chapter 2).

9. Nauta WJ (1972) Neural associations of the frontal cortex. *Acta Neurobiologiae Experimentalis* (Warsaw) 32:125–140.

10. Raichle ME, et al (1994) Practice-related changes in human brain functional anatomy during nonmotor learning. *Cerebral Cortex* 4(1):8–26.

11. Gold JM, et al (1996) PET validation of a novel prefrontal task: Delayed response alternation (DRA). *Neuropsychology* 10:3–10.

12. Walker EH (2000) *The Physics of Consciousness: Quantum minds and the meaning of life.* Cambridge MA: Perseus ISBN 0738202347.

13. Giedd JN, et al (1999 01 Oct) Brain development during childhood and adolescence: A longitudinal MRI study. *Nature Neuroscience* 2:861–863.

14. Amen DG (2000) *Change Your Brain Change Your Life: The breakthrough program for conquering anxiety depression obsessiveness anger and impulsiveness.* NY: Three Rivers Press ISBN 0812929985.

15. Begley S (2001 7 May) God and the Brain: How we're wired for spirituality. *Newsweek*. Religion and the Brain 51–57.

    Newberg AM, D'Aquili EG. Rause V (2002) *Why God Won't Go Away: Brain science and the biology of belief*. Ballantine Books ISBN: 034544034X.

16. RSE (see reference 4, Chapter 2).

17. Amen DG (2001) *Healing ADD: The breakthrough program that allows you to see and heal the 6 types of ADD*. Berkley Books ISBN 039914644X.

18. Goldberg E (2001) *The Executive Brain: Frontal lobes and the civilized mind*. NY: Oxford Press ISBN 0195156307.

    Goldberg E, Harner R, Lovell M, Podell K, Riggio S (1994 Summer) Cognitive bias, functional cortical geometry, and the frontal lobes; laterality, sex, and handedness. *Journal of Cognitive Neuroscience* 6(3):276–296.

Chapter 11

1. Yue G, Cole KJ (1992) Strength increases from the motor program-comparison of training with maximal voluntary and imagined muscle contractions. *Journal of Neurophysiology* 67(5):1114–1123.

2. RSE (see reference 4, Chapter 2).

    Gupta S (2002 18 Feb) The chemistry of love: Do pheromones and smelly T shirts really have the power to trigger sexual attraction? Here's a primer. *Time* 159:78.

Chapter 12

1. Singer RN (2000 Oct) Performance and human factors: Considerations about cognition and attention for self-paced and externally paced events. *Ergonomics* 43(10):1661–1680.

    Salazar W et al (1990) Hemispheric asymmetry, cardiac response, and performance in elite archers. *Research Quarterly for Exercise and Sport* 61:351–359.

    Hatfield BD, Landers DL, Ray WJ (1984) Cognitive processes during self-paced motor performance: an electroencephalographic profile of skilled marksmen. *Journal of Sport Psychology* 6:42–59.

    Landers DM et al (1991) The influence of electrocortical biofeedback on performance in pre-elite archers. *Medicine and Science in Sports and Exercise* 23:123–129.

2. Ramtha (2005 Sept) *A Beginner's Guide to Creating Reality.* Yelm, WA: JZK Publishing ISBN 1578730279.

3. Restak RM (1979) *The Brain: The last frontier.* Warner Books ISBN 0446355402.

4. McCall N (1995) *Makes Me Wanna Holler: A young black man in America.* Vintage Books ISBN 0615004962.

   Elder L (2001) *The Ten Things You Can't Say In America.* St. Martin's Griffin ISBN: 0312284659.

5. Anderson CA, Bushman BJ (2001 Sept) The effects of violent video games on aggressive behavior, aggressive cognition, aggressive affect, psychological arousal and prosocial behavior: A meta-analytic review of scientific literature. *Psychological Sciences* 12(5):353–359. http://www.psychology. iastate.edu/faculty/caa/abstracts/2000-2004/01AB.pdf Accessed 11/16/06.

6. Blakemore C, Cooper GF (1970 31 Oct) Development of the brain depends on the visual environment. *Nature* (Letters to Editor) 228:477–478.

   Ranpura A (2006) Weightlifting for the mind: Enriched environments and cortical plasticity. *Brain Connection* http://www.brainconnection.com/ topics/?main=fa/cortical-plasticity Accessed 11/16/06.

   Hubel DH, Wiesel TN (1962 Jan) Receptive fields, binocular interaction and functional architecture in the cat's visual cortex. *Journal of Physiology* 160:106–54.

   Hubel DH, Wiesel TN (1963 Mar) Shape and arrangement of columns in cat's striate cortex. *Journal of Physiology* 165(3):559–5.

7. Brown BB (1970 Jan) Recognition of aspects of consciousness through association with EEG alpha activity represented by a light signal. *Psychophysiology* 6(4):442–52.

Epilogue

1. Kohler I (1964) The Formation and Transformation of the Perceptual World. Translated by H.Fiss. *Psychological Issues 3.* International Universities ISBN 082362000X.

Restak RM (1979) *The Brain: The last frontier.* Warner Books ISBN 0446355402.

2. Radin D (1997) *The Conscious Universe: The scientific truth of psychic phenomena.* HarperSanFrancisco ISBN 0062515020.

McTaggart L (2003) *The Field: The quest for the secret force of the universe.* Harper Paperbacks ISBN 0060931175.

Jahn RG, Dunne BJ, Nelson RD, Dobyns YH, Bradish GJ (1997) Correlations of random binary sequences with pre-stated operator intention: A review of a 12-year program. Reprint. *Journal of Scientific Exploration* 11(3):345-367. http://freeweb.supereva.com/lucideimaestri/correlations.pdf. Accessed 11/16/06.

INDEX

Figures/illustrations are indicated by **boldface** type.

About the Author

Joe Dispenza, D.C., studied biochemistry at Rutgers University in New Brunswick, New Jersey. He has a Bachelor's of Science degree with an emphasis in Neuroscience from Evergreen State College in Olympia, Washington. Dr. Dispenza also received his Doctor of Chiropractic degree at Life University in Atlanta, Georgia, graduating *magna cum laude*.

Dr. Dispenza's postgraduate training and continuing education has been in neurology; neurophysiology; brain function and chemistry; cellular biology; memory formation; and aging and longevity. He is an invited member of Who's Who in America, an honorary member of the National Board of Chiropractic Examiners, the recipient of a Clinical Proficiency Citation for clinical excellence in doctor-patient relationships from Life University, and a member of Pi Tau Delta—the International Chiropractic Honor Society.

Over the last ten years, Dr. Dispenza has lectured in over seventeen countries on six continents educating people about the role and function of the human brain. He has taught thousands of people how to reprogram their thinking through scientifically proven neuro-physiologic principles. As a result, this information has taught many individuals to reach their specific goals and visions by eliminating self-destructive habits. His approach, taught in a very simple method, creates a bridge between true human potential and the latest scientific theories of neuroplasticity. He explains how thinking in new ways, as well as changing beliefs, can literally rewire one's brain. The premise of his work is founded in his total conviction that every person on this planet has within them the latent potential of greatness and true unlimited abilities.

Evolve Your Brain: The Science of Changing Your Mind connects the subjects of thought and consciousness with the brain, the mind, and the body. The book explores "the biology of change." That is, when we truly change our mind, there is a physical evidence of change in the brain. As an author of several scientific articles on the close relationship between the brain and the body, Dr. Dispenza ties information together to explain the roles these functions play in physical health and disease. His DVD series, *Your Immortal Brain*, looks at the ways in which the human brain can be used to affect reality through the mastery of thought. He also sits as an invited editorial advisor of *Explore Magazine*.

In his research into spontaneous remissions, Dr. Dispenza has found similarities in people who have experienced so-called miraculous healings, showing that they have actually changed their mind, which then changed their health.

One of the scientists, researchers, and teachers featured in the award-winning film *What the BLEEP Do We Know!?*, Dr. Dispenza is often remembered for his comments on how a person can create their day, which he discussed in the film. He also has guest appearances in the theatrical directors cut *What the BLEEP Down the Rabbit Hole* as well as the extended Quantum Edition DVD set *What the BLEEP Down the Rabbit Hole*.

When not traveling and writing, he is busy seeing patients at his chiropractic clinic near Olympia, Washington.